POLICE

SUPERVISION

Theory

and Practice

PAUL M. WHISENAND

california state college at long beach

POLICE

SUPERVISION

Theory

and Practice

PRENTICE-HALL, INC.

englewood cliffs, new jersey

With love and gratitude I dedicate this book to my favorite "supervisors"—
Mildred and Raymond Whisenand and Florence Henderson.

PRENTICE-HALL SERIES IN THE ADMINISTRATION OF JUSTICE
Gordon E. Misner, Editor

© 1971 by *PRENTICE-HALL, INC.*
Englewood Cliffs, New Jersey

Printed in the United States of America
13-686246-2
Library of Congress Catalog No.: 76-129239
Current printing (last digit): 10 9 8 7 6 5 4 3 2

PRENTICE-HALL INTERNATIONAL, INC., London
PRENTICE-HALL OF CANADA, LTD., Toronto
PRENTICE-HALL OF JAPAN, INC., Tokyo
PRENTICE-HALL OF AUSTRALIA, PTY. LTD., Sydney
PRENTICE-HALL OF INDIA PRIVATE LIMITED, New Delhi

Preface

Textbooks are written for a variety of reasons. In producing this volume, I have probably encompassed most of them. However, for me there is a single major stimulus for putting pen to paper and seat to seat. This stimulus centers in a student who approached me shortly after I accepted my first position as a full-time educator. The student had just looked over the course outline I had prescribed for a class in police supervision. Briefly, his comment was, "Why don't you just give us the ten fundamental steps for supervising police officers and skip all the academic jazz?" My response was probably as inept as his question was foolish. In part, this book is directed to the above mentioned student, who was compelled to sit through a semester of "academic jazz."

Three other prominent reasons for writing this text are: First, there is no existing text on police supervision that meets the course requirements for an upper-division class in this subject. This claim is based on my five years of classroom teaching experience at this level and on this topic. Second, the number of upper-division and graduate level programs in police science and, more broadly, criminal justice is growing very rapidly. These programs frequently contain courses in police supervision (for example, the Department of Criminology, California State College at Long Beach, has two upper-division courses in police supervision, one fundamental, the other advanced). Third, this text is different—it incorporates pertinent behavioral research findings in a supportive style for making the practice of police supervision all the more meaningful and effective. Further, it integrates a well recognized format for the teaching of police supervision with the findings from the social sciences. In other words, this text is intended to fill a growing need in local law enforcement for a combined behavioral and practical orientation to police supervision.

To fill this need, this book concentrates on the theoretical concepts of supervision and minimizes the use of the more technique-oriented approach. Concepts are long lasting while techniques are short lived. Thus, no attempt has been made to define in detail the duties and responsibilities of an ideal police supervisor or to describe a set of guaranteed techniques which will work effectively in any local law enforcement organization under all circumstances. What has been attempted is an analysis of the functions of the supervisor, an indication of the scope of supervision in the police environment, and an exposition of those techniques proven to be the most useful in the experiences of successful police supervisors in government and business. The concepts and functions are presented to develop supervisory guides to understanding human behavior. The reader can then perceive the problems of dealing with the human element and keep a certain flexibility in his modes of analyzing and solving both organizational and individual problems.

Most of the anxieties and frustrations to which the police supervisor is subject are characteristic also of the life of the supervisor in private industry; therefore, the author has drawn heavily on the research findings and experiences of industrial supervision. Yet, there are differences. As an example, one significant difference lies in the acute and peculiar police-community relations problem which permeates nearly every function of the police supervisor and his work group.

Special note should be taken of the fact that this volume is designed for both potential and present supervisors in local law enforcement agencies. Local law enforcement denotes municipal police organizations and county sheriff departments of all sizes. To clarify the term police or local law enforcement officer includes the county sheriff as well.

A special word of appreciation is due an outstanding supervisor, Dr. C. Robert Guthrie, formerly Chairman of the Department of Criminology of California State College at Long Beach. It is a shame that his style of supervision is not more prevalent in today's modern organizations. By far, it would make the internal operations of an organization a lot more pleasant for a lot more people. Further, my gratitude is extended to the following colleagues and friends (thankfully they are one and the same): John P. Kenney, A. C. Germann, Harold K. Becker, George T. Felkenes, Ronald H. Rogers, and John H. Good. To Willa K. Nelson, I can merely express many heartfelt thanks for her excellent processing of this manuscript.

This text was supported in part by the National Institute of Law Enforcement and Criminal Justice (NI-122), Law Enforcement Assistance Administration, United States Department of Justice. Views and recommendations expressed herein should not be interpreted as representing the official opinion or policy of the National Institute.

Long Beach, California   **Paul Whisenand**

Contents

part three

TRAINING FOR DEVELOPMENT

part four

THE FUTURE

POLICE

SUPERVISION

Theory

and Practice

1

Introduction:
A Multiview

It is critically important that every present or potential police supervisor understand that there is no *one* right and best way to supervise, regardless of time and place. To grasp this reality requires a multiview of police supervision such as offered in this volume.[1] Police supervisors of long standing are usually quick to acknowledge that there are variations in their particular style of supervising from place to place and from time to time. What is successful practice in one situation may, in a different situation, be unsuccessful. Even given a specific situation there are frequently varying ideas of how most effectively to supervise a group of police officers.

The above thinking leads to the question, "If police supervision depends on a host of intervening variables, why are practitioners, educators, and researchers seeking to advance an art which presumably supports basic principles and endeavors to develop uniform practices in police supervision?" The answer, in essence the reason for the existence of this text, is that attracting capable people to the police service, supervising them properly, and retaining or moving them about as required are important objectives to which all concerned must be dedicated. However, *adhering to rigid precepts and techniques in the belief that there is but a single way to supervise is both ineffective and a disservice to the police organization.* This one-best-way philosophy on the part of police supervisors generates a preoccupation with the enforcement of usually outdated regulations and with the processing of meaningless transactions, while entirely new issues such as the need for a workable system for supervising college-educated police officers in local law enforcement agencies might be ignored. This author has learned that, regardless of the topic, there may be a general rule to assert, but that there are also numerous *if*s, *and*s, and *but*s to describe and explain.

To illustrate let us return to the student mentioned in the preface of this

---

[1] Much of the thinking expressed in this section is derived from Louis J. Kroeger, "A Multi-View of Public Personnel Administration," *Public Personnel Review*, 29 (April 1968), 66–69.

text who was most anxious to get at the heart of the subject by discussing *the* ten or more golden rules for becoming a successful police supervisor. If pushed, this author might respond by citing the following ingredients of a recipe for effective supervision:

> Know your subordinates and what is important to each.
> Listen to subordinates and encourage dicussion.
> Be considerate.
> Be consistent.
> Establish objectives and a sense of direction for your staff.
> When possible, give orders in the form of suggestions or requests.
> Delegate responsibility for details.
> Show your subordinates that you have faith in them and that you expect them to do their best.
> Keep subordinates informed.
> Ask subordinates for opinions and suggestions.
> When a subordinate offers a suggestion, let him know what action is taken on it.
> Give subordinates a chance to participate in decision making.
> Let your subordinates know where they stand.
> Criticize privately and constructively.
> Praise publicly.[2]

Before the reader decides to stop at this point in favor of using the listed guidelines for becoming a good supervisor, he should consider five points. First, is it possible that the above recipe may not contain the proper ingredients—is there another list of things to do superior to the one offered?[3] Second, how does he know when to use a certain ingredient, or does he simply use all the recipe all the time? Third, if a police supervisor employs the above recipe what can he expect as a result? To put it another way, since supervision is a two-way process, what can the supervisor anticipate from his subordinates? Further, what happens if he uses the recipe and his subordinates continue to manifest poor productivity and low job satisfaction? Four, can it be presumed from the list that those items not included should be definitely avoided?

Finally, to conclude this argument, let us look at a few of the guidelines.

---

[2] "Recipe for Effectiveness," *Public Personnel Review*, 29 (April 1968), 121.

[3] Here is an example from "The Key to Success . . . ," *Public Personnel Review*, 28 (April 1967), 88.

The key to being a successful supervisor is the ability to handle people. Here are eight tips on how to make people want to do the things they must do: (1) Get to know the people working for you. (2) Show them how to get ahead. (3) Criticize constructively. A good plan is to get all the facts, stay calm, criticize in private, commend before you find fault, and keep your criticism constructive by emphasizing how to do the job better. (4) Be generous with compliments, but be sincere. (5) Listen to their problems. (6) Throw down a challenge. (7) Make certain you're understood in giving instructions. (8) Check on progress.

How about "Be consistent"? Is it not possible that certain subordinates may respond best to unpredictable supervisory tactics? Should consistency be thought of as applying a series of rules fairly but within discretionary limits rather than with the same degree of precision or frequency? Should consistency mean that the police supervisor consistently use the most appropriate tactic for motivating or controlling a subordinate? Next, let us consider the inherent discrepancy between establishing objectives for the group and allowing the group to participate in the decision-making process. How can the police supervisor do both at the same time? Basically, he cannot; consequently, which one of the two should he select? Consider also the problems of asking subordinates for opinions. What happens if they respond with totally inappropriate suggestions? Or, for that matter, what happens if the suggestions are excellent but not feasible at that particular time?

In summary, there is no one best way to supervise; rigid guidelines or principles are often more damaging than helpful for developing effective supervision because of their overly simplistic design; and both the present and prospective police supervisor should cultivate a multiview of supervision to cope adequately with so complex a process.

THE POLICE SUPERVISOR: NEW DEMANDS, BEHAVIORAL SCIENCES, AND HIS ROLE

Although the term *supervision* was used in the previous section, no attempt was made to define it. The primary reason for waiting until this section to provide a working definition of supervision lies in the basic idea of the supervisory process. Namely, supervision is as highly complex as the nature of individuals and the multiplicity of their relationships. It is comprised of general principles and specific peculiarities and includes all the dilemmas intrinsic to human relations.

Two major concerns are analyzed prior to defining the various terms used in future chapters. First, we review some of the changes and challenges (referred to here as new demands) that have complicated greatly the position of a police supervisor, or, for that matter, job responsibilities of all persons operating within an organizational environment. This particular section is highly relevant as a foundation for an adequate appreciation and understanding of the supervisor's changing role in a local police agency. Second, because this text is mainly a behavioral approach to police supervision, the present and probable benefits of behavioral science research for supervision are reviewed. After these two sections is a third section devoted to the problem of definitions. The police supervisor is described in terms of his emerging role within the police department. Finally, we briefly preview the plan and remaining chapters of the volume.

New Demands on Supervision

Some of the more relevant demands compounding the problems inherent in the position of police supervisor are for new organizational structures, group dynamics, training, tasks and goals, and the over-all job environment. The reader will note that each one of the demands places a greater burden and broadened responsibility on the police supervisor.[4]

Organizational structures. Police organizations are beginning to recognize the importance of integrating their functional units. Traditionally, police work is divided and then assigned, and an endeavor is made to direct the efforts of the work units so as to accomplish the designated mission. Thus, as a police organization grows greater specialization inevitably occurs. This trend of increasing specialization has very serious implications for a police supervisor. First, increased specialization limits the organizational perspective of the police supervisor to achieving a set of narrow objectives. Second, by its very nature, specialization inhibits an organization's ability to integrate its various parts to insure effective total performance. Achieving greater integration and lessening the impact of rigid specialization not only involves a rational redesign of the formal structure but also involves the psychological processes which tend to improve interpersonal communication and functional coordination among the units within the police department.[5] Central to the effectiveness of this psychological process is the police supervisor.

Group dynamics. Groups have a major influence on their members, on other groups, and on the over-all organization.[6] The supervisor is in a unique position to exert beneficial influence on the output and motivation of his assigned group. In regard to groups, it is currently debatable whether the supervisor should attempt to become an integral member of his assigned group. This is to say, can the supervisor be both member and authority figure at the same time? Because of this situation, the police supervisor finds himself in a quandary over his proper relationship with subordinates and superiors. Pfiffner and Fels have aptly referred to the supervisor as the "man in the middle."[7] The police supervisor is also expected to generate "healthy," goal-directed intergroup competition while simultaneously

---

[4] For another list of demands on the supervisor, see Frank P. Sherwood and Wallace H. Best, *Supervisory Methods in Municipal Administration* (Chicago, Ill.: The International City Managers' Association, 1958), pp. 1–5.

[5] The need and possible means for integrating various work groups in an organization can be found in a text by Robert T. Golembiewski, *Organizing Men and Power: Patterns of Behavior and Line-Staff Models* (Chicago, Ill.: Rand McNally and Company, 1967).

[6] Edgar H. Schein, *Organizational Psychology* (Englewood Cliffs, N.J.: Prentice-Hall, Inc., 1965), p. 66.

[7] John M. Pfiffner and Marshall Fels, *The Supervision of Personnel*, 3rd ed. (Englewood Cliffs, N.J.: Prentice-Hall, Inc., 1964), p. 80.

lessening the possible negative consequences. In addition, the police super-visor now realizes that he is being looked to for the development of work groups which fulfill both the needs of the police agency and the individual needs of its members. All three of these group-oriented demands are dis-cussed in a later chapter.

Training. One does not have to search long or hard to find that the con-temporary body of literature pertaining to supervision considers training a major responsibility of this position. In fact, there are some who believe that it should be *the* major responsibility of a supervisor.[8] Training has become all the more critical as occupations have become technically and socially more complex and as organizations have become more highly specialized. Consequently, the police supervisor either *is* or *should be* providing certain organizational training! This is true, if for no other reason, because of his opportunity for interpersonal and group communications. This book places considerable emphasis on the police supervisor as a trainer and devel-oper of human resources. In performing this function, he is instilling and improving not only job skills but also an understanding of the goals of the police service, of its methods for accomplishing these goals, of its organiza-tional philosophy, and of the various career paths available within it. The police supervisor as a trainer can thus assist in: (1) indoctrinating a new officer, (2) teaching him the specific skills and attitudes needed to perform his duties, and (3) providing opportunities for self-development which make it possible for the officer both to grow within his position and to rise within the department. It must be recognized that *how effectively the police supervisor trains his subordinates, as well as the objectives of the training program, have a tre-mendous influence on the capability of the department to meet its goals.* Finally, in the case of training, three significant problems can be discerned: the results of the supervisory training are frequently poorly specified because the police subordinate is at times expected to develop (in broad terms) his general attitudes, capacities, and general knowledge; the training generates pres-sures toward change in other parts of the department; and the training activity must take into account other personnel functions, such as recruitment and job design.

Tasks and goals. The tasks of the police department are becoming more technical, complicated, and unpredictable and thus must depend more on intellect than on muscles. Further, the tasks are fast becoming too complex for a single person to handle. The police supervisor of the future will be dealing with a project or team form of organization. In addition to this new wrinkle, the police will be coping with a multiplicity of goals. Finally, there will be more conflict and more indecision about the criteria of effectiveness. The reason, in part, for this is the high degree of professionalism currently

---

[8] *Ibid.*, pp. 203–72.

emerging in police work. Goal conflict leads to role conflict and ambiguity, and these problems are of direct concern to a police supervisor. Much remains to be researched and accomplished, particularly in the area of police tasks and goals.

Job environment. Those trends and developments already mentioned will continue and increase in force. That is, rapid change and specialization will be with us. Therefore, stability will be reduced. One cause of the accelerating change is the growth of science, research and development activities, and technology. Another is the increase of transactions between organizations. The three main features of the environment will be interdependence rather than independence among organizations, turbulence rather than stability, and large rather than small enterprises. Bennis aptly depicts the evolving job environment when he writes:

> Jobs in the next century should become *more,* rather than less, involving; man is a problem-solving animal, and the tasks of the future guarantee a full agenda of problems. In addition, the adaptive process itself may become captivating to many. At the same time, I think, the future I describe is far from a utopian or a necessarily "happy" one. Coping with rapid change, living in temporary systems, and setting up (in quickstep time) meaningful relations—and then breaking them—all augur strains and tensions. Learning how to live with ambiguity and to be self-directing will be the task of education and the goal of maturity.[9]

Moreover, it appears to be a major task of police supervision.

Police Supervision and the Behavioral Sciences

For nearly a decade managers and supervisors have been exhorted to make more extensive use of the behavioral and social sciences.[10] For approximately the same length of time they have also been urged simultaneously to improve their conceptual skills. Concepts and plans in no way reduce the demand for practical and responsible police supervision. Ideas, in fact, are the very fuel of such supervision. One must recognize that some ideas help and others hinder, that some can be acquired in finalized form and others have to be developed. The ideas available to police supervisors from the behavioral sciences are growing in significance, and the supervisor's job more and more requires him to use these ideas in handling daily problems. This challenge is as exciting as it is filled with responsibility. This section is for those supervisors who are intrigued by the behavioral sciences and who

---

[9] Warren G. Bennis, *Changing Organizations* (New York: McGraw-Hill Book Company, 1966), p. 14.

[10] John M. Pfiffner, "Why Not Make Social Science Operational?" *Public Administration Review,* 22 (September 1962), 109–14.

are especially interested in better understanding what they are attempting to accomplish in human problem solving.[11]

The behavioral sciences have increased in stature for the same reason any science does, namely, because conventional wisdom and practice failed to work. And conventional wisdom began failing when a number of changes in our society began to affect the basic nature of human organization. These changes are manifested in the scale and complexity of modern organizations, the rate of technological change, the influx of professionals into large-scale organizations, and the increase of the general educational level and aspirations of workers. The behavioral sciences have brought about the demise of many well entrenched theories and practices of supervision. For example, the following ideas are now considered reliable (however, the author is quick to admit that many of the ideas are not yet practiced):

Man does not react solely on the basis of economic gain.

Man has a hierarchy of needs which change over time toward social and self-actualization and away from basic physical-economic needs. Quite often, management does not recognize this and hence incentives may be off-target, inappropriate, or both.

Man reacts in unanticipated ways to different forms of leadership.

Man's interpersonal relationships are important, have regularities, are real in their effects, and cannot be subsumed or understood through conventional theory.

Interpersonal relationships affect organizational effectiveness.

Interpersonal relationships cannot be outlawed or ignored. If they are, they go underground and turn up in the oddest places.

Groups establish and enforce norms on their memberships. These norms may or may not be congruent with management goals.

Morale is a complex of variables and not necessarily correlated with productivity.

Communication gets distorted, particularly as it goes up the hierarchy. Subordinates who hold views at variance with their superior tend to withdraw or suppress their point of view, allowing their superior to make mistakes even when they know better.

The validity and frequency of upward communication appears to be dependent upon the degree of interpersonal trust between superior and subordinate, the degree of power held by the subordinate, and the degree of the subordinate's ambition. None of these factors is taken into account explicitly in the theory and practice of bureaucracy.[12]

---

[11] An excellent start in building a workable scheme for relating behavioral science information to real-world problems is offered by Craig C. Lundberg, "Toward Understanding Behavioral Science by Administrators," *California Management Review*, 6 (Fall 1963), 43–52.

[12] This list is adapted from a much longer version in Bennis, *Changing Organizations*, p. 185.

The behavioral sciences include psychology, sociology, cultural anthropology, and the behavioral aspects of political science, economics, educational psychology, and biology. Basically, they deal with how and why people behave as they do, the relationship between behavior and the total environment. In a real sense, behavioral science is the study of the problem-solving behavior of man, and thus its findings are extremely relevant to supervision. Table 1 shows five major categories of behavioral research

TABLE 1: BEHAVIORAL SCIENCE RESEARCH RELATED TO SUPERVISION

Problem	Research and Problem Solving
Interpersonal Communication	
How to improve the interpersonal communication process.	The variables that influence interpersonal communication have been analyzed and organized to increase the understanding of the two-way processes involved. Some of the "filters" that affect listening have been identified. Methods are available for discovering the informal communication system within organizations. The effectiveness of various styles of communication, the values of participation in group behavior, and the relationship of information to a person's commitment to the task are important areas of knowledge for the police supervisor.
Effectiveness of the Decision-Making Process	
How to enhance the quality of organizational decision making.	Research on decision making has challenged some uses of supervisory authority. This research has focused on: the influence of hierarchy in organizations, the sources and supply of information aimed at improving the skills of the administrator, and the complexity of the process itself. For example, no single supervisor makes decisions alone—others always influence him either directly or indirectly, and his conclusions result from the interpersonal dynamics that prevail within the organization. Thus, it is necessary to analyze the sociological and organizational background factors that affect decision making, the perception of the decision maker and those affected by the decision, the evaluative steps involved, and the reaction to the selected alternative.
The Practice and Theory of Leadership	
How to apply better the relevant findings and theories provided by research into organizational leadership.	Early studies on organizational leadership, which focused primarily on the personality traits of the leader, were generally misleading with little agreement about the nature and importance of any particular set of traits. Later studies concentrated on the various styles of leadership (autocratic, democratic, laissez-faire), the functions of leadership necessary to accomplish a certain task, and the leadership activities affecting group action. However, none of the research provided

TABLE 1: (cont.)

Problem	Research and Problem Solving
	a simple, direct answer to the question of what constitutes effective leadership. A new and more useful concept of a leadership continuum has emerged, based on indications that the psychological influences of the leader, of group members, and of the situation make it necessary for a leader to respond with a particular style of leadership appropriate to *that situation* (the situational approach).
Human Resource Development	
How to develop most effectively the human resources within the organization.	The recognition that the vast majority of personnel come into a learning situation with an image of themselves as self-directing and responsible persons—not as dependent individuals—is an important realization for a supervisor trying to train employees. There are different levels of individual change in the development process. People are able to increase their knowledge, insight, understanding, skills, attitudes, values, and interests, but different training methods are involved in developing different levels of these qualities. Learning is more efficient when : the need for training is clear, the learning involves a change in behavior (which frequently tends to be resisted), the learning is facilitated and strengthened through group experience, and the learning is enhanced by evidence of progress.
Planned Change	
How to initiate and facilitate planned organizational change.	Change within organizations and groups is effected by encouragement of cohesiveness, which promotes the acceptance of change if it is generated internally, although it causes resistance if the change is initiated externally. Recent study shows that it is possible to create change by "unfreezing" the equilibrium in the organization, introducing change, and "refreezing" the situation at a new level of behavior or practice. With regard to resistance to attempted planned change by supervision, personnel tend to oppose it when they are not involved in planning for it, it is ambiguous, it does not take into account group norms, it is made for personal reasons, there is poor communication, or the rewards for making it are considered inadequate.

Source: Adapted from Gordon P. Lippitt, Implications of the Behavioral Sciences for Management (*Washington: Society for Personnel Administration, 1966*).

studies of particular concern to police supervision.[13] In essence, each one of the five categories provides a basis for a new concept of man. This new concept is derived from a better scientific knowledge of his complex and

---

[13] For a more comprehensive exploration of the behavioral sciences as they relate to management and supervision, see Maneck S. Wadia, *Management and the Behavioral Sciences: Text and Readings* (Boston, Mass.: Allyn and Bacon, Inc., 1968).

changing needs. In summary, it is primarily because of behavioral science research that we are presently reexamining our assumptions about people and improving our understanding of the supervisory role.

The Police Supervisor's Role and Problems of Definition

Both logic and convention require that we now define the supervisor's role. But what is police supervision? In truth, there is no good definition of supervision. Or perhaps there are good short definitions but no good short explanation. The immediate effect of all one-sentence or one-paragraph definitions of police supervision is conceptual nearsightedness rather than enlightenment and stimulation. This effect results from the continuing confusion concerning what a supervisor is; however, a few attempts have been made to analyze the supervisor's role and to define the position.[14]

Before discussing the role of a police supervisor, let us briefly examine the multifaceted nature of an organizational role.[15] In its broadest sense, a *role* comprises the behavior requirements of a position in an organization. Relatedly, the personality is an arrangement of the particular needs and dispositions of the individual. It is interesting to note that some research studies on leadership conclude that the organizational role tends to be a more basic determinant of behavior than does the personality.[16] For our purposes, we will regard an organizational role as a combination of mutually interdependent sub-roles.[17] One of these, the *institutional role*, is defined as the behavior requirements expected of a person filling a particular position. The institutional role and the organizational position can be easily distinguished by a single term—*behavior*. In other words, a *position* is a static organizational entity that specifies the duties, obligations, rights, and privileges of the present or future incumbent. Once the incumbent assumes a position he is expected to behave according to the specifications. Essentially, the core of position classification is the concept of the position as an abstract entity apart from the employee. From an organizational view-

---

[14] Examples of such attempts can be seen in K. E. Thurley and A. C. Hamblin, "The Supervisor and His Job," in *Management of Human Resources* (2nd ed.), eds. Paul Pigors, C. A. Myers, and F. T. Malm (New York: McGraw-Hill Book Company, 1969), pp. 130–37; Jack W. Jackson and Thomas J. Gazda, "The Nature of Supervisory Effectiveness: A Factorial Study," *Public Personnel Review*, 25 (July 1964), 151–56; and Paul M. Whisenand, "The Role of a Police Supervisor" (unpublished research study, California State College at Long Beach, 1968).

[15] An excellent and exhaustive explanation of role theory can be found in Bruce J. Biddle and Thomas J. Thomas, eds., *Role Theory* (New York: John Wiley and Sons, Inc., 1966). More relevant to this text is Jack J. Preiss and Howard J. Ehrlich, *An Examination of Role Theory: The Case of the State Police* (Lincoln, Neb.: The University of Nebraska Press, 1966).

[16] Bernard Berelson and Gary A. Steiner, *Human Behavior: An Inventory of Scientific Findings* (New York: Harcourt, Brace and World, Inc., 1964), p. 343.

[17] This particular scheme is borrowed from Frank J. Jasinski, "The Dynamics of Organizational Behavior," *Personnel*, 36 (March–April 1959), 60–67.

point, a position is the smallest administrative unit of an agency.[18] In a position classification system an individual employee "fills a position" and achieves promotion by moving from one position to a higher-level position within the organization's structure.

Since position has been defined, let us for a moment review a traditional statement of a police supervisor's position.[19]

Police sergeant

Definition

Under general supervision to supervise patrolmen engaged in investigative, patrol, traffic, records, and juvenile duties; to receive the public and to answer inquiries; and to do related work as required.

Examples of duties

Supervises police patrolmen, policewomen, and clerical personnel in investigative, patrol, traffic, records, and juvenile divisions; supervises dispatching of personnel and personnel cars to investigate complaints; gives information to the public; assists officers in completing crime reports and arrest records and reviews and corrects completed reports; writes crime reports; supervises the maintenance of the radio log; searches and books prisoners; confiscates or stores and gives receipts for prisoners' property; tags exhibits in evidence; fingerprints and assists in questioning prisoners; supervises the inspection of the city jail and enforces discipline, cleanliness, and order.

Minimum qualifications

Knowledge of:

Criminal law with reference to apprehension, arrest, and prosecution of persons committing misdemeanors and felonies, including rules of evidence pertaining to search and seizure

Preservation and presentation of evidence in criminal cases and elements of typical misdemeanor and felony offenses

The geography of the city and of the organization, operation, rules, and regulations of the police department

---

[18] Daniel F. Halloran, "Why Position Classification?" *Public Personnel Review*, 28 (April 1967), 89. As both explanation and justification Halloran further (pp. 89–90) writes that, "Position classification, and its industrial counterpart, job evaluation, are relatively new concepts. The first application of the position classification principle was in 1909 in the Chicago Civil Service. As a coincidence, the first industrial application of job evaluation was also in Chicago in 1912. The development and application of position classification in the United States as an integral part of the civil service reform movement was in reaction to the excesses of the spoils system and the gross pay inequities that were rampant under it. Position classification served well both management and employees of the public service in the early days of reform. It gave management an orderly administrative plan for the utilization of personnel. To employees it assured equal pay for equal work in place of the erratic and meaningless salary situations which had existed. Because of its impersonal approach to salary, it had an aura of democratic fairness about it which strongly appealed to employees who had become accustomed to seeing favoritism shown in matters of pay."

[19] Taken from an announcement for a supervisor's promotional examination. Through the courtesy of the City of Torrance Police Department, Torrance, California (Code 7312, January 1966).

Ability to:
Analyze situations and adopt quick, effective, and reasonable courses of action
Supervise others
Understand and follow directions
Write clear, concise reports

Upon careful analysis, the qualifications for sergeant indicate that, first, the police supervisor is expected to accomplish specific tasks, for which he must possess specified basic qualifications. Second, to a few candidates for the position it may infer that the police organization expects the incumbent to behave in a certain manner while carrying out his duties. Third, totally missing is any indication that the supervisor is expected to provide a leadership role. Finally, it reflects what the police department considers a supervisory position and role. In other words, the previous statement is somewhat static since it focuses on the end result. Any consideration of a person's role while in a formal position must deal also with the dynamic aspects of position, that is, his behavior.

Which role—institutional or social—to emphasize is determined mainly by the supervisor's self-concept. Although the role adopted most frequently is the one in closest harmony with his self-concept, it is untrue that observed behavior is determined exclusively by the response the individual makes to the various roles expected of him. While he may have a clear idea of how he should behave, other influences compel him into a different behavior pattern. Broadly, the demands discussed in an earlier section tend to condition the supervisor's behavior. More explicitly, the supervisor's behavior is affected by the police (institution) organization, its technology, and its value system. To some degree all three of these variables combine to shape the actual role that the police supervisor assumes. The police organization— its structure and method for gaining compliance, allocating rewards, meeting personal needs, and so on—vastly influences the behavior of a supervisor. Consider Scott's list of five organizational problems facing the supervisor:

1. poor downward communications concerning policy
2. little upward influence of the first-line supervisor in policy decisions
3. disagreements regarding supervisory job responsibilities
4. compensation of the first-line supervisor inadequate to sharply differentiate him from his employees, particularly given the advantage of employees of collective bargaining through their unions, which foremen almost unanimously lack
5. poor training opportunities in foremanship[20]

---

[20] William G. Scott, *Human Relations in Management: A Behavioral Science Approach* (Homewood, Ill.: Richard D. Irwin, Inc., 1962), pp. 309–13.

In regard to technology, the police supervisor is confronted by such innovations as: (1) computer-based communications, command, and control systems, and (2) helicopters used as general purpose patrol vehicles. Finally, the police supervisor's role is strongly affected by his value environment. Within his total value environment is the particular set of values that an organization either tacitly or overtly expresses. Each police agency has a history, a way of doing things, a set of conventions, and customs that determine its character of operation. This value system and the supervisors' awareness of it are important controls. In sum, then, the police supervisor's organizational role is a complex and imprecise matter, the result of a number of influences, all significantly conditioning the development and maintenance of his behavior.

We have now arrived at the point of defining the role of a police supervisor. Three research studies furnish the underpinning for this task. First, and foremost, is the study by Jackson and Gazda which primarily focuses on the problem of supervisory assessment in municipal government.[21] They identified 11 basic dimensions or role determinants of supervisory behavior. With some modification by this author, they are

1. organizational control
2. training
3. administrative detail
4. procedure development
5. organizational perspective
6. performance appraisal
7. formal, informal, and personal communication
8. organizational responsibility
9. safety awareness
10. community relations
11. employee morale

While a highly significant contribution to supervisory research, Jackson and Gazda's list is incomplete because it does not provide any consideration of the police supervisor's responsibility to assume the role of an organizational leader. Concerning leadership, four items should be added to this list. These four additional role determinants are derived from a study by Bowers and Seashore.[22] They reported, after comprehensive analysis of relevant behavioral research into organizational leadership, that four role determinants constitute leadership. They are

---

[21] Jackson and Gazda, "The Nature of Supervisory Effectiveness."
[22] David G. Bowers and Stanley E. Seashore, "Predicting Organizational Effectiveness with a Four-Factor Theory of Leadership," *Administrative Science Quarterly*, 11 (September 1966), 238–63.

TABLE 2: THE ROLE DETERMINANTS OF A POLICE SUPERVISOR

Determinant	Definition	Chapter	Example of a Specification for Police Supervisory Training: Subjects*
1. Formal, informal, and personal communication	Supervisory behavior that promotes and sustains the exchange of information and the transmission of meaning between people within the organization.	6 Communication	4
2. Organizational control	Supervisory behavior that influences a subordinate to act in a desired way.	7 Control	6, 10
3. Organizational perspective	Supervisory behavior that sets before a subordinate the fundamental philosophy and over-all goals of the organization.	8 Coordination	
4. Organizational responsibility	Supervisory behavior that both assigns and explains the duties the subordinate is required to perform.	8 Coordination	12
5. Procedure development	Supervisory behavior that facilitates, supports, and guides the subordinate in accomplishing his assigned responsibilities.	8 Coordination	
6. Administrative detail	Supervisory behavior that aggregates and processes numerous small tasks for maintaining organizational health by conflict resolution.	8 Coordination	
7. Support-subordinate	Supervisory behavior that promotes some other member's feeling of personal worth and importance within the department.	9 Leadership	7
8. Interaction facilitation	Supervisory behavior that influences police personnel to develop close, mutually satisfying work relationships.	9 Leadership	7
9. Goal emphasis	Supervisory behavior that creates an enthusiasm for meeting the department's goal or achieving excellent performance.	9 Leadership	7

14

TABLE 2.   *(cont.)*

10. Work facilitation	Supervisory behavior that helps achieve both individual and organizational goals by such activities as deploying, coordinating, planning, and providing organizational resources such as required materials and technical knowledge.	9 Leadership	7
11. Employee morale	Supervisory behavior that augments an employee's faith, loyalty, and satisfaction in the organization.	10 Morale and job satisfaction	9
12. Community relations	Supervisory behavior that develops viable and supportive relationships with the surrounding environment.	11 Community relations	5
13. Safety awareness	Supervisory behavior that reduces the threat of injury to subordinates during the performance of their routine and emergency duties.	12 Personnel safety	
14. Training	Supervisory behavior that assists an employee in developing his job-related talents and requisite body of understanding in order to improve both quantity and quality of the organizational output.	13 Training	13–22
15. Performance appraisal	Supervisory behavior that provides each employee with feedback regarding his organizational endeavors and personal growth.	13 Training	10

The cited specification for police supervisory training is from California's Commission on Peace Officer Standards and Training, The Supervisory Course (Sacramento, Calif.: Commission on Peace Officer Standards and Training,1969). Their subject outline (see below) is designed for a minimum of 80 classroom hours. Notably, all the specified subjects are covered in this text. Those not indicated in the above table are located as follows: Chapter 1, subjects 1 and 2; Chapters 4 and 5, subject 3; Chapters 2–5, subject 8; and Chapter 9, subject 11. Significantly, this book includes other dimensions not traditionally recognized as part of the supervisor's role. The subject outline is as follows: (1) introduction and scope of the course, (2) duties and responsibilities of the police supervisor, (3) the supervisor's relationship to police management, (4) communication principles, (5) handling and preventing complaints, (6) motivating employees to work, (7) leadership, (8) psychological aspects of supervision, (9) morale and discipline, (10) performance appraisal and rating procedures, (11) supervisory decision making, (12) making duty assignments, (13) the supervisory training function, (14) how people learn, (15) job analysis, (16) the four steps of teaching, (17) lesson plans, (18) instructional aids, (19) roll call training, (20) practical application, (21) evaluation of instruction, (22) written examinations.

1. support-subordinate
2. interaction facilitation
3. goal emphasis
4. work facilitation

Finally, this author used these 15 items to analyze specifically the role of a police supervisor.[23] Briefly, the first 11 role determinants were found to reflect the institutional role of a police supervisor. The last four items were manifested, to a greater or lesser degree, in his social role. After combining these 15 determinants, one can observe the actual role of a police supervisor. Table 2 presents the 15 determinants and their definitions in the order they are presented in subsequent chapters. Note that for each determinant the number of the chapter devoted to an analytical discussion of its attributes is included. In respect for established statewide specifications for police supervisory training, the table indicates which chapters contain subjects advocated by a leader in this area, California's Commission on Peace Officer Standards and Training. While each determinant is discussed separately, all are interdependent and susceptible to further division. One final point regarding these role requirements is that while all 15 are relevant, two seem to stand out from the others. Moreover, they do so in practice and in the literature. Simply stated they are *control* and *training*. Since it appears that they will remain dominant role requirements for present and future police supervisors this text gives them special treatment.

Now—what is police supervision? First, and most importantly, it is a process, that is, a human transactional process. The process varies according to the role determinants involved and to the degree that each one is emphasized. To put it another way, the process remains a constant while the determinants included in the process vary over time. Therefore, the supervisory process is both adaptive and relative. Likert concludes that:

> *Supervision is, therefore, always a relative process. To be effective and to communicate as intended, a [supervisor] must always adapt his behavior to take into account the expectations, values, and interpersonal skills of those with whom he is interacting.* This applies to all his relationships with other persons: his superiors, his peers, and his subordinates. This general conclusion is, of course, valid not only for relationships between supervisors and others . . . but any other interaction between persons.[24]

Second, police supervision is a goal-directed process. It is action intended to mount both an individual and collective response for the achievement

---

[23] Whisenand, "The Role of a Police Supervisor."
[24] Rensis Likert, *New Patterns of Management* (New York: McGraw-Hill Book Company, 1961), p. 95.

of either stated or implied organizational goals and personal needs. Thus we have arrived at our destination—a definition of supervision. To summarize, *supervision is an adaptive and relative human transactional process used by one member of the organization on others of a subordinate level to direct their behavior toward the accomplishment of organizational goals and the fulfillment of personal needs.* Perhaps the reader might find it of interest to compare what has been said in this section with the ingredients for successful supervision cited at the beginning of this chapter. In conclusion, any study of the police supervisor's position must recognize that there are separate sets of transactions and interrelationships in which he is involved. Each of these relationships affects his role. Ample research shows that job behavior is conditioned as much by the role determinants as by the personality and the position of the individual performing the role.[25]

Remainder of the Book

Fifteen chapters constitute the remaining body of the text. They are grouped into four major parts. Part One contains four chapters devoted to the organizational environment of the police supervisor. They describe, at successively greater levels of complexity, the multiple environmental dynamics that condition the police supervisor's role. Parts Two and Three deal with the 15 role determinants mentioned previously. In other words, what the reader is about to learn from these two parts is directly related to the *actual* role requirements of a police supervisor. The reason for separating the role requirements into two parts is one of emphasis. Earlier we determined that of the 15 role requirements two, control and training, are dominant. Therefore, Part Two focuses on control and Part Three concentrates on training. Part Four first looks at the supervisor as an innovator and agent of change. Finally, it concludes the volume by forecasting the future organizational environment and role of the police supervisor.

---

[25] Frank P. Sherwood, "The Role Concept in Administration," *Public Personnel Review*, 25 (January 1964), 41–44.

THE
POLICE SUPERVISOR
AND THE
ORGANIZATIONAL
ENVIRONMENT

part one

Introduction

Our society is an organizational society. We are born in organizations, educated by organizations, and most of us spend much of our lives working for organizations. We spend much of our leisure time paying, playing, and praying in organizations. Most of us will die in an organization, and when the time comes for burial, the largest organization of all—the state—must grant official permission.[1]

Clearly, life in organizations is one of experiencing levels of phenomena, of dealing with them, and of combining them together into a plan for rational cooperative action. Consequently, all police supervisors must interact with people, groups of people, and groups of groups, that is to say, the organizational environment.

Organizations are not a modern innovation. The Bible, in regard to the great exodus, relates that

Moses picked out able men from all Israel and put them in charge of the people as officers over groups of thousands, of hundreds, of fifties, and of tens. They rendered decisions for the people in all ordinary cases. The more difficult cases they rendered to Moses, but all the lesser cases they settled themselves.[2]

Other examples can be found in early Egypt, China, and the Catholic Church. Peculiar to our times is man's increasing propensity to draw himself into a web of collective patterns. Modern organizations fulfill a greater variety of societal and personal needs, involve a greater proportion of the population, and account for a larger segment of man's daily life than ever before. This growth in the pervasiveness and influence of organizations has

---

[1] Amitai Etzioni, *Modern Organizations* (Englewood Cliffs, N.J.: Prentice-Hall, Inc., 1964), p. 1.

[2] The author wishes to acknowledge that this particular use of this Biblical quotation was discovered in Robert T. Golembiewski and Frank K. Gibson, eds., *Managerial Behavior and Organizational Demands: Management as a Linking of Levels of Interaction* (Chicago, Ill.: Rand McNally & Company, 1967), p. 2.

generated certain undesirable social and human costs, two of which are personal frustration and alienation. But, there seems no stopping the organizational world, because it is not safe to get off.[3]

Few segments of local government are organized more extensively than the police. The reason is evident: The police are highly dependent on what organization offers. To explain, the police need an established set of relationships among their functions; they need stability, control, and predictability in their internal operations and external transactions. More than ever before, the police need satisfying relationships among the people, process, and technology with which they work.

Part One is devoted to impressing upon the reader that no supervisor is a social island, whatever his specified duties. It is comprised of four chapters. The first chapter examines the individual and his behavior. The following chapter is concerned both with influence in face-to-face situations and with group dynamics and the special problems encountered by police supervisors trying to effectively coordinate their subordinates. The next chapter deals with the formal structure and goals of police organizations. The fourth and final chapter presents the informal nature of police organizations.

Dividing the material in this manner is reasonable both because it provides for systematic development from the single person to the large aggregation of people and because it describes the personal, social, and organizational environment in which the police supervisor operates.[4] The police supervisor is responsible, first, for coping with specific individuals (subordinates, peers, and superiors) who may or may not assist him in meeting his job role and in satisfying his personal needs; second, for utilizing groups of people in teams, which he must direct and lead; and, third, for linking the above individuals and groups of individuals into an established pattern of action for accomplishing the over-all goals of the police organization. Argyris provides a fitting conclusion when he writes:

> To put this another way, we believe that organizations and personalities are discrete units with their own laws, which make them amenable to study as separate units. However, we also believe that important parts of each unit's existence depend on their connectedness with the other. We hypothesize that one cannot fully understand the individual without understanding the organization in which he is embedded and vice versa.[5]

---

[3] *Ibid.*, p. 1.

[4] For an excellent overview of the interrelationship of organizations with their environments see Shirley Terreberry, "The Evolution of Organizational Environments," *Administrative Science Quarterly*, 12 (March 1968), 590–613.

[5] Chris Argyris, *Integrating the Individual and the Organization* (New York: John Wiley & Sons, Inc., 1964), p. 13.

2

The Organizational Environment
And Individuals

When an individual joins a police organization, he brings with him all the characteristics of a whole man—perception, needs, attitudes, motivations and tensions, knowledge, and problem-solving capabilities. Although he has moved from an individual to an organizational environment, we can expect the same laws to shape his behavior. This assumption has been a primary guiding influence in the recent progress toward a better understanding of supervision and organizations. It is presently recognized that the complex behavior observed in organizations can be found in the simpler conditions of individual existence.

> The route from psychology to administration is a two-way street. Going in one direction, we interpret administrative behavior in terms of psychological laws. Going the other way, we use organizational settings as social environments where psychological laws can be tested, and where ideas may be generated for their development and improvement. Thus, it becomes more and more essential for students of administration to have a good basic understanding of psychology, and for psychologists to know something about human behavior as it is observed in organizations.[1]

This chapter is aimed at facilitating the interaction between supervision and psychology. It is organized in terms of categories familiar to the psychologist: perception, needs, attitudes, motivations, tensions, learning, and thinking. Each category contains a discussion of basic psychological theories and knowledge that apply to individuals. Examples are provided of how these theories operate in organizational situations. Immediately preceding these categories is a general description of us as individuals.

Once this chapter is completed, a student of police supervision should be prepared to approach the professional literature of psychology and to extract its implications for individual behavior as it relates to the organiza-

---

[1] Timothy W. Costello and Sheldon S. Zalkind, eds., *Psychology in Administration* (Englewood Cliffs, N.J.: Prentice-Hall, Inc., 1963), p. iii.

tional environment. Hopefully, the nature of this chapter expresses confidence that we have reached a stage in the behavioral sciences where supervision and psychology can interact closely with meaningful advantage to both.

INDIVIDUALS: BASIC ASSUMPTIONS ABOUT PEOPLE

There are a host of assumptions, many of them contradictory, about the nature of people. A few examples are:

> Individuals are motivated by economic rewards versus individuals are motivated by social rewards.
> Individuals are self-controlled versus individuals are controlled by group membership.
> Individuals are most satisfied when provided explicit instructions versus individuals are most satisfied when provided general guidelines for action.

This list could easily be extended. Important here is the recognition that they cannot all be correct. Consequently, what can a police supervisor safely assume about human nature, remembering that he needs a consistent assumption or assumptions for predicting human behavior?[2]

Each supervisor needs an internally consistent theoretical generalization as a foundation for practical action on his part. Some kind of useful theory is just as vital for the police supervisor with his people problems as information theory is for the systems engineer with his computer problems. As previously mentioned, the primary criteria for establishing a theory about people for supervisors are consistency and utility. With this twofold specification in mind, three basic assumptions upon which a theory about individual behavior can be built are now suggested.[3] It is up to the reader to determine whether they are personally helpful or not.

The three major ideas offered by modern psychologists are (1) that behavior is caused (causality), a notion derived from an awareness that both environment and heredity influence a person's behavior, (2) that behavior is purposive, that is to say, besides being caused, an individual's behavior is directed toward a particular goal or goals, and (3) that behavior is motivated by a variety of circumstances, ranging from need fulfillment to anxiety, that tend to move a person along a given path. Combining these three ideas furnishes a beginning for understanding and predicting human behav-

---

[2] For an excellent compilation of research findings on individual behavior, see Bernard Berelson and Gary A. Steiner, *Human Behavior: An Inventory of Scientific Findings* (New York: Harcourt, Brace & World, Inc., 1964).

[3] The three assumptions used here are a product of Harold J. Leavitt, *Managerial Psychology*, 2nd ed. (Chicago, Ill.: University of Chicago Press, 1964), pp. 7–12.

ior. Together they provide conceptual building blocks for constructing a model of human behavior. The model can be referred to as a stimulus-organism-response (SOR) type (see Figure 1).

The assumptions of causality, motivation, and purposiveness apply to all people all the time. Once accepted and used, these assumptions should automatically lead the police supervisor to attempt to discover the motive, and the cause behind it, for a subordinate's behavior. More will be said in a later section about the components of the behavioral model. One further point remains to be covered—that the three assumptions are interrelated in a circular design. Once a person reaches his goal, the cause, motive, and reason for action (behavior) are either eliminated or reduced. Significantly, the goals that eliminate the previous conditions are physical and thus limited. The goals that lessen reasons for the previous steps are psychological and hence unlimited. In other words, we may obtain enough food but seldom sufficient self-esteem.

Thus far we have looked at man in terms of his general, or generic, characteristics. The following sections disclose how and why we as individuals differ from one another. However, before discussing the reasons for our differences (needs, attitudes, motivations, and tensions) we turn to a review of a highly influential conditioner of a person's psychology—perception.

PERCEPTION: REALITY IS
THAT WHICH HAS REAL CONSEQUENCES

All of us sense our world differently. We react to a specific object based on what we see rather than on what it really is. Often we see only what we want to in a given situation. Similarly, how we react depends on what we hear, not necessarily on what was really said. An excellent way to begin applying behavioral science research to supervisory practice is to put aside the attitude of naive realism—an attitude that suggests that our perceptions simply record what is "out there."[4] In fact, they do not. However, this does not mean that we respond only to the subtle or irrelevant cues or to emotional factors. We frequently perceive the obvious, but we are quite likely to react as well to the less obvious and less objective.[5] *Perception* is the complex process by which people select and organize sensory stimulation into a meaningful and rational picture of the world.[6] Since we have mentioned

---

[4] The reader interested in a summary of research findings on the perceptual process should see Jerome Bruner, "Social Psychology and Perception," in *Readings in Social Psychology* (3rd ed.), eds. E. Maccoby, T. Newcomb, and E. Hartley (New York: Holt, Rinehart & Winston, Inc., 1958).

[5] Costello and Zalkind, *Psychology in Administration*, p. 7.

[6] This definition, and others in the chapter, are taken from Berelson and Steiner, *Human Behavior*.

sensation we now define it as the immediate and direct apprehension of simple stimuli—the response of the sense organs to light, sound, pressure, and the like—or the experienced results of that process. Finally, a *stimulus* is a unit of sensory input—for example, some definable unit of light falling on and exciting the receptors in the retina of the eye.

How people come to know and interpret their world is basic to a knowledge of human behavior, since *behavior* (as compared to sheer motion) is action that takes the environment into consideration. Two fundamental theories about human perception are (1) all understanding of the world depends on the senses and their stimulation, but (2) the facts of pure sensory data are insufficient to create or to explain the rational picture of the world as experienced by an individual. The first of these statements is a well established philosophical assumption. The second is an empirical finding that has been documented. In essence, the study of perception is the study of what must be added to and subtracted from pure sensory input to create our picture of the world. Throughout this section the reference is chiefly to vision, man's most widely studied sense. While the preponderance of evidence comes from visual experiments, the general theories apply also to the other senses (hearing, touch, etc.).

Let us consider a few simple but useful examples of the perceptual process. First, how many of us have viewed a particular phenomenon and then attempted to describe it to another person who has also seen it? Most of us were quick to find that our view did not exactly coincide with the other person's. In other words, each of us perceived the phenomenon differently. Second, how many of us have listened to a person speak and then discussed what we heard? Frequently, there are differences expressed over the meaning, that is, perceived meaning, of the message. The perceptual process is seen in action when two psychiatrists pass one of their colleagues on the street. One psychiatrist smiles and says, "Good morning." The other two respond similarly and after walking a few feet, one turns to the other and says, "I wonder what he really meant by that?"[7]

The reasons behind the differences in our perceptions will be explained shortly. Before doing so, a highly critical factor should be stressed at this time—people behave on the basis of the perceived world. Therefore, if we wish to understand an individual we must understand the individual's present perception of the world. Specifically important to a police supervisor is an understanding of a subordinate's perception of his job environment. For if there is any common human relations mistake made by supervisors in their relations with subordinates, it is the error of assuming

---

[7] Another humorous example of the perceptual process was recently observed by this author in the musical comedy *Cabaret*. In one scene an actor dances with a female gorilla and, after a few moments, turns to the audience and expresses his affection for the animal by stating, "If you could only see her through my eyes" (September 3, 1968).

that the real world is all that exists, that everyone works for the same goals, and that the facts are just as he sees them.

If people, and therefore police officers, act on their perceptions and if different individuals perceive things differently, how is the supervisor to know what to expect? In other words, what determines how people perceive their particular environment? Perceptual differences are caused by a series of psychological conditioners (see Figure 1). These conditioners play a major role in determining how we view our world and, subsequently, greatly influence our behavior.

To reemphasize, people's perceptions are determined by a series of conditioners: needs, attitudes, motives, and tensions.[8] All four of these conditioners cause us to employ a process known as *selective perception*. Basically, selective perception results from our attempts to accommodate our desire for need achievement to developed attitudes and tension-producing events. For example, selective perception causes us to magnify either a compliment (need fulfillment) or a word of disapproval (tension) from a superior. This brief illustration exemplifies two of four fundamental rules about selective perception: we look for what will assist us in fulfilling our needs and ignore that which is disturbing (if not a great threat). Note that those things of an immediate and intense threat are not, in most instances, capable of being ignored. At a certain point a dangerous situation becomes so threatening that we reverse our course, discard our perceptual blindfold, and preoccupy ourselves totally with the situation. Hence, the third rule: we pay close attention to that which is really dangerous. Leavitt puts it this way, "People perceive what they think will help satisfy needs; ignore what is disturbing; and again perceive disturbances that persist and increase."[9] The fourth rule about selective perception involves conflict resolution and is considered later in the section on tension.

Thus far we have been talking mainly about the general influences on the perceptual process without regard to the perceiver and his characteristics. There is a fairly substantial amount of research information presently available about individuals as perceivers. Essentially, the research points to a single major problem confronted by the perceiver—accuracy. Somehow we must gain more accurate information about ourselves and others. The most appropriate mechanism available for reducing perceptual distortion is feedback. Other people, by providing us with timely feedback, can help us bring what we see closer to what is real, reducing our uncertainty and

---

[8] It is interesting to note that there are research findings which in turn show that a person's motivations often affect his perception. Briefly, when the real world and the motivations of the individual are at odds, behavior is first designed to bring the real world into line with the motivations. But when this is impossible, for external or internal reasons, the discrepancy can be reduced by attempted changes in the perception of reality. Berelson and Steiner, *Human Behavior*, p. 266.

[9] Leavitt, *Managerial Psychology*, p. 33.

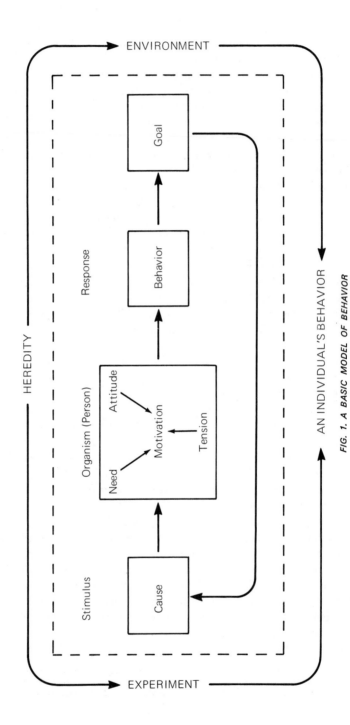

FIG. 1. A BASIC MODEL OF BEHAVIOR

anxiety in the process. Current research suggests certain conclusions about perceivers:[10]

1. *Knowing yourself makes it easier to perceive others accurately.* When a person understands his own personal make-up, he makes fewer mistakes in perceiving that of others.
2. *Your own characteristics, or "mental set," influence the characteristics you are apt to perceive in others.* Thus, the traits which dominate or influence the perceiver will be more often observed when he is forming impressions of others.
3. *In accepting yourself as you are, you are more likely to see the better traits in people.* By accepting ourselves as we really are, we broaden our scope of vision to include the possibility of favorable characteristics in others. Further, as is to be expected, we are more likely to create a favorable image of those having traits we accept in ourselves and to reject those having traits we either do not like or do not have in ourselves.
4. *The ability to be accurate in the perception of others is not a single skill.* It has been shown that a perceiver tends to evaluate the feelings others have about him on the basis of his feelings toward them. Consequently, our ability to perceive others with reasonable accuracy depends on how sensitive we are to the differences between people and to the cultural standards for judging them.

In summary, the police supervisor who desires to perceive someone else accurately must attempt to look at the other person, not at himself. What we perceive in someone else is influenced by our own traits. But if we know our own traits, we can be aware that they provide a background for an evaluation. To put it another way, our own traits help to furnish the categories we use in perceiving others. The question one should ask when viewing another is: "Am I looking at him and forming my impression of his behavior in the situation, or am I just comparing him with myself?"[11]

Before the impression is left that it is only the characteristics of the perceiver that stand between him and others in his efforts to know them, we turn now to some characteristics of the person or persons being perceived which create difficulties in perception. By this it is meant that interpersonal, group, and organizational situations influence one's perception. Recent behavioral science research clearly points out that the process of perception is, at least in part, a function of the social context in which the perception occurs. Much of the research has important implications for a police supervisor. It is possible to identify several characteristics of the interpersonal, group, and organizational climate which have direct effect on perceptual

---

[10] The four conclusions are adapted from an article by Sheldon S. Zalkind and Timothy W. Costello, "Perception: Implications for Administration," *Administrative Science Quarterly*, 7 (September 1962), pp. 218–35.

[11] *Ibid.*, p. 231.

accuracy. Significantly, these are characteristics which can be identified, and, in some cases, controlled in supervisory relationships. How the situation affects the perceptual process is perhaps best understood by citing a few findings. First, when people are given an opportunity to interact in a friendly situation, they tend to see others as similar to themselves. Applying this thinking to a supervisory situation, we can see that some difficulties for supervisory practice develop out of a belief that groups in the organization are made up of different types of people. Once we believe that people in other groups are different, we tend to see the differences. Therefore, would it not be better to create an organizational situation which is cooperative rather than competitive, thus promoting the probability of seeing other people as similar to ourselves? Second, when a work group is comprised of friendly members willing to continue working in the same group, each one's perceptions of the goal-directed behavior of fellow group members are more accurate. The implications for establishing work groups seem clear; namely, do not place together those with a past record of major personal clashes. If they must be in the same group, each must be assisted to see that the other is attempting to accomplish the same goal. Finally, the supervisor's perceptions will be frequently confined to situations which relate specifically to his own department, despite any attempt of his organization to discourage such selectivity. Overlapping group memberships plus continual broad-gauged in-service training programs are two possible ways to reduce selectivity.

In conclusion, perceptual accuracy depends on knowing one's self and one's situation (interpersonal, group, and organization). The probability of developing such knowledge of ourselves and other people is enhanced if the police supervisor: (1) becomes continuously aware of the intricacies of the perceptual process; (2) avoids arbitrary and categorical judgments; (3) seeks reliable information before judgments are made; (4) shifts position as additional information is acquired; and, most crucial, (5) recognizes that we all see things differently because our needs greatly determine the view we have of ourselves and the world. To ignore the importance of the perceptual process is to ignore a major determinant of behavior. However, it remains easy to assume that everyone views a particular person or event from our perspective. Hence, we are constantly challenged to improve our perceptual accuracy and to minimize as far as possible the subjective approach in perceiving others. Supervisors unable to cope with this challenge are seriously handicapped. On the other hand, we must not think that perceptual distortions will not occur simply because the supervisor says he will try to be objective. The police supervisor must guard against seeing only what he wants to see and refuse to mold everything into what he is prepared to see.

NEEDS, ATTITUDES, TENSIONS, AND MOTIVATIONS: A RATIONAL MAN IS ONE WHO CAN HOLD HIS IRRATIONALITIES WITHIN DUE BOUNDS

This section deals with the determinants of human striving: that which we need, that which we avoid (tension), and our attitude toward both. All three determinants precede overt human behavior and, together, provide a basis for understanding motivation theory. We take such needs, attitudes, and tensions for granted as underlying causes of behavior because we constantly experience them.

Let us now define the four terms used in this section. First, a *need* is a requirement, either psychological or physiological, to be fulfilled. Second, an *attitude* is the predisposition of an individual to evaluate some symbol or object or aspect of his world in a favorable or unfavorable manner.[12] One develops an attitude concerning an external object or symbol; that is, an attitude has an objective referent. Third, *tension* is a state of uneasiness produced by either internal or external barriers placed between people and their goals. This definition also encompasses frustration, stress, and conflict. Finally, *motivation* broadly refers to all three of the above determinants. It is an inner state which energizes, activates, and directs, or channels, behavior toward goals. As previously mentioned, a motive results in and therefore can be inferred from purposive, goal-directed behavior.

> One note of caution needs to be stressed at this point. Since motives are both inferred from and taken to account for purposive behavior, there is always the danger of accepting circular reasoning—of taking a motive as an explanation of the very behavior from which it was inferred. When the conditions that produce or arouse a motive are known, or when there are independent measures of it, motives help to explain behavior. When such conditions are not met, motives may serve to describe behavior, but they do not explain it. In short, anyone can make a child hungry, but not anyone can make him ambitious—and therein lies the essential distinction. Being able, truly able, to explain the former, we can predict and control in line with the explanation.[13]

We now proceed to look at each one of the four determinants in more detail.

---

[12] Daniel Katz, "The Functional Approach to the Study of Attitudes," *Public Opinion Quarterly*, 24 (March 1960), 166. Further, there is considerable recent support for emphasizing human values over attitudes. See Milton Rokeach, "A Theory of Organization and Change Within Value Attitude Systems," *The Journal of Social Issues*, 24 (January 1968), 13–34.

[13] Berelson and Steiner, *Human Behavior*, pp. 240–41.

Needs

Current motivational theory questions the validity of limiting our attention to a list of needs. However, it is apparent that our behavior is vastly influenced by our desire for need-fulfillment. A listing of human needs provides a point of departure into the dynamic nature of our needs; however, the list must not be seen as the final answer. Maslow has constructed such an approach. His need-hierarchy model provides a scheme for better understanding individual behavior.[14]

Maslow identified five basic needs possessed by all individuals. Condensed, these are physiological safety, social esteem, and self-actualization. In addition, we are compelled to achieve or maintain the various conditions through which these needs or satisfactions can be obtained. Further, these needs are related to one another in terms of a hierarchy, certain higher needs becoming activated to the extent certain lower ones become fulfilled. Simply, the most potent need will monopolize our behavior, while the less potent needs are minimized. But when one need is fairly well satisfied, the next higher need emerges to dominate and organize our behavior. McGregor described the five needs, in order of their dominance, as follows:[15]

Physiological Needs

Man is a wanting animal—as soon as one of his needs is satisfied, another appears in its place.

Man's needs are organized in a series of levels—a hierarchy of importance. At the lowest level, but preeminent in importance when they are thwarted, are his *physiological needs*. . . . Unless the circumstances are unusual, his needs for love, for status, for recognition are inoperative when his stomach has been empty for awhile.

A satisfied need is not a motivator of behavior! This is a fact of profound significance that is regularly ignored in the conventional approach to the management of ("normal") people. Consider your own need for air; except as you are deprived of it, it has no appreciable motivating effect upon your behavior.

Safety Needs

When the physiological needs are reasonably satisfied, needs at the next higher level begin to dominate man's behavior, to motivate him. These are called *safety needs*. They are needs for protection against danger, threat, deprivation. The fact needs little emphasis that, since every industrial employee is in a

---

[14] For details on this, see A. H. Maslow, "A Dynamic Theory of Human Motivation," *Psychological Review*, 50 (September 1943).

[15] This quotation is excerpted from an address by Douglas M. McGregor, 5th Anniversary Convocation, School of Industrial Management, Massachusetts Institute of Technology, Cambridge, Massachusetts. The address is cited in James V. Clark, "Motivation in Work Groups: A Tentative View: Part One," *Human Organization*, 19 (December-January, 1960–61), 199–202.

dependent relationship, safety needs may assume considerable importance. Arbitrary management actions, behavior which arouses uncertainty with respect to continued employment or which reflects favoritism or discrimination, unpredictable administration of policy—these can be poweful motivators of the safety needs in the employment relationship at *every level*, from worker to vice president.

Social Needs

When man's physiological needs are satisfied and he is no longer fearful about his physical welfare, his *social needs* become important motivators of his behavior—needs for belonging, for association, for acceptance by his fellows, for giving and receiving friendship and love.

Management knows today of the existence of these needs, but often assumes quite wrongly that they represent a threat to the organization.

Yet management, fearing group hostility to its own objectives, often goes to considerable lengths to control and direct human efforts in ways that are inimical to the natural "groupiness" of human beings. When man's social needs—and perhaps his safety needs, too—are thus thwarted, he behaves in ways which tend to defeat organizational objectives. He becomes resistant, antagonistic, uncooperative. But this behavior is a consequence, not a cause.

Self-Esteem Needs

Above the social needs—in the sense that they do not become motivators until lower needs are reasonably satisifed—are the needs of greater significance to management and to man himself. They are the *egoistic needs*.

Unlike the lower needs, these are rarely satisfied; man seeks indefinitely for more satisfaction of these needs once they have become important to him. But they do not appear in any significant way until physiological, safety, and social needs are all reasonably satisfied.

The typical industrial organization offers few opportunities for the satisfaction of these self-esteem needs to people at lower levels in the hierarchy. The conventional methods of organizing work, particularly in mass-production industries, give little heed to these aspects of human motivation.

Self-Actualizing Needs

Finally—a capstone, as it were, on the hierarchy of man's needs—there are what we may call the needs for self-actualization. These are the needs for realizing one's own potentialities, for continued self-development, for being creative in the broadest sense of that term.

It is clear that the conditions of modern life give only limited opportunity for these relatively weak needs to obtain expression. The deprivation most people experience with respect to other lower-level needs diverts their energies into the struggle to satisfy those needs, and the needs for self-actualization remain dormant.

Thus it can be seen that man is a perpetually wanting animal. It should be remembered that the described levels of needs are interdependent and overlapping; hence, each higher-need level can emerge before the immediately lower-need level need has been totally satisfied. As an example, our need for social acceptance normally appears before our safety need is completely satisfied.

As alluded to earlier in this section, a mere listing of needs does not provide an adequate understanding of the dynamics involved in need-fulfillment. Maslow also recognized that there are basic problems connected with his hierarchy of needs theory. A few of those he cited were (1) the problem of values in motivation theory, (2) the relation between appetites, desires, needs, and what is "good" for the person, (3) the nature of the uncompleted act, of success and of failure, and (4) the relation between needs and cultural patterns. In other words, differences are found among individuals when they are responding to the group of needs described by Maslow. The differences are caused by five intervening factors that influence the individual's mode of response to his needs: cognitive style, previous experience, level of aspiration, expectancy, and group memberships. Let us, in a general sense, review each of these factors.

Cognitive style means that each of us form our own way, or style, of handling need satisfaction. Our style is learned through receiving different rewards and punishments for different actions and includes some degree of cognitive (rational) control over our responses. Next, our previous experiences with failure and success directly influence our future level of aspiration. Feelings of failure tend to reduce our level of aspiration while successful experiences raise it. The police supervisor who thinks that his subordinates will be challenged more by the establishment of goals that they cannot reach might well take notice of this failure-success relationship to an individual's level of aspiration. Expectancy also fits into this relationship since either past successes or expectation of future successes increase the attractiveness of a task. Expectancy is based on what a person hopes to get from his endeavor, while the level of aspiration refers to what the person hopes to do (performance level). Finally, because the group influences its members, it also influences the response they make to their needs. Certainly, group norms, the status of the individual in the group, and the amount of interdependency between members for goal achievement operate on the needs of a person.

In summary, a police supervisor cannot afford to think of need fulfillment as a simple matter of matching needs and satisfiers.[16] A complex series of factors intervene between these two elements of any motivational system,

---

[16] To illustrate, "It was found in a series of factor analytic studies . . . that two kinds of need achievement can be distinguished: (a) the need to achieve through one's own efforts—i.e., the need to do a job well—and (b) the need to be a success which results in emulation of the successful rather than hard work." C. G. Costello, "Need Achievement and College Performance," *The Journal of Psychology*, 69 (May 1968), 17–18.

making the needs of human behavior a challenging and frequently a frustrating puzzle.

Attitudes

People differ in their needs. Interwoven with these needs are variations in their attitudes. A police supervisor seeking to influence the behavior of others—subordinates, superiors, co-workers in his own department or in other departments—soon becomes aware of the importance of his attitudes. The supervisor may be amazed at some of the attitudes others have and question how they can hold some of the views they do (especially if these views differ from his own). He may be irritated when others do not change their attitudes even after he has presented facts that obviously should cause them to change.

The behavioral sciences have given a great deal of attention to attitudes, especially in recent years with the expanded use of the sample survey and related techniques. (Remember that attitudes always have to be *about* something—politics, religion, work, and so on.) Scientists have gathered data on the functions of attitudes, the ways in which they develop, the conditions leading to change of attitudes, and the resistance to change of attitudes. The earlier discussion of perception and needs will serve as background for understanding more about attitudes.

Katz informs us that attitudes perform four critical functions for the personality: adjustment, ego-defense, value-expression, and knowledge.[17] Together they furnish an understanding of the reasons that people hold the attitudes they do. Moreover, if we do not comprehend the various reasons for the holding of an attitude we are placed in a poor position to predict when and how it will change. Certainly a more comprehensive discussion of how attitudes serve the four functions is in order.

First, the *adjustment function* is essentially an awareness of the fact that we attempt to maximize the rewards and minimize the penalties in our environment. If a given object is perceived as assisting us in accomplishing a certain goal, then we normally form a positive attitude toward it and vice versa. Hence, the closer an object, person, or idea comes to providing goal attainment, the greater the probabilities of a favorable attitude. Considerable effort has been made both to identify the causes that create job attitudes and to improve their positive influence on the worker.[18] Second, the *ego-defensive function* is an internalized method by which we defend our ego from distasteful or threatening forces and reduce our tension about such problems. This function is helpful in that it reduces sensitivity to impending problems,

---

[17] Katz, "The Functional Approach," pp. 163–76.

[18] For an example, see Paul M. Whisenand, "Work Values and Job Satisfaction: Anyone Interested?" *Public Personnel Review*, in press.

but a handicap in that it makes us unable to cope fully with the actual situation. Third, the *value-expressive function* gives clarity and support to our self-image. As such, this function gives positive expression to our personal values and to our conceptions of ourselves as individuals. Fourth, the *knowledge function* assists us in arranging, in a meaningful way, the informational inputs into our daily lives. In this case our attitudes are a frame of reference for organizing our knowledge into a sensible understanding of the world.

We acquire our attitudes through our learning experiences. The major influences in attitude formation are our society (its customs, habits, and traditions), our family, and our group memberships (socio-economic class to peer relationships). As important as these historical determinants are, new attitudes may be formed and old ones changed by contemporary influences. Certainly, organizations affect an employee's attitudes. In fact, there is relatively firm evidence that an organization tends to shape its members and their attitudes in its own image.[19] Let us look at some of the principles underlying the changing of attitudes.

Before a police supervisor can adequately deal with an individual's attitude, he must know what kind of an attitude actually exists. The identification of attitudes is not an easy chore. Briefly, if the supervisor pays close attention to the person's behavior in various situations, he increases the probabilities of determining correctly which attitudes are present. Once these attitudes are identified, the supervisor is in a good position to select the proper conditions for changing the person's attitude.

The first and most critical step in initiating attitudinal change is to arouse a need for such change. The next step is to show the person that the suggested shift in attitude is beneficial to him and consistent with his other values or goals. The final step is to reinforce the newly acquired attitude through a system of rewards. Now let us again look at the four types of attitudes and see how each might be changed. The adjustive attitude is best modified by making the subordinate dissatisfied with his own existing attitude. Showing a subordinate a better attitudinal route to the achievement of some particular need usually creates dissatisfaction with the current route. Essential here is that the subordinate, not just the supervisor, become displeased with a current attitude. Ego-defensive attitudes are the most difficult to change because they provide protection for the ego. This attitude is best approached as not being connected with the particular individual. The attitude in question should be treated as a part of the organization so as to permit the subordinate every opportunity to voluntarily extricate himself from it. The value-expressive and knowledge-serving attitudes are most effectively changed by conveying to the person both new values and information which seem more meaningful

---

[19] Ivar Berg, "Do Organizations Change People," in *Individualism and Big Business*, ed. Leonard Sayles (New York: McGraw-Hill Book Company, 1963), pp. 61–65.

than the old. To emphasize an earlier point—the need to change an attitude must be aroused in order for the change to occur.

In general, there are two ways to change attitudes: individual and programmatic. The police supervisor needs to use both approaches. The individual approach can be accomplished through two methods: interpersonal contacts and role changes. The former is precarious in that the subordinate may perceive the supervisor as coercing him into a threatening position. It is important that the police supervisor impart information for purposes of discussion rather than as directives based on status. When used properly, this method involves the subordinate in a participative process designed to point out the more advantageous attitudes. The latter individual method is less direct and more influential. In essence, the police supervisor gives a subordinate a specific assignment (group or individual) that quite naturally influences him into adopting new attitudes.[20]

The programmatic approach to attitudinal change embraces a host of training and developmental methods. These organized programs of attitude change range from recruit indoctrination through executive development. Further, the training method employed varies from lectures to nondirective group conferences. More is said about the training programs and the techniques involved in a later chapter.

A final word about resistance to change—we often fail to understand that even a seemingly minor attitudinal change may be resisted. Employees, subordinates, and supervisors alike have vested interests in the established ways; therefore, they are apprehensive over anything new. Seldom do we resist change just to be stubborn; we resist it mainly because it creates psychological and social anxiety. It is imperative, once a police supervisor recognizes resistance to attitudinal change, that he not condemn it as irrational behavior. His immediate reaction should be in terms of the steps outlined above, namely, identification of the attitude in question, selection of proper conditions for changing it, and so on.

Tensions: Frustrations and Conflicts

Our modern environment sees to it that we do not frequently experience tension-free moments. Internal tension is generated whenever one experiences either frustration or conflict or both. Both of these are states of mind

---

[20] Few would argue that social forces do not constrain and change a person's attitudes. Moreover, a number of studies have shown that when a person is induced to behave in a manner opposed to his private attitude, his attitude tends to change to conform more closely to the induced behavior. One explanation for this change is that it is the result of improvisation. According to this view, a person becomes temporarily motivated in favor of the new position and is subject to self-persuasion. As an example, see Phyllis G. Orain, "Induction of Action and Attitude Change: The Function of Role-Self Conflicts and Levels of Endorsement," *The Journal of Psychology*, 68 (January 1968), 39–48.

that induce a person either to overcome a barrier or to adopt defensive action. Let us first acknowledge that these psychological adversities—frustration and conflict—are normal and beset all of us. It is our reaction to them that is occasionally considered abnormal: for example, neurotic behavior and psychosomatic ailments.

Frustration stems either from our attempt to satisfy a need being blocked or from our resistance to required attitudinal change. In either case, we normally try to circumvent, remove, or otherwise master the barrier or necessary change. Conflict is slightly more complex and occurs when two or more needs block each other, when they are mutually exclusive. Obviously our conflicts vary in their intensity from what television program to watch to which occupation to choose. Consider for a moment the police supervisor. Should he identify with management and thus indicate his fundamental loyalty to the work group? Or, is it possible for him to express a dual loyalty?

The police supervisor cannot hope to protect his subordinates from the typical psychological adversities. What he can hope to do, however, is to reduce their negative impact on both the individual and the police organization. If not properly handled by the supervisor, frustration and conflict can increase to the extent that unhealthy behavior results. A positive approach to the handling of tension (conflict resolution) by the police supervisor follows.

First, the supervisor must be quick to recognize tension. Second, he should make every attempt to comprehend the reasons for its existence. Third, he must not consider tension abnormal but rather accept it as a part of our daily lives. Fourth, the police supervisor must not become subjectively involved in the situation but remain to one side to protect his objectivity and ability to act with reasoned judgment. Obviously, the impact of tension varies with the individual. Moreover, tension-producing phenomena affect different people in different ways. Fifth, the supervisor must, therefore, plan his response according to the situation and the individual involved. Last, his response should include a plan for leading the person away from the tension-producing barrier into a better position for need-fulfillment or attitude adjustment.[21]

Motivation

Serious thinkers always have been concerned with ways of motivating man to his best efforts, of encouraging him to bring both buttocks to whatever occupies him.[22]

---

[21] For an interesting and relevant article on psychological conflict in police organizations, see Everett G. Dillman, "A Source of Personal Conflict in Police Organizations," *Public Personnel Review*, 28 (October 1967), 222–27.

[22] Robert T. Golembiewski, *Men, Management, and Morality: Toward a New Organizational Ethic* (New York: McGraw-Hill Book Company, Inc., 1965), p. 187.

One of the central problems of any police organization is to motivate its personnel to attain the goals of the organization. As stated earlier, by motivation we mean an inner state that energizes need-fulfillment, attitude manifestation, and tension reduction and that directs a person's behavior toward an objective. Since our basic concern is the motivation of police personnel to accomplish the goals of their departments, we limit our discussion to job-related motivation. However, our interest also includes, and significantly so, the personal satisfaction of the individual.

Most people in our modern society derive only slight personal satisfaction from their jobs. Likewise, many police personnel are subjected to organizational situations that detract from their job-related satisfactions. Therefore, a major question arises—how might a police supervisor create a situation in which his subordinates can *satisfy their individual needs while, at the same time, work toward the goals (organizational needs) of the department*? Sayles and Strauss list five basic alternative methods for motivating employees: (1) the "be strong" approach, (2) the "be good" approach, (3) implicit bargaining, (4) competition, and (5) internalized motivation.[23] All five approaches have built-in limitations and, in practice, a supervisor uses them in various combinations. In essence, it is the particular job and the specific employees that determine which approach to use.

For many reasons, internalized motivation is the best motivation for use in police organizations, since it provides the greatest opportunity for police personnel to satisfy their needs and to develop healthy job-related attitudes, and an excellent foundation is established for more effectively achieving the goals of the department. However, we must recognize two critical points: first, that the needs of the organization and those of the individual are probably never identical; and second, that personal job satisfaction is not directly related to high productivity. What we are striving for, then, is a form of organizational motivation that encourages an emphasis upon both job requirements and individual needs. Significantly, the police supervisor plays a highly important function in such a motivational scheme.

Internalized motivation attempts to provide this dual emphasis on organizational job requirements and human job-related needs and attitudes. Briefly, this approach seeks to furnish opportunities for personal need fulfillment through doing the job itself and, consequently, internalizes motivation so that people will enjoy doing good work. Internalized motivation lends itself very readily to police work because the job permits the exercise of discretion. Police personnel usually enjoy considerable autonomy in performing their tasks, which offers the greatest possibility for them to satisfy their needs and to develop their personalities.

---

[23] Leonard R. Sayles and George Strauss, *Human Behavior in Organizations* (Englewood Cliffs, N.J.: Prentice-Hall, Inc., 1966), pp. 135–54.

As previously mentioned, the police supervisor can perform a highly meaningful function in fostering internalized motivation. He possesses this faculty since his *principal organizational responsibility is to develop the human resources of a police department by motivating its employees.* This responsibility is accomplished primarily through a style of supervision that supports such conditions as participative decision making, developmental training, and job enlargement, to mention but a few.[24] Future chapters enlarge upon this style of supervision by including a number of immediate, job-related factors that affect the degree to which a police officer can be self-determinative at his work. In conclusion one function of a police supervisor is to motivate his subordinates to achieve job objectives and, of equal importance, personal need satisfaction.

LEARNING: MAN BY HIS VERY NATURE DESIRES TO KNOW

We learn throughout our lives. In fact, every aspect of our human behavior is responsive to learning experiences. Not only can knowledge, language, and skills be learned but also attitudes, value systems, and personality characteristics. Moreover, our activities in a formal work organization (loyalties, role expectations, norms, organizational values) have been learned. Obviously, however, all of our learning experiences do not take place in a job situation. Many occurred previous to entering a work environment. Further, much of our learning while in a formal organization occurs outside its boundaries—in the family, social groups, and community. *Learning*, whether it be in a formal training program or through an individual effort, can be defined as changes in behavior that result from previous behavior in similar situations. In general, learning refers to the effects of experience, either direct or conceptual, on subsequent behavior.

The effectiveness of a police organization is limited by the cumulative effect of each police officer's previously learned abilities, his subsequent learning experiences, and his motivating influences. We concentrate on the learning experiences of an individual occurring after he enters the organization. Further, we approach organizational learning as both a formal and an informal program for imparting new experience or changing existing behavior. This process, in order to distinguish it from learning experiences acquired outside the organization, is hereafter referred to as human resource or personnel development.

---

[24] Significantly, the positive relationship between job size and job satisfaction cannot be assumed to be general but rather is dependent to a great extent on the backgrounds of the workers. See Charles L. Hulin and Milton R. Blood, "Job Enlargement, Individual Differences, and Worker Responses," *Psychological Bulletin*, 69 (January 1968), 41–55.

As mentioned previously, the police supervisor has a major responsibility for personnel development. Although the individual naturally has a basic responsibility for his own development, the supervisor must see that his subordinates develop so that they contribute to the goals of the organization. Also, he must make them responsive to the changes that are a part of a police department; consequently, he must use learning principles and procedures that motivate them to learn what is necessary (as with all human behavior, effective learning is impossible without a motivating influence). This approach to police personnel development assumes that everyone in the organization needs developing, that the development process is continuous, and that development is a dynamic experience.

A police supervisor does not determine whether his subordinate *will* learn (he can count on the fact that the person will learn) but rather *what* is learned. Therefore, his first duty is to establish developmental needs and goals (required behavior, skills, information, and so on). His second duty is to create organizational conditions under which the predetermined developmental needs and goals can be effectively met. Although psychology has provided us with sufficient information concerning the conditions that support the learning process, it is not known how to create these conditions in every organization. In the police organization, the creation of such conditions is a major challenge for the supervisor in his role as a developer of human resources.

This brief section on personnel development is both an indication and an introduction of the vital role a police supervisor plays in the organizational learning process. Other chapters discuss specific developmental needs, principles, approaches, and policies as they relate to improving human capacities.

PROBLEM SOLVING: "THE SCIENCE OF 'MUDDLING THROUGH'"[25]

The terms *decision making* and *problem solving* are frequently used interchangeably. We distinguish between the two by defining *problem solving* as a process of thoughtfully and deliberately attempting to eliminate barriers in the path toward a goal and *decision making* as a strategy for mounting a response to a problem situation. In practice, of course, the two processes are psychologically and organizationally interwoven.

A good argument can be made for viewing the police supervisor as a problem solver and decision maker. In a broad sense, the police organization itself can be viewed as a problem-solving and decision-making system. Facing

---

[25] This provocative title is taken from Charles E. Lindblom, "The Science of 'Muddling Through'," *Public Administration Review*, 19 (June 1959), 78–88.

a problem of moderate complexity, both man and his organization draw from their memory relevant data, obtain data from outside sources, and correlate them to develop a solution. A later chapter investigates, describes, and explains decision making in greater detail. For the present, we will discuss the intellectual factors or stages involved in problem solving.

A group of behavioral scientists found through a recent investigation four significant intellectual factors used in human problem solving: verbal comprehension, conceptual foresight, originality, and sensitivity to the problem.[26] The first factor denotes an understanding of the meaning of words or ideas that describe both the problem and proposed solution. Conceptual foresight means a recognizing of antecedents, concurrents, or consequents of given information so that the information can be properly used. Originality is the generation of a variety of appropriate ways of interpreting the problem. Finally, sensitivity to the problem is accomplished through the evaluation of the antecedents, concurrents, and consequents of given information. Police supervisors possessing these four capacities should be able to solve problems better than those without them.

In addition, current research findings suggest that problem solving should be divided into two distinct but interdependent types.[27] The first type, which appears to be more innovative, is one whereby the solution reached provides new meanings for previous experiences. The second type, found to inhibit the first, is one in which the old meanings influence the resultant solution. Significant here is that our traditional organizational structures tend to promote only the second type of problem solving. Our organizational theorists, along with concerned practitioners, are devoting considerable energy to the design of more fluid organizations for facilitating the more creative type of problem solving—for the police supervisor as well as the entire department. Let us keep in mind that the police organization is essentially a problem-solving system!

SUMMARY

Anyone who has attempted to understand human behavior in an organized and comprehensive manner is usually overwhelmed by the impossibility of describing simultaneously all the facets of even the simplest human act. An individual is an entity that perceives, has needs to be fulfilled, forms attitudes, experiences tension, and, in turn, is motivated. Moreover, he is doing all these things while learning and solving problems. In addition,

---

[26] See P. R. Merrifield *et al.*, "The Role of Intellectual Factors in Problem Solving," *Psychological Monographs*, 76 (1962).

[27] Norman R. F. Mair and Junie C. Janzen, "Functional Values as Aids and Distractors in Problem Solving," *Psychological Reports*, 22 (June 1968), 1021–34.

each phase of a person's behavior must be treated as an integral part of every other phase. Hence, the police supervisor must, when analyzing one aspect of human behavior, consider its simultaneous interaction with all the other facets of a subordinate's potential for response. Finally, a police supervisor can effectively do his job only through motivating his subordinates to work for the goals of the police department. And, it is impossible to motivate an individual without an accurate understanding of his particular needs, attitudes, and tensions.

PROBLEMS

1. "For the life of me, I do not see why you fail to *see* the situation as I do." Explain why people perceive the same situation differently.

2. "What more does a police officer need than the assurance of his continued employment and a living wage?" Do police officers have needs other than job security and an adequate wage? If so, explain.

3. While certain aspects of human behavior are constant or universal, we differ in some rather important ways. These ways primarily determine what motivates us as individuals. Explain how needs, attitudes, and tensions are determinants of our behavior.

4. As a police supervisor, you are responsible for developing the skills of your subordinates, to do which you must know something about the learning process. What is it that you should know?

5. Further, what should you know about the problem-solving process?

3

The Organizational Environment: Interpersonal and Group Relationships

Chapter 3 deals with the next two levels of complexity of human behavior: interpersonal relations (individual interaction) and groups of more than two persons. The first part of this chapter shifts from the singular to the plural, from one person to relationships between people and especially to the attempts of one person to influence and change the behavior of another. The second part focuses on the problem of relationships between the individual and the group. Like interpersonal relations, group behavior is viewed primarily as an effort to influence others through motivating them. Unlike interpersonal relations, however, the group is described as an integrative and coordinative device.

Both sections place a great deal of emphasis on the dynamics of communication because it is the most important prerequisite for any endeavor to influence human behavior. Influence is definitely no small problem for police organizations. It is not only a problem that pervades the internal workings of a police agency, where we find police supervisors continually devoting much of their time and energy to influencing their subordinates, peers, and superiors. It is also a central problem in the family, in education, in politics, and in every other phase of human interaction.

INTERPERSONAL RELATIONSHIPS

> The more psychologists and sociologists actually studied the behavior of people in organizations, the clearer it became that their performance was critically related to the quality of their interpersonal relationships. In particular, their relationships with their supervisors came to be central.[1]

This section has distinctly pragmatic overtones. If you are a police supervisor and wish to influence the behavior or an attitude of another person,

---

[1] Edgar H. Schein, *Organizational Psychology* (Englewood Cliffs, N.J.: Prentice-Hall, Inc., 1965), p. 37.

what strategies are likely to work best? And why? First and foremost, the supervisor must recognize that an exchange of meanings must occur between people prior to any exertion of influence. Most frequently this exchange involves talking and listening, and writing and reading. It can also include gestures, glances, nods, frowns, and any other ways in which meanings can be transmitted from one person to another and back again. The best single word to cover all the various ways for people to express themselves is *interaction*, which refers to communication in its broadest sense. Hence, we first consider the media for exerting influence—interaction, or communication. Second, we describe some of the dimensions of and approaches to influencing others.

Communications

Communication is one of the most important processes of police supervision. Successful communication does not necessarily occur automatically whenever two individuals get together. The basic problem in communication, whether it be face-to-face or otherwise, is that the meaning received by one person may not be what the other intended to send.[2] The transmitter and the receiver of a message are two separate people with different needs, attitudes, and so on; any number of things can distort the interaction between them. At this time we are concerned largely with face-to-face communications between individuals. In Chapter 6, we view communications in terms of the entire police organization.

Let us look at some of the dimensions of communications. To begin, a communication has content. This is to say, we talk about something. It is the content that usually strikes us first when we receive a message. Next, human interaction is affected by varying degrees of "noise" or distortion. Distortion is anything that interferes with the transmission of a message and it can be technological, physiological, or psychological. Besides the content and noise dimensions of interpersonal interaction, there is a third dimension commonly referred to as communications networks. A communication network is created when a sender interacts on an indirect basis with his receiver. The hierarchy of an organization is primarily responsible for determining such networks. Later we discuss how the structure of a network of a particular organization affects the speed and accuracy of members' interaction with one another. A final dimension of the communication process is the direction of interaction—one-way or two-way. We now focus on one of the three described dimensions—distortion. Each of the other three dimensions—content, networks, and direction—are discussed as they

---

[2] Leonard R. Sayles and George Strauss, *Human Behavior in Organizations* (Englewood Cliffs, N.J.: Prentice-Hall, Inc., 1966), p. 238.

relate to the factors that either produce or reduce distortion in the communications process.

The content of communications: distortion and antidistortion. The content of human interaction is susceptible to distortion in a variety of ways. First, there is what Anthony Downs terms a common bias on the part of all organizational members to distort the information they pass upward to superiors in the hierarchy.[3] Specifically, people tend to exaggerate data that reflect favorably on themselves and to minimize data that reveal their own shortcomings. Second, the content of a message is decidedly shaped by our own perceptions, personality, and experiences.[4] Hence, we frequently do not hear what people tell us, but rather what our minds tell us they have said. Third, psychologists report that every individual has a tendency to acquire information consistent with what he already knows. In other words, we tend to ignore information that conflicts with our attitudes or existing body of knowledge. Fourth, to a great extent the source of the communication determines how the content will be received.[5] To put it another way, how reliable is the person or machine as a source of information? When a person we distrust provides information, our reaction is to discount the content of his message. If we trust an individual, our reaction is one of complete faith. Fifth, there is a semantic problem. Obviously, this problem is most difficult with abstract or in-group terms, but even simple words often fail to convey the intended meaning of the interaction. Sixth, the possibility of misconstruing a message increases as one's tensions grow. Our anxieties color everything we hear. (Similarly, when we are comfortable, we sometimes fail to comprehend the problems contained in the content of a communication.)

These possible distortions in the content of a message are presented more as a challenge for solution rather than as a series of impossible barriers. Perfect understanding between people is difficult. The fact is, however, understanding, *meaningful understanding*, can be had through the use of a few proven techniques for improving human interaction. First, and simplest, is face-to-face communications. It gives the receiver an immediate opportunity to clarify contradictory and confusing information. Second are written messages, which can be used for detailed instructions or establishing a per-

---

[3] Anthony Downs, *Inside Bureaucracy* (Boston, Mass.: Little, Brown, and Company, 1967), p. 77.

[4] To explain further, "Each speaker provides a host of cues about himself in both the quality of his voice and his manner of delivery. The substance or content of what he says is an additional determinant of the impression that he conveys, and this content strikes harshly or fairly upon the listener's ears depending upon that person's attitudes toward what is being said. Altogether, the possible combinations of speaker characteristics, communication content, and audience dispositions pose formidable problems of control and manipulation." Elliott McGinnies, "Studies in Persuasion: V. Perceptions of a Speaker as Related to Communication Content," *The Journal of Social Psychology*, 75 (June 1968), 21.

[5] The remainder of this discussion on the content of communication is greatly influenced by Sayles and Strauss, *Human Behavior*, pp. 243–46.

manent record. A written communication is best employed as an adjunct to spoken words. Great care should be taken in both verbal and written communications to use direct and simple terminology. Third, a vital part of both vocal and written interaction is feedback. Feedback plays a dual role in communications by promoting effectiveness in human interaction and maintaining control.[6] The effectiveness of human communication is increased by constantly being on the alert for indicators as to whether our message is understood. In regard to this awareness Weiner explains:

> When I control the actions of another person, I communicate a message to him, and although this message is in the imperative mood, the technique of communication does not differ from that of a message of fact. Furthermore, if my control is to be effective I must take cognizance of any messages from him which may indicate that the order is understood and has been obeyed.[7]

Fourth, the sender of a message must be sensitive to the attitudes and values of the receiver. A sender should be aware of any special symbolic meaning a term or phrase has for the receiver. Further, the timing of a message is crucial to its understanding. If a message can be transmitted when there are no competing messages, the probabilities of its being understood and accepted are vastly enhanced. Fifth, in the presence of distorting influence, a person is wise to communicate more redundantly, to repeat all or parts of the message in the hope that the receiver will better understand. Redundancy is one of the most frequently used weapons for combatting distortion.[8]

The communication network: distortion and antidistortion. The structure of a communications network in a police organization has a great deal to do with the speed and accuracy of the information transmitted between its members. Most of the research on communication networks has been devoted either to the group or to organizational levels. Consequently, much of the discussion on this subject occurs later in this as well as in another chapter. However, there are two types of distortion that are appropriately discussed at this point. To begin, we must keep in mind that a communication system has both horizontal and vertical characteristics. The direction of the information flow can follow the authority pattern of the organization (downward communications); can move between peers at the same organizational level (horizontal communications); or can ascend the hierarchical ladder (upward communication).[9] Of the three flows, the average distortion per message is

---

[6] In regard to the importance of feedback in interpersonal communication, see Robert T. Golembiewski, "The 'Laboratory Approach' to Organization Change: Schema of a Method," *Public Administration Review*, 27 (September 1967), 211–23.

[7] Norbert Wiener, *The Human Use of Human Beings* (New York: Doubleday and Company, Inc., 1954), p. 16.

[8] Harold J. Leavitt, *Managerial Psychology*, 2nd ed. (Chicago, Ill.: The University of Chicago Press, 1964), p. 140.

[9] Daniel Katz and Robert L. Kahn, *The Social Psychology of Organizations* (New York: John Wiley and Sons, Inc., 1966), p. 235.

probably greater in vertical channels than in the horizontal ones. Gordon Tullock informs us that two things occur in a communications network that tend to distort the content of a message from one person to another.[10] First, condensation of a message is a standard procedure within a communication system. Each interpersonal relationship in an organization acts as a screening device, whereby only a portion of the original message eventually reaches the intended receiver. Second, a reduction in the quantity of information in a message usually affects its quality, that is, the substantive content.[11] In fact, the selection criteria used by each sender are likely to be different from those used by other senders. Hence, the information that finally reaches the end receiver has passed through a number of human filters (distorters) which determine the quality of the message.

All the antidistortion techniques used in maintaining a reasonable degree of reliability in the content of a communication can also be applied to communication networks. In addition, there are three other ways specifically pertinent to reducing distortion in communication networks. The first way is to "flatten" the hierarchy of the organization.[12] Basically, this "flattening" is accomplished by broadening the organization's span of control. Having only a few levels in the hierarchy reduces the number of interpersonal screenings of a message and, therefore, keeps the degree of distortion low. Further, widening the span of control in a police organization provides other related benefits such as job enlargement and better opportunities for training on the job.[13] The second way is to design by-pass communication networks for direct interaction between persons that may be three or four levels apart in the organization. In this case an individual circumvents other people in order to have face-to-face contact with the final receiver of the message. Obviously, frequent use of this device can cause a serious loss of morale among those by-passed. The third and final way is to develop distortion-proof messages that cannot be altered in meaning while being transmitted in the communications network. Such messages require both predesignated definitions and coding because they are sent to the receiver without any changes in content. To prevent overloading the network, this method should be used only in special or crisis situations.

---

[10] See Gordon Tullock, *The Politics of Bureaucracy* (Washington, D.C.: Public Affairs Press, 1965), pp. 137–41.

[11] Recent research has substantiated the need for completeness in the content of a message. In fact, it has been suggested that the completeness is more critical in terms of understanding than is the accuracy. See George W. Doten, John T. Cockrell, and Robert Sadaccos, "The Use of Teams in Image Interpretation: Information Exchange, Confidence, and Resolving Disagreements," *Human Factors*, 10 (April 1968), 107–16.

[12] For a more comprehensive treatment of this subject, see Harold S. Green, "The Human Element in Communication," *California Management Review*, 9 (Winter 1966), 3–8.

[13] For a description of these and other benefits attached to a flatter hierarchy, see Robert T. Golembiewski, *Men, Management, and Morality: Toward a New Organization Ethic* (New York: McGraw-Hill Book Company, 1965), pp. 174–76.

The direction of communications: distortion and antidistortion. Let us now turn our attention to the direction, one-way or two-way, of a message. The host of distorting mechanisms described in connection with the content and network of the communication also apply to the direction of a message. Thus, it becomes convenient to discuss one-way and two-way communications in terms of their advantages and disadvantages. First, when one person communicates to another without any return conversation, it is: (1) faster, (2) less accurate because of a lack of opportunity to clarify the meaning of the message, (3) not as psychologically threatening because the sender refuses to receive return information concerning his faults, and (4) more difficult to plan the message since the sender must carefully choose the words he will use. Second, when two people interact with one another, we find that (1) the process of communication is slower, (2) the degree of accuracy improves, (3) the sender opens himself to return messages which may be psychologically frustrating, and (4) the sender does not have to plan his message as carefully because he is provided with additional chances for clarifying its meaning. Both types of communication are presently employed by police supervisors. It is the experienced and more effective supervisor who knows when to use each type. In general, one-way communication has greater utility during emergency or highly routine situations, while two-way communication is more useful for novel problem solving.

In summary, almost every facet of supervisor-subordinate relations involves communications. Moreover, effective supervisor-subordinate interaction is essential to the functioning of a police organization. Nevertheless, every communication system is subject to serious flaws. These flaws or distortions can be seen in the content, network, and direction of a message. Fortunately, however, we have developed antidistortion procedures and mechanisms which partially offset a loss in the meaning of a communication. It is imperative that the police supervisor learn to master the various techniques for facilitating the transmission of understanding between himself and others.

Influence

One communicates in order to influence! And, one attempts to influence someone in order to change his behavior or state of mind. The person seeking to influence another is referred to as a change agent. The recipient of the exerted influence is termed the client. Thus we can see that influence is a process that uses interaction for bringing about change. This process can be one of three types, involving, respectively, authority, power, and self-development. All three are covered in this chapter as they function in an interpersonal situation. Later, they are described as they function in the broader organizational environment. For our purposes, we define *influence* as any action which produces an effect on behavior, psychological state, or any other condition.

Before we look at the three methods of influencing behavior, let us briefly review a few important ideas concerning planned change.[14] In the first place, a person's motivation for initiating change can vary. The major forces motivating a person to bring about change in others are: (1) the simple desire of an individual to do a good job that hinges on his being able to influence another person, (2) the human desire for widening one's power, income, and prestige, and (3) the desire to develop his own self-defense against pressure from external threats. In the second place, we should recognize that no matter how much authority or power a change agent may possess, it is the client who controls the final decision. In the third place, change is basically an uncomfortable experience for the client. This is so because there is safety and security in the established way and uncertainty in the new way. In the fourth place, the final responsibility for changing can rest with the change agent, with the client, or it can be shared. If the client can be convinced to accept a part of the responsibility for changing himself, the outcome is usually a more lasting change.

Now let us turn to the three processes by which one person can influence either the behavior or the state of mind of another.

Influence by authority. Authority is the legitimate right to command another person. In a formal organizational setting this right is conferred upon a position and is subsequently exercised by the individual who occupies the position. Briefly, we can sum up the underlying reason for authority in an organization: Every formal organization has a specified set of activities to be performed, and the primary method for insuring the performance of these activities is to require the members of the organization to obey those in positions of authority. Note that the definition of authority included the term *legitimate*. The basis on which we accept the legitimacy of authority may vary from organization to organization. It was Max Weber who first informed us that there are three major bases of legitimacy for authority—tradition, charisma, and rational-legal.[15]

Tradition as a basis for the legitimacy of authority operates when the individual consents to obey the ruler because it has always been acceptable to do so. A monarchy is the clearest example of this type of legitimacy. One can see that this is not as prevalent as in the past. *Charisma* as a basis for authority occurs in those instances where a magnetic personality is able

---

[14] Readers interested in a comprehensive and detailed treatment regarding the topic of planned change should see Edgar H. Schein and Warren G. Bennis, *Personal and Organizational Change Through Group Methods* (New York: John Wiley and Sons, 1965), and Warren G. Bennis, Kenneth D. Benne, and Robert Chin, eds., *The Planning of Change* (New York: Holt, Rinehart, and Winston, Inc., 1962).

[15] H. H. Gerth and C. Wright Mills, eds., *From Max Weber: Essays in Sociology* (New York: Oxford University Press, 1946).

to gain compliance through a belief in his mystical or extraordinary abilities. Modern-day charismatic leaders are usually found in political and religious movements. However, charisma can be found in organizations, for example, when police supervisors capture the obedience of their subordinate officers purely on the basis of their unique personal qualities. Surely, all of us have, at one time or another, obeyed directives and followed leaders simply because we believed in them wholeheartedly and thus accepted their guidance as the only right way.

Rational-legal principles as the basis of authority tend to be prevalent in our own society. They underlie the concept of a formal organization as outlined in a future chapter. According to its precepts, authority should be assigned on the basis of rational criteria and in terms of procedures contained in formal laws, regulations, and informal norms. Rational criteria state that, in order to be given a position of authority, a person should have demonstrated the ability to fulfill the requirements of the position. In the organizational sphere, these criteria are expressed in the idea of promotion based on merit (ability plus past performance) and in the notion that authority ultimately derives from a person's ability to do something better than those under him, in short, his experience.[16]

Influence by power. Power can be defined as the capacity to command another person. Power and authority are often confused with one another. Although they might be, they are not always synonymous. Nevertheless, one usually looks at an interpersonal relationship in terms of the different levels of authority involved and assumes that power automatically resides with the person who has the greatest amount of authority. Remember, authority is the *right* to command, and power is the *capacity* to command. Authority stems from a position; power originates within the person. An individual's power is based on his superior body of knowledge, unique set of skills, ability to convince, and so forth. Since power is personal, it may or may not be legitimate because the person exerting power may or may not also possess a position of comparable authority. Therefore, we find today people in positions of authority that have the right but not the capacity to influence others. Similarly, we find those who possess considerable power but do not have a great deal of authority. It is a fortunate individual who has power equal to his authority.

Research accords power a prominent role in explanations of behavior in organizations. In fact, it has been said that most of us almost instinctively follow vectors of power.[17] Thus, power is connected with the effectiveness of supervision, whether the power is exercised upward (interpersonal relations with superiors), downward (interpersonal relations with subordinates),

---

[16] Schein, *Organizational Psychology*, p. 12.

[17] Robert T. Golembiewski, *Organizing Men and Power: Patterns of Behavior and Line-Staff Models* (Chicago, Ill.: Rand McNally & Company, 1967), p. 227.

or horizontally (interpersonal relations with other supervisors). For example, Hill and French found that high supervisory power was associated consistently with effective job performance and job satisfaction.[18] Power is a significant means for influencing others, then, especially because it provides the police supervisor with a way for escaping any limitations in the authority delegated to his position.

Influence by motivation. In previous paragraphs we looked at influence largely from the viewpoint of the change agent. We attempted to distinguish between formal authority and informal power. Further, we described their respective bases for influence. The third and last model to be discussed focuses not only on the change agent, but on the client as well. In fact, our discussion emphasizes that the more a changer uses motivational approaches —the more he tries to make new ways of doing things consistent with the client's needs—the more effective and lasting his base becomes for exerting influence.

The basis for being able to use motivation as a method of influence is that man seeks accomplishment, independence, greater self-control, and an opportunity for voluntarily integrating his own goals with those of the organization. Briefly, this form of influence presumes that a person will obtain satisfaction through the use of his capacities for high-quality performance and creativity.

The primary reason for using the motivational approach is that people will, if convinced that a change is of direct benefit to their job success, take most of the responsibility for changing themselves. Consequently, the changer becomes more of a helper rather than a wielder of power or authority. Harold Leavitt refers to this type of an approach as *influence without authority.*[19] A police supervisor, therefore, substitutes for the use of his authority a supportive role which seeks to assist the subordinate in satisfying his needs through his occupation as a police officer.

Each of the above types of influence creates different consequences for the police supervisor and the police organization. This is to say, there will be costs and gains in emphasizing any particular method of influence.[20] In general, the use of authority by one person over another usually results in behavior that is minimally acceptable; the use of power may result in behavior that is above standard and even creative; the use of motivational techniques increases the probability of behavior that is not only above the norm but highly spontaneous and innovative.

In the first part of this chapter we have sought to explore the interpersonal

---

[18] Winston W. Hill and Wendall L. French, "Perceptions of the Power of Department Chairmen by Professors," *Administrative Science Quarterly* (March 1967), 548–74.

[19] Leavitt, *Managerial Psychology*, 189–205.

[20] The costs and benefits inhered in each of the three models of influence are mainly drawn from Katz and Kahn, *Social Psychology*, pp. 347–68.

relationships which constitute the structure in ongoing organizational life. We found that the police organization has means (communications) and techniques for exerting influence. Further, we located the origins or bases of three types of interpersonal influence—authority, power, and motivation. Lastly, we suggested that the type of influence used results in a predictable behavioral response. We are now prepared to move to the next higher level of analysis which deals with collections of individuals, or group behavior.

GROUP RELATIONSHIPS

Without denying the importance of the individual, it can still be said, that a group is often more important, since a great deal of organizational work is carried out either in formal groups or in larger informal groups.[21]

The reason for devoting half a chapter to groups is clear: ample evidence shows that they do have a major impact on their members, on other groups, and on the entire organization. Furthermore, groups can be studied in a number of ways. To illustrate, we can devote our attention to the following phenomena in group relationships: communication, conflict, pressure, motivation, functions they serve both individually and organizationally, how and why they come into existence, types of groups, how they are integrated with each other, their effectiveness, and internal change. In view of these various perspectives on group behavior, our examination begins with an overview of the why, how, and types of groups. Second, we look at the communications networks in groups. Third, we focus on the functions performed by a group. Fourth, our attention shifts to intergroup competition and conflict. Last, we consider problems and possible solutions connected with the coordination of a number of groups.

Groups: How, Why, and Types

A group is a number of people (usually not more than 20) who (1) are aware of one another, (2) interact with one another, and (3) perceive themselves as a group. Therefore, the size of a group is determined by mutual interaction and mutual awareness. A gathering of people does not fit our definition unless they are aware of each other; hence, a crowd watching some event is not a group. Similarly, a total police department, or division of the department, is not a group, regardless of their thinking to the contrary, if they generally do not communicate with everyone and are not all aware of each other. Small work teams, special subunits within a division,

---

[21] Philip B. Applewhite, *Organizational Behavior* (Englewood Cliffs, N. J.: Prentice-Hall, Inc., 1965), p. 36.

cliques, and other informal associations among organization members fit our definition of a group.

Having defined a group, let us now examine five related propositions about groups and group relationships:[22]

> 1. Groups exist; hence, they must be dealt with by police supervisors.
> 2. Groups in a police department are inevitable and omnipresent.
> 3. Groups mobilize tremendous forces that create effects of vital importance to individuals.
> 4. Groups may produce good or bad consequences for their members and the police department.
> 5. An accurate understanding of group dynamics enhances the probability that beneficial consequences will result.

It seems reasonable to ask next, "Why are groups formed?" Essentially, groups are born because they fulfill some very important functions for the individual and the organization. In fact, one can view a group as the primary vehicle for integrating man and organization, while simultaneously satisfying their separate needs. Thus, groups provide man with a social identification in the organization and the organization with a means for effectively using his talents. A group is the bridge between man and his organization.

The answer to "How are groups formed?" is twofold—the organization creates them to achieve better its objectives, and individuals create them (informal groups) to fulfill their needs. Ironically, in forming groups for more effective operations, the organization also acquires all the problems associated with their existence. To explain, a police department necessarily divides the work of its organization into units or divisions. This division, in turn, determines which people will contact each other during the hours of work. Given this prescribed condition, social relations develop which can either support or detract from the operations of the department. To complicate this easily understood situation, people usually belong to more than one group (if not formally, certainly informally), establish their own ways of doing things, and decide on what is an appropriate output for their particular work group. In regard to the first complicating factor, the mere fact that a person holds membership in several groups subjects him to psychological stress when their respective norms or interests differ. Next, once formed, a group creates a customary and stable way of conducting its activities which may conflict with the operational guidelines offered by the organization. Finally, groups tend to set their own standards and goals, both of which frequently take precedence over the broader goals of the organization.

---

[22] These five propositions are taken from Darwin Cartwright and Ronald Lippitt, "Group Dynamics and the Individual," *International Journal of Group Psychotherapy*, 7 (January 1957), 86–102.

Although as mentioned earlier, there are many types of groups, the two major types are formal and informal. Both categories can be further divided. Let us first look at the formal group, created by the organization in order to fulfill organizational goals. These groups have two subtypes, based on their duration, permanent or temporary. Permanent formal groups are units such as patrol work shifts, planning and research, traffic enforcement, and so on. Temporary formal groups are planning committees or special task forces formed to accomplish a particular mission but which, once the mission is achieved, cease to exist until another mission requires them. For example, police departments create tactical squads for handling riot situations and special planning committees for evaluating new technology or programs. On occasion a temporary group may exist for a long time; however, the members understand that they are a part of a group which may at any time lose its reason for existence.

Informal social relationships in an organizational setup frequently develop into informal groups. The tendency to form informal groups arises out of the basic nature of man. How they are formed depends mainly on the physical location of people in an organization, the type of work performed, their time schedules, and so forth. We can see, therefore, that informal groups emerge out of a particular formal structure and human needs. Moreover, informal groups exist even when an organization takes deliberate steps to prevent them. Their omnipresence in an organization attests to the importance of the functions that they serve.

Melville Dalton has categorized informal groups into three subtypes, which he refers to as cliques.[23] The most common subtype is the horizontal clique, an informal group of organizational members who have approximately the same rank and work in the same general area—such groups fulfill individual social needs. Another subtype is the vertical clique, composed of members from different levels within an organization. In this case, the members of the clique are in a superior-subordinate relationship to one another—such groups act as a means for communicating both upward and downward. Finally, there is the random clique, comprised of members from varying ranks, divisions, and physical locations—such groups aid in serving functional requirements not adequately taken care of by the organization. Now, what does all of this hold for the police supervisor? First, it is the police organization that gives birth to groups, both formal and informal ones. Second, the underlying reason for groups created by a police organization is obviously important. Groups are necessary in order to more effectively achieve the objectives of the police department. Imagine, for a moment, a police organization comprised of one hundred people who are not grouped

---

[23] Melville Dalton, *Men Who Manage: Fusions of Feeling and Theory in Administration* (New York: John Wiley & Sons, Inc., 1959).

according to a logical work plan. There would be no detectives, no traffic, juvenile, or vice officers. Further, it is questionable how the officers would be divided among the work shifts. Third, as mentioned, it is the police organization that provides the impetus and environment for groups—all kinds of groups. The police department sees to it that formal work groups are established. The members of the department see to it that informal groups are created. Their underlying reason for doing so lies in their need for developing satisfying social relationships. If properly designed and motivated, an informal group can complement the work of formal groups. Whether this happens is up to the police supervisor. Briefly, where people are involved, informal groups will develop. A police supervisor who is able to effectively influence informal groups greatly increases his chances of organizational success.

Communications: Networks

The relationships among members of a group are restricted by the kinds of communication that occur. As we pointed out earlier, interpersonal communication has several dimensions. At this time we again focus our attention on one of these dimensions, communication networks. The reason for another look at networks is that if more people are added to the communication process, the barriers against the transmission of accurate messages increase. Further, communication networks vastly affect the ways groups solve problems, and most of our problems—organizational and personal—are solved in a group setting. (While we concentrate on networks, we should not forget that content, barriers, and direction play an important part in determining the correctness of a message.)

A communication net is the structure of a group. When we discern this structure, we have discovered how the group is tied together. Thus far, communication networks have been considered as either a static or, more lately, a dynamic process. We look first at group communications as a static process. Figure 2 shows diagrams of various communications networks. Each network depicts the communication channels connecting positions in the particular ways that distinguish the different kinds of networks. Interestingly, all of these can be found in police organizations. Moreover, in many cases, all can be found at the same time in a single police organization. There is not any pat answer to the question, "Which network is best?" The answer to such a question would be another question, "Best for what purpose?" In other words, the task to be performed dictates the type of network to be used. For example, some communication networks permit faster operation than others, but the advantage of speed is usually gained at the cost of accuracy and morale.

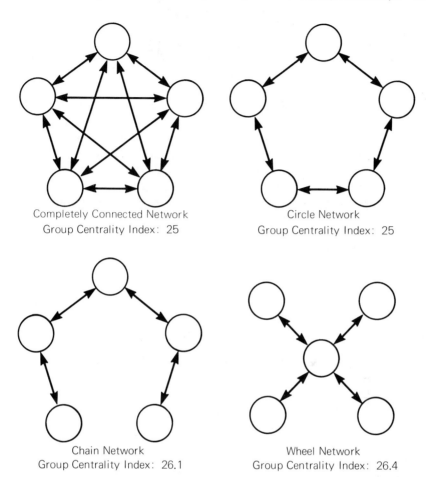

Completely Connected Network
Group Centrality Index: 25

Circle Network
Group Centrality Index: 25

Chain Network
Group Centrality Index: 26.1

Wheel Network
Group Centrality Index: 26.4

(*Source:* Cohen, *"Changing Small Group Communication Networks,"* ASQ, 6 [*March 1962*] p. 448.

FIG. 2. COMMUNICATION NETWORKS AND THEIR CHARACTERISTICS

People are happier in some networks than they are in others, and some networks therefore are likely to keep going longer without blowing up, but these networks may be slower or less accurate than some others. . . . Some networks have fewer errors than others. Some are more flexible than others. All these words may have something to do with what we mean by "efficiency."[24]

Different communication networks cause people to behave differently

---

[24] Leavitt, *Managerial Psychology*, pp. 233–34.

and to be more, or less, satisfied. Arthur Cohen provides one explanation.[25] Each group can be ranked according to its degree of centrality. The degree of centrality is determined by the ratio of the sum of the distances (number of steps to communicate) from all members to all members over the sum of the distances from a given position to all others. The higher the ratio, the greater the inequalities of data received; therefore, the wheel network has the greatest degree of inequality. The wheel molds a problem-solving situation in which the four peripheral members send their information to the center member who decides on an answer and sends it back to them. Of the five types, this one is by far the most structured and hierarchical. The police patrol dispatch network exemplifies this form of communications. As can be seen in Figure 2, the least restrictive and, consequently, the lowest in centrality is the completely connected network. Groups using this network normally solve problems by having members communicate messages to all directly, each member forming his own answers. The police planning and research unit may be an example of this network.

In general, communication networks with less centrality are preferable. Equalitarian networks are better than hierarchical ones because group members in a circular arrangement have higher morale, more self-correctiveness, and better opportunities for creativity.[26] However, certain groups are forced, because of their function, to operate faster and thus one position is highly centralized. Certainly centralization for this reason is understandable, but at times it is also used as a psychological defense device to protect superiors' failings.

Now let us look briefly at group communication networks as a dynamic process. As tasks and their involved problems change, so do communication networks. Cohen has shown that groups modify their communication processes in the light of past experiences. Hence, an organization should provide all members with a training program that presents the various problems they are most likely to encounter. Ample opportunity for exploring the alternative procedures for solving problems is a must in any such program. When finished with the training program, a trainee should be able to adjust easily to networks with varying degrees of centrality. Further, the trainee's reason for selecting and participating in the network will be based on rationality. Therefore, the training program should concentrate on the importance of administrative rationality. Rationality refers to the continuous efforts of group members to select from the available channels of communication those believed to be the most useful for efficient work groups.

---

[25] Arthur M. Cohen, "Changing Small-Group Communication Networks," *Administrative Science Quarterly*, 6 (March 1962), 443–62.

[26] Research evidence indicates a group exposed to noise and complexity during a problem-solving situation is more creative than if not. See Claude Faucheux and Serge Mosocvici, "Studies on Group Creativity: Noise and Complexity in the Inferential Process," *Human Relations*, 21 (February 1968), 29–40.

What does the previous discussion mean to the police supervisor? First, the type of communication network established by the police supervisor can either increase or decrease the performance of his group. Second, the problem at hand should determine which of the various networks is most appropriate. Third, each communication network possesses both benefits and detriments for the members involved. Last, the police supervisor should provide his subordinates with training and experience in using the various group communication networks.[27]

Functions Performed by Groups

The functions performed by a group for the organization are many and varied. Certainly the police supervisor should understand group dynamics because:

> Research in organizations is yielding increasing evidence that the superior's skill in supervising his subordinates *as a group* is an important variable affecting his success: the greater his skill in using group methods of supervision, the greater are the productivity and job satisfactions of his subordinates.[28]

Thus far we have indicated that group processes are important for the organization in a general way and to the supervisor in a more immediate sense. However, we have neglected one other entity that the group serves and supports—the individual. The group is a linking pin that joins man to his organization and simultaneously provides a means for moving both toward the achievement of their respective needs and objectives. Obviously such a complex subject as group dynamics affords numerous ways of investigating and discussing its functions. For our purposes, a group, whether formal or informal, has five functions: organizational, personal, integrative, conformance, and motivational.

Organizational functions. Organizational, or formal, functions, are those that pertain to the accomplishment of the organization's primary mission. Hence, we find formal groups designed to perform formal police functions such as patrolling, investigating criminal events, regulating traffic, and so on. Basically, the organizational functions are the tasks that are assigned to a group and for which it is formally held responsible.

Personal functions. When they join a department, police officers bring with them a variety of needs and motivations. Significantly, it is the group, both formal and informal, that can fulfill many of these needs and motiva-

---

[27] One method of training people to adjust quickly to change is through laboratory training groups. See Chris Argyris, "T-Groups for Organizational Effectiveness," *Harvard Business Review*, 42 (March 1964), 60–74.

[28] Rensis Likert, *New Patterns of Management* (New York: McGraw-Hill Book Company, Inc., 1961), p. 26.

tions. When the formal group fails in this task of need and motivation fulfillment, the organizational members create an informal group for accomplishing the personal functions. Consequently, the greater the need fulfillment provided by formal groups, the less prevalent are informal groups. Groups can furnish the following personal functions:

1. A sense of belongingness; that is, meeting the needs for friendship and approval.
2. A way for acquiring self-determination, or the satisfaction of making decisions about one's own job.
3. A means of self-expression, or the gratification obtained from expressing one's talents and abilities.
4. A means for value expression, or the satisfaction of expressing one's central values.
5. A means of developing, enhancing, or confirming self-identification, or asserting and expressing what one is really like.

Integrative functions. One of the most frequent findings that stems from the study of groups in organizations is that most groups serve the needs of both the organization and the individual members.[29] Groups are, therefore, the key unit for integrating organizational objectives and personal needs. The group that is successful in doing both (achieving organizational objectives and fulfilling personal needs) is invariably more effective. There are four factors which contribute to group integration and thus, in turn, group effectiveness: (1) developing sensitivity and skill of members and leaders in diagnosing and working on group problems, (2) allowing all members to participate in important decisions about group objectives, (3) instilling in each member the feeling that he is making a significant contribution to the over-all group performance, and (4) insuring that all members share in the rewards of the accomplishments of the group. For these four factors to occur there must be some rather major changes in the policy and structure of the common organization. Briefly, the power and authority system would have to be altered so as to give more influence and responsibility to the group and its members.

Conformance functions. A group can pressure members into adhering to its norms. This is to say that group membership frequently gives rise to conformity of thought as well as of feeling. Group pressure for individual conformance can (1) help the group accomplish its assigned objectives, (2) help the group maintain itself as a group, (3) help the members develop validity or "reality" for their opinions, (4) help the group resist change, and (5) ironically, facilitate change. The more attractive the group is for a person, the greater the power of the group over him and, generally, the

---

[29] Schein, *Organizational Psychology*, p. 70.

more it can compel him to conform to its standards. However, once a person feels totally accepted by the group, he may feel more free to deviate from the group's standards than do persons who are not certain they are wanted. One explanation for this feeling might be that the accepted member is valued for a particular skill or for his loyalty, and thus the group probably does not want to lose him.

Most studies on group conformance have shown that the majority of individuals, when confronted with group pressure, shift their behavior and judgments in the direction of the norms and views of the over-all group. Solomon E. Asch has provided a landmark study on this phenomenon.[30] In summary form, his research was based on the performance of a task, which was to match the length of a line (presented at a distance from the group) with one of three unequal lines presented next to it. In one of his group experiments, one member was the subject and the seven other members were accomplices of Asch who had been instructed to vote unanimously on an incorrect matching. The subject, seemingly by random choice, was to express his judgment last. When the seven people before the subject chose an incorrect matching, Asch found that in many instances the subject agreed with the majority opinion even though it was obviously incorrect. However, not everyone was influenced in this manner and there were individual differences. In other experiments, Asch varied the size of the opposing majority. He found the presence in the group of one other individual who responded correctly was sufficient to reduce the power of the majority and in some cases to destroy it. If the opposition to the subject were only one or two people, the subject would not necessarily go against apparent reality. Further, the subject would go along with the majority judgment most often if the majority consisted of three people; majorities of four, eight, and sixteen did not produce pressures any greater than those produced by a majority of three. As might be anticipated, an individual's resistance to group pressure was seen to depend primarily on how wrong the majority was.

In most cases, exerting social pressure upon individuals either keeps the norms constant and preserves the status quo or forces the group members to change in relation to new norms. But, while most research findings show that everyone experiences group pressure, they also show that everyone does not give in to it.[31] Some people succumb to the group judgment, others remain independent, while still others may rebel against the pressure. For those who conform, the conformity may be either superficial and temporary, ending when the group's presence is no longer felt—strictly a matter of

---

[30] See Solomon F. Asch, "Opinions and Social Pressure," *Scientific American*, 33 (November 1955), 31–34.

[31] Harold J. Leavitt and Louis R. Pondy, eds., *Readings in Managerial Psychology* (Chicago, Ill.: The University of Chicago Press, 1964), p. 284.

expediency, with no deeply felt compliance; or it may be profound, reaching deeply into an individual's personality.

> There is a widespread belief that conformity is all bad, that the individual is relinquishing his rugged individuality to the group. But there is another side. *Some* conformity is needed to hold any group (or any society!) together. We are all conforming when we speak the same language, when we honor the same currency, and when we abide by majority rule. Conformity to these and other "social norms" is the price we pay for the benefits of group membership.[32]

Motivational functions. Drawing upon the other four functions, let us now look at group motivation or group supervision. Group motivation and group supervision are not necessarily one and the same, but since they can be identical, the police supervisor should do his utmost to make them so. The advantages to all concerned—police supervisor, police officer, and police department—will be immense.

Before proceeding further with our analysis of the police supervisor as the major source of motivational forces within a group, we must make two points clear. First, the group itself can act to either foster or inhibit achievement-level striving.[33] Second, the use of group methods to motivate the members of a particular group does not preclude the use of authority or power on the part of a police supervisor. Indeed, some have gone so far as to suggest that the supervisor is destined to be a "socio-emotional specialist" handling only interpersonal problems, with little responsibility for such matters as planning and discipline. On the contrary, the supervisor's dual role as both a leader and a motivator of group members expands his responsibilities to include not only achieving the objectives of the organization but also satisfying the needs of the group members through their assigned tasks. In other words, the police supervisor does "something" to make the job of police officer a way for an individual to fulfill his needs. Now let us look at that all important something!

In essence, what the police supervisor first must accept is that a group can be motivated in three ways: to do less than is acceptable, to do the minimum acceptable, and to do as much as possible. Second, the police supervisor must accept his role as a crucial factor in the group's decision on how much to do toward accomplishing the organization's goals. Third,

---

[32] *Ibid.*

[33] It has been suggested that three different reference groups are required to reach maximum performance levels. These are the normative, model, and audience. The first defines the role of the individual, the second shows how the role is to be performed, and the third provides anticipation of rewards. See Theodore D. Kemper, "Reference Groups, Socialization, and Achievement," *American Sociological Review*, 33 (February 1968), 31–45.

the police supervisor must realize that the best way to motivate the group "to do as much as is possible" is to make the job personally rewarding. If these three conditions are met the probability of high output and high job satisfaction is very good. How to meet the third condition is the "all important something" referred to previously. A group's ability to motivate its members will more likely increase if:

1. The personality of the officer and the job requirements are reasonably compatible.
2. The personalities of the members in the group are compatible.
3. There is a broad span of control that promotes independence and interdependence.
4. The supervisory style indicates *at all times* support for the members in the group.
5. The decision-making process allows all members of the group to influence the final choice.
6. The supervisor monitors the task to be performed by the group rather than the members of the group.
7. The supervisor evaluates the results of the group rather than job processes.

Note that the police supervisor has a tremendous opportunity to build high group motivation. His primary technique for accomplishing this feat is *participatory supervision.* And, the amount of group participation hinges on positive support or reinforcement received by each member from the other members and, most importantly, from the police supervisor.[34] One may argue that to permit a subordinate to influence the decision-making process is wrong because it jeopardizes the authority of the supervisor. The answer to this argument is twofold. First, merely allowing a police officer to influence his work environment does not erode the supervisor's authority to make the final choice. Second, permitting a police officer to influence the direction that his group is going to take pays off to the police department in increased output and improved job satisfaction.[35] Likert provides a pertinent summary when he writes that if the supervisor (or manager) supervises by group methods of supervision his department will display greater group loyalty, higher performance goals, greater cooperation, more technical assistance to peers, less feeling of unreasonable pressure, more favorable attitudes toward the police supervisor (manager), and higher motivation to produce.[36]

---

[34] See Theodore R. Sarbin and Vernon L. Allen, "Increasing Participation in a Natural Group Setting: A Preliminary Report," *The Psychological Record*, 18 (January 1968), 1–7.

[35] Robert T. Golembiewski, *Men, Management, and Morality*, p. 227.

[36] Rensis Likert, *Human Organization: Its Management and Value* (New York: McGraw-Hill Book Company, 1967), p. 58.

Intergroup Competition and Conflict

Thus far we have discussed groups as individual units. Obviously, most organizations are comprised of more than one group. Therefore, our concern now shifts to conditions between groups—those conditions that enhance the productivity of each without destroying intergroup relations and coordination. In this section we look at some of the consequences of intergroup competition and conflict. The next, and final, section of this chapter examines the means for evoking group cooperation and coordination.

It is tacitly assumed in most organizations that competition among groups is beneficial for the over-all performance of the organization. By this, of course, is meant moderate competition that stimulates (motivates) groups to work harder on their assigned tasks. Where groups are involved, however, problems of morale, cooperation, and coordination impede over-all goal accomplishment. Competition frequently leads to intergroup conflict which leads to group performances appreciably short of their best.[37]

Let us first look at what happens within each competing group. Second, we will look at what occurs between the competing groups.[38] Within each competing group we find that (1) the group members are more cohesive, (2) greater loyalty is manifested by its members, (3) the group is less concerned with meeting individual needs and more concerned with task performance, (4) the leadership style tends to be more authoritarian, and (5) the group develops more standards and rules. Between the competing groups we find that (1) each group begins to perceive other groups as a threat to their operations, (2) perceptions are more distorted, and (3) communications and interactions decrease in their frequency and meaning. Briefly, competition can improve *intragroup* effectiveness while concurrently reducing *intergroup* effectiveness. Further, when groups engage in a win or lose situation, the loser is usually not convinced that he lost; thus the degree of competition often increases as does the amount of conflict.

There are essentially two ways to keep intergroup competition at a minimum, one pertinent before the competition has developed and the other after. In regard to the former, because of the enormous difficulties of reducing conflict once it has developed, it is advantageous to inhibit its occurrence. Intergroup competition and conflict result from dividing the organization into functional areas. If our modern complex organizations did not force us to divide our work among groups the answer would be rather simple—eliminate groups. But this is impossible. Thankfully, ways

---

[37] *Ibid.*, p. 75.

[38] Currently there are a considerable number of studies dealing with the consequences of intergroup competition. The majority of the findings reported on this phenomena are taken from R. R. Blake and Jane S. Mouton, "Reactions to Intergroup Competition Under Win-Lose Conditions," *Management Science*, 7 (December 1967), 420–35.

are being discovered to lessen the natural tendency of groups to compete with one another. These ways are (1) placing greater emphasis on rewarding groups for their contribution to the *total organizational effectiveness*, (2) promoting frequent interaction and communication on a *common problem* (intergroup conflict cannot be reduced simply by increasing contact between groups), (3) rotating members among groups as often as feasible to build mutual understanding of one another's problems, and (4) refraining from placing groups in a situation where they compete for organizational rewards. Again, place emphasis on "pulling-together" to maximize organizational effectiveness.

To reduce the degree of intergroup competition after it has occurred, the following tactics can be successfully employed: (1) identify an external and common threat which tends to shift the conflict outward and to a higher level, (2) create overlap between the various groups which, in effect, takes a few members from each group and places them into a subgroup (this informs those involved of common problems, and subsequently this information is transmitted to those in the competing groups), (3) create common objectives which require cooperative effort on the part of the competing groups.

Not all intergroup conflict can be eliminated. And, even if we wanted to do so, it would not be wise, mainly because there are not one but two types of intergroup conflict—task and nontask. Conflict and competition at the level of the assigned group task is not only beneficial but essential for the achievement of the best solutions to problems. What is harmful is intergroup conflict in which the task is considered secondary, while gaining advantage over others is deemed primary. Significantly, the steps described above can be used to combat both types of conflict. Interestingly enough, research data suggests that task-relevant conflict which improves over-all organizational performance is greater under coordinative and cooperative conditions because groups trust each other enough to be candid and open in sharing information.[39] Consequently, we now turn to an examination of the crux of intergroup effectiveness—coordination.

Coordination

Coordination (integration) is the unification of effort among the various groups in the accomplishment of the organization's goals. The importance of coordinative devices can be seen in their growing number. Hence, according to Lawrence and Lorsch,

> Although coordination is undoubtedly an important part of the top manager's job, there is considerable evidence that many organizational systems develop

---

[39] Schein, *Organizational Psychology*, p. 87.

integrative devices in addition to the conventional hierarchy. Litterer recently suggested three main means of achieving integration: through the hierarchy, through administrative or control systems, and through voluntary activities. It is our view that these "voluntary" activities, which managers (supervisors) at lower echelons develop to supplement the hierarchical and administrative systems, are becoming increasingly formalized. One has only to note the proliferation of coordinating departments (whether called new product, marketing, or planning departments), task forces, and cross-functional coordinating teams to find evidence that new formal devices are emerging to achieve coordination.[40]

Our previous discussion of integration dealt with intragroup behavior; here our interest centers on coordinative or integrative intergroup behavior.

Unfortunately, the trend toward greater specialization in police work is compounding the already serious problem of how to achieve coordination in a police organization. Since concerted action comes about through coordination, considerable time and effort are being expended on improving it. This is to say, coordination is not an inexpensive item for the organization to develop and maintain. Good coordination results from high levels of cooperative behavior, an overlapping group structure, an effective communications system for exerting influence, and participation in important decisions about the organization's objectives and procedures. These four conditions cannot occur unless the previously mentioned tactics for minimizing intergroup competition and conflict are successfully employed. Let us proceed to an analysis of each one of the four conditions for achieving effective coordination. In doing so, note that these conditions, which improve human cooperation in intergroup situations, are *interdependent* and are thus discussed as they relate to one another.

Of the four conditions, by far the most fundamental is that of a multiple, overlapping group structure which links one group to another. Briefly, this means that a person will have more than a single group membership. For example, an individual will be a permanent member of a line group (patrol), a permanent member of a special task force (riot squad), a temporary member of a research committee (evaluation of new weapons), and a temporary member of an advisory committee (developing standard operating procedures for uniform and investigative officers). The overlapping of groups should be both vertical (linking different levels of authority) and horizontal (linking different functions). A police organization using this structural design builds an impetus for cooperative behavior, a relevant communications network, and a means for more effective group decision making. Hence, the group is capable of receiving and transmitting influence later-

---

[40] Paul R. Lawrence and Jay W. Lorsch, "Differentiation and Integration in Complex Organizations," *Administrative Science Quarterly*, 12 (June 1967), 12.

ally, upward, and downward. When operating properly, these four conditions give rise to the motivational forces needed for the *total* coordination of effort.

Finally, it is rather obvious that the group pattern recommended for achieving effective coordination requires significant changes in the formal structure of a highly specialized police department. Basically, two major changes are necessary. First, the linking of groups through the overlapping of memberships adds a new, formal structure to the existing one of the department. Normally, when the tasks of the present personnel are unreasonably increased by adding coordinative tasks, it is necessary to increase the number of people in the organization. This is not always so, however. Frequently, the addition of coordinative tasks to the standard functional tasks sufficiently enhances an employee's efficiency to the point where he finds that the new task has lessened the burden of the others. In other words, assuming a coordinative role makes the performance of the functional one easier. The second major change deals with the way the organization makes decisions. This change is group decision making, which involves all members of the group in the decision process. When decisions are the product of an entire group, they are made with a broader orientation and greater consensus. More will be said about coordination in a later chapter. At this time, we again look at Likert, who provides for us a summary statement concerning coordination.

> The more often he uses group methods of decision making, the greater is the capacity of his organization to achieve highly coordinated efforts toward accomplishing its objectives, and the greater is its success in attaining these objectives.[41]

SUMMARY

In this chapter the reader has confronted the major ideas underlying interpersonal and group relationships. Interpersonal relations are the primary vehicle for exerting influence. Further, the performance of this vehicle depends on the accuracy of the message and the lack of distortion in the communication network. Communication has four dimensions: content, noise, network, and direction. Noise or distortion in a communication is bound to occur for a variety of reasons. Even so. what is important is that meaningful understanding can still be had if the police supervisor uses a series of proven antidistortion techniques. Finally, the primary reason for attempting to influence another person is to change him in some way. Basically there are three types of influence: authority, power, and self-development. Essentially, authority resides in the position, power resides

---

[41] Rensis Likert, *Human Organization*, p. 69.

in the person, and self-development in the relationship between the changer and the client. When applied, each method results in a different behavioral response. The latter method yields the most innovative and spontaneous reactions.

Groups are created in two ways, for a variety of reasons, and are of basically two types. Briefly, the organization forms groups to perform specialized activities and, in other instances, individuals form them to meet their personal needs. Hence, we see that groups are formed both to meet the objectives of an organization (a formal group) and to fulfill the needs of its members (an informal group). Groups develop various networks for communication among members, the effectiveness of which is determined by the problem at hand. Because they create and maintain communication networks, groups can perform five functions: organizational, personal, integrative, conformance, and motivational. It is in the performance of all five of these functions that we can comprehend the true importance of a group. As do individuals, groups tend to compete with each other, which naturally leads to intergroup conflict. All conflict is not injurious; in fact, a certain degree of task-relevant competition is beneficial for attaining the goals of the police department. Last, there is the critical and continuing need for effective coordination of the groups that constitute a police organization. There are various methods for achieving effective coordination, each one of which depends to a great degree on the performance of the police supervisor.

PROBLEMS

1. As a newly appointed police supervisor you are aware that the content of the messages you receive and send tends to be distorted. What are the reasons for such distortion? Can distortion of the content of communications be completely eliminated? What are some techniques that can be employed to reduce distortion and thus improve the accuracy of communications?
2. Similarly, you observe that the communication network of the police department seems to be distorting the meaning of your messages. What are the reasons for this distortion? What changes might you recommend to reduce distortion in the communications network?
3. Finally, you recognize that the direction of a message should depend on the situation at hand. When is a one-way message preferable to a two-way, and vice versa?
4. There are essentially three types of influence that can be exerted by a police supervisor. Describe each one by distinguishing their major characteristics.
5. Why are groups formed by an organization? Why are they formed by individuals?

6. What are some of the implications that a group's communication network holds for the police supervisor?

7. In general, groups perform five functions. What are they?

8. Not all intergroup conflict is bad—in fact, a certain amount and a certain type is desirable. Explain.

9. A system of effective coordination rests on four conditions. What are they? Why is the coordination of the various groups in a police department so vital?

4

Police Organization:
the Formal Side

That the phenomenon known as *organization* continues to be poorly understood and appreciated by most people is ironic, for organizations are among the most important institutions in every part of the world and have a pervasive influence in almost all human activity. Because of their growing influence, we find an ever increasing interest in the "why and wherefore's" of organizations.

Organizations are not a modern invention. The pharaohs of Egypt and the emperors of China depended upon organizations for constructing a variety of complex structures. However, conscious interest in theories or principles of organization began in ancient Greece. The immediate antecedents of organizational theory are in the development of the social sciences and business and public administration. In regard to the present scene, Waldo relates that:

> The increasing interest in the study of organization no doubt arises also from the increase in the number, size, and importance of organizations: the so-called "Organizational Revolution." Much of the recent swelling of interest is caused and given its distinctive qualities by the Behavioral Movement and attention to the social sciences. Much of the interest is interdisciplinary. Indeed, it is the focus on organization as a phenomenon to which we address ourselves, but among social sciences disciplines as established and defined in the United States, the center of the interest is at present most closely associated with Sociology.[1]

Organizational theory is problem centered, the problem being how to construct human groupings that are as rational as possible and simultaneously to produce a minimum of side effects and a maximum of satisfaction. There is a record of both progress and setbacks in the search for the best combination of these objectives. Significantly, the supervisor can either add or detract in an attempt to more effectively organize. He plays a critical

---

[1] Dwight Waldo and Martin Landau, *The Study of Organizational Behavior: Status, Problems, and Trends* (Washington, D.C.: American Society for Public Administration, 1966), p. 2.

role in coordinating human efforts to accomplish organizational goals. This chapter and the next seek to describe for the supervisor the changing aspects of organizational theory and behavior. More specifically, the two chapters describe for the police supervisor the state of the art and future trends in police organization.

This chapter is first historical, since it deals primarily with the formal side of organization, and second, contemporary, because much of the historical or classical thinking remains in practice. In the next chapter we look at both a reaction and an emerging synthesis. The reaction is to those who could not see beyond the mechanistic doctrine of the traditionalists—it is referred to as the informal side, or human relations in organizational theory. The synthesis combines these two theoretical concerns—formal and informal —into the much more sophisticated systems theory of organization.

ORGANIZATION DEFINED

Organizations are social units (human groupings) deliberately constructed and reconstructed to seek specific goals.[2] Corporations, armies, schools, hospitals, churches, and police departments are included; tribes, ethnic groups, friendship groups, and families are excluded. An organization is characterized by (1) goals, (2) a division of labor, authority, power, and communication responsibilities in a rationally planned, rather than a random or traditionally patterned, manner to enhance the achievement of specific goals, (3) a set of rules and norms, (4) the presence of one or more authority centers which control the efforts of the organization and direct them toward its goals.

In defining organization, it is helpful to define some other concepts frequently confused with it. First, let us consider management. *Management* is action intended to achieve rational cooperation in an organization. Second, there is *administration*, which is, quite simply, organization and management. The crux or central idea of administration is to deliberately construct a rational plan of human action for goal accomplishment. Third is the much discussed and cussed concept known as *bureaucracy*. Bureaucracy often carries a negative connotation for the layman, while organization is a neutral term. Further, bureaucracy implies for those familiar with Weber's work that the unit is organized according to the principles he specified. But many organizations are not bureaucratic in this technical sense. Hospitals, for instance, do not have one decision-making center, whereas bureaucracies, by definition, do. Since many police departments are to a

---

[2] Talcott Parsons, *Structure and Process in Modern Societies* (New York: The Free Press of Glencoe, Inc., 1960), p. 17.

great extent, if not totally, bureaucratic, this concept is covered in more detail later in the chapter. For now, bureaucracies (1) are organizations that have numerous *formalized* rules and regulations, and (2) are among the most important institutions in the world because they not only provide employment for a very significant fraction of the world's population, but also make critical decisions that shape the economic, educational, political, social, moral, and even religious lives of nearly everyone on earth.[3]

The next section is devoted first to a general overview of organizational goals, and second, to goals as they specially relate to the police department. There are two reasons for organizing this chapter in this way: (1) goals are philosophical, specific to a particular organization, and enduring, and (2) the organizational theorists remain chiefly interested in structural-functional relationships.

ORGANIZATIONAL GOALS

Goals: In a General Sense

The goals of an organization serve many uses. Etzioni asserts that

> They provide orientation by depicting a future state of affairs which the organization strives to realize. Thus they set down guide lines for organizational activity. Goals also constitute a source of legitimacy which justifies the activities of an organization and, indeed, its very existence. Moreover goals serve as standards by which members of an organization and outsiders can assess the success of the organization—i.e., its effectiveness and efficiency. Goals also serve in a similar fashion as measuring rods for the student of organizations who tries to determine how well the organization is doing.[4]

The very reason for an organization's existence lies in its goals. However, once the goals are decided upon, organizations frequently generate unforeseen needs (for example, providing job satisfaction to their employees in order to retain them). In such instances, organizations usually reduce their preoccupation with their initial goals in order to satisfy their acquired needs. At times organizations go so far as to abandon their initial goals and pursue new ones more suited to the organization's needs. We will return to this and other problems concerning goals in a few moments. First, let us look at what goals are, how they come into being, and their benefits.

---

[3] Anthony Downs, *Inside Bureaucracy* (Boston, Mass.: Little, Brown and Company, 1967), p. 1.

[4] Amitai Etzioni, *Modern Organizations* (Englewood Cliffs, N.J.: Prentice-Hall, Inc., 1964), p. 5.

What is a goal? "An organizational goal is a desired state of affairs which the organization attempts to realize."[5] The organization may or may not be able to bring about this hoped-for image of the future. For example, it is highly unlikely that our American police system will ever be able to attain its principal goal of maintaining social order at all times. But if a goal is reached, it ceases to be a guiding image for an organization and is either dismissed or replaced with another. In reality, a goal never exists; it is a state which we seek, not one we have. Further, we should distinguish between *real* and *stated* goals. At times they are one and the same, but often we are able to detect that an organization is pursuing a direction different from that which they expressed as their goal. The reasons for this phenomenon vary from a lack of awareness that this is happening to hiding the real goal so that it can be more easily achieved. The real goals of an organization are those future states toward which a majority of the organization's resources are committed, as compared with those that are stated but receive fewer resources. The distinction between real and stated goals is important because they should not be confused with the important difference between intended and unintended consequences. Real goals are always intended. Stated goals can be intended or not.

How are goals derived? All formal organizations have an explicitly recognized, legally specified means for creating the initial goals and also for changing them. Regardless of the formal means, in practice goals are often established in a complicated power play involving (1) organizational subdivisions (groups), (2) individuals, and (3) environmental influences. The outcome of the three-cornered power play provides direction for (1) sharpening and clarifying goals, (2) adding new goals, (3) shifting priorities among goals, and (4) eliminating irrelevant goals. In summary, goal formation is the result of policy making. Policy making is based upon decision making, which, in turn, draws upon numerous decision centers in order to reach the final choice—in this case, which organizational goals to adopt.

What are the benefits of goals to an organization? We can list the primary benefits of a goal or a set of goals as providing a means for:

1. presenting the general purpose and ideology of the organization
2. guiding and supporting organizational decision making
3. developing and maintaining a useful information system
4. integrating the planning process
5. performing the control function
6. motivating the people in the organization
7. delegating responsibility

---

[5] *Ibid.*, p. 6.

8. integrating the activities between the operating subunits within the organization

On the basis of this analysis of the meaning and development of goals, we are better able to understand "goal dynamics," the concept that goals are not static but moving and changeable. We now consider multiple goals, goal displacement, and goal succession.

Most modern organizations possess multiple goals. Pfiffner and Sherwood emphasize this when they write, "organizations have more than a single goal, some of which may have been provided from outside the organization."[6] Further, Argyris' "Mix Model" defines one of the essential properties of organization as "The achievement of *goals* or *objectives*."[7] As an illustration, besides apprehending offenders, the police also act to prevent offenses. Interestingly, the latter goal seeks to make the former unnecessary. One final comment in regard to multiple goals—organizations that serve more than a single goal do so more effectively than single-purpose organizations of the same category. The reasons for this are twofold: first, serving one goal often increases the achievement of another goal; and second, there is a much improved recruitment appeal because the nature of the work provides more variety and, therefore, enhanced job satisfaction.

With respect to goal displacement, we find that the attainment of a goal or goals is vastly increased when goal displacement is kept at a minimum.[8] Briefly, goal displacement occurs when an organization substitutes for its legitimate goal some other goal for which it was not created, for which resources were not allocated, and which it is not known to serve.[9] Since goal displacement is injurious to the effectiveness of an organization, what can be done to avoid it? Making the goals more tangible is the simple answer, for goal displacement is minimized when goals are tangible. Gross, however, takes exception to the importance of goal tangibility in his "Clarity-Vagueness Balance" when he writes that

> There is no need to labor the need for clarity in the formulation of an organization's objectives. Precise formulations are necessary for delicate operations. They provide the indispensable framework for coordinating complex activity . . . yet in the wide enthusiasm for "crystal-clear goals," one may easily lose sight of the need for a fruitful balance between clarity and vagueness. . . .[10]

[6] John M. Pfiffner and Frank P. Sherwood, *Administrative Organization* (Englewood Cliffs, N.J.: Prentice-Hall, Inc., 1960), p. 413.

[7] Chris Argyris, *Integrating the Individual and the Organization* (New York: John Wiley & Sons, Inc., 1964), p. 150.

[8] W. Keith Warner and A. Eugene Havens, "Goal Displacement and the Intangibility of Organizational Goals," *Administrative Science Quarterly*, 12 (March 1968), 539.

[9] Etzioni, *Modern Organizations*, p. 10.

[10] Bertram M. Gross, "What are Your Organization's Objectives: A General Systems Approach to Planning," *Human Relations*, 18 (August 1965), 213.

Gross supports the virtues of vagueness again by writing:

> If all points on a set of interrelated purpose chains were to be set forth with precise clarity, the result would be to destroy the subordination of one element to another which is essential to an operating purpose pattern. The proper focusing of attention on some goals for any particular moment or period in time means that other goals must be left vague. This is even truer for different periods of time. We must be very clear about many things we aim to do today and tomorrow. It might be dangerously misleading to seek similar clarity for our long-range goals.
>
> Apart from its role in helping to provide focus, vagueness in goal formation has many positive virtues. It leaves room for others to fill in the details and even modify the general pattern; over-precise goals stifle initiative. Vagueness may make it easier to adapt to changing conditions; ultra-precision can destroy flexibility. Vagueness may make it possible to work toward many goals that can only be attained by indirection. Some of the deepest personal satisfactions from work and cooperation come as by-products of other things. If pursued too directly, they may slip through one's fingers; the happiest people in the world are never those who set out to do the things that will make them happy. There is something inhuman and terrifying about ultra-purposeful action proceeding according to blueprint and schedule. Only vagueness can restore the precious element of humanity.[11]

Gross's thinking leaves us in somewhat of a quandary. Should we create tangible goals in order to better accomplish them or vague goals in order to be more flexible? The solution to this apparent dilemma is not perfectly clear. Perhaps it lies in better and more frequent organizational analysis. This is to say, if an organization will subject its goals to periodic study and evaluation the opportunity for changing them is improved. Hence, the necessity of vagueness becomes less because the tangible goals are kept updated and relevant. At the same time, the over-all mission or philosophy of an organization can remain vague to facilitate adaptation and innovation. For example, the police philosophy, "to protect and serve," leaves considerable room for creating and changing the more tangible goals of a police department.

To summarize, it appears that more effective ways should be developed for changing organizational goals from unanalyzable abstractions to meaningful descriptions of a desired state of affairs. At the present we can see two such ways to make an organization's goals more concrete: planning, programming, and budgeting systems (PPBS), and automated data processing systems (ADP).[12]

---

[11] Bertram M. Gross, *The Managing of Organizations* (New York: The Free Press of Glencoe, Inc., 1964), p. 497.

[12] Examples of pertinent literature on these subjects can be found in *The Police Chief*, 35 (July 1968); and Paul M. Whisenand, *Automated Police Information Systems* (New York: John Wiley & Sons, Inc., 1970).

Not only do modern organizations usually have multiple goals and experience goal displacement, but they also tend to find new goals when the traditional ones have been attained or cannot be attained. This latter tendency on the part of an organization is known as goal succession. Therefore, *goal succession* is the replacement of a goal or goals with another goal or goals, or merely acquiring new goals. The police organization is a case in point. To the more traditional goals of arresting and recovering stolen property have been added those of maintaining public order. Initially, the newer goals, and this holds true for the police, are justified in that they improve the accomplishment of the traditional goals, but often they become equal in importance. We have arrived at a point where it seems worthwhile to provide some limited discussion on the goals of our police organizations.

Goals: In a Police Sense

A police organization is designed to deal, for the most part, with the actions and behavior of human beings. More often than not, police work is defined in terms of criminal behavior.

> There are at least four different types of criminal behavior. First, there are the so-called major crimes: felonious homicide, rape, robbery, aggravated assault, burglary, larceny, auto theft, forgery, counterfeiting, embezzlement, fraud, blackmail, arson, and kidnapping. Second, there are offenses against public morals: vice, gambling, liquor, drugs, and offenses against the family. Third, there are offenses which have to do with the maintenance of the peace: disorderly conduct, possession of weapons, assault, trespassing, and vagrancy. And finally there are violations of traffic and other regulations not covered by the first three classifications.[13]

But the police department has evolved into much more than a law-enforcing agency. It has an enormously broader social responsibility with regard to the activities previously mentioned. One benchmark text in the police field asserts that a police department now has five goals. In order of priority, they are:

1. *The Prevention of Criminality.* This goal is one of the newer responsibilities of the police. It is being more and more clearly realized that a constructive approach to the crime problem must go to its very roots—to the factors in community life which create criminal tendencies and lead the criminal to indulge in anti-social behavior. Case studies must be made to determine the causes that led to delinquency, and on the basis of these facts attempts must be made to eradicate the causes.

---

[13] This classification is adapted from that employed by August Vollmer, *The Police and Modern Society* (Berkeley: University of California Press, 1936).

2. *Repression of Crime.* This function is more firmly imbedded in police practice. Adequate patrol plus continuous effort toward eliminating or reducing hazards is stressed as a means of reducing the opportunities for criminal activity.

3. *Apprehension of Offenders.* Quick apprehension and certain punishment discourage the would-be offender by making the consequences of crime seem less pleasant. In addition to its repressive influence, apprehension enables society to punish offenders, prevents a repetition of their offenses by restraining their movements, and provides an opportunity for their rehabilitation.

4. *Recovery of Property.* This activity is intended to reduce the monetary cost of crime, as well as to restrain those who, though not active criminals, might benefit from the gains of crime.

5. *Regulation of Noncriminal Conduct.* Many police activities are concerned only incidentally with criminal behavior. Their main purpose is regulation; apprehension and punishment of offenders are means of securing obedience. Other methods used to obtain compliance are education of the public to the dangers inherent in the disobedience of regulations; and the use of warnings, either oral or written, which inform the citizen of the violation but do not penalize him. Examples of such activities are the regulation of traffic and the enforcement of minor regulations concerning sanitation and street use.

 This type of regulation is time consuming and drains police energies from those tasks which are more important in the eyes of the public.[14]

While still relevant, the previous list of goals is considered incomplete and in need of modification. Because of emerging contemporary demands for new services, police organizations need to add still another goal to their over-all mission. Let us consider one of the more salient possibilities. Before doing so, however, the fifth goal in the previous list should be redefined in more tangible terms. This redefinition is caused by the growing awareness that the police organization is an institution for social control. We rely on a recognized authority for needed assistance in this task, namely, Quinn Tamm, Executive Director, International Association of Chiefs of Police. In referring to this newer goal for police organizations, he writes:

> But the social climate of our times has immensely broadened this concept to where the police find themselves the arbiter between rival social factions, where they find themselves involved in the most delicate problems of human relations in the rapidly changing social structure of our modern society. It is no exaggeration to say that the type of duties normally performed by social workers occupy as much as fifty percent of the long day of both police administrators and line officers.
>
> To meet these demands requires abilities, training, and understanding far beyond what was ever conceived as necessary police characteristics in the not-

---

[14] *International City Managers' Association Municipal Police Administration*, 5th ed., rev. (Chicago: International City Managers' Association, 1961), pp. 7–8.

too-distant past. Today any plan of action must be carefully considered from the standpoint of the human factors involved. . . .

Most police executives recognize this problem and are actively eliminating the basic cause through increased emphasis on sociological training and developing expertise in human relations among the personnel under their supervision.[15]

Los Angeles Police Chief Thomas Reddin adds further credence to the above thinking when he states that

Times change and we must change with time.

The policeman of the future will be more effective and will function at a more personal level than in the past. He will be much more sociologist, psychologist, and scientist than his present-day counterpart. He will have many more scientific and technological aids to assist him.

In short, he will utilize space-age techniques of the physical sciences coupled with a type of police work that draws upon the best lessons learned from the social scientists.[16]

Finally, we can now see the news media offering support for a broader social role for the local police when one of their members editorialized "Changing Role for the Police—Today's urban policeman is expected to be, along with an enforcer of complex laws, *sociologist, psychologist, social worker.*"[17]

Included in this expanded responsibility is the power by which a culture exercises supervision and control over matters involving the peace, good order, health, morals, and general welfare of its people. Under this broad and often vaguely described power, cities pass ordinances relating not only to public peace and order but also to health, morals, public convenience, and general welfare. *Social control* may be defined as those mechanisms and techniques used to regulate the behavior of persons to meet societal goals and needs.[18] In a formal way, social control is exercised by the state, through such sanctions as the criminal and civil codes and general legislation affecting "police power." The notion of social control has given rise to police powers frequently questioned by those concerned with the role of police in our society. It is in the latter area of general legislation that we find the rationale for many of the new police services and responsibilities undertaken by American cities during the past few decades. In fact, it is thought by some that the police are the most important local agency of social control.[19]

---

[15] Quinn Tamm, *The Police Chief,* 33 (November 1966), 6.

[16] Tom Reddin, "The Police, the People, the Future," *Los Angeles Times,* May 19, 1968, sec. g, p. 4.

[17] Editorial Views of the Week, *Los Angeles Times,* May 19, 1968, sec. g, p. 4. [Italics added.]

[18] Robert L. Derbyshire, "The Social Control Role of the Police in Changing Urban Communities," *Excerpta Criminologia,* 6 (May-June 1966), 316.

[19] *Ibid.,* 318.

Based on this redefinition, the proposed sixth goal becomes somewhat of an expected sequel to the fifth. Briefly, it requires the establishment of detailed civil disaster plans for the care and control of the population during either emergency or unusual circumstances. On the surface this goal may appear similar to other well-established operational goals intended to accomplish the over-all police mission. It differs, however, in three significant dimensions: It is basically designed to cope with a noncriminal problem —that of either survival or restoration of general community peace; it involves an advanced planning program infused with a high capability for change; it requires a much greater degree of intra- and extra-jurisdictional coordination and liaison. This goal has imposed upon the local police department an organizational requirement for short and long range planning. Further, it requires the design of a complex man-machine system that reacts quickly to individual and total community threats. Through training and experience, for example, most police departments are becoming qualified to handle dangerous substances, control demonstrations, render first aid, determine unsafe areas, and perform rescue operations.

In summary, to over-all mission of a police organization is to effectively discharge the foregoing six goals. Each goal includes the performance of numerous functions not exclusively confined to the more traditional concept of police protection and service. We find this especially true in the case of the latter two objectives, as now defined. To repeat, we have identified and described six goals that provide a framework of responsibility for a local police agency. Briefly, these goals are: (1) prevention of criminality, (2) repression of crime, (3) apprehension of offenders, (4) recovery of property, (5) provision of social control, and (6) participation in the implementation of civil defense, disaster, and disorder services. When combined, these six goals provide the underpinning for the over-all mission or ideology of a local police department, namely, *to maintain the peace, and to protect life and property.*

ORGANIZATIONAL THEORY: THE CLASSICAL APPROACH

By classical theory of organization is meant the theory that developed over a number of centuries and finally matured in the thirties. It is exemplified in Luther Gulick's essay "Notes on the Theory of Organization,"[20] in Mooney and Reiley's *The Principles of Organization,*[21] and in Max Weber's

---

[20] Luther Gulick, "Notes on the Theory of Organization," in *Papers on the Science of Administration,* eds. Luther Gulick and Lyndall Urwick (New York: Institute of Public Administration, 1937), pp. 1–45.

[21] James D. Mooney and Alan C. Reiley, *Principles of Organization* (New York: Harper & Row, Publishers, 1939).

writings on bureaucracy.[22] All these theorists were strongly oriented toward economy, efficiency, and executive control. These values, when combined, create a theory of organization that has four cornerstones. Briefly, they are the division of labor, hierarchy of authority, structure, and span of control. Of the four, division of labor is the major cornerstone. In fact, the other three are dependent on it for their very existence. The hierarchy of authority is the legitimate vertical network for gaining compliance. Essentially, it refers to the chain of command, the sharing of authority and responsibility, the unity of command, and the obligation to report. Structure is the logical relationships of positions and functions in an organization, arranged to accomplish the objectives of the organization efficiently. Structure suggests system and pattern. Classical organization theory usually works with two basic structures, the line and the staff. According to Gulick, both structures can be arranged four ways: purpose, process, clientele, and place where services are rendered.[23] The span of control concept deals with the number of subordinates a superior can effectively supervise. It has significance, in part, for the shape of the organization. Wide span yields a flat structure; short span results in a tall structure.

Our approach to classical organization theory is divided, for better understanding, into three broad areas. The first area deals with rationality and its critical role in a bureaucratic structure. The principal theorist in this case is Max Weber. The second area is devoted to maximizing efficiency by making management a true science. In this instance, the majority of our thinking is derived from Frederick W. Taylor. The third area is best termed principles and here we turn to the works of Gulick, Urwick, Mooney, and Reiley.

Weber: Rationality

Max Weber was one of the leading scholars of the early twentieth century. Significantly, he was a founder of modern sociology as well as a pioneer in administrative thought. The major theme underlying most of Weber's work is the derivation and development of rationality. This led him to study different kinds of organizations—economic, governmental, religious, and political—in terms of their interactions with society as a whole. From his studies, Weber described the development of Western rationality through capitalism, science, and bureaucracy. We concern ourselves here with the latter vehicle for creating rational relationships.

---

[22] The best known translation of Max Weber's writings on bureaucracy is H. H. Gerth and C. Wright Mills, trans., *From Max Weber: Essays in Sociology* (New York: Oxford University Press, Inc., 1946).

[23] Gulick, "Notes."

Weber probed bureaucracy, here essentially synonymous with large organization, to uncover the rational relationship of bureaucratic structure to its goals. His analysis led him to conclude that, as discussed in Chapter 3, there are three types of organizational power centers. In review, they are (1) traditional—subjects accept the orders of a supervisor as justified on the grounds that it is the way things have always been done, (2) charismatic —subjects accept a superior's order as justified because of the influence of his personality, and (3) rational-legal—subjects accept a superior's order as justified because it agrees with more abstract rules which are considered legitimate. The type of power employed determines the degree of alienation on the part of the subject. If the subject perceives the power as legitimate he is more willing to comply. And, if power is considered legitimate, then, according to Weber, it becomes authority. Hence, Weber's three power centers can be transformed into authority centers.

Of the three types of authority, Weber recommended that rational structural relationships can be obtained best through the rational-legal form. The other two forms were seen to lack systematic division of labor, specialization, stability, and to have nonrelevant political and administrative relationships.

Still, Weber was aware of the weaknesses of the rational-legal structure. Not only are there constant pressures from external forces for the administrator to follow norms other than those of the organization, but over a period of time an individual's adherence to the bureaucratic rules declines. Etzioni describes this decline as a typical organizational dilemma.

> For the organization to be effective, it requires a special kind of legitimation, rationality, and narrowness of scope. But the ability to accept orders and rules as legitimate, particularly when they are repugnant to one's desires— frequently the case in bureaucracies—requires a level of self-denial that is difficult to maintain. Hence bureaucratic organizations tend to break either in the charismatic or the traditional direction where discipline relations are less separated from other, more "natural," "warmer" ones. Moreover, the capacity for self-denial which the rational organization requires cannot be developed within it; it depends upon the more encompassing social relationships that exist in the traditional family or charismatic movement.[24]

In each principle of bureaucracy described shortly, one can see Weber's constant concern for the frailness of a rational-legal bureaucracy. His primary motive, therefore, was to build into the bureaucratic structure safeguards against external and internal pressures so that the bureaucracy could at all times sustain its autonomy.

---

[24] Etzioni, *Modern Organizations*, p. 53.

According to Weber, a bureaucratic structure, to be rational, must contain these elements:[25]

1. *Rulification and routinization.* "A continuous organization of official functions bound by *rules.*" Rational organization is the opposite of temporary, unstable relations, thus the stress on continuity. Rules save effort by eliminating the need for deriving a new solution for every situation. Further, they facilitate standard and equal treatment of similar situations.

2. *Division of labor.* "A specific sphere of competence. This involves (a) a sphere of obligations to perform functions which have been marked off as part of a systematic division of labor; (b) the provision of the incumbent with the necessary authority to carry out these functions; and (c) that the necessary means of compulsion are clearly defined ánd their use is subject to definite conditions." Each participant must know his job and have adequate power to carry it out. He also must know the limits of his job and power so as not to overstep the boundaries of his role and thus interfere with the functioning of the entire structure.

3. *Hierarchy of authority.* "The organization of offices follows the principle of hierarchy; that each lower office is under the control and supervision of a higher one."

4. *Expertise.* "The rules which regulate the conduct of an office may be *technical* rules or norms. In both cases, if their application is to be fully rational, specialized training is necessary. It is thus normally true that only a person who has demonstrated an adequate technical training is qualified to be a member of the administrative staff. . . ." What Weber is saying here is that the basis of an administrator's authority is his job-related knowledge—not that knowledge replaces legitimation, but that his capability for exercising technical skill and knowledge is the basis on which legitimation is granted to him.

5. *Written rules.* "Administrative acts, decisions, and rules are formulated and recorded in writing. . . ." These rules are commonly referred to as red tape. Weber, however, emphasized the need to maintain a written interpretation of norms and enforcement of rules for consistency and accuracy.

6. *Separation of ownership.* "It is a matter of principle that the members of the administrative staff should be completely separated from ownership of the means of production or administration. . . . There exists, furthermore, in principle, complete separation of the property belonging to the organization, which is controlled within the spheres of the office, and the personal property of the official. . . . " Weber advocated such a separation for two reasons: to keep the administrator's organizational position from being influenced by the requirements of his nonorganizational roles and to keep the resources and people of the organization free from outside control or inside monopoly.

---

[25] Max Weber, *The Theory of Social and Economic Organization*, ed. Talcott Parsons, trans. A. M. Henderson and Talcott Parsons (New York: Oxford University Press, Inc., 1947), pp. 329–30.

The above features of a bureaucracy are expressed by Weber as an "ideal type." That is, it does not suggest goodness or badness but rather a standard or a model. Weber did not expect any bureaucracy to have all the elements he listed. However, the greater the number and intensity of these elements an organization possessed the more rational and, therefore, the more efficient would be the organization.

Weber's theory on bureaucracy contained two other essential aspects. First, he stressed the universality of bureaucracy. In other words, since bureaucracy is the best known means for achieving rationality in human behavior, it is equally applicable in both the private and the public sector of society. Second, for bureaucracy to work, man has to be a free agent. This is to say that the relationship between man and bureaucracy has to be contractual rather than master-slave.

Weber's concept of bureaucracy has not been without criticism. Those who find fault with Weber have done so over his method, purpose, and ideas.[26] Most frequently, the critics take exception to his ideal type of bureaucracy and to the sharp distinction he makes among the three types of power or authority. The former criticism is made because Weber's concept of an imaginary ideal type does not provide understanding of concrete bureaucratic structures, such as a large-scale police organization. The latter criticism is lodged because the three types of authority are not discussed as they are most often experienced—in mixed forms. Indeed, all three forms, some to a far lesser extent of course, can be found in a police department.

Weber's contribution to organizational theory is becoming more recognized and appreciated. In fact, his thinking is spreading into the more pragmatic management literature. Certainly our modern police organizations would find it hard to deny that he has to some degree influenced their structure.

Taylorism: Scientific Management

Frederick W. Taylor, production specialist, business executive, and consultant, applied the scientific method to the solution of factory problems and from these analyses built up orderly sets of principles which could be substituted for the trial-and-error methods then in use. The advent of Taylor's thinking opened a new era, that of "scientific management." Taylor probably did not invent the term or originate the approach. Taylor's enormous contribution lay first in his large-scale application of the analytical, scientific

---

[26] For an excellent analysis and critique of Weber's writings, see Alfred Diamant, "The Bureaucratic Model: Max Weber Rejected, Rediscovered, Reformed," in *Papers in Comparative Public Administration*, eds. Ferrel Heady and Sybil Stokes (Ann Arbor, Mich.: Institute of Public Administration, University of Michigan, 1962), pp. 59–96.

approach to improving production methods in the shop.[27] Second, while he did not feel that management could ever become an exact science in the same sense as physics and chemistry, he believed strongly that management could be an organized body of knowledge and that it could be taught and learned. Third, he originated the term and concept of "functional supervision." Taylor felt the job of supervision was too complicated to be handled effectively by one supervisor and should therefore be delegated to as many as eight specialized foremen. Finally, Taylor believed that his major contribution lay in a new philosophy for workers and management.

> Now, in its essence, scientific management involves a complete mental revolution on the part of the workingman engaged in any particular establishment or industry—a complete mental revolution on the part of these men as to their duties toward their work, toward their fellow men, and toward their employees. And it involves the equally complete mental revolution on the part of those on the management's side—the foreman, the superintendent, the owner of the business, the board of directors—a complete mental revolution on their part as to their duties toward their fellow workers in the management, toward their workmen, and toward all of their daily problems. And without this complete mental revolution on both sides scientific management does not exist.[28]

Interestingly, Taylor's contributions to the practice of management stem from a question he constantly sought to answer—How does one get more work out of workers, who are naturally lazy and engage in systematic soldiering? His desire for an answer to this problem led Taylor into the analysis of work methods, a field rarely entered by previous engineers. Based on this analysis, he recommended that managers use scientific research methods to discover the "one best way" of performing every piece of work. This research would enable management itself to evaluate how much work should actually be accomplished in a specific period of time. It would also involve significant changes in the specifications for tools and materials, and in the selection, supervising, and training of workmen. When this foundation had been laid, and only then, would it be possible to make proper use of incentives for higher individual output. He consistently maintained—and successfully demonstrated—that through these techniques it would

---

[27] Frederick W. Taylor, *Shop Management* (New York: Harper & Row, Publishers, 1911).

[28] Frederick W. Taylor, "The Principles of Scientific Management," in *Classics in Management*, ed. Harwood F. Merrill (New York: American Management Association, 1960), p. 78. A comprehensive account of Taylor's achievements in this field is found in three basic documents: "Shop Management," a paper presented to the American Society of Mechanical Engineers in 1903; "The Principles of Scientific Management," which Taylor wrote in 1909, when his work was becoming an object of public attention, but which was not published until 1911; and his 1912 "Testimony before the Special House Committee," which consisted largely of a justification of his views in the light of public attack. These three documents have been published in one volume, *Scientific Management* (New York: Harper & Row, Publishers, 1947).

be possible to obtain appreciable increases in a worker's efficiency. Furthermore, Taylor firmly believed that management, and management alone, is responsible for putting these techniques into effect. Although it is important to obtain the cooperation of the workers, it must be "enforced cooperation." He emphasizes this point as follows:

> It is only through *enforced* standardization of methods, *enforced* adaptation of the best implements and working conditions and *enforced* cooperation that this faster work can be assured. And the duty of enforcing the adaptation of standards and of enforcing this cooperation rests with the *management* alone. . . . All those who, after proper teaching, either will not or cannot work in accordance with the new methods and at the higher speed must be discharged by *management*. The *management* must also recognize the broad fact that workmen will not submit to this more rigid standardization and will not work extra hard, unless they receive extra pay for doing it.[29]

Taylor prescribed five methods for scientifically managing an organization. First, management must carefully study the worker's body movements to discover the one best method for accomplishing work in the shortest possible time. Second, management must standardize its tools based on the requirements of specific jobs. Third, management must select and train each worker for the job for which he is best suited. Fourth, management must abandon the traditional unity of command principle and substitute functional supervision. As mentioned, Taylor advocated that a worker receive his orders from as many as eight supervisors. Four of these supervisors are to serve on the shop floor (inspector, repair foreman, speed boss, and gang boss) and the other four in the planning room (routing, instruction, time and costs, and discipline). Fifth, management must pay the worker in accordance with his individual output.

Taylor's ideas were opposed by management and unions. A revolutionary change in the thinking of managers and workers threatened their established patterns of operation. Its challenge to the accepted way of doing things made it a widely controversial subject—so much so that the House of Representatives in 1911 appointed a special committee to investigate it and other systems of shop management. In January 1912, after many hearings during which Taylor believed scientific management had been distorted and misrepresented, he took the stand before a Special House of Representatives Committee in order to clarify and defend his ideas.

Let us consider for a moment functional supervision. It was rejected for two reasons. First, the concept of multiple supervision seemed to violate the sacred unity of command precept so deeply ingrained in management's thinking. Second, job specialization had not reached such a point as to

---

[29] Frederick W. Taylor, *Scientific Management*, p. 83.

force attention to his theory. However, specialization has been increasing at such a steady rate in recent years as to raise the issue of functional influence. As a matter of fact, an examination of the tasks and duties of Taylor's functional supervisors reveals that these supervisors do exist in today's manufacturing organizations. Modern systems of production control have shop planners, clerks, and timekeepers located right in the shop.

Ironically, Taylor's general approach to management is widely accepted today in production-oriented business organizations. In brief, scientific management became a movement, which still has a tremendous influence on industrial practice. More specifically, it had a major effect on the reform and economy movements in public administration and thus also influenced police administration. Its impact on public organizations is readily apparent at the present. One can find numerous managers and supervisors (private and public alike) who firmly believe that if material rewards are directly related to work efforts, the worker consistently responds with his maximum performance.

Gulick and Urwick: the Principles

While the followers of Taylor developed more scientific techniques of management and work, others were conceptualizing broad principles for the most effective design of organizational structure. Luther Gulick and Lyndall Urwick were leaders in formulating principles of formal organization. Not only did they develop such principles, but Gulick went even further and defined administration as comprising seven activities.[30] Together these activities spell out the familiar acronym POSDCORB.

> *P*lanning: working out in broad outline what needs to be done and the methods for doing it to accomplish the purpose set for the enterprise;
> *O*rganizing: the establishment of a formal structure of authority through which work subdivisions are arranged, defined, and coordinated for the defined objective;
> *S*taffing: the whole personnel function of bringing in and training the staff and maintaining favorable conditions of work;
> *D*irecting: the continuous task of making decisions, embodying them in specific and general orders and instructions, and serving as the leader of the enterprise;
> *CO*ordinating: the all important duty of interrelating the various parts of the organization;
> *R*eporting: keeping those to whom the executive is responsible informed as to what is going on, which includes keeping himself and his subordinates informed through records, research, and inspection;

---

[30] Gulick's seven elements of administration are drawn from Henri Fayol's list of five: planning, organization, command, coordination, and control. See Henri Fayol, *General and Industrial Management*, trans. Constance Storrs (London: Sir Isaac Pitman & Sons, Ltd., 1949), pp. 43–110.

*B*udgeting: all that goes with budgeting in the form of fiscal planning, account-ing, and control.[31]

Importantly, POSDCORB continues to serve as a starting point for innumerable scholars and practitioners interested in dealing with different administrative processes. Many writers on public or business administration take this list and through additions, subtractions, and modifications adapt it to meet their interests and needs.

The Gulick-Urwick principles deal primarily with the structure of the formal organization. Underlying all their principles was the need for an organizational division of labor. In other words, their approach rests firmly on the assumption that the more a specific function can be divided into its simplest parts, the more specialized and, therefore, the more skilled a worker can become in carrying out his part of the job. Moreover, the more skilled the worker is in his particular job, the more efficient the whole organization is. According to Gulick, any division of labor should be homogenous, and homogeneity can be achieved if one or more of four determinants are used to characterize the type of work each individual is performing.

The major *purpose* he is serving, such as furnishing water, controlling crime, or conducting education;

The *process* he is using, such as engineering, medicine, carpentry, stenography, statistics, or accounting;

The *persons* or *things* dealt with or served, such as immigrants, veterans, Indians, forests, mines, parks, orphans, farmers, automobiles, or the poor;

The *place* where he renders his service, such as Hawaii, Boston, Washington, the Dust Bowl, Alabama, or Central High School.[32]

This four-determinant approach has been subject to criticism. Namely, determinants are difficult to apply to a specific organization since they often overlap, are sometimes incompatible with one another, and are quite vague. For example, when looking at a police organization, it would be difficult not to conclude that the four principles fail to provide a satisfactory guide to division of labor in that organization. Furthermore, it can be seen that these determinants are prescriptive rather than descriptive, that they state how work should be divided rather than how work is divided. The planning of the division of labor in a given organization is affected by many considerations not covered by the four principles. The division may be deter-mined by the culture in which the organization is situated, by the environ-ment of the organization, by the availability and type of personnel, and by political factors. In the final analysis, organizations are made up of a combi-

---

[31] Gulick, "Notes," p. 13.
[32] *Ibid.*, p. 15.

nation of various layers which differ in their type of division. The lower layers tend to be organized according to area or clientele and the higher ones by purpose or process. Even this statement, however, should be viewed only as a probability. In a police organization, all four determinants operate at the same time, and it is their particular mix that makes the department either effective or ineffective.

In addition to Gulick's and Urwick's central principle of division of labor there are seven other related principles which merit our attention.[33]

1. *Unity of command.* "A man cannot serve two masters."[34] This principle is offered as a balance to the division of labor. In other words, the tasks have to be broken up into components by a central authority, the efforts of each work unit need to be supervised by a single supervisor, and the various job efforts leading to the final product have to be coordinated.

2. *Fitting people to the structure.* People should be assigned to their organizational positions "in a cold-blooded, detached spirit," like the preparation of an engineering design, regardless of the needs of that particular individual or of those individuals who may now be in the organization.[35] Every effort must be made to adapt or force-fit people to the structure.

3. *One top executive (manager).* Both Gulick and Urwick strongly supported the principle of one-man administrative responsibility in an organization. Hence they warned against the use of committees or boards, especially in government, for purposes of administration.

4. *Staff: general and special.* The classical writers' concern for staff assistance to top management deserves special attention. This concern became increasingly necessary when management expressed a need for help from larger and larger numbers of experts and specialists. Their need immediately raised the question of the relation of these specialists to the regular line supervisors and employees. In this instance, Gulick recommended that the staff specialist obtain results from the line through influence and persuasion, and that the staff must not be given authority over the line. The next question to be answered was that of coordination. Top management would have more people to supervise since they would be responsible for not only the line but the special staff as well. The Gulick-Urwick answer to this problem was to provide help through "general staff" as distinguished from "special staff" assistance. Significantly, general staff are not limited to the proffering of advice. They may draw up and transmit orders, check on operations, and iron out difficulties. In so doing, they act not on their own but as representatives of their superior and within the confines of decisions made by him. Thus, they allow him to exercise a broader span of control.

---

[33] This list is in part suggested by Gross. See Gross, *The Managing of Organizations*, pp. 145–48.

[34] Gulick, "Notes," p. 9.

[35] Lyndall Urwick, *Elements of Administration* (New York: Harper & Row, Publishers, 1943), pp. 34–39.

5. *Delegation.* Urwick emphasized that "lack of the courage to delegate properly and of knowledge how to do it is one of the most general causes of failure in organization." In larger organizations, we must delegate even the right to delegate.[36]

6. *Matching responsibility with authority.* In this case, Urwick dealt with both sides of the authority-responsibility relationship. It is wrong to hold people accountable for certain activities if "the necessary authority to discharge that responsibility" is not granted. On the other side, "the responsibilities of all persons exercising authority should be absolute within the defined terms of that authority. They should be personally accountable for all actions taken by subordinates." He set forth the widely quoted principle that "at all levels authority and responsibility should be coterminous and coequal."[37]

7. *Span of control.* Again, Urwick asserted that, "No supervisor can supervise directly the work of more than five, or at the most, six subordinates whose work interlocks." When the number of subordinates increases arithmetically, there is a geometrical increase in all the possible combinations of relationships which may demand the attention of the supervisor.[38] Regarding the span of control, Gulick posited some conditions that influence the optimum span, particularly the capacity of an individual manager, the type of work performed, the stability of an organization, and the geographical proximity to those who are supervised.[39]

Before moving on to the next subject, two other leaders in the area of formulating principles should be mentioned. James D. Mooney and Alan C. Reiley attracted attention with the publication of *Onward Industry*, a book which reappeared in 1939 under the title *The Principles of Organization.*[40] Based primarily on years of executive experience with General Motors, these two authors proposed four major principles for organizing: (1) the coordinative principle—the first and most encompassing principle which provides unity of action, (2) the scalar principle—the vertical division of authority and assignment of duties to organization units, (3) the functional principle—the specialization of work tasks, and (4) staff and line—the line represents authority and the staff advice and ideas.

While Gulick, Urwick, Mooney, Reiley, and others of similar thinking accepted the need for principles of supervision and a single center of authority and control in the organization, they differed on how these principles should be implemented. The disagreement centered on (1) the most efficient way to distribute the work among the production units and (2) how the organizational pyramid of control should be designed. Besides failing to provide a workable guide to the division of labor, all these principles are

[36] *Ibid.*, pp. 51–52.
[37] *Ibid.*, pp. 45–46, 125.
[38] *Ibid.*, pp. 52–53.
[39] Gulick, "Notes," pp. 7–9.
[40] Mooney and Reiley, *Principles of Organization.*

prescriptive and consequently fail to allow for the numerous differences in real as compared with ideal organizations. Finally, the human relations movement, which overlapped this era, demanded a new approach because of the increasing awareness of limitations in the proposed principles of organization.

In Retrospect

In review, classical organization theory was built on three interlocking cornerstones: rationality of structure, scientific management, and principles of organization. One way of classifying these three concepts is as follows: first, Weber's writing was primarily descriptive; however, it did indicate that a particular form of organizational structure is preferable. Second, the theories of both Taylor and the Gulick-Urwick team were prescriptive; that is, they expressed the one right way to manage and organize. Interestingly, Taylor's notion of a scientific management, while being purely mechanistic at first glance, is at the same time motivational. Taylor viewed man as a rational-economic animal; hence, the way for management to motivate him is through economic incentives that include improved work methods.

Having considered some of the antecedents and components of the classical approach, we turn now to the present results of its teachings. This era lives on in the form of our contemporary formal organizational structures. It keeps those that listen to its tenets constantly gazing at the formal hierarchical jobs, positions, and procedures. Hence operations are stressed over people. Classical organization theory has given rise to not one but four formal structures. Since we live with these structures on a daily basis it seems worthwhile to discuss them further.

FORMAL ORGANIZATIONS: THE FOUR STRUCTURES

As the foregoing sections indicate, the first half of this century has resulted in the development of a very substantial body of literature dealing with the formal hierarchy. The four types of structures that have emerged from the literature are (1) job-task, (2) rank, (3) skill, and (4) pay.[41]

The Job-Task Structure

The job-task structure embodies people working at specialized tasks. There is a division of labor, which in the assembly-line process is broken

---

[41] The remainder of this section is drawn primarily from the work of Pfiffner and Sherwood, *Administrative Organization*, pp. 66–71.

down into the smallest repetitive operations. In small organizations these positions develop rather naturally and are not formalized in writing. As organizations grow and become more complex two developments usually occur: (1) classification of duties and (2) centralization of the authority to establish new positions. Both these developments provide a basis for establishing a system of position classification. Briefly, position classification is the grouping of positions, according to the similarity of duties and responsibilities, into job categories having identical job descriptions. Job descriptions spell out roles and give official legitimacy to the organization. Note that position classification or job description (analysis) is a study of tasks, not people. The widespread movement toward job standardization that began in the late 1930s is gaining momentum, and the police organization is vastly influenced by this trend.

The Structure of Rank

The structure of rank involves an officer class, an obvious example being the police. Other examples include the United States Foreign Service and the military. A structure of rank differs from the job hierarchy in that status does not attach to the particular job; a police sergeant is a sergeant whether supervising a patrol unit or conducting an investigation. He remains a sergeant until promoted to lieutenant or retired. The job structure emphasizes the duties to be performed, while the concept of rank stresses the personal status, pay, and authority of the incumbents. This is not to say that the latter has no relation to the tasks and level of job responsibility; a police sergeant, for instance, is considered a first-line supervisor; however, some sergeants that spend time in this rank never supervise.

The Structure of Skills

An organization is constructed from a structure of skills. The job descriptions used for personnel administration contain a statement of the required training and experience for each position, in addition to the duties to be performed. At or near the top of the organizational structure are the positions demanding the managerial skills of organizing, planning, controlling, and coordination. These are the skills of the generalist, the person who sees the organization as a whole. He may also possess specialized skills as a detective or narcotics investigator, but his tasks as a manager do not depend upon them. Beneath the top managers are the middle managers, in police terminology the captains and lieutenants. These men (and in some cases, women) are also coordinators, but their objectives are coordinating day-to-day operations and not over-all policy making. Finally, under them are the first-line supervisors of the rank and file.

In addition to this structure of managerial skills, there is also a hierarchy of professional and technical skills. In any large- or medium-scale police organization we find numerous functional specialists such as records analysts, juvenile officers, trainers, researchers, public information officers, and the like. Interestingly, these skills are becoming more concerned with and, in some instances, dependent upon college training. Formal education is a natural and necessary adjunct to professionalization. Importantly, the theory of formal organization views this structure of skills as job requirements. Individuals are placed in certain jobs because they are thought to possess the necessary skills or to have the potential for developing them in a reasonable time. In modern police organizations, the more general positions (patrolman) are broken down into specialized positions (robbery detective, narcotics investigator, juvenile officer, and so forth).

The Pay Structure

The larger police organizations tend to have a standardized pay structure, often referred to as a compensation plan. Indeed, police departments set up more formal controls for administering compensation than does industry. Frequently salary and wage administration incorporates some elements of scientific method, using statistical approaches. Consequently, levels of difficulty of positions are established, which helps in the internal comparison of various jobs. This method is less widely used in local police agencies where the comparative evaluation of different jobs is based largely on the individual judgment of personnel technicians.

All four of these organizational structures can be found in our contemporary police departments. In concluding this chapter we look briefly at these four structures as they constitute a formal police organization.

FORMAL POLICE ORGANIZATIONS: THEIR STRUCTURES

A review of the literature pertaining to the police indicates that the following phenomena are generally experienced by today's police organization:

1. Growing size
2. Complexity
3. Specialization of skills
4. Multiplicity of goals
5. Constant and rapid environmental change
6. Continuous interaction with its immediate environment
7. Goal conflict

When viewing a police organization we find three primary characteristics. First, one segment of the organization provides police services—through patrol, crime investigation, vice control, traffic control, and other activities. Second, these operational services cannot be efficiently provided unless supported through the provision of supplies, the maintenance of equipment, the processing of information, and the other internal activities sustaining the field divisions. Finally, there must be planning, command-control, and organizing; further, the organization must be staffed and provided with buildings, equipment, and supplies. These are the administrative services. However, typically a police organization is perceived as a series of duties assigned according to a time period and place of performance.[42]

1. The police are organized primarily according to the nature of the tasks to be performed (job-task structure). Therefore, the organization is divided into units so that similar and related duties may be assigned to each. For example, most members are assigned to patrol duties, but some may be assigned to such specialized functions as traffic control, crime investigation, and so on (structure of skills). It may be pointed out here that these divisions encompass all the services, including support and administrative activities, that must be provided by the police department.

2. The functional units are also divided into shifts or watches according to the time of day when the members are to work as a platoon.

3. A territorial distribution of the platoon, accomplished by assigning patrolmen to beats, is necessary to direct and control the officers and to ensure adequate patrol coverage. Patrolmen are usually under the supervision of a patrol sergeant. When the number of patrolmen is large, they are often separated into squads and assigned to specific sectors of the jurisdiction, with a sergeant in charge of each squad. A large city is divided into geographical districts and the patrol force apportioned among them; hence the organization of the patrol activity reflects that of the territory. In some departments personnel engaged in specialized tasks (crime investigation, traffic, vice and juvenile-crime control) are apportioned among the several districts, with their control vested in the district commanders. An often used alternative has the commander of each specialized unit retain direct control over all personnel performing tasks in his field, even though they may be physically decentralized in district stations.

4. The department is also divided according to the level of authority; for example, patrolmen, sergeant, lieutenant, and so on. Vertical combinations of superior officers, with each rank (rank and pay structures) at a different level of authority, form the formal channels through which operations may be directed. Similar to a majority of organizations, these chains of command, or lines of direct control, enable the delegation of authority and the placing of responsibility.

---

[42] O. W. Wilson, *Police Administration*, 2nd ed., rev. (New York: McGraw-Hill Book Company, 1963), p. 49.

SUMMARY

Since the nineteenth century modern society has been experiencing what is commonly referred to as an organizational revolution. However, organizations are not a new phenomenon in our world; in fact, they are ancient activities. In contrast with earlier organizations, those of today place a high value on rationality, efficiency, and basic principles. This stress has created an organizational ethic that emphasizes production and administrative efficiency. This ethic is supported by classical organization theory, or the formal side of organizations.

An organization is a social unit intentionally constructed to seek specific goals. An organizational goal is a desired state of affairs which the social unit seeks to realize. Organizations (especially police organizations) have more than a single goal. Further, most organizations experience goal displacement, the substitution for a legitimate goal of some other goal for which the organization was not originally created. Finally, organizations frequently change their goals through replacing the older goals with newer ones. Currently, there is reasonable justification for ascribing six goals to a local police department: (1) prevention of criminality, (2) repression of crime, (3) apprehension of offenders, (4) recovery of stolen property, (5) provision of social control, and (6) participation in the implementation of civil defense, disaster, and disorder services. Together, these six goals form a fundamental philosophy for local policing—to maintain the community peace, and protect life and property.

Classical organization theory stresses division of labor, hierarchy of authority, structure, and span of control. Its proponents, or contributors, include Max Weber, Frederick W. Taylor, Luther Gulick, and Lyndall Urwick. Their contributions have ranged from an explanation of bureaucracy to an analytical plan for scientific management to universal principles for organization. From their thinking we have constructed our structures which either singularly or in various mixtures constitute our formal organizations of today: job-task, rank, skills, and pay structures. The police organization contains elements of all four.

The next chapter continues our examination of the organizational revolution by reviewing the human relations movement (informal organization) and by previewing the systems era.

PROBLEMS

1. In your own words, what is an organization? What are some of its characteristics?

2. There are conflicting opinions on how specific (tangible) or how general (vague) goals should be. Discuss this dilemma.

3. Discuss the six goals cited for a local police organization. Do you agree with them? Rank them in terms of their priority of accomplishment.

4. Of the three described pioneers of classical organization theory (Weber, Taylor, and Gulick-Urwick), which do you feel has made the most significant contribution to the formation of our present-day formal organizations? Why?

5. Of the four structures (job-task, rank, skills, and pay) which constitute an organization, which one, if any, do you think provides the major cornerstone for organizing a police department?

5

Police Organization: the Informal Side and the Systems Era

The assembly line doesn't receive a complete human being. It receives a role—a foreman or a mechanic or a painter or an upholsterer. From the point of view of industrial management it is not only desirable, but absolutely essential, that the workers leave some of their human-ness behind when they enter the factory gate. Organized industrial effort, by its very nature, demands the subordination of individual human existence to the existential requirements of a task or final product. Under these circumstances, to insist that human beings working on an assembly line assume an independent existence is to insist that the industrial world become fantastic. Indeed, it is precisely this kind of juxtaposition that leads to so much misunderstanding between members of a work force and the management of a factory. If management assumes a relentlessly rational posture vis à vis the requirements of its task—that is, maximum production with minimum cost—and members of the work force assume a relentlessly rational posture vis à vis the requirements for individual existence, then the world of management is fantastic to the workers, and the world of workers is fantastic to management. Under these conditions, one can perhaps begin to understand why misunderstandings arise.[1]

In the 1920s the classical approach to organization experienced a reaction to its mechanistic prescriptions for managing and organizing. This reaction is commonly referred to as either the human relations approach or the neoclassical theory of organization. It evolved out of the discovery that within formal organizations man tends to establish informal organizations. This theory emphasized communication, shared decision making, and leadership. The two major assumptions underlying the human relations approach are (1) the most satisfying organization (for the worker) is the most efficient and (2) it is necessary to relate work and the organizational structure to the social needs of the employee. We are currently witnessing in modern organization theory an attempt to rectify the shortcomings of both the traditional (classical) and human relations (neoclassical) ap-

---

[1] Robert Boguslaw, *The New Utopians: A Study of System Design and Social Change* (Englewood Cliffs, N.J.: Prentice-Hall, Inc., 1965), p. 155.

proaches. These shortcomings include incompleteness, limited perspective, and a lack of integration among the many facets constituting an organization. This chapter first discusses the human relations era. Second, it looks at systems theory as it now influences our organizations—this is referred to as modern organization theory.

NEOCLASSICAL ORGANIZATION THEORY: THE INFORMAL ORGANIZATION

The origins of neoclassical theory are customarily associated with the Hawthorne studies and, in particular, the writings of Elton Mayo, John Dewey, Kurt Lewin, and Mary Follett.[2] The general direction of neoclassical theory was away from the structural, mechanical, rational patterns of classical theory. It stressed the affective and the social, and was both caused by and a cause of increasing attention of psychology, social psychology, and sociology to contemporary organizations. This theory "discovered" the small (or face-to-face) group in large organizations and, in broad terms, emphasized the notion that formal organizations also have a large informal, that is, social and emotional, component. An *informal organization* includes both the social relations that develop among the personnel and the organizational operations as they naturally evolve from the formal organization and from the needs of the individual workers. In essence, classical organization theory failed to recognize that formal organizations tend to breed informal organizations within them and that in the informal organization, workers and managers are likely to establish relationships with each other which influence the manner in which they carry out their jobs or fulfill their roles.[3] To clarify this point, we look to a highly significant piece of research— the studies conducted by Mayo, Roethlisberger, and Dickson in the Hawthorne plant of the Western Electric Company in Chicago, Illinois.

The Hawthorne Studies

The well-known Hawthorne studies were conducted during the late 1920s through the mid-1930s. This series of studies (we review only a part of them)

---

[2] Edgar H. Schein, *Organizational Psychology* (Englewood Cliffs, N.J.: Prentice-Hall, Inc., 1965), p. 27.

[3] Mary Follett's contribution to neoclassical organization theory is beginning to be better understood and certainly more appreciated. In essence, she developed a theory of human interaction based on the "law of the situation," which means the bringing together of various inputs and acting in accord with their syntheses. An excellent overview of her thinking can be found in Elliot M. Fox, "Mary Parker-Follett: The Enduring Contribution," *Public Administration Review*, 28 (November-December 1968), 520–29.

produced some very important, unexpected findings.[4] To begin, a group of girls who assembled telephone equipment were selected as subjects for a series of studies designed to determine the effect of their working conditions, length of the working day, number and length of rest pauses, and other factors relating to the "nonhuman" environment on their productivity. The girls were located in a special room under close supervision.

As the researchers varied working conditions, they found each major change was accompanied by a substantial increase in production. Further, when all the conditions to be varied had been tested, they decided to return the girls to their original, poorly lighted work benches for the usual long working day without rest pauses and other benefits. To the astonishment of the researchers, *output rose again, to an even higher level than it had been under the best of the experimental conditions.* In light of this fact a new hypothesis had to be found. The hypothesis was that motivation to work, productivity, and quality of work are all related to the nature of the social relations among the workers and between the workers and their boss. New groups were created for additional experimentation. The findings of the study are summarized as follows:

1. The productivity of the individual worker is determined more by his social "capacity" than his physical capacity.
2. Noneconomic rewards play a prominent part in motivating and satisfying an employee.
3. Maximum specialization is not the most efficient form of division of labor.
4. Employees do not react to management and its norms and rewards as individuals but as members of groups.

The tendency of experimentally chosen groups to show increased productivity and job satisfaction is now termed the "Hawthorne effect" and is certainly one of the most widely recognized findings of the social sciences. However, the findings from this study have come to be misused in the literature to refer to any favorable effect on the performance of an experimental group resulting not from the specifics of the experimental treatment but merely from the special recognition and attention of being selected as an experimental group. In the Hawthorne experiments treatment was the significant factor. The girls selected for the experiment were (1) assigned the best supervisor in the plant, (2) accorded special privileges of genuine importance to them, and (3) *made into a cohesive group* by encouragement of patterns of interaction. First, note that the group was created at the beginning of the experiment. Consequently, the group did not hold previously

---

[4] A more comprehensive description of these researches can be found in F. J. Roethlisberger and W. J. Dickson, *Management and The Worker* (Cambridge, Mass.: Harvard University, 1939).

established norms on what its level of production should be. Follow-up studies attempting to achieve similar results failed when the researchers did not create new groups. Essentially, the workers' cohesion around their own norms was too strong to change.[5] Apparently, these researchers forgot the primary lesson contained in the original study—that the level of production is set by social norms (man's social capacity), not by physiological capacities. Second, it is extremely difficult to make permanent changes in a group merely through the special attention it receives as an experimental group. What this study brought home to the social scientist was the importance of the social factor—the degree to which work performance depended not on the individual alone, but on the network of social relationships within which he operated.

Neoclassical Organization Theory after the Hawthorne Studies: The Human Relations Era Continues

In the years since the Hawthorne experiments a long line of research has added to the evidence that group solidarity and loyalty is associated with productivity, effectiveness, and job satisfaction. Moreover, these experiments have provided a better understanding of organizational leadership, decision making, and communication. In regard to leadership, it was observed that the leader is able to set and enforce group norms through his particular style of leading a group.[6] Also, considerable time was devoted to analyzing the difference between informal and formal leadership. Elton Mayo and Kurt Lewin directed their attention to the importance of communication between levels in the organization and of participation in decision making (permitting the lower-level employee to share in the decision-making process with his supervisors).

The human relations approach to managing and supervising is still widely accepted in administrative circles. Our fundamental reason for discussing it, however, is that this period in management thinking set the stage for identifying and understanding the informal organization. After man's social capacity was discovered, others began to notice the social scientists directing their attention to how such factors as power, expertise, and so on operated in a nonformal or informal sense. Thus we see the human relations

---

[5] There are numerous studies showing the tremendous degree of compliance that can be exerted over a person through group cohesion. Two of the leading studies in this area are Stanley E. Seashore, *Group Cohesiveness in the Industrial Work Group* (Ann Arbor, Mich.: Institute for Social Research, 1954), and A. Zalernik, C. R. Christensen, and F. Roethlisberger, *The Motivation, Productivity and Satisfaction of Workers: A Predictive Study* (Boston, Mass.: Harvard Graduate School of Business Administration, 1958).

[6] See, for example, R. Lippitt and R. K. White, "An Experimental Study of Leadership and Group Life," in *Readings in Social Psychology*, eds. G. E. Swanson, T. M. Newcomb, and E. L. Hartley (New York: Holt, Rinehart & Winston, 1952), pp. 340–55.

approach to organization carving out a neoclassical theory, which devoted most of its study to an improved knowledge of the informal organization. John M. Pfiffner and Frank P. Sherwood have described most convincingly and in excellent fashion not one but five informal organizations that can, and usually do, exist within a formal structure. We now look at their work in detail.[7]

Neoclassical Organization Theory: Organization as Overlays

The formal structure of an organization represents as closely as possible the framer's intended processes of interaction among its members. In the typical work organization this structure involves a definition of task specialties and their arrangement in levels of authority, with clearly defined lines of communication from one level to the next (see Figure 3).

It must be recognized, however, that the actual processes of interaction among the individuals represented in the formal plan cannot adequately be described solely in terms of its planned lines of interaction. Coexisting with the formal structure are myriad other possibilities for interaction among persons in the organization which can be analyzed according to various theories of group behavior. It must not be forgotten, however, that in reality those other ways never function so distinctively and that all are intermixed together in an organization which also follows to a large extent its formal structure.

These modified processes must be studied one at a time; a good way to do so without forgetting their "togetherness" is to consider each as a transparent overlay superimposed on the basic formal organizational pattern. The totality of these overlays might be so complex as to be nearly opaque, but it will still be a closer approach to reality than the bare organization chart so typically used to diagram a large group structure.

Five such overlay patterns are considered here; many more or fewer might be chosen from the studies that have been made, but these five might well be considered basic.

> The sociometric network
> The system of functional contacts
> The grid of decision-making centers
> The pattern of power
> Channels of communication[8]

---

[7] Reprinted with permission of authors and publisher from *Administrative Organization* (Englewood Cliffs, N.J.: Prentice-Hall, 1960), pp. 18–27. Footnotes and figures have been renumbered.

[8] For much of the conceptual underpinnings of this chapter we are indebted to John T. Dorsey, Jr., "A Communication Model for Administration," *Administrative Science Quarterly*, 3 (December 1957), pp. 307–24. While Dorsey seems to view communication as the central component of administration, we put it on a level with others dealt with here.

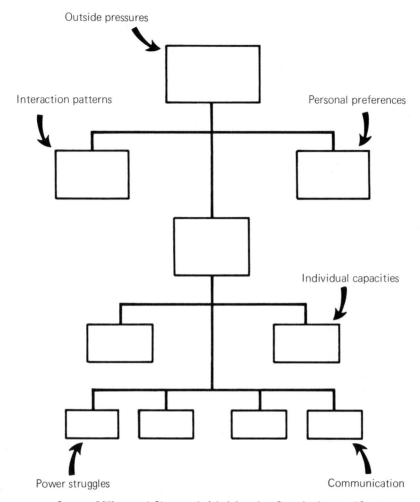

Outside pressures

Interaction patterns

Personal preferences

Individual capacities

Power struggles

Communication

Source: Pfiffner and Sherwood, Administrative Organization, *p. 18.*

FIG. 3. THE TYPICAL JOB PYRAMID OF AUTHORITY AND SOME OF ITS INTERACTING PRO-CESSES

The idea that these processes are overlays upon the conventional job-task pyramid does not require that the latter take a subordinate position, although much of the research in organization might give this impression. The overlay approach aims to be realistic in recognizing that organization also consists of a wide variety of contacts that involve communication, sociometry, goal-centered functionalism, decision making, and personal power. Let us consider this complex of processes one at a time.

The job-task pyramid. The job-task pyramid constitutes the basis from which all departures are measured. It is the official version of the organization as the people in the organization believe that it is and should be. In most production organizations today, whether private or public, this official version of the organization-as-it-should-be reflects the view of those in the top echelons of the job-task pyramid. The operating organization may differ in some respects from the formal organization; this difference can be expressed by showing the manner in which the other networks vary from the job-task hierarchy.

Job-task hierarchy as foundation. Variations of the other networks from the job-task hierarchy do not mean that the latter is being undermined or has no acceptance in the organization. It is well recognized in practice that there is an operating organization that varies from the chart with the full knowledge of those in authority. Day-to-day and hour-to-hour adjustments must be made, and there is no need to revise the chart for each of these. Nevertheless, the job-task hierarchy as depicted by the organization manual does set forth the grid of official authority as viewed by those in the organization. Without it the other networks would simply not exist.[9]

The sociometric overlay (see Figure 4). In any organization there is a set of relationships among people which is purely social; it exists because of feelings of attraction or rejection. This pattern of person-to-person contact is called sociometric because it is revealed in the kind of group testing given that name by its originator, J. L. Moreno. Some investigators have felt that individual attitudes lending themselves to sociometric measurement include

1. The *prescribed* relations, identical with the official or formal organization
2. The *perceived* relations, the people's interpretation of the meaning of the official network
3. The *actual* relations, those interactions which in fact take place among persons
4. The *desired* relations, people's preferences regarding interactions with other persons
5. The *rejected* relations, relationships with other people which are not wanted[10]

It is, however, the last two categories that are primarily sociological in nature and that are considered sociometric here. Desired and rejected relationships are fairly easy to ascertain with statistical reliability and are found to be very responsive to the other dynamics of the group. Ohio State studies of naval leadership have effectively utilized sociometric charts (socio-

---

[9] William Brownrigg deals with the job-task hierarchy most provocatively in *The Human Enterprise Process and Its Administration* (Birmingham, Ala.: University of Alabama Press, 1954).

[10] Fred Massarik, Robert Tannenbaum, Murray Kahane, and Irving Weschler, "Sociometric Choice and Organizational Effectiveness: A Multirelational Approach," *Sociometry*, 16 (August 1953), 211–38.

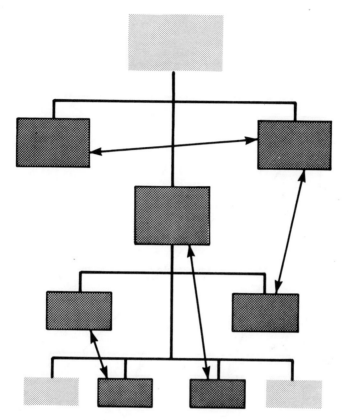

Source: Pfiffner and Sherwood, Administrative Organization, *p. 20.*

FIG. 4. SOCIAL OVERLAY—THE SPECIAL FRIENDSHIPS IN THE ORGANIZATION ("I'LL TALK TO MY FRIEND GEORGE IN PURCHASING. HE'LL KNOW WHAT TO DO.")

grams—graphic representations of social relations) superimposed on the traditional job-task charts.[11]

The functional overlay (see Figure 5). Within the organization is a network of functional contacts important to and yet different from the formal authority structure. Functional contacts occur most typically where specialized information is needed; through them the staff or other specialist, the intellectual "leader," exerts his influence upon operations without direct responsibility for the work itself. This relationship, something like that between a professional man and his client, is a phenomenon of the twentieth century and more markedly of the mid-century period.

---

[11] Ralph M. Stogdill, *Leadership and Structure of Personal Interaction*, Monograph No. 84 (Columbus: Ohio State University, Bureau of Business Research, 1957), p. 10.

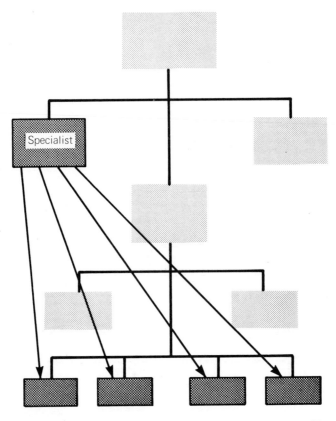

Source: Pfiffner and Sherwood, Administrative Organization, *p. 22.*

*FIG. 5. FUNCTIONAL OVERLAY—THE DIRECT RELATIONSHIPS BETWEEN THE SPECIALIST ASSIS-
TANT AND THE OPERATING DEPARTMENTS ("YOU HAVE TO SEE PERSONNEL FOR
APPROVAL TO TAKE THAT COURSE.")*

Frederick Taylor was so perceptive as to understand the importance of the network of functional contacts in a management institution. Taylor called these functional contacts "functional supervision"; a term which upset many theorists who worshipped the concept of clear-cut supervisor-subordinate authority relationships.[12]

While Taylor's original concept of multiple supervision was rejected at the time, it is still true that most organizations exhibit a system of functional supervision. Many charts of formal authority structures, such as those of

---

[12] A collection of excerpts from the literature of the early scientific management movement relating to staff specialization and functionalism is contained in Albert Lepawsky, *Administration* (New York: Alfred A. Knopf, Inc., 1949), pp. 299–306.

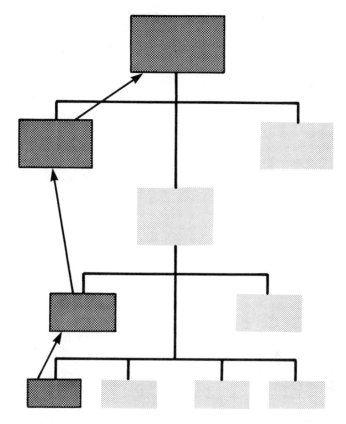

Source: Pfiffner and Sherwood, Administrative Organization, *p. 23.*

FIG. 6. DECISION OVERLAY—FLOW OF SIGNIFICANT DECISIONS IN THE ORGANIZATION ("DON'T
WORRY ABOUT JOE. HE DOESN'T CONCERN HIMSELF ABOUT THIS. OUR NEXT STEP
IS TO GO TOPSIDE.")

the military, also show functional contacts through such devices as broken
connecting lines.

The decision overlay (see Figure 6). Herbert Simon maintains that the best
way to analyze an organization is to find out where the decisions are made
and by whom.[13] Normally in an organization the decision pattern follows
the structure of the formal hierarchy, that is, the job-task pyramid. However,
the power and authority network, together with the functional network,
may cut across hierarchical channels. It is in this sense that they take on the
configuration of a grid, or network. Thus the network pattern of approach

[13] Herbert A. Simon, *Administrative Behavior*, 2nd ed., rev. (New York: The Macmillan
Company, 1947), p. xix. Simon's decision model is discussed in detail in Chapter 21.

is helpful, not in undermining the concept of hierarchy, but in conveying the real operational picture. It modifies the harsh overtones of hierarchy by pointing out that organizations permit a great many cross-contacts.

It might be more correct to say that there is a network of influence, rather than a network of decision, depending on one's definition of decision making. If one insists on there being a clear-cut choice between alternatives by a person in authority, then decision making usually follows clear hierarchical channels. However, if we think in terms of a decision process rather than a decision point, the sense of interaction and influence is more appropriately conveyed. In this connection it is helpful to refer to Mary Parker Follett's concept of order giving, in which she says "an order, command, is a step in a process, a moment in the movement of interweaving experience. We should guard against thinking this step a larger part of the whole process than it really is."[14]

The power overlay (see Figure 7). Any discussion of power as a factor in organizational dynamics quickly encounters difficulties of definition and terminology. Since this is a subject upon which there is to be considerable discussion at a later point in this book, let it be noted here that many of these problems arise from a confusion between power and authority.[15] These terms are not necessarily synonymous; yet there has been a tendency to look at the organization chart, note the various status levels, and assume that power increases as one rises in the pyramid. Much of this attitude is based on old concepts of authority as they are found in jurisprudence. Within this framework is the assumption that a rule laid down by a political superior who is ultimately sovereign can be enforced by the imposition of sanctions. Translated into the terminology of management institutions, this means that authority, and hence power, rests with those at the top echelons of the job-task pyramid.

However, there has been a considerable rebellion against this narrow view of the power factor in organization environment. Almost everyone who has had any experience in a management institution has encountered a situation in which the boss's secretary, his assistant, or the executive officer is the "person to see." For a great variety of reasons, these people may be effective decision makers in a particular situation. Thus power is really personal and political and it may or may not be legitimate, depending on whether it has been authorized by formal law or has achieved hierarchical legitimization. In a person-to-person relationship, power exists when one has the ability to influence someone to behave in a particular way or to make

---

[14] Henry C. Metcalf and L. Urwick, eds., *Dynamic Administration: The Collected Papers of Mary Parker Follett* (New York: Harper and Brothers, 1940), p. 49.

[15] See Pfiffner and Sherwood, *Administrative Organization*, Chapter 5, "Authority, Policy, and Administration as Organization Factors."

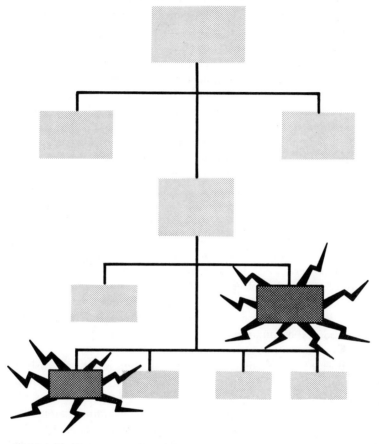

Source: Pfiffner and Sherwood, Administrative Organization, *p. 24.*

FIG. 7. POWER OVERLAY—CENTERS OF POWER IN THE ORGANIZATION ("BEFORE YOU GO FURTHER, YOU HAD BETTER CLEAR THAT WITH JACK IN PRODUCTION PLANNING.")

decisions. As a result, the mapping of power centers would seldom follow the pattern of a typical hierarchy.

It seems desirable to emphasize that management institutions are political and that the basis of politics is power. While the use of the adjective political may be jarring to students of business administration, who regard politics and government as synonymous, the fact remains that business organizations are also political to an important degree. The maneuvering for proxies to gain control of an industrial corporation is certainly a political act, as are struggles on the part of individuals to build empires or the use of artifice to gain the ear of the president.

The important consideration from the standpoint of organization theory is that there is a network, or grid, of personal power centers, though sometimes latent and not expressed, which may or may not coincide with the official structure of authority.[16] Power is not institutionalized in the sense that one can look in the organization manual and find where it resides. As a matter of fact one might find it in unsuspected places. A person of comparatively low status may be a power center because he has been around so long that only he knows the intricate rules and the regulations well enough to make immediate decisions.

The communication overlay (see Figure 8). Perhaps nowhere is the interrelationship of the various overlays more clearly seen than in communication. The information process is central to organizational system. It affects control and decision making, influence and power, interpersonal relationships, and leadership, to name only a few facets. Dorsey, in making a case for the significance of communications, says that "power consists of the extent to which a given communication influences the generation and flow of later communications. Points in the patterned flow where this occurs . . . are positions of power. . . ."[17] Furthermore, the communication net "consists physically of a complex of *decision centers* and *channels* which seek, receive, transmit, subdivide, classify, store, select, recall, recombine and retransmit *information*."[18] This net consists not only of the technical information apparatus but also of the human nervous systems of the people who make up the organization.

It is important to recognize that communication is itself a clearly identifiable facet of behavior. Redfield tells, for example, of the consultant who "starts his studies in the mail room, for, by plotting the lines of actual communication, he can sometimes build a more accurate organization chart than the one that hangs on the wall in the president's office."[19] Such a chart is, of course, one of communications. And it may tell a great deal more about how life is really lived in an organization than the formal authority picture. Thus an important and useful means of taking a look at an organization is to ask the question, "Who talks to whom about what?"

Answers to the question often reveal that patterns of communication are at variance with official prescriptions. Furthermore, there have been enough experiments with small groups to give great strength to the proposition that "the mere existence of a hierarchy sets up restraints against communication

---

[16] Robert Dubin, *Human Relations in Administration: The Sociology of Organization* (Englewood Cliffs, N.J.: Prentice-Hall, Inc., 1951), p. 173. See also Dubin, *The World of Work* (Englewood Cliffs, N.J.: Prentice-Hall, Inc., 1958), pp. 47–54.

[17] Dorsey, "A Communication Model for Administration," *Administrative Science Quarterly*, 3 (December 1957), 310.

[18] *Ibid.*, p. 317.

[19] Charles Redfield, *Communication in Management* (Chicago: University of Chicago Press, 1953), p. 7.

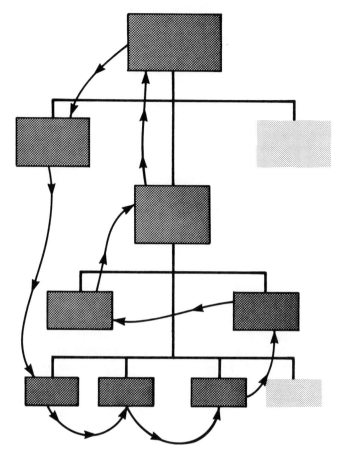

Source: Pfiffner and Sherwood, Administrative Organization, *p. 26.*

FIG. 8. COMMUNICATIONS OVERLAY—THE ROUTE OF TELEPHONE CALLS ON A PARTICULAR MATTER ("IF WE HAD TO GO THROUGH CHANNELS, WE'D NEVER GET ANYTHING DONE AROUND HERE!")

between levels."[20] Gardner points out that factory production reports on productivity are sometimes rigged to give higher echelons the type of information which makes them happy.[21] Such blockages and distortions are certainly frequent enough to force us to recognize that the communications overlay represents an important dimension of organization analysis.

---

[20] Burleigh B. Gardner and David G. Moore, *Human Relations in Industry*, 3rd ed. (Homewood, Ill.: Richard D. Irwin, Inc., 1955), pp. 213ff.

[21] Leon Festinger, "Informal Social Communication," in *Group Dynamics*, eds. Dorwin Cartwright and Alvin Zander (Evanston, Ill.: Row Peterson, 1953), p. 201.

Conclusion

The recognition of and the intense interest in the informal organization was brought about by the weaknesses inherent in the formal structure. According to one author:

> The informal organization is nature's response to management's artificial structuring of an orderly business event. Driven by assumptions about functional division of work, the formal organization splits the natural unity of a business event into segments according to title authority. Informal organization attempts to heal the managerial rupturing by weaving an authority of knowledge about the fracture.[22]

The classical and neoclassical organization theories are in many ways directly opposed to one another. The attributes one theory considers important, the other usually does not mention at all. However, the two theories do hold one thing in common: an organization's desire for rationality and human happiness could be completely resolved if each theory's particular body of knowledge was utilized. To explain, the classical theorists assumed that the most efficient organization would also be the most satisfying one, because it would maximize both productivity and the employees' salary. In this instance, man was viewed as an economic entity striving to increase his wages—therefore, the greater the pay the happier the worker. In contrast, the neoclassical theorists assumed that the happier the employees were made through satisfaction of their social needs, the greater would be their cooperation and efficiency. It rejected man as an economic entity and defined him as a social animal. Accordingly, once man's social problems were solved, management would be able to make the worker's organizational existence a happy one.

In summary, both theories said, "Hey, manager and supervisor, follow me and I'll provide you with efficiency and your workers with happiness." Thus they were saying that a perfect balance between organizational goals and employee's needs could be found in their own specific approaches to the problem of organizing and managing. The reason for their different approaches to the utopian dream rests mainly in their view of man—economic versus social. These views automatically caused, moreover, the earlier theory to deal primarily with formal organization and the latter with informal organization. Hence, it remained for the systems theorists to point out the relationship between formal and informal organizations; to show that alienation and tension are inevitable (and even to some degree desirable)

---

[22] Arthur L. Svenson, "Lessons from the Informal Organization," *Systems and Procedures,* 19 (May-June 1968), 14.

in an organizational setting; and to emphasize the close ties and influence transmitted between the organization and its environment.

Before proceeding to the third, or modern, theory, note that there is no sharp discontinuity between the usages of the three theories, that the new is added to and more or less modifies the old rather than displacing it. Classical theory is still very much alive, is widely used and has its defenders, and while there is now a tendency to regard "human relations" as passé, as associated with certain excesses and naivetés of the past, there is a massive carryover of concepts, attitudes, and research interests into the modern theory.

MODERN ORGANIZATION THEORY: THE SYSTEMS APPROACH

> Every system is a system of some larger system and is itself made up of a hierarchy of subsystems, sub-subsystems, sub-sub-subsystems, etc., each of which is a system in its own right.[23]

This logic reminds one of the old rhyme:

> Big fleas have little fleas upon their backs to bite 'em;
> Little fleas have lesser fleas
> And so ad infinitum

All of this is to say that the diversity and number of systems is great. The molecule, the cell, the organ, the individual, the group, the society are all examples of systems. Further, there are communication, information, computer, and a host of hardware systems. In some respects they are alike. However, they differ in their level of complexity and over a host of other dimensions such as living, nonliving, or mixed; material or conceptual; and so forth. This section describes the organization, more specifically a police organization, as an open social system. Increasingly, organizations are considered through a systems perspective.[24] Accordingly, the modern organization is dominated by the systems approach which, in turn, is itself a set of theories, analytical methods, and plans.

---

[23] Albert Shapero and Charles Bates, Jr., *A Method for Performing Human Engineering Analysis of Weapon Systems*, USAF Technical Report 59–784 (Wright Patterson Air Force Base, Ohio: Air Research and Development Command, September, 1959), p. 6.

[24] Perhaps the most outstanding contribution and convincing argument for viewing an organization as a social system is Daniel Katz and Robert L. Kahn, *The Social Psychology of Organizations* (New York: John Wiley & Sons, Inc., 1966). Another example supporting a systems approach to organizations is Stanley Young, *Management: A Systems Approach* (Glenview, Ill.: Scott, Foresman, and Co., 1967).

The police supervisor functions in a system. Russell L. Ackoff informs us that a system is any entity, conceptual or material, which consists of interdependent parts.[25] Certainly this broad definition encompasses a police organization. The primary difference between an organization and a system is that the former has a goal or goals to accomplish. While we have referred to the police organization as an open social system, it is in reality a mixed social system, since it contains men, machines, and materials (living and nonliving entities). Moreover, it relates (integrates) them in a dynamic fashion in order to conduct the work of the system (goal attainment). Consequently *our idea of an organization is changing from one of structure to one of process.* In order to foster the view of an organization as a process, or system, this section continues with reasons for the development of a systems approach and its benefits for modern organizational theory. Next, we consider what is meant by a systems approach. Finally, the characteristics and subsystems of an open social system are described as they relate to a police organization.

Forces toward a systems point of view. Hopefully the reader has begun to question the reasons (or needs) for approaching organizations as open social systems. The first reason for doing so is found in the increased complexity and frequency of change in our society. This is evident in both our social relations and technological innovations. Further, such complexity and change is equally prevalent within the organization itself. The second reason is seen in the limitations of the previously discussed organizational theories, namely that both the classical and neoclassical theories viewed an organization as a *closed* structure. Such nearsightedness produces an inability to recognize that the organization is continually dependent upon its environment for the inflow of materials and human energy. Consequently, we often find supervisors coping with organizational problems as if they were independent of changes in the environment. Thinking of an organization as a closed structure, moreover, results in a failure to develop a feedback capability for obtaining adequate information about changes in environmental forces and goal accomplishment. Hence, today we find societal change, complexity, and inappropriate organizational theories generating an urgent need for an open-system approach to organizations.

Beyond the more general reasons are specific and compelling ones which cause a police organization to consider itself an open system. These reasons are in terms of the benefits to be derived from such consideration. Briefly, ample evidence supports the contention that the systems approach offers, at least, five significant benefits to a police organization: (1) a vehicle for permeating organizational boundaries of a police structure, (2) a way to deal with complexity, (3) a new perspective on organization, (4) a conceptual

---

[25] Russell L. Ackoff, "Systems, Organizations and Interdisciplinary Research," *General Systems*, 5 (1960), 1.

underpinning for an empirical tool (system analysis and design), and (5) a potential fund of scientifically pragmatic information.[26]

First, we are beginning to recognize that police organizations are a component of, and positioned within, a system of relationships. And, these relationships are not exclusively confined to a single organizational environment such as a city government. The police agency can be thought of logically as either a system (a single police department) or a subsystem. In viewing the police organization as a subsystem, it is naturally involved in a complex set of interface patterns with other subsystems external to its particular organizational boundary, such as the district attorney, parole agencies, courts, and so on. The systems approach effectively helps us to cross boundaries to identify, establish, and make use of meaningful interrelationships between various organizations. Police departments presently undergoing analyses for either computer-based information systems or planning-programming budgeting systems are being made more aware of the requirement for external transactions.

Second, many police agencies are growing aware of the limitations of simplistic research. Organizations and problems in the sphere of law enforcement, as in other fields of endeavor, are more and more seen to exist within a broader system. While the use of a systems approach is new, as a concept it is a product of the past decade. In essence, it has been and remains an attempt to synthesize the research contributions of relevant fields into a single approach for the solving of a given problem. In terms of organization theory, therefore, the systems approach is attempting to gather the necessary research information to construct a better organization.

Third, a systems approach provides us with a new perspective on the internal operations and environmental relationships of police organizations. Further, the use of a systems approach may result in a highly creative process, and its outcome is predominately dependent on its users and the resources on which they draw. It compels the involved researcher to view the phenomena in an entirely different manner. The solutions arrived at are not likely to be overt in the data or in the stated objectives; yet they must be consistent with existing data and current objectives. Additionally, the available data and theoretical framework are likely to be incomplete and somewhat ambiguous so that certainty is out of the question. In essence, those that use the systems approach need imagination, judgment, and courage to generate a new perspective. The set of possible future environments in which an organization must remain valid have to be imagined. Even the way the police organization under study is subdivided demands

---

[26] The majority of the cited benefits are drawn, in part, from Paul M. Whisenand and Targ Tomaru, *Automatic Police Information Systems* (New York: John Wiley & Sons, Inc., 1970).

originality. Significantly, the traditional subdivisions along governmental or organizational lines, or in terms of the standard academic disciplines, are not necessarily the best and certainly not the only options. In short, the systems approach offers us a highly useful way to fulfill the need of a new perspective on police organizations.

Fourth, the systems approach relies greatly on empirical data. The data of interest to us generally include not only facts on a particular police department but also data on the processes, interactions, goals, and other characteristics of all organizations (public and private) that exert an influence on it. Many police agencies now know that, with the proper facilities and technical resources, even very large quantities of data may be stored, manipulated, organized, reduced, and used rapidly and effectively. The systems approach, besides being an aid to understanding and providing a framework for organizing data, aids us in the search for new data.

Fifth, an important benefit of the systems approach for those in police work is that it is intended to be action-oriented. Data are gathered not merely to inform or to describe a relationship, and ideas are evaluated not merely on their cleverness; these activities are pursued because they are instrumental in fulfilling a set of objectives or in solving a problem. Hence the activities of a police organization influence the interests of many other organizations and individuals that have economic, professional, social, political, and personal stakes in what results. Furthermore, their decisions and activities are input to a repository of operational information which has relevance for many organizations.

Stanley Young provides a fitting capstone for these benefits when he writes:

> Only when the organization is designed (organizational planning) from a systems orientation will it be able to take full advantage of the new and emerging managerial technologies, which include quantitative methods, the computer, the information sciences, and the behavioral sciences.[27]

The Systems Approach: Theory, Analysis, Design

We approach the idea of a system as broadly encompassing systems theory, analytical techniques and technologies, and various designs needed to cope with a given problem. We combine, therefore, systems theory, analysis and design into a single framework called the "systems approach," which differs from the more abstract concept of a system in that it incorporates a plan of action and the "doing." The problem at hand assists us as investigators in deciding which analytical tools and design would be most

---

[27] Stanley Young, "Organization As A Total System," in *Management: A Decision Making Approach*, ed. Stanley Young (Belmont, Calif.: Dickenson Publishing Company, Inc., 1968), p. 125.

appropriate to employ. If we integrate theory, tools, and design in a systematic and rational fashion, along with stated objectives, criteria, we are then using a systems approach. From systems theory we gain new perspective, from systems analysis we gain a group of methodological tools, and from systems design we gain a plan of action. To repeat, systems theory, analysis, and design constitute the systems approach, which is characterized by a systematic and rational approach, with an explicit means for conceptualization analysis, and clearly defined design objectives and criteria. In essence, the systems approach is a model that stimulates our intuition and judgment. In contrast to a single scientific method, it extracts everything possible from existing scientific methods, and therefore its virtues are the virtues of those methods. Research efforts to date offer considerable support for the use of a systems approach in analyzing police organizations.

We must keep the supportive relationship between theory, analysis, and design constantly within the same field of vision because together they provide an improved means for handling the problems of changing reality. We now proceed with a separate look at the three components of the systems approach.

Systems theory. Our attention now focuses on systems theory in order to provide us with a better appreciation and a broader understanding of systems in general. Importantly, the theory serves as the primary basis for our particular analytical and design schema. Simply stated, theory predates analytical methods and planned courses of action; therefore, good theory can, and often does, lead to sound programs of action. We must recognize that *an analytical and design schema is only as useful as the theory is reliable.*

Dorsey gives a framework for theoretically identifying a system by describing it as

> A bounded region in space and time, within which information and/or energy are exchanged among subsystems in greater quantities and/or at higher rates than the quantities exchanged or rates of exchange with anything outside the boundary, and within which the subsystems are to some degree interdependent.[28]

Of immediate interest to us is the fact that we see the police officer positioned in the middle of a system of relationships, out of which he must design a role that will accomplish personal and organizational goals. A system is created wherever there is a sequence of operations performed in a regular or predetermined order by people or equipment. Let us look, for example, at the decision-making process in a police organization. Police decision

---

[28] John T. Dorsey, "An Information-Energy Model," *Papers in Comparative Public Administration*, eds. Ferrel Heady and Sybil L. Stokes (Ann Arbor, Mich.: Institute of Public Administration, 1962), p. 43.

making is a matter of flows and processes. Decisions are the product of thinking and action through time on the part of many people and machines. The modern police organization is a manifestation of this interrelational phenomenon. Appropriately, it has been concluded that, "Modern organization theory and general systems theory are closely related with organization theory as a special element of general systems theory."[29] Further, Rensis Likert also expresses cogent support of this viewpoint in a chapter from his book *Human Organization* entitled "The Need for a Systems Approach."[30]

To emphasize the scope and significance of systems theory, let us consider a few illustrative examples from a variety of fields. In the natural sciences, the systems concept has been widely used to comprehend celestial, planetary, chemical, nuclear, and other phenomena. In the biological sciences man has applied systems theory frequently in the study of plant and animal life at a variety of levels. In the engineering fields the growth in the use of systems theory has been rapid, particularly in man-machine combinations, such as described by Shapero and Bates in *Method for Performing Human Engineering Analysis of Weapon Systems*.[31] Operations research and decision making tend to be based on system models, as reflected in Hitch and McKean's *Economics of Defense in the Nuclear Age*,[32] Kershaw and McKean's *Systems Analysis and Education*,[33] and McKean's *Efficiency in Government Through Systems Analysis*.[34] Information processing, and in particular EDP (electronic data processing), is infused with system concepts, as we can easily see in Lockheed's *State of California Information System Study*,[35] the Space-General Corporation's *Prevention and Control of Crime and Delinquency*,[36] and the Systems Development Corporation's *Los Angeles Police Department Information System (Phase I): Preliminary System Description*.[37]

In anthropology the key element of analysis is cultural systems. In sociology, particularly as developed by Parsons, the concept of social systems is

[29] Richard A. Johnson, Fremont E. Kast, and James E. Rosenzweig, *The Theory and Management of Systems* (New York: McGraw-Hill Book Company, 1963), p. 51.

[30] Rensis Likert, *The Human Organization* (New York: McGraw-Hill Book Company, 1967), pp. 116–27.

[31] Shapero and Bates, Jr., *Human Engineering Analysis*.

[32] Charles J. Hitch and Roland N. McKean, *The Economics of Defense in the Nuclear Age* (Cambridge, Mass.: Harvard University Press, 1963).

[33] J. A. Kershaw and Roland N. McKean, *Systems Analysis and Education*, Research Memorandum (Santa Monica, Calif.: Rand Corporation, 1959).

[34] Roland N. McKean, *Efficiency in Government Through Systems Analysis* (New York: John C. Wiley & Sons, Inc., 1958).

[35] Lockheed Aircraft Corporation, *State of California Information System Study* (Sunnyvale, Calif.: Lockheed Aircraft Corporation, 1965).

[36] Space-General Corporation, *Prevention and Control of Crime and Delinquency* (El Monte, Calif.: Space-General Corporation, 1965).

[37] Systems Development Corporation, *Los Angeles Police Department Information System (Phase I): Preliminary System Description* (Santa Monica, Calif.: Systems Development Corporation, 1965).

of crucial importance.[38] In political science the works of Easton, Riggs, North, Eisenstadt, Almond, and Coleman have as a central focus the use of systems theory. Briefly stated, systems theory is present in most areas of scientific inquiry and in many applied fields. Significantly, our local police agencies are just now beginning to detect the presence of systems thinking and to experience its influences.

Systems analysis. Since the late 1940s a variety of new analytic techniques for understanding complex organizational processes have been developed and refined from the disciplines of physical science, mathematics, and economics. The simultaneous development of high-speed computers has provided added means and incentive to a few police executives to tackle some of the more difficult problems of management. One can find these techniques grouped under such titles as operations research, management science, probability theory, game theory, input-output analysis, and operational gaming.[39] However, the solutions for various problem areas do not always fall neatly into one or another of these categories. Nearly all scientific investigations into one or more dimensions of administration incorporate several of these techniques. Systems analysis incorporates all of the aforementioned plus other analytical techniques into a plan for assisting us, as problem solvers, to identify a preferred choice among possible alternatives. Marvin Adelson views systems analysis as

> The set of methods, techniques and intellectual tools that collectively are known as system analysis was brought forth, gradually and unsystematically, *in response to the growing need to deal effectively with complex and important problems.* The methods themselves are incompletely developed and tend to be improved with each application. Some are very complicated and mathematical. Others are simple and commonsensical.[40]

Using systems analysis, many basic and applied sciences have developed sophisticated research procedures. The Blalocks suggest that such analysis may be carried out from three perspectives:

1. that involving the relationship between system and environment;
2. that involving interaction between several systems;
3. that involving one type of system composed of other types of systems.[41]

---

[38] A strong and highly readable argument for the use of systems theory in improving the understanding of social systems is found in Joseph H. Monane, *A Sociology of Human Systems* (New York: Appleton-Century-Crofts, 1967).

[39] A brief explanation of these analytical tools can be found in Franklin A. Lindsay, *New Techniques for Management Decision Making* (New York: McGraw-Hill Book Company, 1958).

[40] Marvin Adelson, "The System Approach-Perspective," *SDC Magazine,* 9 (October 1966), 1.

[41] H. M. Blalock and A. B. Blalock, "Towards a Classification of System Analysis in the Social Sciences," *Philosophy of Science,* 26 (1959), 84.

Hopefully, any research into the design and establishment of new systems, whether technical, managerial, maintenance, or otherwise, will require an examination of organizational processes from all sides, all levels, and all angles. Such an examination suggests that the elements of a systems methodology be used (that is, provide principles of procedure). Let us consider one illustration of recent support for the application of systems analysis to problem solving in police agencies:

> The criminal justice system is an enormous complex of operations. Subjecting such a system to scientific investigation normally involves making changes in its operations in order to observe the effects directly. Whenever practical, this kind of controlled experimentation is clearly the best kind. But experimentation inside a system is often impractical and even undesirable, not only because the costs could be prohibitive, but because normal operations are frequently too critical to be disrupted. Instead, the scientist may be able to formulate a mathematical description or "model" of the system in order to illuminate the relationships among its parts. Systems analysis involves construction and manipulation of such mathematical models in order to find out how better to organize and operate the real-life systems they represent. It is desirable to conduct such analysis of the criminal justice system. . . .[42]

In this case, we observe an analytical framework, with internally consistent procedural steps applicable to simple and complex problems, which is capable of grouping or separating elements of problems, that is to say, systems analysis. Such a framework provides an analytical foundation for the creation of a modern police organization.

Systems design. It is in the early stages of the design process that inventiveness and ingenuity offer the biggest payoff in the development of new and different patterns of organization. Stoller and Van Horn put it this way: "The design process is a blend of science and art, whether the final product is a missile or an organization chart."[43]

There are different goals that can be set when designing or redesigning an organization. We consider three types of designs. Perhaps the most common one is *equipment and method improvement.* Very significant developments in equipment during the past 15 years have resulted in extensive emphasis on better ways to mechanize the processes of an organization. Equipment and method improvement is usually well received because it reduces the amount of change necessary on the part of the organization. If we decide on such a design, any analysis of, and changes in, the existing organization

---

[42] President's Commission on Law Enforcement and Administration of Justice, *The Challenge of Crime in a Free Society* (Washington, D.C.: U.S. Government Printing Office, 1967), pp. 261–62.

[43] David S. Stoller and Richard L. Van Horn, *Design of a Management System* (Santa Monica, Calif.: The Rand Corporation, 1958), p. 1.

are discouraged and most of the interest is directed toward automation or mechanization of the current procedures with only limited, if any, changes in the structure or the output of the organization per se. We should recognize that equipment or method improvements are certainly worthy in situations where the goals are well defined, such as some routine record keeping or statistical compilations. However, in a police organization the end results are often ambiguous. In fact, in many police agencies the paramount problem lies in ascertaining what should be the primary, as well as secondary, goals of the organization.

A second approach is *increased output*. One adopts this design by increasing the types and amounts of organizational output. The main disadvantage of an increased output design is that it tends to either overload the organization or emphasize quantity over quality of output. This design is perhaps best confined to short-term, exploratory organizational revisions.

The final approach can be referred to as *organizational effectiveness*. In essence, this design consists of (1) specifying the managing and operating decisions prerequisite to better accomplishment of the goals of a police organization, (2) linking or integrating the various subsystems in order to facilitate greater effectiveness, (3) determining the data requirements implied by each organizational decision, and (4) developing preferred courses of action for attaining improved effectiveness data. The organizational effectiveness approach is suited to making long-term improvements in police departments. Admittedly, improvements of a short-term nature in a police bureaucracy can, with some limited degree of effectiveness, draw from the previous two approaches. If we are seeking long-term benefits (and it is hoped that we are), they will be found in the third design for organizing police agencies.

Modern Organizational Theory: The Police Organization as an Open Social System

Thus far we have covered the reasons for a systems perspective and the nature of a systems approach to organization. In summarizing these two topics, it can be said that they form the distinctive qualities of modern organization theory—its conceptual-analytical base, its devotion to empirical research data, its process orientation, and, most significantly, its integrating nature.[44] With due regard for these qualities, the police organization as an open social system provides the point of departure for our forthcoming discussion.

Social systems (police organizations) are contrived systems; they are

---

[44] William G. Scott, "Organization Theory: An Overview and an Appraisal," *Journal of Academy of Management*, 4 (April 1961), 19.

made by men and hence are anchored in the needs, perceptions, attitudes, and motivations of human beings. Further, they form patterns of internal relationships for processing inputs (man and materials) into outputs (the handling of called-for services). Figure 9 presents a graphic description of this model.

All open systems possess the following nine characteristics:[45]

1. *Input.* Open systems input various types of energy from their external environment.
2. *Processing.* Open systems process the energy available with an output.
3. *Output.* Open systems output products or services into the environment.
4. *Cyclic character.* The product or service output furnishes the source of energy for an input and thus the repetition of cycle.
5. *Arresting of disorganization.* Social systems process and store energy in order to combat the natural trend toward disorganization.
6. *Information: input, processing, output, and feedback.* Information is handled much the same as energy. In fact, information can be considered a form of energy.
7. *The steady state.* Open systems seek to maintain a viable ratio between energy input and service output. This state is not to be confused with the status quo. A steady state allows for change by constantly adjusting the input and the output so as to achieve a healthy relationship between the two.
8. *Specialization.* Open systems move in the direction of specialization.
9. *Equifinality.* Open systems can reach the same final state from differing initial conditions and by a variety of paths.

In addition to these nine characteristics, all modern social systems are comprised of five subsystems. The total system requires these subsystems to accomplish its goals and to survive. These subsystems are (1) operations subsystems to get the work done, (2) maintenance subsystems to indoctrinate people and service machines, (3) supportive subsystems for procurement and environmental relations, (4) adaptive subsystems concerned with organizational change, and (5) managerial subsystems for the direction, coordination, and control of the other subsystems.[46] If we were to reshape the present structure of a police organization according to the five subsystems the result would appear quite different (see Figure 10). It would be even more revolutionary when experienced in terms of its new processes—the *new* way of conducting its business. Table 3 contains a more detailed explanation of the purpose, functions, and activities of each subsystem.

Regretfully, space does not permit a more thorough description of the police organization as a system. Such an attempt would require the writing

---

[45] These common characteristics are drawn from Katz and Kahn, *Social Psychology*, pp. 19–26.

[46] This typology of subsystems is suggested in *ibid.*, pp. 39–44.

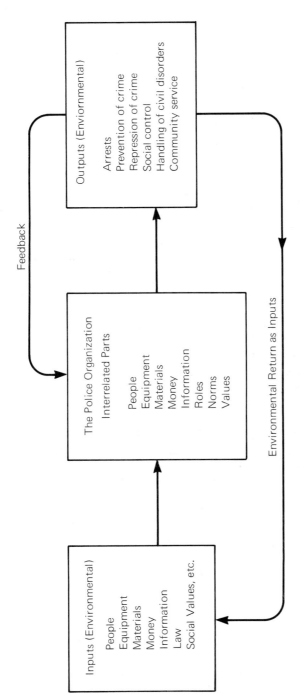

FIG. 9. POLICE ORGANIZATION AS A SYSTEM: A SIMPLIFIED MODEL

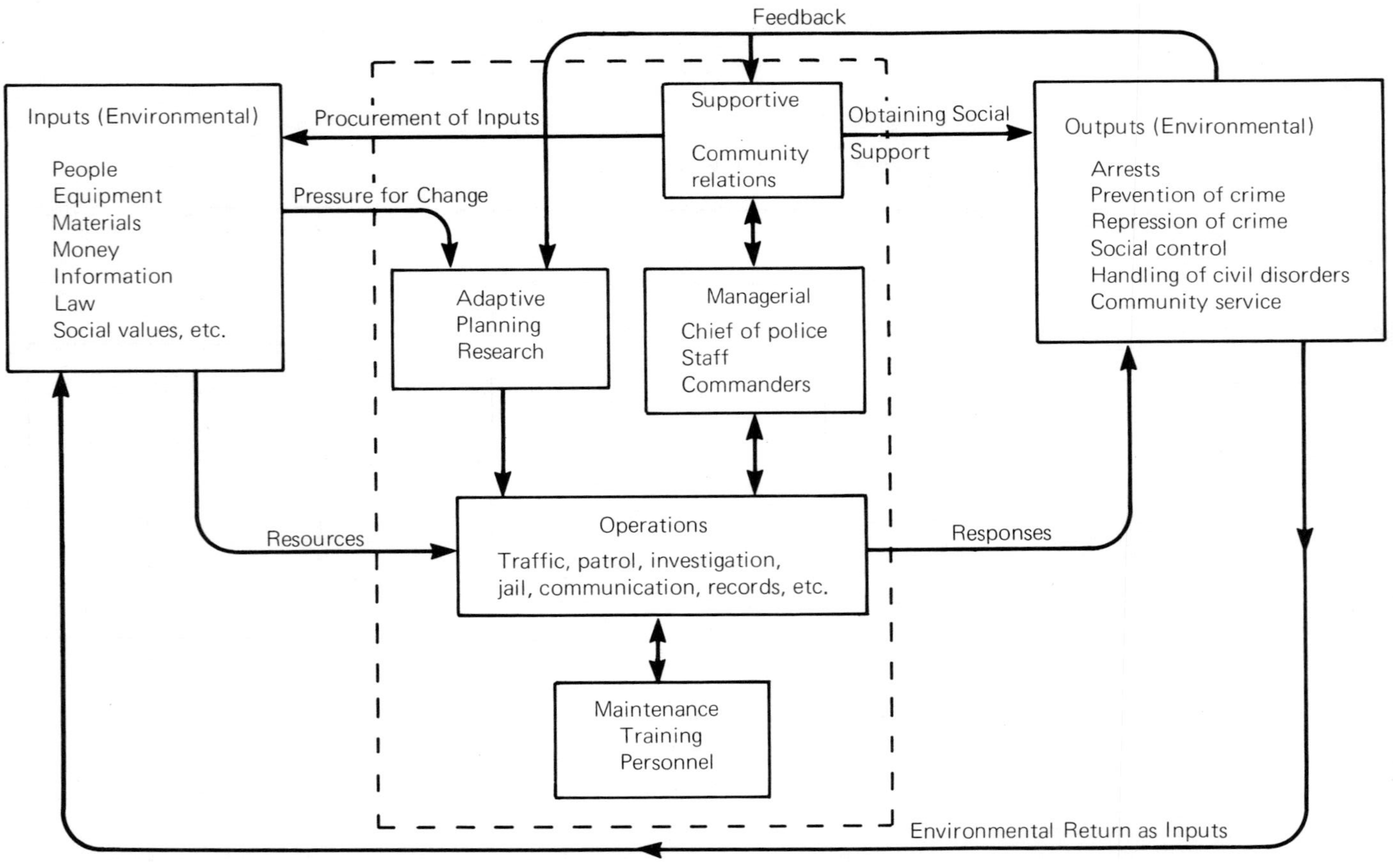

FIG. 10. THE POLICE ORGANIZATION AND ITS SUBSYSTEMS

Outputs (Environmental)

Arrests
Prevention of crime
Repression of crime
Social control
Handling of civil disorders
Community service

Environmental Return as Inputs

Responses

Obtaining Social Support

Feedback

Supportive
Community relations

Managerial
Chief of police
Staff
Commanders

Operations
Traffic, patrol, investigation, jail, communication, records, etc.

Maintenance
Training
Personnel

Adaptive
Planning
Research

Procurement of Inputs

Pressure for Change

Resources

Inputs (Environmental)

People
Equipment
Materials
Money
Information
Law
Social values, etc.

TABLE 3: *THE SUBSYSTEMS OF A POLICE ORGANIZATION: THEIR PURPOSES, FUNCTIONS, AND ACTIVITIES*

Subsystem	Purpose	Function	Activities
1. Operations Patrol, traffic, investigation, jail, communications, etc.	Efficiency in field operations	Task accomplishment—processing of inputs within the organization	Division of labor: specialization and job standards
2. Maintenance Training, personnel	Maintenance of subsystems: their functions and activities	Mediating between organizational goals and personal needs, indoctrination, and servicing man-machine activities	Establishing operating procedures, training, and equipment maintenance
3. Supportive Community relations	Environmental support for the organization	Exchange with environment to obtain social support	Building favorable image by contributing to the community and by influencing other social systems
4. Adaptive Planning and research	Planned organizational change	Intelligence gathering, research and development, and planning	Making recommendations for change and implementing planned change
5. Managerial Chief of police, staff and subsystem commanders	Control and direction	Resolving internal conflict, coordinating and directing subsystems, coordinating external requirements and organizational resources and needs	Use of authority, adjudication of conflict, increasing of efficiency, adjusting to environmental changes, and restructuring the organization

of another text, in addition to considerable research. For those interested in a start in this direction, see the texts *The Human Organization* and *Organizing Men and Power: Patterns of Behavior and Line-Staff Models.*[47] Both of these works suggest new organizational structures for integrating the efforts of employees for greater effectiveness. While they differ in several respects, both possess a common focus: the organization as a system of interdependent relationships.

Conclusion. Admittedly, the reader has been exposed to some rather "heady" material. It was not intended to impress or depress any of you. The purpose of this section was to indicate the dimensions of an emerging theory —an organizational theory that has as its major underpinning the systems approach. For those that either rejected systems thinking or failed to comprehend it, all is not lost. You may still impress others and thus remain in vogue by speaking systems. The following information will prove most useful in influencing friends, co-workers, and superiors. While initially designed by the Canadian Forces Headquarters for use in defense matters, the buzzphrase generator also provides its users with instant expertise in systems level concepts.[48] The buzzphrase generator consists of three columns of buzzwords numbered zero to nine:

Column 1	*Column 2*	*Column 3*
0. integrated	0. management	0. options
1. total	1. organizational	1. flexibility
2. systematized	2. monitored	2. capability
3. parallel	3. reciprocal	3. mobility
4. functional	4. digital	4. programming
5. responsive	5. logistical	5. concept
6. optional	6. transitional	6. time-phase
7. synchronized	7. incremental	7. projection
8. compatible	8. third-generation	8. hardware
9. balanced	9. policy	9. contingency

From this point the procedure is simple and straightforward. Select any three-digit number at random. Then select the corresponding buzzword from each column. Put them together and you sound just like a systems expert. To illustrate, take the number 257. Take word two from column one, word five from column two, and word seven from column three. You now have "systematized logistical projection." You don't know what it

---

[47] Respectively, Likert, *Human Organization*, and Robert T. Golembiewski, *Organizing Men and Power: Patterns of Behavior and Line-Staff Models* (Chicago, Ill.: Rand McNally & Company, 1967).

[48] As quoted in an excerpt entitled, "Need Instant Expertise," *Public Administration Review*, 28 (November-December 1968), 519.

means, but don't worry, neither does anyone else. The important thing is that the buzzphrase generator provides the user with the perfect aid for preparing anything on the subject of systems. Automatically you have 1,000 different combinations, all of which give you that proper ring of a decisive, progressive, knowledgeable authority on systems and, in turn, modern organizational theory.

Now, in a more serious note, what does modern organizational theory with its systems concept mean to the police supervisor? In essence, because of the newer forms of organization, the police supervisor will eventually find himself

1. using many styles of supervising rather than just one
2. monitoring results rather than concentrating on techniques
3. observing constant structural changes at all levels
4. working under a system with mutual dependence and an absence of compartmentalized responsibilities
5. observing shifting boundaries between groups
6. working with multiple objectives
7. initiating reciprocal action rather than merely orders and reports

Complexity and change—moreover, ever increasing complexity and change — is in the future (if not already the present) of the police supervisor.

SUMMARY

Chapters 4 and 5 have presented three theories of organization. The first two, classical and neoclassical, are reasonably well understood and presently in use. The latter theory is just now becoming known. It is referred to as "modern" and its basic attributes are derived from the systems approach.

The neoclassical theory grew out of a recognition by social scientists that the classical, or traditional, theory was sadly lacking in an understanding of the human component in organization. The Hawthorne studies furnished a major cornerstone for the neoclassical movement when they reported that man had a social capacity and that he responds to supervision as a group member and not as an individual. Out of these early studies came an interest in the informal organization. Moreover, we have found that there is more than one type of informal organization. These organizations exist because organizational man has found them necessary to better fulfill his personal needs and organizational tasks.

Modern organization theory is much more than an amalgamation of the classical and neoclassical theories. First, and foremost, modern organization theory treats the organization as an open social system. Therefore, the organization is viewed as a *process* that seeks to take an input (equipment, materials, people, etc.) and transform it into an environmental output (product or service), which eventually returns to the system as an input. In doing so the process integrates the internal parts of the system into a unified entity and, in turn, relates the entity to its environment. When dealing with an organization as a system, however, we include more than theory. To properly use the idea of a system, we choose to call it the systems approach. This approach includes systems theory (concept), systems analysis (research method), and systems design (plan of action). The potential of the systems approach is great, because it offers the vehicle for merging what is valuable in the classical and neoclassical theories into a systematic and integrated theory for making police organizations more effective. Significantly, the police supervisor figures to play an even more important role in the resultant modern police organization.

PROBLEMS

1. Discuss where the "Hawthorne effect" might be found in a police organization.
2. List the major differences between the classical and neoclassical theories of organization.
3. Develop your own argument for treating, or even redesigning, the police organization in terms of systems thinking.
4. Review the material on organizational subsystems. Are there other ways of conceptualizing these subsystems? First, draw your systems-subsystems model of a police organization. Second, describe the purpose, function, and activity of each subsystem.
5. Why is some understanding of modern organizational theory relevant to a police supervisor? In a single paragraph, justify the inclusion of such information in a text on police supervision. (The last part of the conclusion to the section on modern organization theory can serve as a point of departure for your justification.)

SUPERVISORY
BEHAVIOR

part two

Introduction

Up to this point we have been talking about some of the essential components constituting a police organization: individuals, groups, formal structure, and informal relationships. Each of these components is an integral part of a police organization. The remainder of this book relates the police supervisor to his organizational world. This world provides him with certain role requirements that he is expected to meet. Part Two is designed to cover 14 of the 15 role requirements mentioned in Chapter 1. To refresh your memory, they are

1. formal, informal, and personal communication
2. organizational control
3. organizational perspective
4. organizational responsibility
5. procedure development
6. administrative detail
7. support-subordinate
8. interaction facilitation
9. goal emphasis
10. work facilitation
11. employee morale
12. community relations
13. safety awareness
14. performance appraisal
15. training

The last requirement, that of training, is the subject of Part Three.

While examining all 14 role requirements, Part Two is admittedly biased in terms of organizational control, since, as we established earlier, the provision of organizational control is one of two major role requirements for a police supervisor. Chapter 6 discusses communications, which is the vehicle of control. Basically, organizational control is the attempt on the part of one person (in this case, a police supervisor) to influence another and influence cannot be transmitted or received unless a message is exchanged. Hence, we begin Part Two with a look at the means by which control is exercised. Chapter 7 is devoted entirely to the control mechanism itself—the types of control and their impact on the people involved. In Chapter 8 we learn that a police supervisor must exercise control for coordination. Briefly, in order for his subordinates to effectively accomplish their assigned tasks, the police supervisor must coordinate both their individual activities with one another and their group activities with the other groups that constitute the police organization. Chapter 9 examines the importance of the supervisor in fulfilling the role requirements of an organizational leader. In essence, by becoming a leader, the supervisor enhances his ability to exert control over his subordinates. Chapter 10 discloses the results of effective and ineffective supervisory control—high or low morale and job satisfaction. In Chapter 11 we see a very special requirement of the supervisor: he is expected to build and maintain healthy relationships with outside groups and the general public. Finally, a much newer role requirement is previewed in Chapter 12, that of personnel safety.

Together, the chapters that form Part Two provide a major portion of the multiview approach to an improved understanding of police supervision. Also, each chapter ends with a concise list of recommended supervisory behavior. These recommendations are not to be confused with principles or the-one-best-way thinking. They are intended to furnish the present or prospective supervisor with some basic techniques that have proven to be successful on most (not all) occasions. Here's hoping that they work for you!

6

Communication in
Police Organizations:
the Flow of Information

Information is a name for the content of what is exchanged with the outer world as we adjust to it, and make our adjustment felt upon it. The process of receiving and of using information is the process of our adjusting to the conting encies of the outer environment, and of our living effectively within that environment. The needs and the complexity of modern life make greater demands on this process of information than ever before, and our press, our museums, our scientific laboratories, our universities, our libraries and textbooks, are obliged to meet the needs of this process or fail in their purpose. To live effectively is to live with adequate information. Thus, communication and control belong to life in society.[1]

Communication is the vehicle for supervisory control. In other words, the police supervisor is a key person in building and maintaining effective organizational communications as he interacts with subordinates, peers, superiors, and the citizenry. To succeed in this task, he must communicate in many directions for the basic purpose of exerting his control. Thus we can understand why a major portion of our consideration of police supervision deals with the subject of communication.

A communication, or in terms of organizational setting a communication system, provides the means by which information, statements, views and instructions are transmitted through an organization. Although one often speaks of the "flow" of communications, in fact, this flow consists of a series of discrete messages of different length, form, and content. These messages are transmitted through certain channels (or lines of communications), which make up the communication system or network. Each message is sent by a transmitter (an individual, a group, a division, a computer) to a receiver or several receivers. It may induce action or provoke a reaction in the form of a counter-message or both. Every individual or division in a police organization acts as a transmitter and a receiver, though not for the

---

[1] Norbert Wiener, *The Human Use of Human Beings: Cybernetics and Society* 2nd ed., rev. (New York: Doubleday & Company, Inc., 1954), pp. 17–18.

same messages. Some individuals, depending on their role and function in the organization, transmit more than they receive, others receive more than they transmit. Significantly, the supervisory role and function is filled with a heavy volume of transmissions and receptions. What we must keep in mind, then, is that messages in a communication network *are a manifestation of interactions in the system and of the control mechanisms at work.*

Like other organizational phenomena, communications can be viewed at the organizational level as interpersonal and group (the reader may find it useful at this point to review the two sections in Chapter 3 dealing with communications). In organizational terms, we cover, in the order they appear here,

1. relevance of communications to the police supervisor
2. types of communication channels
3. direction of communication
4. volume and types of messages
5. cybernetics
6. the computer
7. basics of effective communication

Only brief or indirect reference is made to the external systems of police communications such as the police radio, teletype, and so on.[2] Our discussion of communications, therefore, is built around the internal channels for transmitting and receiving messages.

THE RELEVANCE OF COMMUNICATIONS TO THE POLICE SUPERVISOR: WHY COMMUNICATE?

Why communicate? First and most importantly, a police supervisor decides issues based on information received in conjunction with previously developed strategies, procedures, or rules. Consequently, the communication process is necessary because the flow of proper information to the decision points throughout the organization is such a vital requirement for task accomplishment. In fact, if supervision were thought of primarily as decision making and if the decision process were considered essentially a communication process including a network of communication systems, then supervision could be viewed as a communication process. According to Dorsey, and with equal validity for supervision,

---

[2] For those in need of information pertaining to the technological aspects of police communication systems, see *Task Force Report: Science and Technology,* Report to the President's Commission on Law Enforcement and Administration of Justice, prepared by the Institute for Defense Analyses (Washington, D.C.: U.S. Government Printing Office, 1967); and International Association of Chiefs of Police, *Design and Operation of Police Communications System* (Washington, D.C.: International Association of Chiefs of Police, 1964).

Structurally, administration can be viewed as a configuration of communication patterns relating individuals and collectivities of varying sizes, shapes, and degree of cohesion and stability. Dynamically, administration appears as a patterned swirl and flow of communications, many of them channeled through transactional "circuits" between persons and persons, persons and groups, and groups and other groups.[3]

Thus the several concepts, communications, control, information, and decision making, are interwoven. Plainly, the closer we look at control and decision making the more we become aware of the basic significance of information exchange.

The term *information-decision system* is used to emphasize the fact that available information should be transmitted in light of the decisions to be made throughout the organization. Thus an information-decision system is a communication process relating the necessary new inputs to the already stored information and the desired decisional outputs. It is likely that decisions at a given stage in the organization represent output from one communication process and input information for a subsequent decision at the same level, a lower level, or a higher level. The over-all information flow is a communication system with many interdependent elements and subsystems.

In summary, a police supervisor communicates in order to transmit or request information for the making of a decision on the direction of subordinate officers. Hence, we design communication systems to carry the requisite information for decision making on the provision of task-oriented control. Such a system may also be referred to as an information-decision system. It may be formal or informal or both. Further, it may be manual or automated or both. Specifically, then, why does a police supervisor depend on a communication system? The answer, simply, is because control is achieved through communications. By analyzing communications in detail we find that its capacity for control is based on five things. First, it provides sufficient information to accomplish assigned tasks. This communication function may be satisfied through a variety of forms such as periodic training, provision of technical reference manuals, daily coaching, orders, and so forth. Second, communication clarifies perceptions and expectations of responsibility. Organization charts, job descriptions, work plans, schedules, routes, performance ratings, orders, and other devices may serve this function. Third, communication facilitates the *coordination* of men and materials in achieving specific objectives. Fourth, an effective communication system makes possible organizational problem solving (task oriented) and conflict resolution (interpersonal problems). Fifth, communication furnishes general

---

[3] John T. Dorsey, Jr., "A Communication Model for Administration," *Administrative Science Quarterly*, 2 (December 1957), 310.

direction not only on what to accomplish, but also on the way it should be accomplished. Johnson, Kast, and Rosenzweig provide a fitting conclusion for this section when they write:

> Throughout history the transmission of information has been a key to progress. Efficient communication is important in all fields of human endeavor. However, as society has become more complex, as technology has increased at an accelerating rate, and in spite of improvements in communication media, it is becoming more and more difficult to communicate effectively. The growth of organizations and increased specialization and functionalization have developed barriers to communication in many spheres of activity. Scientists and researchers find it more and more difficult to communicate on a broad scope. Managers of business and industrial organizations find communication an increasing problem in their day-to-day operations.[4]

TYPES OF COMMUNICATION CHANNELS

Various channels of communication are available to the police supervisor for exchanging information. Commonly, a communications system is divided into formal and informal channels. We modify this list by dividing the informal communication channels into three subclasses: subformal, personal task directed, and personal nontask directed.[5]

Formal Communication Channels

All organizations develop formal communication channels as a response to large size and the limited information handling capability of each individual. The formal channels adhere to the recognized official structure of the organization. Accordingly, the formal communication channels transmit messages expressive of the legitimate structure of authority. Hence, one usually sees formal orders and directives, reports, official correspondence, standard operating procedures, and so on. Those persons who emphasize going through channels are doing so in deference to the unity of command principle within the formal hierarchy.

Strict compliance with formal channels can be dysfunctional. These dysfunctions are primarily in terms of time, creativity, and experience. To explain, first, it takes a long time for a formal message from a supervisor in one division to pass to another supervisor in another division. Second, formal messages are on the record and thus restrict the free flow of ideas.

---

[4] Richard A. Johnson, Fremont E. Kast, and James E. Rosenzweig, *The Theory and Management of Systems* (New York: McGraw-Hill Book Company, 1963), p. 87.

[5] This classification is suggested in part by William M. Jones, *On Decisionmaking in Large Organizations* (Santa Monica, Calif.: The Rand Corporation, 1964).

As an example, police officers may not want to expose their ideas to their supervisors for the time being, even in rough form; yet any formal communication is immediately routed through the originator's supervisor. Third, in practice a formal communication system cannot cover all informational needs. Informational needs change quite rapidly, while the formal channels change only with considerable time and effort. Therefore, the most urgent need for informal communication channels is to "plug" the gaps in the formal channels.

Informal Communication Channels

Regretfully, there are some who consider formal communication channels as the only way to transmit information so necessary to the functioning of the organization. However, this precept is no longer as sacred as it once was. Not only are we witnessing an interest in acquiring a better understanding of the informal organization, but along with it has come an awareness of its potential use. This interest and awareness quite naturally leads to a different perspective on the structuring of communication flow. In essence, this perspective does not confine organizationally useful communication to purely formal channels. It includes all the social processes of the broadest relevance in the functioning of any group or organization. Consequently, we now treat informal and personal communications as a supportive and frequently necessary process for effective functioning. Further, the unofficial communication channels become a prime means for studying the informal organization.[6] In fact, police supervisors are often expected to seek information through channels not officially sanctioned.

The prevalence of informal channels means that formal channels do not fully meet the important communications needs in a police department. Therefore, it is futile for police administrators to establish formal channels and assume that those channels will carry most of the messages. Ironically, the more restricted the formal channels, the greater the growth of informal ones. However, while the informal system attempts to fill the gaps in the formal one, the leaders of a police organization can severely curtail the development of the former by simply ordering subordinates not to communicate with each other, by physically separating people, or by requiring prior clearance for any communication outside a certain division. In doing so, the number of meaningful messages is sharply reduced, thus affecting the over-all effectiveness of the organization.

We next proceed to an analysis of three kinds of informal communication channels. The first two are task, or goal, oriented, while the third is oriented toward the individual.

---

[6] Jacob Jacoby, "Examining the Other Organization," *Personnel Administration* (November-December 1968), 36.

Informal communication channels: subformal. Subformal channels carry those messages arising from the informal power structure existing in every police organization. Every member of the department must know and observe informal rules and procedures about what to communicate and to whom (see the first part of Chapter 5). Such rules are rarely written down and must be learned by experience and example, a necessity which causes difficulties for newcomers.

There are two types of subformal communications: those that flow along formal channels, but not as formal communications; and those that flow along purely informal channels. Both types have the distinct advantage of not being official; therefore they can be withdrawn or changed without any official record being made. As a result, almost all new ideas are first proposed and tested as subformal communications. Significantly, the vast majority of communications in police organizations are subformal.[7]

As mentioned above, subformal channels of communication develop whenever there is a functional need for police personnel to communicate but no formal channel. Formal channels are normally vertical, following the lines of the formal authority structure. Hence, most of the gap-filling subformal lines of communication are horizontal, connecting peers rather than subordinates and superiors. This characteristic is one reason that police supervisors find subformal channels so important in their job. Through subformal communications a police supervisor can interrelate his unit and their efforts to others. Further, even when subformal channels link police personnel of different ranks, the informality of the information exchanged reduces the variations in organizational status. Subformal communications provide a means for subordinates from all levels to speak more freely to their superiors.

While in general it has been indicated that subformal channels meet the communication requirements not met by formal channels, they become all the more necessary under certain conditions. First, the greater the degree of interdependence among activities within the department, the greater the number and use of subformal channels. Second, the more uncertainty about the objectives of the department, the greater the number and use of subformal channels. When the environment is relatively unpredictable, men cannot easily determine what they should be doing simply by referring to that environment. Consequently, they tend to talk to each other more to gain an improved understanding of their situation. Third, when a police organization is operating under the pressure of time, it tends to use subformal channels extensively, since there is often no time to use the formal channels. Thus, police administrators reach out for information whenever they can

---

[7] Anthony Downs, *Inside Bureaucracy* (Boston, Mass.: Little, Brown and Company, Inc., 1967), p. 113.

get it from whatever channel is necessary. Fourth, if the divisions of a police organization are in strong competition, they tend to avoid subformal channels and communicate only formally. Conversely, closely cooperating sections rely primarily upon subformal communications. Hence, strong rivalry has significant communications drawbacks. Fifth, subformal communications channels are used more frequently if departmental members have stable, rather than constantly changing, relationships with each other.

Informal communication channels: personal task directed. A personal task-directed communication is one in which an organization member deliberately reveals something of his own attitude toward the activities of his own organization.[8] While personal, this communication is also in terms of the goals or activities of the organization. Thus we can refer to it as task directed. It possesses the following characteristics. First, task-directed personal channels are nearly always used for informing rather than for directing. Second, before a person acts on the basis of information received through personal channels, he usually verifies that information through either subformal or formal channels. Third, this channel transmits information with considerable speed because there are no formal mechanisms to impede its flow. Fourth, because task-directed personal messages are transmitted by personnel acting as individuals, they do not bear the weight of the position emitting them. To this extent, they differ from subformal messages, which are transmitted by individuals acting in their official capacity—but not for the record.[9]

Informal communication channels: personal nontask directed. As suggested by its title, this form of communication apparently does not contain information related to the tasks of the organization. Note the emphasis on the word *apparently.* Paradoxically, this channel may handle information on occasion far more valuable to the achievement of organizational goals than any other channel, including the formal ones. An example of this channel is the supervisor learning through a friendly subordinate of the reasons for growing job dissatisfaction. A discussion of its characteristics should provide an explanation of its utility. First, nontask-directed channels furnish a vehicle for an individual to satisfy his social needs. In doing so, he experiences a certain degree of need-fulfillment which carries over into his job, and as described in earlier chapters, a person is more likely to remain with an organization if he is satisfied. Second, this channel provides a way for an individual to blow off steam over things that disturb him. This pressure release valve often reduces a person's level of tension to point where he does not engage in acts injurious to the functioning of the organization. Third, nontask-directed channels frequently supply useful feedback information to the management and supervisory levels. This feedback is normally comprised of unexpected information not obtainable in any other way.

---

[8] Jones, *On Decisionmaking*, p. 5.
[9] Downs, *Inside Bureaucracy*, p. 115.

Fourth, personal channels offer the best medium for a person to become socialized in his organizational setting. Unwritten standards, group values, and "the way we do things here" are conveniently expressed through non-task-directed channels.

In conclusion and to reemphasize a point made earlier in this section:

> The efficiency of a large formal organization is sizably enhanced when its own chain of command or decision or communication is tied into the informal network of groups within the organization, so that the network can be used to support the organization's goals.[10]

COMMUNICATIONS: DOWN, UP, AND LATERAL

Chapter 2 revealed that communications flow in more than a single direction. Traditionally, communication flow was envisioned as being exclusively downward and synonymous with the pattern of authority. The pattern of authority provides, of course, the structure of an organization, but almost invariably it is found to represent an idealized concept of what the organization is like, or what it should be like, and this is why students of organization theory constantly need to investigate the informal structure for other directions of communication flow. The formerly described formal and informal channels indicate the three directions of communications in an organization. Furthermore, the content of the message varies with the direction of flow. As mentioned in Chapter 2, the three directions possible for a message to flow are downward, upward, and laterally (horizontally).[11] We begin our discussion by a look at the downward flow of messages.

Downward

Communications from supervisor to subordinate are of primarily five types:

1. Specific task directives: *job instructions*
2. Information to produce the understanding of the task and its relation to other organizational tasks: *job rationale*
3. Information concerning organizational *procedures and practices*
4. *Feedback* to the subordinate officer about his performance
5. Information to instill a sense of mission: *indoctrination of goals*

---

[10] Bernard Berelson and Gary A. Steiner, *Human Behavior: An Inventory of Scientific Findings* (New York: Harcourt, Brace & World, Inc., 1964), p. 370.

[11] This particular section is drawn from Downs, *Inside Bureaucracy*, pp. 235–47.

The first type of message is most often given priority in police organizations. Instructions about the position of police officer are communicated to the person through direct orders from his supervisor, training sessions, training manuals, and written directives. The objective is to insure the reliable performance of every police officer in the organization. Less attention is given to the second type, which is designed to provide the police officer with a full understanding of his position and its relation to related positions in the same organization. Many police officers know what they are to do but not why. Withholding information on the rationale of the job not only reduces the loyalty of the member to his organization, but it also means that the organization must rely heavily on the first type of information, detailed instructions about the job. If a man does not understand why he should do something or how his job relates to other jobs performed by his co-workers, then there must be sufficient repetition in his task instructions so that he behaves automatically. This problem is dramatically illustrated in the conflict about the information to be given to police officers about their functions. Some city and police administrators are in favor of reducing the policeman's behavior to that of a robot; others want to use his intelligence by having him act on his understanding of the total situation. It can be seen, therefore, that the advantages of giving fuller information on job understanding are twofold: If an officer knows the reasons for his assignment, he will often carry out his job more effectively; and if he has an understanding of what his job is about in relation to the over-all mission of his department, he is more likely to identify with its goals. Third, information about organizational procedures supplies a prescription of the role requirements of the organizational member. In addition to instructions about his job, the police officer is also informed about his other duties and privileges as a member of the police organization. Fourth, feedback is necessary to insure that the organization is operating properly. It is also a means for motivating the individual performer. However, feedback to the individual about how well he is doing in his job is often neglected or poorly handled, even in police organizations in which the managerial philosophy calls for such evaluation. Where emphasis is placed upon compliance to specific task directives, it is natural to expect that such compliance will be recognized and deviation penalized. Fifth, the final type of downward-directed information has as its purpose to implant organizational goals, either for the total organization or a major unit of it. Consequently, an important function of a police supervisor is to describe the mission of his police department in an attractive and novel form. For example, a police supervisor may depict the role of his police department as the work of professional officers engaged in a constructive program of community improvement.

The size of the loop in downward communications affects organizational morale and effectiveness. In terms of morale, communications about the goals of the police organization cover in theory a loop as large as the organization itself. In practice, however, the rank-and-file officers are touched only minimally by this loop. Their degree of inclusion within the loop depends mainly upon how they are tied into the police organization. If they are tied in on the basis of being rewarded for a routine performance, information about the goals and policies of the over-all structure will be of no interest to them. Therefore, the police supervisor should make every effort to see that his subordinates are involved members of the organization. Next, the size of the loop affects the degree of understanding contained in a communication. Messages from top management addressed to all organizational personnel are often too general in nature and too far removed from the daily experiences of the line police officer to convey their intended meaning. To be effective, messages about departmental policy need to be translated at critical levels as they move down in the organization. Hence, the police supervisor is required to translate a received message into specific meanings for his subordinates. This does not necessarily mean that a police officer should get all his job directives from a single supervisor, but it does mean that additional supervisors should be used only if experts on a specialized function. To illustrate, the patrolman, in addition to complying with the orders of his immediate supervisor, on occasion can also find relevant direction from a superior of a traffic, vice, or juvenile unit.

Upward

Communications from subordinate to supervisor are also of chiefly five types:

1. Information about his *performance* and *grievances*
2. Information about the *performance* and *grievances* of others
3. Feedback regarding organizational *practices* and *policies*
4. Feedback concerning what needs to be *done* and the *means* for doing it
5. Requests for *clarification* about goals and specific activities

However, there are great constraints on free upward communication for a variety of reasons. Most prominent is the structure itself. Simply stated, bureaucracies or highly formalized organizations tend to inhibit upward informal communications. In doing so, a tremendous amount of important information never reaches the upper-level decision centers.[12] Other factors adversely affecting the upward flow of messages are as follows. Superiors are less in the habit of listening to their subordinates than in talking to them. Further, information fed up the line is often used for control purposes.

---

[12] Berelson and Steiner, *Human Organization.*

Hence, the superior is not likely to be given information by his subordinates which would lead to decisions affecting them adversely. They not only tell the superior what he wants to hear, but also what they want him to know. Employees do want to get certain information up the line, but generally they are afraid of presenting it in the most objective form. Full and objective reporting about one's own performance and problems is difficult. For all these reasons the upward flow of communication in police organizations is not noted for spontaneous and objective expression, despite attempts to formalize the process of feedback up the line. Importantly, it is not a problem of changing the communication habits of individuals, but of changing the organizational conditions responsible for these habits.

Horizontal

Communications between people at the same hierarchical level are basically of four types:

1. Information necessary to provide task *coordination*
2. Information for identifying and defining *common problems* to be solved through cooperation
3. Feedback from co-workers which fulfills social needs
4. Information needed to provide social (not organizational) control for a group so that it can maintain the members' compliance with its standards and values

Organizations face one of their most difficult problems in procedures and practices concerned with lateral communication. In essence, a working balance must be found between unrestricted and overrestricted communications amongst peers in an organization. To explain, unrestricted communications of a horizontal character can detract from maximum efficiency because too much nonrelevant information may be transmitted. At the opposite extreme, efficiency suffers if an employee receives all his instructions from the person above him, thus reducing task coordination. Our position here is that some lateral communication is critical for an effective police organization. Police tasks cannot be so completely specified from above to rule out the need for coordination between peers. The type and amount of information that should be circulated on a horizontal basis is best determined by answering the question, "Who needs to know and why?" To put it another way, the information transmitted should be related to the objectives of the various units in the police organization, with primary focus on their major task. An interesting hang-up in horizontal communications occurs when people overvalue peer communication to the neglect of those below and above them. Sergeants talk only to sergeants, and lieutenants only to lieutenants. However, in many instances the really critical information is at levels below or above them.

Finally, as organizations move toward a greater authoritarian structure, they exert more and more control over any flow of horizontal information by outlawing the forms of free communication among equals. Consequently, employees cannot organize cooperative efforts and, in turn, the organization is adversely affected.

MESSAGES: VOLUME AND TYPES

Communication is costly! Every message involves the expenditure of time to decide what to send, time for composing, the cost of transmitting the message (which may consist of time, money, or both), and time spent in receiving the message. Consequently, the volume of messages in an organization is of real concern to an administrator. Not only do they take time and money, but they can also seriously hamper an individual because they subtract time from his working day. Plainly, the more time a person spends in searching or communicating, the less he has for other types of activity. Furthermore, every individual has a saturation point regarding the amount of information he can usefully handle in a given time period. In this case, both the volume and the length of the message can overload an individual beyond his saturation point. If he should become overloaded, he will be unable effectively either to comprehend the information given to him or to use it. All of this means that the particular methods used by a police organization to collect, select, and transmit information are critically important determinants of its success. First, we take a closer look at the volume of messages; second, at the types of messages.

Volume

The volume of messages in a police organization is determined by six basic factors:

1. The total number of members in the organization
2. The nature of its communications networks (downward, upward, or horizontal)
3. The transmission regulations controlling when and to whom messages are sent
4. The degree of interdependence among the organization's various activities
5. The speed with which relevant changes occur in its external environment
6. The search mechanisms and procedures used by the organization to investigate its environment

High message volume usually results in overloading. Attempts are automatically made to reduce any overloading. Police supervisors can react to this situation in one or more of the following ways. First, they can slow down their handling of messages without changing the organization's network structure or transmission rules. This action will cause the police department to reduce its speed of reaction to events, and thereby lessen its output. Second, they can change the transmission rules so that their subordinates screen out more information before sending messages. This reaction also reduces the quantity of the department's output. Third, they can add more channels to the existing network to accommodate the same quantity of messages in the same time period. This reaction provides more opportunities for message distortion and is more expensive. Fourth, they can relate tasks within the organization so that those units with the highest message traffic are grouped together within the over-all communications system. This action reduces the volume of messages sent through higher levels in the network and facilitates the coordination of effort. Fifth, they can improve the quality of the messages in order to reduce the time needed for receiving, composing, and transmitting them. Further, besides bettering the content and format of the message, the supervisor can decide on more advantageous methods for handling them. In conclusion, a police organization compelled by its functions to maintain a high volume of messages must inevitably suffer certain disadvantages over a department functioning with a low message volume. This conclusion applies to all police organizations with high message volumes, whether their high volumes are caused by large size or proportionally high message traffic.

Types

Messages vary in content and form. There are reports, statements, inquiries, questions, accounts, comments, notes, records, recommendations, rejoinders, instructions, and so on.[13] Each message may have a different purpose in control procedures and lead to a different response. Further, messages can be transmitted either formally or informally by one of three media: (1) written communication, (2) oral communication in face-to-face meeting of two or more individuals, and (3) oral communication in telephone conversations.

Written messages. Samuel Eilon groups written messages into six categories (see Table 4): routine reports, memoranda, inquiries, queries, proposals, and decisions.

1. *Routine report.* A routine report is a message that supplies information as part of a standard operation. There are two ways in which a report can be created: (1) time triggered—a report called for at set time intervals (for

---

[13] The majority of this section is elicited from the article by Samuel Eilon, "Taxonomy of Communications," *Administrative Science Quarterly*, 13 (September 1968), 266–88.

example, a police supervisor is required to send weekly reports on the activities of his subordinates) and (2) event triggered—a report called for when certain tasks are completed (for example, a report is to be sent when a case is finished, or when certain training has been provided to his subordinates).

In each of these examples, the initiative to make a report does not lie with the supervisor; the circumstances under which a report is issued are clearly specified by organizational procedures; the supervisor is required only to determine that the circumstances conform to the specifications. Frequently, the contents of the report are prescribed, either in the format the report is to take (as in the case of a predesigned form) or in the information it is expected to furnish, although the supervisor can exercise limited initiative as to the content and coverage.

TABLE 4: TYPES OF MESSAGES IN A COMMUNICATIONS SYSTEM

Types	Subtypes
Routine report	1. Time-triggered report 2. Event-triggered report

Memorandum	Statement, following an inquiry or event triggered
	Comment
	Details on data collection and processing, as follows, may be included:
	    data from available records
	    ad hoc data collection
	    routine data processing
	    ad hoc processing

Inquiry	1. Inquiry covered by standing procedures 2. Inquiry about a novel situation
Query	1. Query about problems covered by regular procedures 2. Query for novel situations or to clarify ambiguities and inconsistencies
Proposal	1. Proposal about procedures or recurrent events 2. Proposal on an ad hoc issue
Decision	1. Decision on procedures affecting recurrent events 2. Decision on ad hoc issues
Meeting, the outcome of which may be any or several messages above	
Telephone discussion	

Source: Adapted from Samuel Eilon, "Taxonomy of Communications," Administrative Science Quarterly, 13 (September 1968), 278.

2. *Memorandum.* A memorandum also supplies information but not as a part of a routine procedure. A memorandum can be: (1) *a statement of fact,* submitted in response to an inquiry, to aid in evaluating a problem, or to prepare proposals for action; (2) *a statement that is event triggered,* released when circumstances have changed in an unprescribed manner, calling for some initiative by the transmitter in drawing attention of others to the change so

that a plan of action can be formulated; or (3) *a comment*, made in response to some other statement to add information or to give a different interpretation of data.

This explanation does not mean that all routine reports are devoid of initiative, whereas all memoranda are not. If a memorandum is made in response to a request, then the initiative for generating the memorandum lies with the requesting individual, not with the person who created the memorandum. And although event-triggered routine reports do not call for any initiative to create them, initiative may be exercised in composing their content, while event-triggered memoranda may not call for a great deal of initiative with respect to content. There is a distinction between a prescribed event, which triggers a report, and an event that generates a memorandum: the first is described by "*When* event such and such occurs, then, . . .," the second, by "*If* the following event occurs, then, ..." The first describes an event that is expected to occur; the second, an event that may occur. This is the basic difference between the circumstances that lead to reports and those that lead to memoranda.

The creation of a message containing information (report or memorandum) may include one or several of the following activities: (1) extracting data from records; (2) processing data, including computations and analysis, on a routine basis; (3) collecting data as needed; and (4) processing data as needed. In the case of reports, activities are generally confined to the first two activities, whereas memoranda may include all four.

3. *Inquiry*. An inquiry is a message requesting information to assist in evaluating a given problem, usually before making recommendations for action. The response to such a request would be a memorandum, which would include a statement with the necessary information and an analysis of the data. An inquiry usually involves information not included in reports, unless the reports are time triggered and the information is required before the next report is due. Relatedly, an inquiry may meet with a comment, which asks for clarification or points out the difficulties in providing certain information in the time specified. Such a comment is usually generated when the inquiry is ambiguous.

4. *Query*. A query is a message defining the characteristics of a problem and asking for instructions or proposals about courses of resolution. A query is often made by a subordinate concerning problems not fully covered by standing regulations, either because of the novelty of the situation or because of ambiguities or inconsistencies in procedures. Further, a query may also be generated by a supervisor seeking advice and direction from his peers or subordinates.

5. *Proposal*. A proposal describes a course of action the writer feels should be taken. It can be the result of several exchanges of queries, inquiries, reports, and memoranda. It may be generated by a subordinate, on his

own initiative or at the instigation of a supervisor; or it may be created by a supervisor wishing to test the reactions of his peers or subordinates. A response to a proposal may take the form of a comment or a counter proposal. The absence of a reaction to a proposal is usually viewed as tacit approval.

6. *Decision.* A decision states the action to be taken. This message may be of two kinds: (1) a decision that affects recurrent events—which provides direction, not only on how to handle the particular event that caused the discussion prior to the decision, but also similar events in the future (such a decision is made to avoid handling similar problems on an ad hoc basis in the future and to delegate the action for such problems to a lower level in the organization) and (2) a decision on an ad hoc problem—which does not formally affect future procedures.

A decision can take a number of forms. It may begin with a request to review the causes that necessitate making a decision to resolve certain problems; it may continue by outlining alternative courses of action and explaining the reasons for the rejection of some; it may then specify what has been decided and how the decision is to be implemented; next it may indicate what feedback is expected to keep the decision maker informed of progress in implementation.

Oral messages. Oral messages are of two varieties: meetings (face-to-face) and telephone conversations (ear-to-ear).

7. *Meetings.* A meeting involves a discussion among two or more people. Meetings have four purposes: (1) to provide a means for exchanges to take place quickly, (2) to provide a job environment in which members are stimulated to new ideas by the rapid exchange of views between individuals, (3) to reduce the amount of semantical difficulties through face-to-face interaction,[14] and (4) to get the members attending the meeting committed more strongly to given proposals or procedures than they would be otherwise.

There are two types of meetings: routine meetings, such as those of permanent committees, and ad hoc meetings, called to discuss particular issues. The difference between a routine and an ad hoc meeting is similar to that between a routine report and a memorandum. Like a routine report, a routine meeting can be either time or event triggered, while an ad hoc meeting may either be called in regard to a request to consider a particular problem or be event triggered. Further, a meeting can result in the issuance of any one or several of the messages listed earlier: a report, a memorandum, an inquiry for further information, a request for instructions, a proposal, or a decision. Significantly, a meeting can also fizzle out and end inconclusively.

---

[14] The importance of semantics for a supervisor is explained in Gerald H. Graham, "Improving Superior-Subordinate Relationships through General Semantics," *Public Personnel Review,* 30 (January 1969), 36–41.

8. *Telephone Conversations.* Many of the comments made on meetings are pertinent to telephone communications. The distinction made earlier between routine and ad hoc communications may be useful here. There are, however, some noteworthy differences between the two media: (1) a telephone conversation is generally confined to two participants and (2) it lacks certain unique characteristics of interaction which take place in a face-to-face exchange.

CYBERNETICS: COMMUNICATIONS AND CONTROL

Since the late 1940s a new technology has begun to take hold in our modern social organizations, one so new that its significance is only now beginning to be understood. While many aspects of this technology are yet uncertain, it seems clear that it will move into the supervisory scene rapidly, with definite and far-reaching impact on the police organization. In this and the next section we first explain and then speculate about this new technology. We refer to this new technology as *information technology.* Implied in this title is our major concern, communications. Information technology is composed of several related components. One includes the machinery and techniques for processing large amounts of information rapidly. A second component is in the offing though its applications have not yet emerged very clearly; it consists of the simulation of higher-order thinking. Both of these components are epitomized by computer systems. A third part centers around the application of statistical and mathematical methods to decision-making problems; it is represented by techniques like mathematical programming and by methodologies like operations research. A fourth part is the control and communication of information for the purpose of feeding it back into certain areas of the organization. These last two parts also frequently use computers. In this section we focus on the fourth component, feedback. The next section discusses the computer.

First we take time to justify our review of information technology. Broadly speaking, it is certain to have a significant impact on police supervision. Specifically, information technology either will or presently is (1) placing more responsibility for planning on the supervisor, (2) requiring the supervisor to be innovative in performing his role, (3) freeing the supervisor from red tape, and (4) asking the supervisor to put this new technology to work solving problems.

Feedback and cybernetics are often considered synonymous. Granted, they are more similar than not. The distinction between them, however, is meaningful. To explain, certain aspects of communication imply that organizations have a built-in capacity to correct their errors, enhancing their potential for rational behavior. Cybernetics (a word coined from the

Greek *kubernetes*, "steersman") focuses strongly upon the role of feedback in the learning process. Feedback is defined by Norbert Wiener as a method of controlling a system by reinserting into it the results of its past performance.[15] He further described cybernetics as "the entire field of control and communication theory, whether in the machine or in the animal."[16] Wiener explained his own rationale for linking communication and control into cybernetics thusly:

> When I control the actions of another person, I communicate a message to him, and although this message is in the imperative mood, the technique of communication does not differ from that of a message of fact. Furthermore, if my control is to be effective, I must take cognizance of any messages from him which may indicate that the order is understood and has been obeyed.[17]

Feedback is extended here to mean any information that influences an organization's or an individual's current action. Cybernetics denotes both the process by which feedback is furnished (communications) and a special purpose for feedback (control). The computer fits neatly into this picture because, by being hooked up with electronic data processing machines, the new communication-control systems are capable of responding more quickly and accurately to changes in a large number of variables. Hence, the most obvious impact of cybernetics has been in the acceleration of technological change through new machines that can replace routinized mental labor. As with other technological advances, these new "machine brains" change the technological environment of police organizations and police supervisors.

A word of caution, however; there are some who seek to use cybernetics in shaping human organizations—in other words, to change our organizations to operate like self-controlled machines. This concept envisions a self-steering network composed of receptors, transmitters, and feedback controls. Such thinking refutes what we have learned thus far about the purpose, will, consciousness, autonomy, integrity, and meaning of man and his organizations. Simply, its mechanistic doctrine looks like what we might call neo-scientific management. The benefits of cybernetics are many for our human organizations. We must keep in mind, though, that the information provided through cybernetics is for control and subsequent correction or reinforcement. More importantly, the control function over people is best exercised by people, not by machines. Machines can select, carry, and process information. *It remains for man to act upon it!*

---

[15] Wiener, *The Human Use of Human Beings*, p. 61.
[16] Norbert Wiener, *Cybernetics* (New York: John Wiley & Sons, Inc., 1948), p. 19.
[17] Wiener, *The Human Use of Human Beings*, p. 16.

ENTER THE COMPUTER

The electronic computer is basically a device for ingesting, judging, and otherwise processing or usefully modifying knowledge. Thus it enlarges brainpower as other man-made machines enlarge muscle power. Like man, the computer expresses knowledge in terms of symbols. Man's symbols are letters and numbers; the machine's symbols are electro-magnetic impulses that represent letters and numbers. There are two categories of computers: (1) the analog, which measures and compares quantities in one operation and has no memory and (2) the digital, which solves problems by counting precisely and sequentially and has a memory. The analog computer is about 50 years old, enjoys a big and growing use in simulation and process control, and is "hybridized" with digital computers in some applications. But it accounts for a very small percentage of the over-all computer market and its potentialities at present are not so universal as are those of the digital machine. The police field is now using, for many purposes, digital computers. First let us briefly discuss the machinery; next we will examine some of its uses.

Automatic Data Processing (ADP) denotes both electronic data processing (EDP) and electric accounting machines (EAM). EDP means the kind of automatic handling of information which is done by the million-operations-a-second electronic computer, as contrasted to the limited mechanical handling done by EAM. The five major phases of any information system are: *input*, acquisition of data and placement into the system; *storage*, to file data either temporarily or permanently; *processing*, to manipulate data according to specified rules; *output*, to present the results of the processing or the status of any data stored in the system; and *communications*, to transmit the data from one point in the system to another. A very important subphase, especially to those in local law enforcement, is that of *inquiry*. (See Figure 11 which depicts the relationship of the various phases to one another.) An integrated law enforcement information system is highly dependent on remote inquiry and receiving devices. An inquiry involves both the input and output functions at a single location.

A recent survey into police ADP systems provides us with an appreciation of computer usage by police organizations.[18] Note that the findings are limited to local police departments and, therefore, do not supply data on county, state, or federal policing agencies. In 1968 all municipal police agencies servicing cities of populations over 25,000 were mailed a questionnaire regarding both present and future automated police data processing systems, and existing or anticipated applications. Out of the 592 city

---

[18] Paul M. Whisenand and John D. Hodges, Jr., "Automated Municipal Police Information Systems," *Datamation*, 15 (May 1969), 91–96.

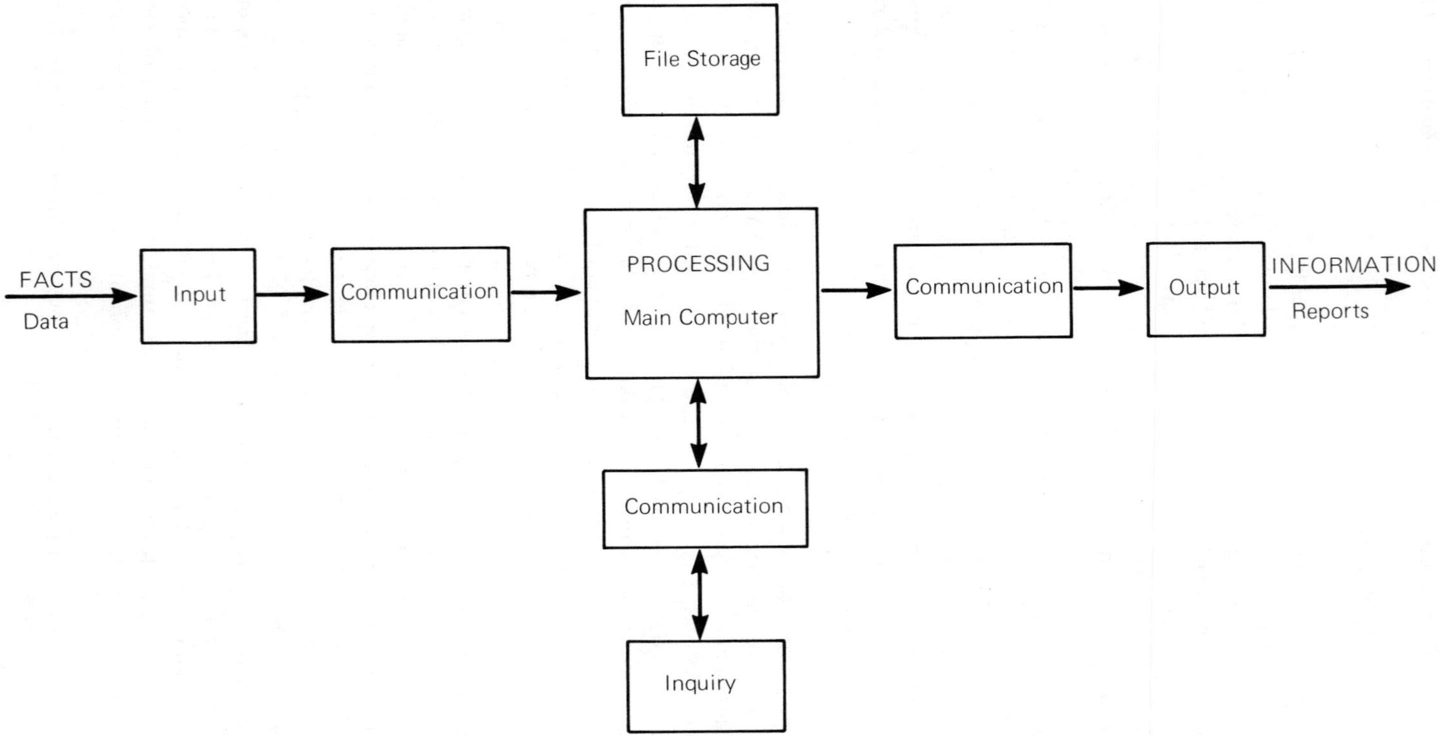

Source: *Hearle and Mason, A Data Processing System for State and Local Governments, p. 4.*

FIG. 11. A DATA PROCESSING SYSTEM

police departments sent questionnaires, 251, or 42 per cent, responded with a complete set of answers. To determine the effects of city size on the responses, the population was broken down into five subpopulations as follows:

City Size (Population)	Total Number of Cities	Number of Cities that Responded
500,000 or over	27	18
250,000–500,000	27	15
100,000–250,000	96	48
50,000–100,000	153	66
25,000– 50,000	289	104
Total:	592	251

The response to the questionnaire was directly related to city size (67 per cent of the cities with populations over 500,000 responded, while only 36 per cent of cities with populations under 50,000 responded), as was the use of ADP. Of the police departments responding, 110, or 44 per cent, indicated that they were using some form of automatic data processing. The proportion of cities using ADP in the five categories ranged from 100 per cent of the cities of 500,000 population or more to only 18 per cent of the cities with populations below 50,000. The police departments were also asked if they had plans to implement a data processing system in the next three years; an additional 49, or 19 per cent, indicated that they had plans firm enough to allow them to indicate a year for installation.

The basic results of the survey as related to ADP use are summarized as follows:

1. Of the police departments responding (251 of 592, 42 per cent), a group of 110, or 44 per cent, indicated that they were using automatic data processing.
2. By 1971, this group should increase to 159, or 63 per cent, of the departments responding.
3. A vast majority of the ADP equipment being used are computer systems (84 per cent) as compared to electronic accounting machines (16 per cent).
4. The future trend is definitely in favor of computer systems, although the proportion of computers to EAM will remain about the same.
5. The use of ADP is directly related to city size, with larger cities more likely to use ADP than smaller ones, as would be expected.
6. There seems to be no definite trend at this time that establishes a pattern of control, operation, or location of ADP equipment. Some 50 per cent of the departments reported that they operate their own equipment, and the sentiment in law enforcement is absolutely in favor of police control of their own systems.

Finally, Tables 5 and 6 show current and projected police ADP applications. The computer is performing an additional service to local law enforcement

TABLE 5: CURRENT ADP APPLICATIONS BY POLICE DEPARTMENTS

Rank	Current ADP Applications	Number of Departments*	Per Cent of Departments
I	Traffic accidents	56	51
II	Parking citations	55	50
III	Traffic citations	54	49
IV	Arrested persons	45	41
V	Criminal offenses	44	40
VI	Personnel records	43	39
VII	Financial–budget	40	37
VIII	Police activities	39	36
IX	Patrol distribution	33	30
X	Juvenile activity	33	30
XI	Stolen property	31	28
XII	On-line inquiries	30	27
XIII	Vehicle registration	29	26
XIV	Vehicle maintenance and costs	29	26
XV	Warrant file	28	25
XVI	Offense location	25	23
XVII	Inventory control	21	19
XVIII	Message switching	4	4

*N = 110.

Source: Paul M. Whisenand and John D. Hodges, Jr., "Automated Municipal Police Information Systems," Datamation, 15 (May 1969), 94.

TABLE 6: PROJECTED ADP APPLICATIONS BY POLICE DEPARTMENTS

Rank	Projected ADP Applications	Number of Departments*	Per Cent of Departments
I	Arrested persons	106	96
II	Traffic accidents	103	94
III	Criminal offenses	102	93
IV	Personnel records	100	91
V	Traffic citations	99	90
VI	Warrant file	96	88
VII	Police activities	95	86
VIII	Stolen property	93	85
IX	Parking citations	92	84
X	Patrol distribution	88	80
XI	Financial–budget	88	80
XII	Juvenile activity	86	78
XIII	On-line inquiries	80	77
XIV	Offense location	77	70
XV	Vehicle maintenance and costs	75	68
XVI	Inventory control	74	67
XVII	Vehicle registration	64	58
XVIII	Message switching	42	38

*N = 110.

Source: Paul M. Whisenand and John D. Hodges, Jr., "Automated Municipal Police Information Systems," Datamation, 15 (May 1969), 94. Reprinted with permission of Datamation magazine : copyright 1969 by F. D. Thompson Publications, Inc., 35 Macon Street, Greenwich, Conn. 06830.

—that of linking the numerous individual police ADP systems into a unified, or total, network. The local ADP system is fast becoming a building block for a nationwide computer-based police information system. California's Law Enforcement Telecommunications Systems (CLETS) is one example of a significant effort to put together a total statewide ADP system. Further, it is also an example of highly important federal-state linkage. Consequently, let us look at CLETS a little closer. Essentially, CLETS is a soon to be operational $5 million computer system to link more than 450 California law enforcement agencies to computer crime files in Sacramento and Washington, D. C. It enables any urban or rural law enforcement agency to transmit messages to any other agency in the state and to receive instant information on wanted persons, stolen or lost property, and firearms. Further, any agency will be able to broadcast a message to all other agencies within the state or to any combination of agencies. CLETS results from two and a half years of study by a committee composed of representatives of the California Peace Officers Association, the California Sheriffs Association, the League of California Cities, the County Supervisors Association, and officials of various state agencies. Of invaluable importance is the fact that the state's law enforcement agencies will be linked to computers at the California Department of Justice, the California Department of Motor Vehicles, the California Highway Patrol, and the Federal Bureau of Investigation's National Crime Information Center in Washington, D. C. CLETS will be a cooperative effort of the California Department of Justice and local agencies. Computers, switching center personnel, and the backbone circuitry with one terminal point per county are being provided by the state. Each local agency will provide the circuitry and equipment to link itself to its county terminal point. When CLETS is operating, a police officer can, in a few seconds, ask and receive information from a statewide data base that contains facts on persons, vehicles, property, and firearms.

Certainly the computer looms large in the future, if not the present, of a police supervisor. The benefits to the supervisor were listed earlier in the preceding section. Basically, the computer will upgrade the status and responsibilities of the supervisor's role in the police organization and permit him more time for personal interaction. In other words, the computer will assist the supervisor in accomplishing one of his primary duties, organizational control. Simultaneously, it will free him for performing another primary duty, training. For those police supervisors who have remained on the sideline, while their co-workers have increased their physical and intellectual accessibility to the computer,[19] it seems inevitable that they will become involved in the computer progress and problems of their department.

---

[19] An excellent discussion of the importance and relationship between intellectual and physical accessibility to computers can be found in Herbert H. Issacs, "Computer Systems Technology: Progress, Projections, Problems," *Public Administration Review*, 28 (November-December, 1968), 488–94.

BASICS OF EFFECTIVE COMMUNICATIONS

The importance of maintaining effective communications was never more vital than it is today. Every aspect of human endeavor within a police organization depends in some way on communication. Although it is a vital part of every police supervisor's job, communication remains a highly personal art. Human beings have been communicating with each other by gestures and signs since the origin of the species, by spoken words for perhaps half a million years, and by some form of writing for more than 4,000 years. We should be experts at it by now! The major problem today is not that we are not experts at communication, but that the demands now being placed on human communication threaten to exceed its capacity. Since communications is a human activity, even though machines may be used to assist man in interacting, we emphasize a fundamental principle: The effectiveness of communication tends to be directly proportional to the degree to which both the sender and the receiver regard and treat each other as "human," in the sociocultural context of the event.[20] The following techniques or basics for effective communication should be evaluated and implemented with this principle in mind.

A tremendous number of techniques have been developed whereby supervisors may remove or bypass the blockage at each point in the communication process. The major techniques may be broadly classified in terms of the blockage they remedy. There are five areas where blockage might occur in a communication system: (1) senders—those who initiate a message, (2) message—the vehicle for transmitting information, (3) symbol—the content and format of the information, (4) channel—the means for interchanging messages, and (5) receivers—those who receive a message. The major techniques for overcoming the blockages are as follows:[21]

Sender blockage	Special positions or units whose function is to disseminate information inside or outside the organizations
	Formal and informal reporting systems
Message blockage	Standards for the preparation of reports
	Summarization of long or complex messages
Symbol blockage	Improved style
	Training in use of special terms
	Visual aids

---

[20] Edward E. Marcus, "The Basis of Effective Human Communication," *Public Personnel Review*, 28 (April 1967), 111.

[21] *Ibid.*

Channel blockage	Liaison officers and special intermediaries
	Routing, screening, and clearance procedures
	Reeducation of hierarchic levels and number of intermediaries
	Exploitation of informal channels and polyarchic relations
Receiver blockage	More use of face-to-face communication
	Indoctrination in common frame of reference

The use of such techniques is, by itself, no guarantee of better communication. Any one of them, in helping to cope with one source of blockage, may create still another kind. If many of them together resulted in much more communication, the result could be a serious increase in the information overload. The appropriate use of well-known techniques and the invention of new ones are rooted in the broader reasoning of police supervisors who have acquired an interest in the communication process and the ability to communicate. The supervisor with an interest in communication is one who, instead of taking communication for granted, is always aware of the possibility of blockage at any point. Perhaps of greatest importance is that the police supervisors understand the communication system in their organization. They become familiar with the strengths and weaknesses of both formal and informal communication channels in the organization's structure. Further, they learn through their analysis of the communication process about personal judgments and values, the meanings which individuals attach to certain facts, and self-enforcing group attitudes. Even poor supervisors often develop certain obvious skills of oral or written presentation. The more successful supervisors, however, develop the skills of listening also, thereby facilitating their entry into two-way communication interchanges. Both types of skill reach the level of art only when the supervisor as sender-receiver is able to "regard and treat each other as 'human' in the sociocultural context of the event."

SUMMARY

Communications is the media for organizational control. Since one of the primary role responsibilities of a police supervisor is to control subordinates, he depends a great deal on the existing communication in the police organization. Without an effective way of transmitting information, the police supervisor becomes organizationally impotent. Specifically, a police supervisor communicates so that (1) adequate information can be provided to his subordinates for their accomplishment of assigned tasks, (2) perceptions and expectations can be clarified, (3) coordination of man and materials can be achieved, (4) problem solving and conflict resolution can occur, and (5) the means for accomplishing a task are better understood.

The available channels for transmitting information are either formal or informal. The former basically conforms to the official structure of the organization. The latter can be subdivided into subformal, personal task directed, and personal nontask directed. Further, these channels are both vertical and horizontal. The vertical channels transmit information both downward (usually formal) and upward (formal and informal). The horizontal channels carry information between peer groups (usually personal task directed and personal nontask directed).

The volume and types of messages circulated within the communication channels differ for a variety of reasons. If the volume of messages becomes too high, the police organization suffers what is known as "information overload." The supervisor can play a most useful role in keeping the volume at an acceptable level.

Cybernetics is logically included at this time because of its status as one form of our modern information technology. Essentially, cybernetics provides (usually by a mechanical communication device) organizational feedback for the purpose of control. Correspondingly, we find the electronic computer as the next subject. Not only is the computer well qualified to store and process information in a very rapid fashion, but it can also act as a vehicle for transmitting highly useful operational information. Its impact on police organizations will continue to grow at an ever increasing rate. The police supervisor is just now getting involved with its potential. In closing, we see that the effectiveness of organizational communications tends to be directly proportional to the degree to which both the sender and the receiver regard and treat each other as "human" in the sociocultural context of the interaction.

PROBLEMS

1. What kinds of information are transmitted within a personal task-directed communication channel? What kinds are transmitted within a personal nontask-directed communication channel? Why do both of these channels exist?

2. Justify the importance of lateral, or horizontal, communication channels in a police organization.

3. As a police supervisor, what steps would you take to insure yourself, as well as others in the police organization, against a situation involving information overload?

4. What are some possible uses a police supervisor might make of a computer-based information system? How can it help him better perform his role?
5. Review the section on effective communications. Either modify the given list or create a list of your own techniques for more effective communications.

7

Organizational
Control:
the Road to Effectiveness

The purpose of organizational control is twofold: first, to insure that rules are obeyed and orders followed and, second, to bring about coordination of effort. If a police organization could select people who would automatically conform and cooperate, there would be no requirement for organizational control. This has never been the case however. The reasons for this are discussed in the coming pages. At this point it is emphasized that the twofold purpose of control is underpinned by its very reason for existence: to promote organizational effectiveness. In other words, organizational effectiveness is based upon conformance to rules and cooperative behavior.

A knowledge of interpersonal influence is antecedent to any understanding of control (the reader may find it helpful to review certain sections of Chapter 2). Influence has been defined as an interpersonal transaction in which one person acts in such a way as to affect the behavior or psychological state of another in some intended fashion. A policeman steps into the street and raises his hand; a driver steps on the brake and brings his car to a halt. We infer, in the absence of other evidence, that the policeman *positively*, or successfully, influenced the driver and that he intended to do so. However, suppose the policeman raised his hand, and the driver speeded up. This is influence of a kind; apparently the act of the policeman caused the behavior of the motorist. However, the driver's response was quite opposite to what the policeman intended. We refer to this influence as having a negative effect. Further, not only may the effect be exactly as intended or exactly opposite to that intended, it may be nothing at all. If the policeman raised his hand to stop the driver, and the driver failed to see it and continued as before, the influence of the policeman would have been zero. There was an attempt to influence, but no reception of it, and therefore no influence was exerted.

When one exerts influence and is successful in affecting another's behavior or psychological state as he intended, we can then say that he controlled the other person or groups of persons. This usage seems very close to the traditional meaning of control, which is getting people to do what we ask. Lack of control does not imply a lack of attempt to influence; it does not even imply lack of influence. It does imply that other forces in the situation are stronger than the agent's influence, and that the response he desires is not attained. Control can be defined, therefore, as *"that process in which a person (or group of persons or organization of persons) determines, i.e., intentionally affects, what another person, (or group, or organization) will do."*[1] (Italics added.)

CONTROL: PROCESSES AND PROBLEMS

Nowhere is the tension between the organization's needs (effectiveness) and the member's needs more apparent than in the area of organizational control. It should be recognized, however, that at times the two sets of needs support each other. For example, an increase in the budget of a police organization might allow it to increase the salaries it pays, or an increase in the prestige of a police department might increase the prestige of the police officers who work there. To the degree that the two sets of needs are in agreement little control is necessary. The members tend to do what is best for the police organization to satisfy their own needs, and the organization in seeking to meet its needs will meet theirs. But such meshing of needs is never complete. A certain degree of dissatisfaction, even disaffection, is usually present in a formal organization. Consequently, deliberate efforts are made by the organization to reward those who conform to its rules and to penalize those who do not. Plainly, the internal effectiveness of a police organization is primarily dependent on its power to control its members. Etzioni explains:

> All social units control their members, but the problem of control in organizations is especially acute. Organizations as *social units* that serve specific purposes are *artificial social units*. They are planned, deliberately structured; they constantly and self-consciously review their performances and restructure themselves accordingly. In this sense they are unlike natural social units, such as the family, ethnic groups, or community. *The artificial quality of organizations, their high concern with performance, their tendency to be far more complex than natural units, all make informal control inadequate and reliance on identification with the job impossible.* Most organizations most of the time cannot rely on most of their participants to internalize their obligations, to carry out their assignments voluntarily, without additional incentives. Hence, organizations require formally structured distribution of rewards and sanctions to support compliance with their norms, regulations, and orders.[2]

---

[1] Arnold S. Tannenbaum, "Control in Organizations: Individual Adjustment and Organizational Performance," *Administrative Science Quarterly*, 2 (September 1962), 236–57.

[2] Amitai Etzioni, *Modern Organizations* (Englewood Cliffs, N.J.: Prentice-Hall, Inc., 1964), p. 59.

In order to maintain control the police organization must allocate its rewards and sanctions according to performance—those whose performance conforms with organizational standards are rewarded and those whose performance does not are penalized. First, we look at the control processes; next at the problems of establishing and sustaining organizational control.

Control Processes

Control processes in organizations are dominated by the need for a group of administrators or supervisors to appraise and successfully influence the behavior of their subordinates. The basic processes in the formal control function are described shortly. As can be seen, our description of the control function emphasizes the central location and importance of organizational feedback. To begin:

> First, a superior issues a set of orders.
> Second, he permits his subordinates time to act on each order.
> Third, he selects certain orders to appraise his subordinates' performance—feedback.
> Fourth, he seeks to discover what has been done as a result of the orders he is appraising—feedback.
> Fifth, he compares the effects of his order with his original intentions—evaluation.
> Sixth, he decides if these results are effective enough to require no more attention, or partially effective and capable of being improved by further orders—decision.
> Seventh, he issues further orders.

Control Problems

If a superior's foresight were perfect, if all members of the police department were flawless organization men, and if the environment of the police organization were static, the problems of police administrators and supervisors might be at an end once the structure had been created and the functions explained. The organization could be given an initial push and would operate thereafter without intervention. There would be no continuing need for control and coordination; the parts and their functions would be coordinated in the initial statement of functions and relationships. But, since organizations are imperfect (they are neither totally effective nor do they completely meet the needs of their members), control is necessary. The greater the imperfection, the greater the requirement for organizational controls. To put it another way, the most fundamental problem for the achievement and maintenance of control is that we find imperfect people, using imperfect techniques, within an imperfect structure to bring about organizational effectiveness and, simultaneously, make the members happy. Let us now analyze this over-all problem in more detail. Our analysis shows that most control problems arise from the intrinsic difficulties of running police organizations, rather than from any specific incompetence on the part of individual police personnel.

Nontask-oriented behavior: hang-ups and payoffs. Organizational behavior that is not organizationally useful can be one indication of an absence of organizational control. But what is meant by "useful"? All of us are quick to agree that wasteful (nontask-directed) behavior occurs in police organizations (and, for that matter, in all social organizations). What we fail to comprehend, however, is that a certain amount of wasteful behavior is beneficial to the organization and its members. A case in point is individual need fulfillment which, in turn, positively affects morale and job satisfaction. The police organization has a responsibility for making their work as pleasant as possible. Retention, motivation, and work output hinge on the ability of a police agency to provide a satisfying job environment. Hence, behavior producing such satisfactions is not wasted at all!

The major challenge to police management and supervision is in deciding how much wasted behavior should and can be eliminated. This challenge is not a simple one because the decision on what behavior is wasteful yet useful demands judgment and opinion rather than logic or empirical measurement. In essence, those in supervisory positions are confronted with creating an acceptable balance between task-directed and nontask-directed behavior. The police supervisor must first decide, after careful examination, how well the existing job environment serves both man and organization. Next, he must experiment with the limits and types of wasteful behavior to see what most favorably affects job satisfaction and least detracts from the achievement of the organizational goals. Truly, he becomes the "man-in-the-middle." The police supervisor thus finds it constantly necessary to resist the easy way out, which would be to adopt a supervisory style that supports, on the one side, total effectiveness or, on the other side, total satisfaction of human needs. We live in the real world; consequently, man is not going to be completely happy in his work, nor is the organization going to completely eliminate wasteful activities on the part of its members.

Uncertainty: the delegation of authority. As orders and the authority necessary to accomplish them move downward in the organization, they are made more specific and therefore expanded. Changing general policy into detailed programs of action allows considerable individual interpretation. Hence, delegation breeds uncertainty, and uncertainty weakens organizational control.

Uncertainty is accelerated when self-interest and many levels of authority are involved. Because of their self-interest, individual members of the organization have varying goals, and each uses his discretion in translating orders from above into commands going downward. The purposes the superior had in mind are not the exact ones his subordinate's orders convey to people farther down the hierarchy. Since some loss of control usually occurs whenever orders pass down through the levels of the hierarchy, such a loss tends to become cumulative when many levels are involved. There are very few orders so precise and certain that they cannot be distorted by a factor of 10 per cent; consequently, if a police organization has four levels in its structure, the lowest level receives its instructions embodying only 81 per cent of what the top level really desired.[3] Therefore, in any large, multilevel police organization a very significant degree of all the activity being carried out is completely unrelated to the organization's formal goals, or even to the directives of its topmost administrators. Is there any wonder why police administrators and supervisors experience the feeling of uncertainty when they delegate authority!

TYPES OF CONTROL

Amitai Etzioni informs us that there are basically three kinds of control: physical, material, and symbolic.[4] The use of a gun or club, for example, is physical since it affects the body; the threat to use physical control is viewed as physical because the influence on the person is similar, though not in intensity, to the actual use. Material rewards consist of goods, services, and money received. Pure symbols include *individual* symbols, those of prestige and esteem, and *social* symbols, those of love and acceptance. Symbolic individual control can be exercised by those in higher ranks to influence those in lower ranks directly, as when a football coach gives a pep talk to his team. Symbolic social control can be indirect, as when a superior appeals to the peer group of a subordinate to control him.

Organizations can be distinguished from one another by the predominant type of control used. It can be either physical (prison), material (business), symbolic (professional associations), or a mixture of the three (for example, material-symbolic, a labor union). Each type of control results in a different kind of involvement on the part of the organizational members. The three types of possible involvement are (1) alienative—the person is not psychologically involved but is coerced to remain as a member, (2) calculative— the person is involved to the extent of doing a fair day's work for a fair day's pay, and (3) moral—the person values the purpose of the organization and his job within it, and performs his job primarily because he values it. Table 7 shows the nine logical organizational relationships which could

---

[3] This formula is suggested by Anthony Downs. Interestingly, if an organization has seven levels, only 53 per cent of an order received at the lowest level arrives undistorted. *Inside Bureaucracy* (Boston, Mass.: Little, Brown, and Company, 1967), p. 135.

[4] Etzioni, *Modern Organizations*.

TABLE 7

	Physical	Material	Symbolic
Alienative	*		
Calculative		*	
Moral			*

Source: Adapted from Amitai Etzioni, Modern Organizations (*Englewood Cliffs, N.J.: Prentice-Hall, Inc., 1964*), pp. 58–67.

result from this typology. The type of personal involvement possible depends to a large extent on the kind of control used by the organization. Hence, organizations tend to collect in groups on the table, primarily along the diagonal from upper left to lower right. Thus, if we look again at the various controls an organization might use, we further see that organizations listed under physical control tend to have alienated members who would rather not belong but are forced to stay; organizations listed as material tend to have calculative members who expect primarily monetary rewards for their efforts but who do not feel they have to enjoy their work or like their employer; organizations listed as symbolic tend to have members who belong because they value the goals of the organization and like their organizational roles, and therefore consider it morally correct to belong. To summarize, the use of symbolic control tends to convince people, that of material control tends to promote their self-interests in conforming, and the use of physical control tends to compel them to comply.

The previous typology represents pure types of organizations which seldom, if ever, exist. Most organizations are a complex mixture of the types. The use of pure types is helpful, however, in giving us perspective. Usually an organization can be classified according to the predominant pattern of control; for example, a prison uses primarily physical controls. But it must be recognized that the guards and administrators in a prison are controlled by material-symbolic means. Therefore, we see that the controls organizations use differ mainly by the rank of the members controlled. In general, most organizations use less alienating means to control their higher rather than their lower ranks.

Comparing the controls applied to the lower levels of different organizations is the best way to classify organizations as using a certain type of control. In doing so, however, we must keep in mind that most organizations most of the time use more than one control. As police organizations have become more complex and more dependent on high-quality performance from police administrators, supervisors, and line personnel, a trend has been established toward the use of more material-symbolic controls. Consequently, police departments are seeking to establish new kinds of relationships with their members. These new relationships to some degree abandon material conceptions in favor of symbolic ones. Police personnel are increasingly expected to like their work, to be personally committed to organizational goals, and to be innovative in the attainment of these goals; in exchange, they are given more influence in the decision-making process (for example, subordinates who regularly meet with their commanders to plan the work of the department). The position of the police supervisor offers tremendous opportunity for either supporting or hindering this trend.

AMOUNT OF CONTROL

There are very broad differences in the amount of control needed in one organization as compared with another because of differences in recruitment and socialization of personnel. Recruitment (selection) is based on the qualities of police officers as they enter the police organization; organizational socialization subsequently adapts these qualities to make them functional for the satisfactory performance of assigned tasks. Socialization includes much more than mere training. It encompasses training and all other learning experiences acquired through particularization in the organization. Training is but a small, however important, part of the over-all socialization process for a police officer.

Control is most often viewed in terms of the position or person exercising it. Thus, there are numerous analyses of the distribution of control, the amount of control exercised by each level or person in the organization. The sum of levels of control at all hierarchical levels may be considered the total amount of control in an organization.[5] The total amount of control exercised in an organization is a phenomenon frequently neglected by behavioral scientists. In fact, most purport that once organizational control is redistributed and increased at the lower levels it is automatically decreased at the top. Furthermore, control removed from an upper level may result in a reduction of total control in the organization. For example, if police chiefs, for some reason, issue fewer directives, it cannot be assumed that the power of field personnel will necessarily be increased; it is more likely that fewer organizational objectives will be accomplished. Reducing the amount of total control beyond a certain level may endanger the coordination and effective functioning of the over-all police organization.[6]

In an analysis of membership participation in four labor unions it was reported that the membership as a whole exercised more influence than their executives, that is, the control curves tended to be positively sloped.[7]

---

[5] Philip M. Marcus and Dora Cafagna, "Control in Modern Organizations," *Public Administration Review*, 25 (June 1965), 122.

[6] *Ibid.*

[7] Arnold S. Tannenbaum and Robert L. Kahn, *Participation in Union Locals* (New York: Row & Peterson, Inc., 1958).

But when officers of the two most effective unions were compared with those of the other two, the membership indicated that the more effective officers used more control. Members also reported that they exerted greater control in the effective unions than in the ineffective ones, thus affirming the assumption that effectiveness is related to the total amount of control exercised in an organization. To put it another way, the more effective organizations had greater control given to both executives and workers alike.

In conclusion, it can be stated that most respondents of the organizations studied wanted more control, not only for themselves but also for others within the organization. Ironically, the way to acquire greater total control is to reduce certain forms of overt organizational control. The trade-off works thusly. Through proper selection and socialization of police personnel we can vastly increase the total amount of control in a police department because we reduce the need for guarding against deviant behavior. Relevantly, various studies indicate that a small increase in the selectivity of an organization often results in a disproportionately large decrease in the investments required for formal control. One reason is that a high percentage of deviant acts are committed by a small percentage of the members; hence, if these members are screened out or better trained, the need for formal control declines sharply. So, while the need for formal control is decreased, the amount of real control has improved because the individual experiences less external or formal restraint and greater internal restraint on his behavior. The employee with "built-in" controls is much preferred and is certainly more effective than any set of organizational "do's and don'ts." Hence, what we are proposing or arguing for in this text is greater total control through the individual internalization (selection and socialization) of controls with a concomitant reduction in formal organization controls. Both the individual, regardless of his position, and the organization stand to benefit immeasurably. Since selection and socialization are the crux of increased organizational control, and since the police department has ample opportunity to implement both processes, it is worthwhile to discuss them further.

Selection and Socialization

The ineffectiveness with which a police organization selects its personnel is proportional to the amount of effort needed to maintain the level of control considered necessary. The degree of selection varies among the three types of organizational control. Physical organizations (prisons) are the least selective, accepting virtually everyone sent by such agencies as the courts and the police. Typical material organizations are highly selective. They often use formal mechanisms—examinations, psychological tests, probation periods—to improve the selection of their members. Normally, the higher the rank of the person, the more carefully he is selected and the less he is formally controlled once selected. Why? Simply because the higher the position, the higher the probabilities that the individual has internalized the controls required for effective behavior. Finally, symbolic organizations vary in their degree of selectivity. Some are extremely selective while others are very unselective. In general, the more selective organizations are more effective and instill a deeper commitment in their participants than do organizations of lower selectivity.

In regard to socialization, Simon asserts that the more effective the socialization, the less the need for control.[8] Relatedly, socialization is itself affected by the means of control used, since some kinds of control more than others create a relationship between higher and lower ranks that is supportive to effective socialization. The socialization efforts of physical organizations are usually poor. Organizations which rely heavily on symbolic control are the most successful in terms of their socialization achievements. Material organizations tend to delegate socialization to other organizations, such as vocational schools and universities, and prefer careful selection of presocialized persons to socialization by the organization. Please note that socialization and selection may be partially substituted for each other. For example, the same level of control can be maintained by high selectivity and a low level of organizational socialization or by low selectivity and a high level of organizational socialization. Consequently, the amount of control needed is lower when selectivity and socialization are both high. This latter possibility is, by far, the ideal situation for a local police department.

Police organizations are usually well suited to be highly selective and to foster socialization. In more cases than not, the hang-up has been, however, that better use is not made of the existing selection process. Moreover, once selected, the individual is not receiving what might be termed appropriate socialization. In other words, the mechanisms for improved control are present and in use by many police departments. The next step is to perfect them. Significantly, the police supervisor has little to do with the initial selection. But, he can and should have a great deal to do with the selection process. After all, the police supervisor is in the best position to determine if the person selected should be retained (the probation period is considered an important phase of selection). Further, the police supervisor pretty well determines whether the organization should promote the individual to higher levels. Most important is the realization that the police supervisor provides a major portion of an officer's socialization (the subject of Part Three). Therefore, we have arrived at a point where it can be seen that the police supervisor is capable of exerting both formal (external to the person being controlled) and informal (internal to the person being controlled) controls. To date, the former has received undue emphasis. Our mission

---

[8] Herbert A. Simon, *Administrative Behavior*, 2nd ed. (New York: Macmillan, 1957).

here is to redress the balance. Ideally, there should be no need for the exercising of formal controls. In practice, we find a real need for them. More significantly, in practice we are beginning to find a real need for both (formal and informal) of them.

Span of Control

Attacking the principle of the span of control seems appropriate at this time. Certainly this author is not the first to do so. Simon attacks this principle on the ground that one can also state an equally plausible contradictory proverb. In essence, he takes exception to two of our pioneers. According to Urwick, "No supervisor can supervise directly the work of more than five, or at the most, six subordinates whose work interlocks."[9] Further, Gulick identifies various factors that may influence the optimum span, particularly the capacity of an individual executive, the nature of the work performed, the stability of an organization, and geographical proximity to those supervised. He is less certain about the maximum number of subordinates, but no less confident concerning the general validity of the principle.[10] Simon relates that a narrowing of the span of control, desirable from one point of view, usually has the undesirable effect of hampering communication by increasing the number of organizational levels. This principle does not, he laments, cast light on how to reconcile these conflicting considerations.[11] What does all this mean to a police supervisor? First, and foremost, there is no such thing as an "ideal" span of control. The span of control is determined by the training of the subordinates, the objectives of the group, the situation in which they find themselves, and the communication networks available to them. Haire states the "idea of the span of control . . . is often discussed as if there were some absolute answer to the question—How many subordinates can a superior manage?—as if the span were a kind of inflexible constant in social organizations."[12] It is not inflexible because it depends on the organization and group that uses it. Second, the broader the span of control, the greater the chances for personal growth and job enlargement. Hence, the job becomes more rewarding and satisfying to the police officer. The supervisor is in a position to affect the size of the span of control. If he

---

[9] Lyndall Urwick, *The Elements of Administration* (New York: Harper & Row, Publishers, 1943), pp. 52–53.

[10] Luther Gulick, "Notes on the Theory of Organization," in *Papers on the Science of Administration*, eds. Luther Gulick and Lyndall Urwick (New York: Institute of Public Administration, 1937), pp. 7–9.

[11] Simon, *Administrative Behavior*, pp. 26–28.

[12] Mason Haire, "Biological Models and Empirical Histories of the Growth of Organizations," in *Modern Organization Theory*, ed. Mason Haire (New York: John Wiley & Sons, Inc., 1959), p. 294.

provides his subordinates with proper training, an appreciation of the group's objectives, a supportive interpersonal relationship, and an effective communications system, the probabilities for a larger span of control are greatly enhanced. Close supervision is necessary, however, when (1) subordinates are much less qualified to do their jobs than their superiors and (2) there is a marked difference between the goals of the subordinates and those of their superiors. It presently appears that the trend toward professionalization in local law enforcement will force broader spans of control within our police organizations.

ORGANIZATIONAL CONTROL AND ITS RELATIONSHIP TO EFFECTIVENESS

Police organizations can function at a high level of effectiveness for various reasons. Technically, they can possess the finest machinery and the most modern automated equipment. Financially, they can be provided with a proportionately high level of income. Organizationally, they can work out an unusually sound means for accomplishing their tasks. In this section we are concerned with another reason for the level of organizational functioning: the controlling of people within the organization.

Though information about organizational control has been growing as a result of behavioral research, there has been little systematic application of this knowledge to organizational functioning. In brief, the approach taken in exercising organizational control has been either oversimplified or too general. Supervisors have either assumed that the organization was like a single individual or that there was a single problem of control for the entire organization with a single answer. The use of rewards in blanket fashion for all organizational members is an instance of oversimplification; the concept of a universal morale an example of generalization.

The distribution, amount, and type of control significantly affect individual behavior and adjustment to organizational life. Several studies have shown that total control, the distribution of control, and the type of control are related to organizational effectiveness.[13] More significantly, evidence suggests that the type of control exercised is more crucial in terms of increasing effectiveness than the total amount or distribution of control.

Since the type of organizational control used in a police department so strongly influences its level of effectiveness, we concentrate on the various types that might be employed. First, however, we must determine what various behaviors a police agency needs to be effective. Once we answer this question, we are in a position to study the types of organizational control

---

[13] Marcus and Cafagna, "Control in Modern Organizations," 126.

available for producing the various kinds of needed behavior. In essence, we will see that a given type of control may be very effective in bringing about one necessary behavior and completely ineffective in producing another. Finally, we will identify the conditions for applying a particular type of control in a police organization. Hence, our forthcoming analysis depicts (1) the behavior required for organizational effectiveness, (2) the control patterns that can be used to bring about the required behavior, (3) the conditions needed for implementing certain control patterns, and (4) the use of discipline.

Required Behavior

First of all, sufficient personnel must be recruited and retained within the police department to perform its essential functions. The desired rate of recruitment is determined by the amount of retirement and defection. High turnover and absenteeism are costly to a police department and hence can be considered as yardsticks of organizational effectiveness. Second, there must be dependable behavior. The great range of possible human behavior must be reduced to a limited number of relevant patterns. In other words, the assigned tasks must be carried out in ways that meet some minimum standard of quantity and quality. A third (and most frequently neglected) set of behavioral requirements includes those actions not specified by the position but which assist in the accomplishment of organizational goals. The agency's need for actions of an innovative and spontaneous nature is inevitable. No police planning can foresee all contingencies within its own operations. The capability of police personnel for innovation and spontaneous cooperation are thus vital to organizational effectiveness. A police organization which depends solely upon its blueprints of prescribed behavior is a very fragile department.

Types of Control Patterns

The reader will recall the three basic types of control: physical, material, and symbolic. The latter two are pertinent to a police organization. Each type of control includes a series of control patterns: material control subsumes legal compliance and tangible rewards, while symbolic control involves social rewards, self-expression, and internalized values. Let us consider each in more detail.[14]

Material patterns of control. The first pattern in this category, that of legal compliance, does not include a monetary influence. Legal compliance is a

---

[14] The majority of this section is drawn from Daniel Katz and Robert L. Kahn, *The Social Psychology of Organizations* (New York: John Wiley & Sons, Inc., 1966), pp. 337–68.

material pattern of control because it manifests a tangible legitimacy. Thus, police officers obey rules because they stem from legitimate sources of authority and because they can be enforced by organizational sanctions. The working of legitimacy to secure control rests upon two sources of influence: an external influence, which can be mobilized to compel obedience, and a psychological acceptance of legitimate authority. Joining a police agency means that its authority and its rules, formalized in the prescribed manner, are accepted as binding. A person cannot join a police department and make himself the arbiter of what he will accept or reject in its requirements. He can attempt to influence or alter the rules and regulations but, once made, they are binding upon him regardless of his own ideas.

The second control pattern involves material rewards. In this case the police department links a certain kind of reward to a desired behavior. The tangible rewards can be divided into two subtypes: general and individual. General rewards can be earned merely through membership in the police department and increase with seniority. For example, local police agencies offer retirement pensions, sick leave, health examinations, and other forms of fringe benefits. They may furnish cost-of-living raises and other across-the-board wage increases. Further, some provide attractive educational incentive programs. Most of these benefits are available to all members in the department; others are apportioned on status or seniority. But all are benefits, rewarding a large group of people for remaining with the organization. In addition to the more general rewards are the individual rewards of pay increases, promotion, and special recognition. In the police service, these rewards are often apportioned on the basis of an examination process which includes the evaluation of an individual's work history.

Symbolic patterns of control. The various patterns of symbolic control (social rewards, self-expression, and internalized values) furnish a conceptual basis and operational plan for motivating people into desired courses of action. This approach is, by far, the most preferred means of controlling organizational behavior. While more complex, this form of control is the best way to handle the complexities of human behavior. Symbolic control is a socio-psychological stimulus for assisting man and, therefore, his organization to become more effective. Some may think of it as subliminal control. In essence, we take a certain type of organizational control and use it to motivate man toward the fulfillment of specified behavioral requirements. Comparing symbolic control with material control, we see that the former involves external reminders of the rules and sufficient policing to reinforce acceptance of legitimacy and material rewards. The latter deals with activities designed for the attainment of positive rewards. In other words, in the latter case motivation is so internalized that performance is automatic. The police supervisor does not constantly have to oversee and correct. The tasks carry their own rewards; they are so much an integral part of the pattern of personal satisfaction that they need no further incentive. One of three control patterns for motivating subordinates is based on the social rewards imparted through the approval received from the supervisor and one's own work group. In regard to supervisory approval, we are not referring to the approval of the superior interpreted by the officer as a promise of a good personnel rating. It refers to the gratification a subordinate finds in praise by a respected leader. A similar social reward can be had from approval by one's own group. The strength of the peer group in influencing behavior is a continuing source of surprise to supervisors. Social approval of the immediate work group motivates members toward organizational requirements, however, only to the extent that the organizational requirements concur with the norms of the group. Hence, this type of motivation can aid or hinder attainment of organizational objectives, depending upon the group norms.

Another control pattern for motivating police officers includes self-expression (gratification derived from expressing one's talents and skills) and self-determination (the satisfaction of making decisions about one's own behavior). Together they constitute the basis for job identification, which is the gratification derived directly from doing a particular kind of work.

The last symbolic control pattern involves value expression (the satisfaction of expressing one's central values) and self-identification (the desire to establish and maintain a satisfying self-concept). Value expression and self-identification lead to the internalization of organizational goals. The goals of the organization become instilled as part of the individual's value system or as part of his conception of himself. Consequently, considerable gratification is provided to the person by the expression of attitudes and behavior reflecting his values and self-image. A police officer who considers himself an enlightened professional, a prudent worker, and a devoted departmental employee is motivated to actions which express these values. Workers so stimulated usually have a deep sense of mission and commitment. In most police organizations there is a small group of such dedicated members who have internalized the values of the organization. It is up to the police supervisor to see that this small core eventually grows into a large majority of the personnel.

Conditions Conducive for Implementing Control Patterns

The preceding analysis of the various behaviors required for organizational effectiveness and of the different control patterns available for developing and channeling such behavior strongly indicates that there will be costs and benefits in stressing any single desired outcome. We need to examine in detail the differing effects of two patterns of control upon organizational behavior and the conditions most likely to create these patterns.

Conditions influencing the implementation of material control. The conditions conducive to material control can be divided between legal compliance and tangible rewards. Legal compliance is implemented by (1) the use of recognized sources of authority, (2) the clarity of legal norms, (3) the use of specific sanctions, and (4) the threat to the individual's security in the system. Now, what can be anticipated in the way of organizational behavior if the employees are subjected to the above conditions? In terms of legal compliance, it most often can (1) produce minimally acceptable quantity and quality of work, (2) reduce absenteeism, (3) increase turnover, and (4) adversely affect innovative and other behavior beyond the call of duty.

Tangible rewards are manifested through their being perceived as (1) large enough in amount to justify the additional effort required to obtain them, (2) directly related to the required performance and following directly on its accomplishment, (3) equitable by the majority of department members, (4) relatively advantageous over general rewards in other available organizations, and (5) uniform for all members or for major categories. Tangible rewards can result in (1) possible reduction in turnover, (2) some reduction in absenteeism, (3) possible increases in productivity, (4) no necessary increase in cooperative or protective behavior, and (5) possible increases in creative suggestions. Consequently, in general, material control produces minimal accepted behavior, especially in the police service where incentive pay, or piece rates, as reliable methods for raising the quality and quantity of work cannot be used. One final point, the five conditions for activating tangible rewards can be divided accordingly: the first three are individual and the latter two general. It is well to keep in mind that general rewards have a logic of their own. Since they accrue to police personnel by virtue of their membership or length of service in a police department, they will be perceived as inequitable if not uniformly provided.

Conditions influencing the implementation of symbolic control. The conditions promoting symbolic control are arranged in accordance with the three patterns discussed earlier—social, self-expression, and internalized goals. Social rewards can be split into supervisory and peer group. Combined, they provide the individual with the feeling of social approval. The only means for implementing social rewards is through group cohesion. The outcome is (1) decreased turnover and absenteeism, (2) possible increases or decreases in productivity, and (3) no cooperative behavior beyond the call of duty. It is in the pattern of symbolic control using self-expression that we find the greatest chance for the achievement of high quantity and quality of job performance.

The conditions facilitating self-expression involve (1) complexity and skill requirements of job and (2) responsibility and autonomy of job. The results of providing such conditions are (1) no necessary change in turnover, (2) decreases in absenteeism, (3) high productivity, and (4) some increase in cooperative activity but usually little direct relation with behavior beyond the call of duty. Before reviewing the next pattern, some explanation concerning one of the above conditions seems necessary. Let us consider the aspect of job complexity for a few moments.

If job satisfaction or identification with the work is to be aroused and sustained, then the job itself must provide adequate variety, complexity, challenge, and exercise of talent to engage the abilities of the employee. If there is one definite finding in all the studies of worker morale and satisfaction, it is the correlation between the variety and challenge of the job and the satisfactions which accrue to workers.[15] There are instances where people do not want more responsibility and become demoralized by being placed in positions too difficult for them, but they are the exceptions. In the main, people seek more responsibility, more skill-demanding jobs than they hold, and, as they acquire these more demanding jobs, they become happier, better adjusted, and more effective.

The conditions which bring about the internalization of organizational goals are (1) hazardous character of organizational goals, (2) organizational goals expressive of cultural values, (3) organizational leader as model, (4) sharing in organizational decisions, and (5) sharing in organizational rewards. The outcomes expected are (1) reduced turnover and absenteeism, (2) increased productivity, and (3) cooperative and innovative behavior. Note that the five conditions necessary for goal internalization are based on value expression and self-identification, which are generally confined to the upper levels of the police organization. Concerted effort should be made to extend such expression and identification to the rank and file of the department. The path for doing so, though not easy, is fairly well mapped out. The previous five conditions indicate the route to be taken.

The police supervisor is central to any movement toward goal internalization. For example, the imaginative supervisor can help develop an attractive picture of the police organization by a new conceptualization of its mission. Policemen responsible for the routine and sometimes dirty business of law enforcement can be motivated by seeing themselves as a corps of professional officers devoted to the highest form of public service. As suggested, the other steps to be taken include participating in important decisions about organizational and group objectives; contributing to organizational and group performance in a significant way; and sharing in the rewards of organizational and group accomplishment. When the above conditions are met, the individual can regard the police organization and specific work group as his. The first step for a police officer has been taken; the goals to be achieved are frequently hazardous. Hence, we know the conditions that must be brought about for improved acceptance of a department's goals.

---

[15] *Ibid*, p. 364.

Indeed, the first one is in existence. It remains for the police supervisor to initiate the other four conditions. The payoff to all concerned is much to be desired, that is, reduced turnover and absenteeism, increased productivity, and cooperative and innovative behavior. The first two conditions can be achieved by other patterns of control, including material. But the third is exclusive to this particular form of control. Cooperation is critical because it serves as the basis of coordination, the vehicle for maximizing organizational effectiveness. Self-expression and self-identification which, in turn, create the internalization of an organization's goals furnish this vehicle with its road bed. Consequently, from this came the title of this chapter, "Organizational Control: the Road to Effectiveness" (in the next chapter we concentrate on the vehicle). In conclusion, a police organization can function with limited effectiveness under other control patterns. In fact, most of them do. We find, however, in the last symbolic pattern a way to develop the coordination of effort! Therefore, we can say that *effective supervisory control is the very basis of coordination which, in turn, provides the major cornerstone for the building of organizational effectiveness.*

DISCIPLINE

Discipline has purposely been left to the end of this section so that we could discuss the more positive means for attaining required behavior first. Discipline is needed only when all the previously discussed patterns of organizational control have failed. Suppose we have clearly instructed a police officer on his duties, used one or more of the patterns of control, and yet he still fails to meet standards. Then what? Then, reluctantly, we are forced to resort to discipline. And, the principal responsibility for exercising discipline should be lodged in the police supervisor. To perform this responsibility adequately the supervisor needs support. He should know organizationally that it is his duty to exercise disciplinary action firmly and, of course, wisely. He must be assured by police management that his sincere and competent efforts to do a good disciplining job will be supported at all times. Moreover, he must be made to feel that should discipline enter the hearing stage, his efforts will be evaluated upon their merits and will not be abrogated by sentimentality or legal technicality.

"There can be no specific rules of supervision which will work well in all situations."[16] Similarly, there can be no specific rules concerning the spirit, extent, or degree of disciplinary action that brings the optimum return. Should discipline be strict and severe or tolerant and easy going? The answer

---

[16] Rensis Likert, *New Patterns in Management* (New York: McGraw-Hill Book Company, 1961), p. 95.

is not in any set of universal principles. It can be found, however, in the nature of the wrongful act, the particular organization, and the person being disciplined. This is to say, discipline is by nature both organizational and individual. It is organizational in that its quality must depend on the regulations of the formal organization and on the social attitudes of the informal organization. It is also individualistic in philosophy and clinical in method because it deals with human feelings. Hence the approach to discipline is through both the individual and the organization and not within the framework of a theoretical ideal approach. To say that a flexible posture in disciplining, through good organizational and individual reprimands, cannot be accomplished would be to surrender the hope of ever producing a satisfactory way of life within a police organization.

Types of Discipline

In the police service, the supervisor's disciplinary discretion is usually limited by official rules, most of which are reasonable and will produce desirable results if given a chance to work. Often the police supervisor adopts a defeatist attitude when the employee has a chance to appeal through some grievance procedure. But if the supervisor is a systematic fact-finder and if he makes adequate records to justify his personnel actions, he should not have to worry about appeal board reversal in the great majority of cases. Consequently, every disciplinary action must be bolstered by possession of all possible facts. Therefore, most of the significant happenings in a police officer's work life in the police organization should find their way into his personnel folder. The recording of these matters, other than the difficulty in getting police supervisors to commit themselves in writing, is the least difficult part of the record-keeping process. It is the interpretation of past events which, if not "professionally" handled, can lead to great difficulty.[17] One final point regarding fact gathering, personnel record keeping should not become entirely a negative procedure in the evaluation of employees. Good, as well as wrong, performance should be recorded, especially if it indicates improvement in an area related to a previous disciplinary action.

The types of discipline the police supervisor may use or recommend in the police service range from warning or reprimand to requirement of overtime work, reassignment of duties, demerits or reductions in service ratings, loss of seniority rights, suspension without pay, fines, demotion, simple discharge, dismissal with continuing disability for reemployment, and even judicial prosecution. Reprimand, suspension, and dismissal are used most often. Again, the nature of the act, the particular organization, and the individual

---

[17] John M. Pfiffner and Marshall Fels, *The Supervision of Personnel,* 3rd ed. (Englewood Cliffs, N.J.: Prentice-Hall, Inc., 1964), p. 113.

determine which type of discipline should be administered. The cardinal guideline when applying discipline lies in its purpose: *the purpose of discipline is to obtain compliance with established rules of conduct—that is, to correct improper conduct.* It must not be punitive in nature. Rather, it must be exercised in an open and positive manner.

Procedures for disciplining. Inflicting discipline places the police supervisor in a dilemma. How can he expect his subordinates to regard him as a source of support when discipline is by nature distasteful? Can he inflict discipline without causing resentment? Yes—that is, if he wants to. Once the type of discipline has been decided upon, certain procedural steps can be taken to reduce, if not totally eliminate, any resentment on the part of the police officer. The steps are

1. *Immediate discipline.* The police supervisor should initiate the disciplinary action as soon as possible after he notices a violation of the rules.

2. *Explicit policies.* If discipline is to be accepted without resentment, both the police officer who is being disciplined and his fellow officers must regard it as fair. Unexpected discipline is almost always considered unfair. This means that (1) there must be clear policy indicating that a given violation will lead to discipline and (2) there must be clear indication of the amount of discipline that will be imposed for a specific violation.

3. *Consistency.* Consistent discipline helps to establish boundaries (that is, to notify police personnel what they can and cannot do); inconsistent discipline leads to confusion and anxiety. Consistent discipline is crucial if the work environment is to be kept stable. When some rules are permitted to be violated, employees may decide to disregard all forms of control.

4. *Impersonality.* The police supervisor can minimize the danger of destroying the necessary relationship with a subordinate by imposing discipline in an impersonal way. Impersonality occurs if the individual feels that only his behavior at the particular moment is being criticized and not his total personality.

5. *Interaction.* The disciplinary interview is not much different from most other interviews. First, state the problem as you see it; then encourage the subordinate to state his point of view. Listen to his story, then ask how it happened, not why. Provide him every chance to explain himself. Listen!

6. *Learning.* Administer the discipline so that it provides the individual with a learning experience. In essence, the person should fully understand (1) *why* he was disciplined, (2) *why* a particular type of discipline was used, and (3) how to avoid future disciplinary action.[18]

Labor Relations: the Grievance Procedure

The police supervisor should be familiar with the civil service regulations that circumscribe his disciplinary choices. He is now beginning to witness another delimiting influence—the growth of union membership in the police

---

[18] Leonard R. Sayles and George Strauss, *Human Behavior in Organizations* (Englewood Cliffs, N.J.: Prentice-Hall, Inc., 1966), p. 329.

service. With this growth have come formalized grievance procedures and strikes. While illegal, government employees have struck and will continue to strike. Police departments have experienced a form of organized employee dissatisfaction known as work stoppage, for example, large numbers of police officers reporting in ill. An established and respected grievance procedure does much to avoid injurious "show-downs."

A grievance procedure can be thought of as a continuous process for the adjustment of human rights. It appears that the grievance procedure will become more of an integral part of formalized police personnel procedures. Ironically, this trend challenges the theory that civil service law automatically gives public employees more protection and advantages than they would obtain doing similar work elsewhere. Personnel practices in private organizations have so improved of late that the advantages under civil service may in many instances have been eliminated.

The great majority of grievances can be placed under the heading of problems of job evaluation, which is another way of saying that they are related to compensation and pay.[19] Closely associated with these issues are grievances that usually disturb police officers as group rather than as individuals. Examples are the allotment of overtime assignments, the allocation of vacation periods, and the assignment of shifts.

Police supervisors naturally resist the idea of a grievance procedure. They regard it as a way of "bypassing them," or "going behind their backs." The increasingly judicial nature of personnel administration has influenced the role of police supervisor by requiring that he be ready to supply substantial proof to justify his actions involving the handling of police personnel. As in disciplinary actions, this means that he must keep records that will refresh his memory and serve as proof when he may find it necessary to defend his actions before police management, the personnel director, a grievance committee, an arbitrator, or a civil service commission.

The new personnel jurisprudence is not only emerging as a pattern of semijudicial procedure, it also has a definitely legalistic aspect. The great labor statutes and collective bargaining agreements, combined with civil service rules and regulations, have created a set of fundamental personal rights and liberties and a procedure akin to due process of law in the management realm.[20] The main effect of this trend upon supervision is to deprive the police supervisor of any powers that he may once have had to deal arbitrarily with employees. Consequently, the impact of organized labor on the police supervisor can be viewed as having a positive outcome. First, it reduces the chances of a police supervisor wrongfully exercising control

---

[19] Pfiffner and Fels, *Supervision of Personnel*, p. 117.

[20] For further information on this subject, see Kenneth O. Warner, *Management Relations With Organized Public Employees* (Chicago, Ill.: Public Personnel Association, 1965); and Executive Committee of the National Governors' Conference, *Report of Task Force on State and Local Government Relations* (Chicago, Ill.: Public Personnel Association, 1968).

and discipline. Second, it demands a more humanistic approach to the handling of people.

The presence of a union need not impair the police supervisor's attempts to implement an effective disciplinary policy. Unions seldom object strongly to discipline if it is applied consistently and if the rules are clearly publicized and generally considered fair.[21] Most union contracts require (1) that the organization may discipline employees only for "just cause" and (2) that any employee who feels he has been unreasonably disciplined may appeal to management through the grievance procedure, and, if management's answer is unsatisfactory, to arbitration. The arbitrator makes the final decision on whether the discipline had just cause. He may be able to sustain the organization's action completely, reduce the penalty, or decide the penalty was entirely unwarranted and eliminate it altogether. The grievance procedure including the possibility of arbitration provides a valuable protection to the individual employee, awkward though it may be for the police supervisor.

Collective bargaining contracts frequently provide for arbitration of grievances that cannot be settled by negotiation. An arbitration procedure also tends to become semijudicial in nature. Hence, there is again a need for the police supervisor to be well prepared to defend his disciplinary action. A systematic four-step plan is the best guarantee of the police supervisor's success: (1) receive the grievance properly, (2) get the facts, (3) take action, and (4) follow up. When there is an appeal, hearing and grievance boards usually request two types of proof: (1) detailed evidence of offenses with times, dates, and places and (2) assurance that every possible step has been taken to caution, assist, and rehabilitate the employee. If he fulfills these expectations, the police supervisor can anticipate being "backed up."

BASICS OF CONTROL

The essentials or basic techniques required for a police supervisor to exert effective organizational control have to a major extent already been discussed (missing is the use of the computer to provide control).[22] They are selection and socialization, an appropriate span of control, and material and symbolic patterns of control.[23] The most fundamental is, of course, an

---

[21] Sayles and Strauss, *Human Behavior*, p. 338.

[22] For an excellent treatment of this subject, see Thomas L. Whisler, "The Impact of Information Technology on Organizational Control," in *The Impact of Computers on Management*, ed. Charles A. Myers (Cambridge, Mass.: The M.I.T. Press, 1967), pp. 16–48.

[23] One study concerned itself with an analysis of three other dimensions of employee control. It reported that as the supervisory style and the number of formal policies varied so did the degree of organizational control. William R. Rosengren, "Structure, Policy, and Style: Strategies of Organizational Control," *Administrative Science Quarterly*, 12 (June 1967), 140–64.

effective program for selecting and continuously socializing (remember socialization includes but is not limited to training) the police personnel. Without such a program the other controls are extremely difficult to successfully apply. Since the span of control is dependent upon proper selection and socialization, it varies accordingly. The greater the success in choosing the correct person for the job and the better indoctrinated he becomes afterward, the broader the possible span of control. The more narrow (the fewer the number of subordinates supervised by a single supervisor) the span, the less the success in selection and socialization. Similarly, material and symbolic controls are also based on these two processes. The better the selection and socialization, the greater the probabilities of using the more beneficial patterns of control including self-expression and internalization of organizational goals, and vice versa. Remember, it is the latter pattern that does so much to foster cooperative behavior. Significantly, all three of these control processes also act as positive factors in any arsenal of motivators. Therefore, the controls suggested here are all the more valuable because they, at the same time, provide psychological motivation toward organizationally desired behavior. Hopefully, the reader by now has recognized that this author, in essence, has recommended a program of organizational control that is firmly entrenched in motivational theory.

Other supervisory control techniques are:[24]

1. Issue orders that require minimal review. The less ambiguous and general a supervisor's orders are, the less discretion is delegated to subordinates. Hence, subordinates are provided less of an opportunity to modify the intent of an order.
2. Create the information necessary for discovering what subordinates are doing. Some valid measures of performance must be designed to report on activities, even when the performance involved is hard to quantify. These reports have two major purposes: (1) they inform the supervisor about what is happening and (2) the necessity of preparing routine reports serves to remind each subordinate that he must meet certain standards of performance.
3. Select only small segments of the total activity for review. The supervisor should be selecting (1) those matters that create strong feedback from the clientele served, (2) significant deviations from standard performance targets, (3) those decisions about which subordinates cannot agree, and (4) a number of matters selected entirely at random.

By merging the previous processes and techniques into a well-planned program of organizational control, the police supervisor can more effectively

---

[24] For a more comprehensive examination of these control devices, see Downs, *Inside Bureaucracy*, pp. 144–55. Additionally, Downs describes three other control devices designed for the administrative level: (1) bypassing antidistortion techniques for gaining compliance, (2) separate monitoring units, and (3) the use of staff personnel to aid in controlling line employees.

move men and materials in the direction of goal achievement. Furthermore, such a program enhances his chances of making the police officers reasonably happy while accomplishing their assigned tasks. Finally, it is important that we keep in mind that "how to develop and maintain control" can be learned. Effective organizational control, therefore, is a habit; that is, a complex of useful techniques—and techniques can always be learned.

SUMMARY

The objectives of organizational control are (1) to assure those in supervision and management that their rules and orders are obeyed and (2) to effectuate the coordination of effort. Both are required to achieve organizational effectiveness. We define control as a process by which a person (or group of persons, or organization of persons) intentionally affects what another person (or group, or organization) will do.

The control process begins with an order and includes feedback and a series of decisions which eventually result in the issuance of another order. One does not have to belabor the point that all organizations experience control problems. Importantly, what should be stressed is that *the difficulties of controlling the actions of police personnel do not reside in human incompetence but rather in the omnipresent internal problems of any social organization.* We find that one of these problems has to do with a much too common supervisory misconception. Basically, supervisors and administrators alike are constantly pushing for maximum effectiveness, or maximum individual satisfaction, and in some instances both. Many are beginning to realize that neither can completely occur. What we must seek, therefore, is a workable balance between the two.

Control can be classified into three types: physical, material, and symbolic. Most organizations favor one of the types but always include the others to a lesser degree. We suggest that our local police agencies are today primarily utilizing material control. However, we can detect a definite trend toward greater use of symbolic control. Related to the type of control is the question of the amount of total control that exists at various levels in a police organization. Briefly stated, the amount of control can be simultaneously increased at the supervisory and line levels. One level receiving an increase in control does not preclude another from also receiving additional control. The amount of control necessary in a particular police department is dependent mainly upon the quality of its selection and socialization of members.

The type of control used in a police agency vastly influences its degree of effectiveness. Three kinds of behavior are required to achieve high levels of organizational effectiveness: (1) people must join and remain in the organization, (2) they must perform dependably the roles assigned to them, and (3) they must engage in innovative and cooperative behavior beyond the requirements of the role but always in the service of organizational objectives. Furthermore, there are two (out of a possible three) major types of control that can be used to control the behavior of police personnel: material and symbolic. Material control comprises legal compliance and tangible rewards. Symbolic control encompasses social rewards, self-expression, and internalized goals. In the latter device we find a means for promoting and maintaining cooperative behavior prerequisite to the coordination of effort and organizational effectiveness.

If these control patterns fail, disciplinary action enters the picture. For discipline to be accepted, the rules must be effectively communicated and the sanctions inflicted must be consistent. Discipline helps police personnel learn the requirements of their job; and if discipline is applied impersonally, the respect shown the police supervisor by his subordinates need not decrease and may even increase. Where unions or protective associations exist, an accepted disciplinary policy does much to reduce the possibility of grievance procedure being instigated by a penalized employee.

In conclusion, the police supervisor's chances of exerting organizational control are considerably improved if (1) the organization's selection and socialization programs are sound, (2) he has a tailored span of control, and (3) he uses symbolic control patterns. As a result of these policies, less overt control is needed because the employee becomes motivated (internalization of organizational goals) to act in a highly desired manner (latent controls). Three other techniques have proven helpful to the police supervisor in maintaining control: (1) issue orders that require little review, (2) generate information that indicates what the subordinates are doing, and (3) select only small samples of the over-all activity for review.

PROBLEMS

Rather than solve a group of problems as in previous chapters, let us analyze a case study that involves organizational control.[25] The case presented occurred in a local law enforcement agency. Naturally, names and certain details have been changed to maintain anonymity for both the department and its members. However, the general problem in the case remains intact. You are asked to apply your recently acquired knowledge on organizational control to this specific situation. This is to say, how would you have attempted to either avoid or solve the situation described below?

---

[25] Permission to use the case, "Roy Bruce—Police Supervisor," was granted by its author, William F. Stovall, Jr.

Roy Bruce—Police Supervisor

Occasionally, a member of the supervisory team suddenly seems to turn against his peers and become an abrasive factor in the machinery of efficiency. But, is this so often a sudden turn? Retrospection on this problem may suggest that positive corrective action taken at the earliest indication could possibly have saved the organization from damage and may even have salvaged the services of the supervisor who triggered complications.

Roy Bruce, police supervisor, is a case in point. It appeared that his intelligence, ambition, and job knowledge made him a likely candidate for the accomplishment of the supervisory role. The first 12 years of his career were quite satisfactory in that no severe problems had been noted by those with whom, or for whom, he worked. But, at some point near the completion of his formal schooling, something happened to effect a change in him. This change progressed from a mild discontent to an ultimate climax in a major disruption which had to be reckoned with.

To begin, Roy Bruce was a supervisor in the Metropolitan Police Department. This department of 840 personnel is located in a densely populated area of southern California and serves a community of nearly 400,000 persons.

When I first met Roy he was a sergeant working in the Traffic Division on the Parking and Intersection Control detail. He had been in the department about 13 years and had been going part time to the University of California at Los Angeles for several years. Though he performed his job and ran his detail satisfactorily, he complained regularly about the policies and decisions of his superiors and did little to conceal his feelings from those working under him. Apparently, his growing state of job dissatisfaction motivated him to earn his college degree and, subsequently, a teaching credential.

I met him about the time he graduated. I came to know him quite well and he confided in me that policework was growing less and less interesting to him and that, between his job and the congested area, he was just about fed up. He indicated that he wanted to quit the police department and go into teaching. Consequently, he began searching out different areas of the country and submitting applications for teaching positions.

One day he told me he was requesting a leave of absence to accept a teaching position in a small town somewhere in southern Michigan. In August he sold his house and he and his wife left for his new job. Quite frankly, I really didn't expect to see him again.

The following February Bruce returned. Though I, at first, thought he was just here visiting between semesters, I soon learned that he had resigned his teaching job and returned to resume his former position. When questioned about his return, he would talk at length about the unsatisfactory working conditions and an impossible school administration which he could no longer tolerate. I also learned that his wife was violently opposed to the winter she had experienced there and had given him an ultimatum: she was coming back to California—with or without him.

Whatever the reasons, Bruce had returned. And, being well within the period of his authorized leave, he was reinstated as a police sergeant. His former position in the Traffic Division was filled, so he was assigned to the afternoon Patrol Division, a job he had often commented most unfavorably about. Furthermore, it wasn't long before he began complaining and disagreeing with the persons and policies controlling departmental operations. However, I noticed that his complaints were not generally taken up with his superior officers but were more often voiced in the presence of his subordinates in a manner which seemed to solicit support. This action began to result in a close-knit group of malcontents forming around him and turning to him for support of their complaints; a sort of self-serving group subverting departmental goals.

Roy had been working less than a year when two important changes occurred within the department. A large, modern police facility was built and the chief of police retired. Interestingly, it was within a few months of these changes that Roy placed high on a promotional examination and was subsequently promoted to lieutenant. The new chief initiated a program of up-dating his entire department. He cleaned out the old cliques which had been functioning in a most archaic and unprofessional manner for years and instituted recruiting and training programs which soon increased the competency of the entire department and resulted in an increased feeling of pride and esprit de corps among the personnel.

I had little contact with Roy over the next couple of years, but I would have thought, with his reaching the command level and with the department growing and progressing so well, that his discontent would have been reduced. Actually, the opposite had occurred! I had been assigned to the Administrative Division for a scant three months when I became acutely aware of a morale problem which had developed on the afternoon watch. I learned that Roy Bruce was one of the two men commanding that watch.

Discreet observation revealed that he was manifesting the same attitudes and behavioral patterns that had been so much a part of him in the years before. There were now several important factors which differed however. Being on the command level, Roy had a position which influenced greater numbers of police personnel. His opinions carried the authority of a command rank. Further, Roy now directed his attacks not only against departmental leadership, but also against the personalities of the leaders as well. He spread rumors regarding the personalities and private lives of city and departmental administrators with the apparent purpose of discrediting their ability to properly administer their responsibilities.

Lieutenant Bruce had developed a cohesive group of dissidents which surrounded him and facilitated his subversion by spreading false rumors throughout the rank and file of the department.

Roy openly failed to support departmental orders and policies issued to his division. This is not to say that he defied orders, for he was careful to follow all orders and to comply with all policies. But he continued to engage in a verbal sabotage of needed supervision. The effect that his attitude was having on his men was damaging to departmental efficiency. As his disciples spread his word to the young and impressionable rookies on his watch, his following grew. It certainly seemed that dissent begat dissent.

Soon Roy's watch began a work slowdown to protest an alleged inequity in their pay scale (it took months to restore the Patrol Division to its former level of operation). The damage to departmental morale was severe and was spreading throughout the entire Patrol Division. The damage was accentuated by some of his rumors which found their way into a weekly newspaper published and distributed as an advertising throw-away throughout the city. Becoming aware of the problem, the chief transferred Roy from his present position and reassigned him to the Communications Division. In this new assignment he would command a very small number of persons and thus be in a poor position to directly influence the operating divisions. It seems that at this point Lieutenant Bruce intensified his vendetta toward the executives of the department. He was careful, however, and operated primarily through some of the older malcontents he had nurtured.

Shortly after his transfer to the Communications Division, departmental promotional examinations began. Roy placed high on the written exam for captain. The ensuing oral interview offered a capstone for his dissatisfaction. In short, Roy circulated a story that the chief was responsible for sending a special letter to the oral board denouncing his loyalties and abilities. He next went into the interview room with a recording device strapped to his leg and attempted to elicit from the interviewers a statement that they had been furnished with a letter denouncing him. His actions became known to the interviewers and eventually to others. Needless to say, the newspapers made prime news of the allegations of Civil Service misconduct. When the promotional list was published, Roy petitioned for and received an injunction against the use of that particular list until a hearing was conducted into what he alleged were irregularities in the Civil Service actions regarding this examination (Roy's final exam score was very low). The promotional list was suspended for 10 months while court action was pending, and no evidence was submitted to substantiate Lieutenant Bruce's accusations. His actions brought about a strong resentment toward him by his peers who were anxious to see the list implemented.

Naturally, this incident was told and retold with variations several times in the newspapers, and though the case was never substantiated, enough adverse publicity was developed to embarrass every man in the department. Not long after this incident Roy Bruce retired—as you might suspect—as a lieutenant. He had lost considerable respect from his peers. To put it mildly, Roy's career will always be remembered by his superiors, peers, and subordinates.

8

Coordination:
the Vehicle for Organizational
Effectiveness

This chapter builds upon and around a central proposition: *effective supervisory control leads to human cooperation; human cooperation provides an impetus for the coordination of effort; and, through the coordination of effort, organizational effectiveness is optimized.* If this proposition were expressed as a formula it might look like this: self-identification + self-expression → internalization of organizational goals → cooperative behavior → coordination of effort = organizational effectiveness. Admittedly, we daily see organizations that have failed to develop coordination and yet still survive. In fact, many of them can be considered, to a limited extent, effective. It is because of effective coordination, however, that we are able to attain an optimal state of organizational effectiveness.[1]

Our consideration of organizational coordination begins with a discussion of the various meanings and ideas contained within and tangential to it. Next we proceed to an examination of the human and organizational costs and benefits connected with the furtherance of coordination. We then discuss the four determinants of the police supervisor's organizational role which are interdependent upon coordination, namely: (1) organizational perspective, (2) organizational responsibility, (3) procedure development, and (4) administrative detail. Subsequently, we touch upon an innovative concept presently known (or unknown) as "team policing." Finally, as in previous chapters, we suggest some techniques that may prove useful in promoting greater coordination within a police department.

---

[1] For those interested in a highly relevant discussion of optimal versus suboptimal levels of police service, see William W. Herrmann, "Public Order in a Free Society," in *Law Enforcement, Science and Technology—II*, ed. S. I. Cohn (Chicago, Ill.: Port City Press, Inc., 1969), pp. 297–306.

COOPERATION, COORDINATION, INTEGRATION, SPECIALIZATION, DIFFERENTIATION: WHICH?

At this point let us define our terms and look at their conceptual development. First comes cooperation. Police supervision, similar to police administration, is cooperative human action.[2] Indeed, Simon defines administrative organizations as systems of cooperative behavior.[3] Cooperation usually suggests willingness on the part of those involved in a particular task. In the case of formal organizations, however, we frequently observe mutually supportive acts performed unwillingly. The acts may be done solely because they have been ordered by a superior. Hence, cooperative behavior can be attained either willingly or unwillingly. The successful police supervisor advances human cooperation by developing his subordinates' willingness to assist one another in the accomplishment of assigned duties. Chester I. Barnard, perhaps the foremost advocate of the need for cooperation, provides us with a strong warning that human cooperation is not easy to come by.

> Formal organization is that kind of cooperation among men that is conscious, deliberate, purposeful. Such cooperation is omnipresent and inescapable nowadays, so that it is usually contrasted only with "individualism," as if there were no other process of cooperation. Moreover, much of what we regard as reliable, foreseeable, and stable is so obviously a result of formally organized effort that it is readily believed that organized effort is normally successful, that failure of organization is abnormal.
>
> But in fact, successful cooperation in or by formal organizations is the abnormal, not the normal condition. What are observed from day to day are the successful survivors among innumerable failures. The organizations commanding sustained attention, almost all of which are short-lived at best, are the exceptions, not the rule.[4]

The importance of coordination to an organization was well known by our so-called pioneers in administrative thought. Henri Fayol listed it as one of five elements of administration, while Gulick included it as one of seven administrative activities. Mooney went one step further and analyzed coordination as being both perpendicular (vertical) and horizontal (for references regarding the works of these authors, see Chapter 4). Perhaps we can clarify our discussion by using the term *cooperation* for activity in

---

[2] Dwight Waldo, *The Study of Public Administration* (New York: Random House, Inc., 1955), p. 5.

[3] Herbert A. Simon, *Administrative Behavior*, 2d ed., rev. (New York: Macmillan Company, 1957), p. 72.

[4] Chester I. Barnard, *The Functions of the Executive* (Cambridge, Mass.: Harvard University Press, 1938), pp. 4–5.

which the participants share a common goal, and *coordination* for the process of organizationally interrelating individuals to one another, and groups to each other. Hence, coordination is usually ineffective—does not reach its goal, whatever the intentions of the participants—in the absence of cooperation.

To continue, the police supervisor has a constant problem of relating all his manpower and resources in a manner which avoids unnecessary expenditure and duplication of effort. It is obvious that coordination does not represent a tight or neat package within which certain ideas and practices fall. Rather, everything that has been previously said about individuals, groups, and controlling and gaining cooperation has primary relevance to the coordinative process. The problem is complicated, moreover, by the frequent reliance upon technical skill as a criterion in supervisory selection, as well as a tendency to pay mere lip service to the human relations element in police administration. Clearly, the individual police officer must be made to feel a part of the work group before he can identify with its objectives and values. Coordination may sometimes require the acceptance of objectives inconsistent with the immediate, personal values of the individual. Thus essentially, emotional appeals are often necessary to evoke individual loyalty. Again, we see that a police organization, like a nation, must possess a system of commonly shared values and objectives.

The term *integration* is similar to coordination. We use them interchangeably. Schein emphasizes the importance of the coordinative process when he writes that, "one of the major problems organizations face is the integration of their various parts to insure effective overall performance."[5] The use of the term *integration* is, however, more encompassing in scope. Basically, it can be utilized in one of three ways: (1) individuals can be integrated into a group or an organization,[6] (2) groups can be integrated with one another, and (3) organizations can be integrated with their surrounding environment. We focus on the first and second meanings. To conclude, Bennis describes the significance of coordination (integration) to modern organizational structures by writing that:

> The social structure in organizations of the future will have some unique characteristics. The key word will be "temporary"; there will be adaptive, rapidly changing *temporary systems*. These will be organized around *problems-to-be-solved*. The problems will be solved by groups of relative *strangers* who represent a set of diverse professional skills. The groups will be conducted on *organic* rather than mechanical models; they will evolve in response to the problem rather

[5] Edgar H. Schein, *Organizational Psychology* (Englewood Cliffs, N.J.: Prentice-Hall, Inc., 1965), p. 14.
[6] A benchmark text devoted to the subject of integrating individuals into formal organizations is by Chris Argyris, *Integrating Individual and the Organization* (New York: John Wiley & Sons, Inc., 1964).

than programmed role expectations. The function of the . . . [police supervisor] thus becomes *coordinator*, or "linking pin" between various project groups.[7] (Italics added.)

Finally, we look at two other terms which mean approximately the same thing, *specialization* and *differentiation*. The growth in numbers and size of modern organizations has occurred through more intensive division of labor, as well as through greater extension of given techniques and functions. Intensive specialization or differentiation generates an extremely complicated web of relationships among individuals. The reason for this occurrence is obvious: organization as a process depends primarily upon specialization. In today's police departments the work is divided, then assigned, and an attempt is made to control the efforts of the component groups in such a way as to achieve a given goal. With a large police agency greater specialization is an inevitable result. Size, however, is not the only determinant. More emphasis is being placed on the expert rather than on the generalist. Police officers have been forced to concentrate their knowledge in very limited areas in order to establish competence in such fields. Witness, for one example, the detective unit. One usually finds burglary, forgery, homicide, and robbery specialists within this particular unit. To put it another way, the work of the detective has been differentiated.

Regardless of the causes, increasing specialization has very serious implications for police supervision. Essentially, it tends to separate the officer from the end result of his endeavor. In the early part of this century, a single officer usually performed all police functions. Today he has a very small part to play in the completion of any single police function and finds it exceedingly difficult to identify his own contribution to the success of the entire department. Certainly, this does not instill a sense of over-all responsibility. If a police officer is motivated by a need to complete a specific assignment, this situation can cause a very critical problem in police supervision.

When one attempts to consider the dual need for coordination and specialization within our modern police organizations, he is apt to adopt one of two possible positions. First, it would seem reasonable to concurrently push for increased coordination and specialization, thus making the department all the more effective. Or, second, one might quickly conclude that it is best to promote coordination over specialization or vice versa. Both of these two positions are feasible. Feasible—yes, but beneficial—no! The fact of the matter is that coordination and specialization are antagonistic states. With this in mind, it appears timely to begin our analysis of the costs and benefits connected with coordination and specialization.

---

[7] Warren G. Bennis, *Changing Organizations* (New York: McGraw-Hill Book Company, 1966), p. 12.

COORDINATION VERSUS SPECIALIZATION: THE COSTS AND THE BENEFITS

Specialization is a necessary evil! The reader can correctly assume that this review of the coordinative process and technical specialization is biased in favor of coordination. Remember, however, that the division of labor is an essential aspect of organization and that this division results in the specialization of the various means by which a given goal is to be accomplished.

Specialization

The origin of our modern police organization lies mainly in the need for technical skills. Trained in a certain skill, performing it again and again, and viewing his position as a career, the police officer should develop a high degree of proficiency. Specialization is reinforced by the fact that entry and advancement are based upon technical preparation. In our police organizations, the demand for technical expertise continues to grow. Professional societies abound, and career training becomes increasingly specialized. Thus the police organization is both a cause and an effect of police specialization and professionalization, bringing to routine matters greater precision and speed of operation. More specifically, specialization has these clearly recognizable benefits to a police organization:

1. *Reduces training costs.* It reduces training costs, for a worker learns more quickly when he concentrates on a single function.
2. *Saves time.* It avoids the waste of time involved in shifting a man from one kind of job to another, and enables each man to develop fully his skills for a particular job.
3. *Optimizes the use of equipment.* It makes unnecessary the duplication of equipment that would otherwise be used on only a part-time basis.
4. *Enhances the use of specialized equipment.* It enables the company to purchase more specialized equipment.
5. *Promotes job control.* It simplifies the problem of developing job controls.[8]

Now let us look at the other side of the coin: what are the hang-ups in specialization? Broadly speaking, the disadvantages are two: psychological and operational. While the two problem areas are interdependent, for clarification they are described separately. Importantly, together they reduce the over-all effectiveness of the organization. Consequently, we are confronted with the realization that *specialization both assists and impedes an organization.* Further, research has shown that specialization inhibits group

---

[8] This list is drawn, in part, from Leonard R. Sayles and George Strauss, *Human Behavior in Organizations* (Englewood Cliffs, N.J.: Prentice-Hall, Inc., 1966), p. 394.

productivity at the analysis phase of problem solving, efficiency, and risk taking.[9] Furthermore, specialization also seems to attenuate one of the beneficial characteristics of group processes, competition for respect. Police management and police supervision have a fundamental responsibility for determining just how much specialization is healthy for their particular local law enforcement operation. The psychological costs are

1. *Job dissatisfaction.* Specialization can create serious morale and motivational problems. In the typical police organization, many police officers have little sense of autonomy, or identification with work.

2. *Risk-taking behavior.* Specialization causes less risk-taking behavior, especially when ideas are expressed within a group. To explain, in order for an idea to be acted upon by a specialized group, the person who generates the idea must defend his view and advocate the idea before the rest of the group. By attempting to promote the idea, the person is identified with it. If the group acts upon the idea and it is subsequently proven unsound, the individual who advanced the idea experiences failure in the eyes of his specialized group, a risk few people are willing to take.

3. *Suboptimization.* When an organization divides and assigns its work to specialized units, it also establishes limited objectives for these units to attain. Therefore, often the "big picture" is lost by these units. As an example, we find vice officers thinking of themselves as being solely vice officers—not police officers, but vice officers! Their focus is thus narrowed to performing only their own unique specialized tasks. Subsequently, the person loses sight of the over-all mission of the police department and stresses only a portion of it.

4. *Competition.* Directly connected to the suboptimization is the fact that many of the attitudes, and informal procedures, reflect a growing loyalty to the unit to which the person belongs. As he identifies with it, his self-esteem is tied to its performance, and it becomes increasingly difficult for him to understand the problems of other units and of the organization as a whole. Increasingly, he may work for his own unit and become indifferent or hostile to others. The organization often encourages this process by rewarding competition between groups. The gains may justify such competition but, at the same time, create intergroup coordination problems.

The operational costs are

5. *Loss of productivity.* First, and foremost, specialization causes a loss in productivity. The presence of specialization in an organization curtails three highly useful organizational processes: feedback for error correcting, social support to individual members, and motivation of people to win the respect and esteem of their co-workers.

---

[9] Edwin M. Bridges, Wayne J. Doyle, and David J. Mahan, "Effects of Hierarchical Differentiation on Group Productivity, Efficiency and Risk Taking," *Administrative Science Quarterly*, 13 (September 1968), 305–19.

6. *Poor personnel development.* While the specialization of work is extremely important in understanding the difficulty police supervisors encounter in motivating certain people, it is also significant that specialization tends to narrow the perspective of the potential supervisor. People who become supervisors should have a broad experience and background; yet modern organizations force them into narrow niches. In some ways public agencies have been perhaps less guilty than their private counterparts. For example, the police department customarily has a rotational policy which ostensibly insures that all prospective police supervisors will have a wide range of experiences. In general, however, it must be acknowledged that most people are not as well equipped, in terms of background, as they might be for supervisory responsibility.

7. *Less efficiency.* Specialization produces less efficient operations. When a collection of individuals come together to form an organization, they have the potential to produce more in concert than separately; however, the potential is not realized until a pattern of interpersonal relations develops. Highly specialized differences among the members is an obstacle that delays the development of this pattern. Low status members of specialized organizations and groups hesitate to become actively involved in solving the problem until the specialist (expert) indicates through his behavior the kind of role he will play in the problem-solving situation.

In conclusion, we can presently see attempts being made by some organizations to reduce the degree of specialization to a more favorable level. While this author does not advocate the merging of the police and fire services, an interesting and pertinent illustration of despecialization can be found in this area. One case study of the combining of police and fire departments reported benefits were gained by all concerned.[10]

Coordination

Police supervisors sometimes believe that they can get something for nothing, that they can get the advantages of increased specialization by dividing up more complex assignments into simpler assignments. However, they ignore the possibility that the problems of coordination so created may outweigh the advantages gained. Dividing up work is easier than putting the parts back together again. The purpose of any police organization is to accomplish its goals effectively. Individual task performance is only useful insofar as it facilitates the attainment of these goals. No matter how hard a police officer works, his efforts are wasted unless they integrate with those of his fellow officers.

One way to look at the need for coordination is as a problem in human relations. Police administrators anticipated that, if highly motivated spe-

---

[10] Barnard H. Baum and Robert H. Goodin, "The Effective Despecialization of Jobs: A Case Study," *Public Personnel Review,* 29 (October 1968), 222–26.

cialists could be trained and if each did his work correctly, coordination would take care of itself. But if we watch these police specialists (detectives, juvenile officers, traffic officers, vice officers, and so on) at work, we commonly see human relations problems. Clearly, the problems of coordination have increased as more police specialists have been created, more tasks subdivided, and thus more human relations created. Coordination is a human relations problem: how to get *A* to do his job so that it fits into the way *B* and *C* are doing their work. Moreover, it entails how to get group *A* to do their job so that it fits into the way groups *B* and *C* are doing their work. The modern large-scale police organization is characterized by ever greater series of interrelationships between all levels of the hierarchy.

There are many human relations problems to be resolved if police work is to be accomplished and over-all departmental goals attained. In other words, specialization has increased the relative importance of horizontal relationships, as distinct from hierarchical (superior-subordinate) relationships. Significantly, police supervisors spend considerable time in contact with other people in the organization (and some outside the organization) who are neither their superior nor their subordinate. In a typical medium-sized department, for example, supervisors should maintain close working relationships with as many as 20 to 30 people who are not superiors or subordinates. Broadly, the benefits to be gained by an increased level of coordination within a police department can be summarized as offsetting costs connected with specialization. Specifically, these benefits are

1. *Job satisfaction.* Improved job satisfaction results from the individual experiencing a sense of accomplishment, self-expression, self-identification, and completion.

2. *Risk-taking behavior.* Ideas are expressed in terms of bettering the entire group or organization and are a product of a group and not a single individual.

3. *Optimization.* Police officers are prevented from identifying with their own specialty and thus losing sight of the over-all organization. Police officers integrate their work activities so that ideas, materials, and information pass smoothly from unit to unit.

4. *Mutual support.* Greater coordination provides not only a rational redesign of the formal organization, but also psychological procedures which improve communications, and mutual understanding and support among the groups within the police organization.

5. *Enhanced productivity.* Better coordination does not automatically guarantee higher productivity. However, it does guarantee an opportunity for increasing it. This is to say, good coordination provides a basis for greater productivity.

6. *Effective personnel development.* Coordination facilitates broadened job knowledge by allowing members of the organization to observe and experience the variety of functions performed. This form of a job enlargement insures police management of having personnel capable of understanding the over-all operations and objectives of the department. Eventually, these personnel furnish the police

organization with a valuable pool of supervisory talent, in that they bring to the supervisor's position wide experience and background.

7. *Improved efficiency.* The above six benefits, as does this one, hinge on better interpersonal relationships. In police organizations that stress coordinated plans of operation, police personnel can begin immediately to develop a pattern of interpersonal relationships, since they are not hindered by the need to adjust and readjust their behavior to the status offered to a specialist. This means that the process of developing interpersonal relationships requires more time in highly specialized groups than in less specialized groups. As a result, specialized groups are slower than nonspecialized groups and, therefore, less efficient in successfully moving toward the goals of the department. Further, operational efficiency increases because greater coordination causes a lessening in intergroup struggles, which frequently enable men to avoid responsibility, to "pass the buck." Hence, better coordination leads to the pinpointing of responsibility.

In regard to the disadvantages inherent in coordination, there is one that has considerable magnitude. First, the very act of organizing generates specialization. Consequently, the development of specialized units immediately challenges the police supervisor's ability to coordinate. Second, the creation of specialized units causes strong psychological forces in the members of these units to identify with their particularistic interests and objectives. Third, traditional organization theory prescribes tasks as being the basis of dividing work. All this is to say that it appears specialization has everything going for it. Important here is the growing knowledge that the flow of work suffers in such a structure.[11] Many are coming to the realization that the flow of work in the police organization requires viable horizontal and vertical integration, that is, coordination across and perpendicularly in the structure. Added to this problem is the previously mentioned fact that specialization and coordination are essentially incompatible and that one can be obtained only at the expense of the other.[12] To summarize, the disadvantage of increased coordination lies in the twofold difficulty of overcoming the strong emphasis on specialization and reconciling the need for specialization with the need for coordination. In the next section we examine some possible ways to escape this seemingly impossible dilemma.

COORDINATION: THE ROLE OF THE POLICE SUPERVISOR

Up to this point we have questioned the contribution of specialization to police work. Further, we have emphasized that a police supervisor's prob-

---

[11] Possibly the strongest argument for less specialization and greater coordination is made by Robert T. Golembiewski, *Organizing Men and Power: Patterns of Behavior and Line-Staff Models* (Chicago, Ill.: Rand McNally and Company, 1967).

[12] Paul R. Lawrence and Jay W. Lorsch, "Differentiation and Integration in Complex Organizations," *Administrative Science Quarterly*, 12 (June 1967), 47.

lems do not end when he has broken a single job into parts that can be handled by specialists. Supervisory success depends on being able to put these parts together again and on developing coordination among various individuals and groups so that the total departmental goals can be achieved. Of concern is the fact that the division of labor and the technology formalize a pattern of human relations; change one and you change the other. Supervisors typically underestimate the human relations consequence of even slight changes in specialization or equipment. Yet these have a direct impact on who must do what with whom, when, and where. Obviously, the role of the police supervisor includes the furtherance of coordination. In order to bring about increased coordination the police supervisor must engage in the following types of behavior: (1) organizational perspective, (2) organizational responsibility, (3) procedure development, and (4) administrative detail. Each of these four items forms a part of the police supervisor's role in the organization, and, moreover, provides a means for strengthening coordination, which, in turn, assists the department in more effectively achieving its goals. Before we take a closer look at each role determinant, one extremely important point should be made. The four processes or role determinants are behavioral. Little attention has been given to what might be accomplished in a structural way to foster coordination. The now to be described role determinants are present and ready to be used by the police supervisor. In the next section we discuss what could be done structurally to support the supervisor in his efforts to fulfill his role as coordinator.

Organizational Perspective

If those in a police organization do not think in terms of the over-all goals of the organization, their endeavors are bound to be fragmented and inadequate. The police supervisor who can impart an organizational perspective which encompasses all the goals of his department directly enhances its effectiveness. The supervisory role requirements for developing organizational perspective and goal emphasis are somewhat similar, in that they both deal with the goals of the department. However, they differ in a significant way: *the former role is informative in nature, while the latter is an obligation to set constantly higher levels of desired achievement.* Essentially, the goals of a police department are dependent upon two organizational perspectives. The supervisor should impart both. One, *external perspective,* has to do primarily with the complex which we may call organization-in-environment. We have earlier shown that an organization should be defined as an ongoing, open system, in a state of dynamic interaction with its environment. This environment is made up in part of other organizations: criminal justice agencies, other related governmental agencies, service organizations, private business firms, and the public.

External perspective requires the police supervisor to build for himself and his subordinates a sensitivity to the demands which the police organization must meet to satisfy its environment. Further external perspective requires developing a sensitivity to changes in the environment, which is characteristically in a state of movement, both with respect to the demands it makes on police organizations and to the opportunities it affords to them. Obviously, the police supervisor is not the sole source of external perspective. Indeed, he may depend heavily on others in the police department to assist him. The basic demand on the police supervisor for external perspective remains, nevertheless, and the importance of instilling such perspective increases as one ascends upward in the police organization. Lack of such perspective has led once successful police departments to persist in the service of conventional goals when the majority of the community was interested in other services as well.

The idea of internal system perspective is similar in many ways to the notion of external perspective. Every police organization consists of suborganizations, or groups. These groups have different needs, and the perspective in them portrays characteristically different strivings. It is an unavoidable task of police supervision to attempt to integrate these group differences; indeed, coordination and control of groups. To perform this role successfully requires constant awareness and perceptiveness of the changing requirements of the groups and their members. Consider, for a moment, the staff and the uniform service divisions. The staff division judges police service very largely on how efficiently it is performed. The uniform division, on the other hand, is in direct touch with the public and is more concerned with meeting the needs of the public than with conforming to efficiency requirements. For the supervisor who must relate the different strivings of these and other groups, interpersonal skills are useful, but something more is still required. The police supervisor will be more effective if he understands the dynamics, needs, and potential of these groups and if he can express that understanding in terms of the mission of the department. Therefore, to provide organizational perspective, external and internal, the police supervisor must first possess it himself.

Organizational Responsibility

The police supervisor must first have a sound knowledge and appreciation of the responsibility of police personnel to their public before he can effectively impart it to his subordinates. Furthermore, this knowledge is also externalized and internalized. Beside the broad responsibility to the general public, the police supervisor must develop an internal sense of responsibility on the part of the members to their department. The first can be measured by one's contribution to society, the second by the amount of loyalty to the police agency.

In regard to one's contribution to society, four basic duties must be fulfilled: (1) welfare, (2) equity, (3) achievement, and (4) participation.[13] Together they form a standard of public responsibility that the police supervisor should practice; in fact, he should make them a part of his personal philosophy and conduct. Each of the four duties should be further divided into more specific functions for accomplishment. Concerning a police officer's internal responsibility, he is expected to do certain tasks in certain ways. The supervisor has a role for both assigning tasks and explaining them. If performed, and in the desired manner, we can say that the person is expressing loyalty, that is, adhering to his organizational responsibility.

Organizational responsibilities are easily stated but not simple to achieve. Of the previous two, the internal set of duties is more readily comprehended and performed. Responsibilities to the external environment of public interest are more vague and thus difficult to instruct. Regardless, however, the role of police supervisor includes a requirement for motivating himself and others to perform a set of duties that constitute an individual officer's dual responsibility to his particular police organization and the public interest.

Procedure Development

Procedure development is supervisory behavior that supports a subordinate in the performance of his duties. It is related to two other supervisory role requirements, support-subordinate and work facilitation. The distinction among the three role behaviors is that the former consists of establishing *work methods and rules* that directly assist the individual in his job. The second deals with the *human dimension* (job satisfaction, self-expression, and self-identification). The third interrelates the work through *appropriate planning and organizing*.

That the police supervisor should be constantly striving to identify and formalize operational procedures that aid the police officer in his work seems a truism. Frankly, we have to admit that there are supervisors, yes—police supervisors, that either ignore or completely violate this requirement. Consequently, on occasion we find supervisors intentionally constructing barriers between the officer and the successful achievement of assigned duties. Certainly this poses a severe problem for police management. Our position is more optimistic; namely, most police supervisors are interested in supporting the work activities of their subordinates and coordinating them with the activities of other work groups. Our main concern in this section switches, therefore, away from the procedure itself to the process from which it is derived.

Briefly, and this is an underlying theme in the text, subordinates should

---

[13] Harlan Cleveland, "A Philosophy for the Public Executive," in *Perspectives on Public Management*, ed. Robert T. Golembiewski (Itasca, Ill.: F. E. Peacock Publishers, Inc., 1968), p. 20.

be allowed to *participate in the making of those decisions that affect them.* To put it another way, as a group, subordinates should be involved in the establishment of the procedures that guide their working efforts. Ample evidence shows that the use of group methods for decision making results in improved performance.[14] More will be said about group methods in the section on team policing. One word of clarification is vital at this point, however. It deals with the responsibility of the police supervisor for the outcome of group decisions.

> It is essential that the group method of decision making and supervision not be confused with committees which never reach decisions or with [the] "wishy-washy," "common-denominator" sort of committee about which the superior can say, "Well, the group made this decision, and I couldn't do a thing about it." Quite the contrary! The group method of supervision holds the superior fully responsible for the quality of all decisions and for their implementation. He is responsible for building his subordinates into a group which makes the best decisions and carries them out well. *The superior is accountable for all decisions, for their execution, and for the results.*[15]

Administrative Detail

As previously stated, the supervisor's role includes the handling of administrative detail. This means, basically, that the police supervisor is responsible for keeping the numerous small tasks that are an integral part of any formal organization at a minimum. Moreover, he must prevent these small tasks from adversely affecting coordination within and between police units. Administrative detail can (and usually does) detract from the efforts of a police unit. The unit, in essence, spends time on details when it should be attending to the store.

By either reducing the amount of administrative detail or by processing it himself, the police supervisor provides the department with two important benefits: (1) less nonproductive activity by the subordinates and (2) increased motivation and time for coordinative efforts. While doing so, the supervisor may well become the great "detail artist," which must also be avoided. There are two major ways to extricate the police supervisor from time-consuming small tasks. One deals with operating procedures and the other with the computer. Hence one means is readily available and the other, for most, lies in the future. Both are capable of taking small tasks and processing them as a matter of routine. Consequently, much of the processing can

---

[14] Philip B. Applewhite, *Organizational Behavior* (Englewood Cliffs, N.J.: Prentice-Hall, Inc., 1965), p. 78.

[15] Rensis Likert, *The Human Organization: Its Management and Value* (New York: McGraw-Hill Book Company, 1968), p. 69.

be handled either by clerks or by automated equipment, thus freeing the police supervisor for more important activities.

In summary, in order to achieve coordination within and among police units, the members of these units must not be burdened with administrative detail. It is the responsibility of the police supervisor to see that this does not happen to his work group or to himself. Administrative details susceptible to "programming" ought to be handled by clerical personnel or automated machinery.[16] The ultimate reward is more time for integrating the efforts of individuals and groups into a cohesive system for goal attainment.

TEAM POLICING: STRUCTURAL COORDINATION

The police organization should be more than a structure for exerting authority, communicating information, and coordinating roles. To explain, the police organization, like most others, emphasizes that the authority structure is by far the most important of the three. However, in general, organizational growth, professionalization, and new knowledge have all tended to reduce the significance of authority in our thinking about structure and to increase the weight of other dimensions like communication and coordination. Significantly, we are really just beginning to reattack the structural problem after leaving it alone for many years. It is an important issue, both because the structure we work in clearly has a great deal to do with how happy we are while in the organization, how effective the organization is in reaching its goals, and how we behave, and also *because structure is susceptible to manipulation and change.* If we could learn more about what effects to expect from particular changes in the structure, we might be able to answer a key question in modern organizational theory: "*Which organizational* designs are appropriate for which tasks?" More specific to our interests: "Which organizational design is most appropriate for local law enforcement?" While it may not be the best answer, team policing does offer (with proper recognition of the importance of authority) a structural design that not only facilitates but also advances the cause of improved communications and coordination. Naturally, the traditional structure is violated to exploit full potentialities inherent in a new and modern approach to organizing the police service. Therefore, *underpinning the over-all need for team policing is the development of a modern structure that integrates all components of the police organization into a coordinative pattern of action for better accomplishing its goals.*

To continue our analysis and description of team policing, let us again consider the need for cooperation in an organization, remembering that it

---

[16] For further information on this concept, see Herbert A. Simon, *The Shape of Automation: For Men and Management* (New York: Harper and Row, Publishers, 1965), pp. 68–75.

is the basis of coordinated activity. The patterned activity which makes up a police organization is so intrinsically cooperative and interrelated that it tends to resemble habitual behavior. Within every unit of a police department one can find countless acts of cooperation without which the organization would break down. Most of us take these everyday acts for granted, and few are included in the formal role prescriptions of a position. One officer assists another in solving an investigative problem. Patrol officers supply vice officers with pertinent information on observed vice situations. The list of such examples is infinite. Police supervisors lend credence to the need for cooperative relationships by raising specific questions about an officer's capacity for them when he is considered for an assignment. How well does he relate to his co-workers; is he a good team man; will he fit in?

By now, hopefully, we fully understand and appreciate the reasons for advocating greater coordination in a police organization. Simply stated, team policing fosters coordination and communication. More important still is the fact that it fosters horizontal coordination and communication, two processes highly difficult to attain. Relatedly, team policing is also a structural tool for combating Downs' Law of Decreasing Coordination: "*The larger any organization becomes, the poorer is the coordination among its actions.*"[17] In regard to this law, he explains:

> Certain types of organizational structures provide better coordination than others. Nevertheless, no accounting systems, high-speed computers, or structural reorganizations can ever overcome [it]. . . .[18]

Let us remain optimistic over the possibilities of team policing for rescinding the Law of Decreasing Coordination.

Well, just what is team policing? Bennis provides a generalized description of team policing as: adaptive, temporary systems of diverse specialists, solving problems, linked together by coordinating and task-evaluative specialists, in organic flux. As no catchy phrase comes to mind, let us call this an "*organic-adaptive*" structure.[19] In other words, it is the merging of all program (line) units into a single whole. This larger group of generalists and specialists is then divided into a number of work teams, each comprised of a combination of generalists (patrolmen) and specialists (vice, traffic, detective, and juvenile officers). Next, the teams are assigned the responsibility for performing all program functions necessary to accomplish the goals of the department. The mix of generalists and specialists on the teams is determined by the area to be serviced. To illustrate, let us suppose that a depart-

---

[17] Anthony Downs, *Inside Bureaucracy* (Boston, Mass.: Little, Brown, and Company, 1967), p. 143.
[18] *Ibid.*
[19] Bennis, *Changing Organizations.*

ment decides to divide its geographical area into six patrol beats, or areas. Each beat would be allotted three Police Teams (Team 1, days; Team 2, nights; and Team 3, mornings). The mix of police personnel on the Teams on beat 1 depends on the type and number of services to be performed. Hence, we might find Team 1 comprising ten patrolmen, two traffic officers, four detectives, and two juvenile officers; Team 2 comprising 14 patrolmen, two traffic officers, one detective, and one vice officer; and Team 3 comprising ten patrolmen. Similarly, the other beats would vary according to the particular services required.

Organizing around team policing demands other changes beyond the grouping of generalists and specialists together in a work unit. First, the generalists and specialists rotate among the three teams within a beat, and among the various assignments within a team. Second, the organizational structure has to be decentralized (there are new and growing arguments for greater decentralization of operations).[20] Third, related to decentralization is the facing downward of the locus of effective decision making. Fourth, the hierarchical shape of the organization becomes susceptible to, in fact influenced toward, a reduced number of vertical levels within its framework. Finally, and of greatest consequence, is the need for vastly improved training programs. All of the above points are dependent upon a better qualified— in every sense of the word—police officer. In other words, the "compleat cop."

We have thus far described an innovative, and admittedly untested, way of reorganizing the police structure. However, the President's Commission on Law Enforcement and Administration of Justice has recommended that the police "experiment with team policing combining patrol and investigative duties."[21] It is seen that our proposed course of action extends beyond their original thinking. What are some other compelling pressures for a changed organizational form? To cite a few of the more outstanding pressures, our present system of policing

1. Fragments the operational components in geographical, expertness, and psychological senses.
2. Creates suborganizations which suboptimize in terms of the more encompassing goals.
3. Decreases the likelihood of horizontal integration (viable lateral relations between the suborganizations).

---

[20] Salient among the growing body of literature in decentralization is a collection of articles contained in the *Public Administration Review*. All are commendable; however, of particular merit is the article by Herbert Kaufman, "Administrative Decentralization and Political Power," *PAR*, 29 (January–February 1969), 3–14.

[21] *Task Force Report: The Police*. Prepared by the President's Commission on Law Enforcement and Administration of Justice (Washington, D.C.: U.S. Superintendent of Documents, 1967), p. 53.

4. Increases intersuborganization conflict by causing the suborganizations to compete for success.

The necessary changes are not going to occur, however, unless certain objectives are overcome and other issues are resolved. Let us list some questions that will have to be asked and subsequently answered. These questions deal with, among other things, rank, salary, quality of performance, level of required expertise, training, retention, discipline, and job rotation.[22] Whether the police organization is amenable to team policing is, in essence, the major question. A simple *no* to this question lacks proper thought and optimism. Only well-planned research and experimentation can provide the answer we are looking for, the correct one.

In conclusion, what does team policing hold for the police supervisor? Most significantly, organizing for team policing substantially improves the supervisor's chances of meeting the assigned objectives of his particular work team. This is so because (1) coordination is enhanced, (2) more opportunity exists for motivating higher levels of performance, (3) errors are more easily spotted and corrected, and (4) training and development programs are reinforced by the new structure.[23] One final note—the above description is incomplete. Missing is a very critical concern for the overlapping of multiple groups (teams) within the structure. Figure 12 attempts to depict a police department organized for team policing and with overlapping (linking) group relationships. The intent of this section has been, therefore, to stimulate thought and eventually action in regard to better forms of organizing for police work.

BASICS OF COORDINATION

The list following shortly includes both the behavioral and structural techniques for bringing about increased coordination in a police department. Those of behavioral nature are immediately (not necessarily easily) available for application. In other words, the police supervisor is able to apply them right now. Those of a structural nature are not, in most cases, at hand. Furthermore, they are exceedingly difficult to attain because considerable

---

[22] For example, in regard to job rotation, Rensis Likert indicates that "Rotation and changed personnel assignments are valuable and needed for such purposes as developing personnel, stimulating creativity, pumping new blood into old groups, and handling technological changes and organizational growth, but they tend to prevent work groups from becoming highly effective. In order to achieve and maintain a high level of cooperative working relationships, rapid changes in personnel assignments should be avoided insofar as possible." *New Patterns of Management* (New York: McGraw-Hill Book Company, 1961), p. 184.

[23] For a comprehensive explanation of these four points, see Golembiewski, *Organizing Men and Power*, pp. 188–232.

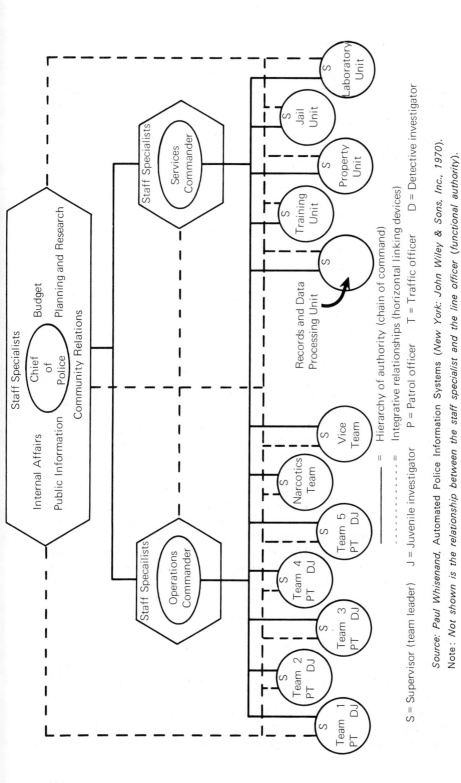

Staff Specialists

Internal Affairs
Public Information

Chief
of
Police

Budget
Planning and Research
Community Relations

Staff Specialists

Operations
Commander

Staff Specialists

Services
Commander

Records and Data
Processing Unit

Team 1
PT DJ
S

Team 2
PT DJ
S

Team 3
PT DJ
S

Team 4
PT DJ
S

Team 5
PT DJ
S

Narcotics
Team
S

Vice
Team
S

S

Training
Unit
S

Property
Unit
S

Jail
Unit
S

Laboratory
Unit
S

====== = Hierarchy of authority (chain of command)

======== = Integrative relationships (horizontal linking devices)

———— = Line relationships

S = Supervisor (team leader)   J = Juvenile investigator   P = Patrol officer   T = Traffic officer   D = Detective investigator

Source: Paul Whisenand, Automated Police Information Systems (New York: John Wiley & Sons, Inc., 1970).

Note: Not shown is the relationship between the staff specialist and the line officer (functional authority).

FIG. 12. A POLICE DEPARTMENT ORGANIZED ACCORDING TO MODERN ORGANIZATIONAL THEORY.

203

reorganization is required. All techniques are offered to assist the police supervisor in implementing four of his assigned role requirements: (1) organizational perspective, (2) organizational responsibility, (3) procedural development, and (4) administrative detail. As indicated, it is through the fulfillment of these requirements that coordination can be achieved.

As mentioned, the following list of techniques for achieving coordination comprises both behavioral and structural approaches. The first five are behavioral and the remaining two are structural.

Participation. The police supervisor must permit his subordinates to influence the job environment within which they work. There are, of course, degrees and types of participation. We refer here, however, to the engagement of an officer in the department so that he is involved in decisions which affect him as a departmental member. The effect is—he has both a voice and a vote in the work unit in which he functions and a voice and a vote in the representation of that work unit in the entire department. *And,* this type of participation guarantees an opportunity to coordinate his thinking and activities with others in his work unit.

Job enlargement. The police supervisor must plan the work so that it allows his subordinates more variety and more individual responsibility for the over-all work cycle. Job enlargement is decidedly applicable to police work. In essence, it does not promote coordination as much as it reduces the need for it. To explain, since the officer is handling an enlarged set of work tasks, there is less of a requirement for close coordination of efforts. The need for coordination remains even with the job enlargement. The major benefit here is that false or unnecessary coordination because of poor work design is abated through job enlargement.

Group decision making. Akin to participation is the need for group decision making, a simple if revolutionary technique for developing coordination. A typical application involves the setting by a police supervisor of general objectives to meet increasingly growing crime rates. Work units in the department, cognizant of these general objectives, determine and enforce a level of output. Traditional supervisory practice countenances no such silliness—an order would suffice. Despite the newness surrounding the concept, group decision making increases the probability of participation in decisions by those who must execute them. And, significantly, such participation vastly increases coordination.

Job rotation. Related to job enlargement is job rotation. In fact, it might be considered one form of job enlargement. Simply stated, job rotation is the transferring of personnel from one position to another. The process is quite complex, however. Moreover, the results can be highly supportive of a coordinative effort. This is so because job rotation builds an improved (1) knowledge of the total job and (2) an appreciation for the activities and objectives of other work units. Job rotation is also a means for circumventing those areas within the department that are incapable of employing job enlargement.

Integrated training. Training, just as the police organization, tends to become fractured and splintered into a series of unrelated programs. The training officer usually finds his day divided into training efforts that do not integrate the various work units into a systematic pattern of cooperative behavior. "Systems" training, involving all officers, is of importance here. In other words, detectives, patrolmen, and so on, must be trained as a team, a unified group of personnel trained to coordinate their work efforts.

Team policing. Most of the argument for this particular technique is given earlier in this chapter. As discussed, team policing is an innovative plan for structuring coordination. Considerable organizational change must be made in order to achieve it. In this case, the police supervisor rearranges his work unit or team into a body of police personnel that possess the responsibility for handling and making decisions about all of the line police functions. The police supervisor thus assumes a coordinative role for relating a group of police generalists and specialists in such a fashion that they become all the more effective.

Linking of teams. Police supervision can and should extend from the bottom to the top of the hierarchy, linking successive teams and work groups together as supervisors, alternately, are superiors in one group and subordinates in the second. This linking tends to set a stage for good coordinative action, depending, of course, on the manner in which policy is suggested and carried out through these overlapping small groups. A basic assumption in this revised structure is that *the linking of teams through a superior-subordinate overlap has major implications for greater coordination and productivity.*

SUMMARY

Our fundamental argument is that effective supervisory control stimulates human cooperation; human cooperation gives impetus to the coordination of effort; and, it is through the coordination of human effort that a police department is able to become more effective. Cooperation can be thought of as activity in which the organizational members share a common goal. Further, coordination is the process of organizationally interrelating individuals and groups to one another. The interrelationships can and should occur in two directions: vertical and horizontal. The latter is most often neglected and difficult to establish.

Our modern police departments, similar to other organizations, have fallen victim to the demands of modern society. As modern society grows larger and ever more complex it automatically demands an ever-increasing level of specialization on the part of men and machinery. Now the hang-up—specialization and coordination are basically incompatible, and yet the need for both is constantly increasing. Hence, this dilemma continues not only to exist but also to become all the more injurious to our formal organizations. Modern police supervisors are very familiar with this issue. They are constantly struggling with the difficulty of reconciling the need for specialization with the need for coordination of effort. Thankfully, we now have data that provides some clues to conditions that seem able to make it possible to achieve high specialization and high coordination simultaneously. Our analysis suggests that any balance between these two states should favor coordination.

As indicated in the first chapter, the police supervisor plays a highly critical role in developing and maintaining a high degree of coordinative effort. To fulfill this role, he must provide for his subordinates: (1) organizational perspective, (2) an understanding of their organizational responsibility, (3) procedure development, and (4) administrative detail. These requirements are behavioral. Little attention has been devoted to what might be done structurally to enhance coordination. Two substructural innovations, both untested, are team policing and overlapping group memberships. The two approaches combined link the organizational units vertically and, moreover, horizontally.

The four role determinants mentioned previously can be fulfilled by providing the subordinates with a job environment that has as its principal characteristics: (1) participation, (2) job enlargement, (3) group decision making, (4) job rotation, (5) integrated training, (6) team policing, and (7) linking of teams. All seven techniques are designed to aid the police supervisor in bringing about heightened levels of coordination.

PROBLEMS

The problem, while singular, incorporates all the ideas and techniques discussed in this chapter. Construct a futuristic plan which assures a police department of an unusually high degree of coordination. Your plan encompasses both behavioral and structural considerations. Prepare a one-page justification for your new, model police department. Additionally, relate some of the more important barriers to implementing your model. Be as specific as possible in terms of the requisite structure and job design necessary to promote coordination.

9

The
Police Supervisor
as a Leader

This chapter poses for the reader both questions and answers on the theory and practice of leadership as it relates to police supervision. Admittedly, more questions are asked than answers furnished. The reason for this disparity is that (although for centuries writers and researchers have studied the subject) the literature on leadership remains vast, discursive, and without a conceptual framework for shaping the requisite information into a meaningful body of knowledge. Thanks to a study by Bowers and Seashore we are able to approach leadership in an unusually organized manner.[1] Further, we should also thank various people dating from Aristotle to modern day behavioral scientists for their ideas and data. Therefore, we are concerned with developing informational consistencies, exploring some neglected issues, and finding the techniques for acquiring the role of organizational leader. Our message, simply stated, is: *Supervisory leadership is the product of making correct decisions on how to* (1) *support subordinates,* (2) *facilitate interaction,* (3) *emphasize high goal performance, and* (4) *facilitate work.* When all four tasks are performed, we can say that the supervisor is fulfilling his leadership role. Before continuing, the reader should take a few minutes to refresh his memory about organizational controls (Chapter 7) and decision making (Chapter 2, the section on problem solving; and Chapter 5, the section pertaining to the decision overlay).

To truly and fully appreciate the perplexities revolving in and around any discussion of supervisory leadership, we should keep in mind that

> Leadership is not a familiar, everyday idea, as readily available to common sense as to social science. It is a slippery phenomenon that eludes them both. What leaders do is hardly self-evident. And it is likely that much failure of

---

[1] In the estimation of this author, either *the* or at least *one of the* outstanding contributions to the study of leadership during the 1960s is contained in the article by David G. Bowers and Stanley E. Seashore, "Predicting Organizational Effectiveness with a Four-Factor Theory of Leadership," *Administrative Science Quarterly,* 11 (September 1966), 238–63.

leadership results from an inadequate understanding of its true nature and tasks.[2]

Some are quick to say, "If the subject of leadership is so darn difficult, why bother?" The police supervisor is not permitted the luxury of such a response. More and more he is expected to behave as a leader. The reason for this expectation can be divided into two parts. In the first place, considerable evidence shows that the productivity of a work unit is affected by the kind of supervisory leadership the unit receives. In the second place, ample evidence also indicates that the satisfaction and general morale of the individuals in a work unit is influenced by the kind of leadership exerted. The crux of the question is, consequently, what should a supervisor do in order to become a leader and, of equal significance, how should he do it? To put it another way, "What is the appropriate leadership role and style (behavior) for a supervisor in a police department?"

The previous introductory material is suggestive, in part, of the roadway and roadblocks in the remaining sections of this chapter. We encounter, in the following sequence, (1) leadership defined, (2) the need for leadership, (3) the role of a supervisory leader, (4) the various styles of leadership, (5) supervision—leadership—decision making, and (6) the basic techniques for effective leadership.

LEADERSHIP: WHAT IS IT?

Fortunately, it is beginning to look as if a theory based on empirical findings is finally in the making. No one yet knows precisely what its ultimate content will be, but its framework can now be perceived and—even more valuable—put to use to improve supervisory practice. Leadership has been studied both by observing the lives of great men (descriptive) and by attempting to identify the personality traits of acknowledged leaders through assessment techniques (empirical). As mentioned earlier, a review of the research literature from these studies, however, reveals few consistent findings. Since World War II research emphasis has shifted from a search for personality traits to a search for behavior that makes a difference in the performance or satisfaction of the followers. Our focus is naturally on the latter approach.

To eventually understand leadership we must first be aware that the position of a police supervisor includes only the opportunity to be an organizational leader. Thus, an individual assigned to the formal position of

[2] Philip Selznick, *Leadership in Administration* (New York: Harper & Row, Publishers, 1957), p. 22.

police supervisor does not receive any guarantee that he either automatically or ultimately will assume the role of an organizational leader. A supervisory position merely provides the opportunity for an individual to become a formal leader. Failing to grasp this all-important leadership opportunity can be, and much too frequently is, a serious fault on the part of the police supervisor. The police supervisor capable of incorporating the role of formal leader into his position offers his department the probability of obtaining optimum personal effectiveness. Obviously, decisions about which style of leadership to adopt must to some extent be made for the department as a whole rather than being left to the intuitions of individual supervisors. More pointedly,

> History, administrative experience, behavioral science research all testify that when leadership is defined without reference to destination or to the particular waters to be navigated, we may be led around in circles or indeed, simply drift.[3]

We have reached a point where a few basic assumptions are required. First, *leadership in a police department is definitely not limited to positions of command or extensive formal authority*. In fact, all personnel, regardless of their position, are capable of exerting leadership. In our case, however, interest centers on supervisory leadership. Second, *the ability of a police supervisor to act as a leader is determined both by his personality* (to a limited extent) *and by his formally assigned work role* (to a major extent). Hence, leadership is a function of the formal work role as well as of the personality. We now define what we mean by leadership or leader.

Leadership, in social science literature, has three major meanings: as the attribute of a situation, as the characteristic of a person, and as a category of behavior. To be a police supervisor is to occupy a position of authority, and to be a chief of police is to occupy a position of greater authority. Yet, certain supervisors exercise considerable authority, and the chiefs of some departments exercise very little. Authority is the right to command! In a police department, authority resides in a position. Thus the question, if two supervisors occupy the same type of position in an organization, why might their amount of actual authority differ? Basically, the position is static, that is, it contains certain rights. And, equal positions command equal authority. Not inherent in the position is the ability to command. This ability resides in the supervisory position itself, in the individual assigned to that position, and in the characteristics of the over-all work situation.

---

[3] James W. Fesler, "Leadership and Its Content," *Public Administration Review*, 20 (Spring 1960), 122.

The ability to command is another way of saying power or influence. All of us, to some extent, exert influence. Thus we witness situations where the supervisor is led by a follower. In other words, because of a particular situation and a subordinate's personality, the supervisor may be so influenced as to accept (usually on a temporary basis) the leadership of a subordinate.

Since we have mentioned the terms *personality* and *situation*, it is important that we pause and specifically relate them to leadership. For a long time the study of leadership followed two notions: (1) that leadership could be narrowly equated with position in an organization and (2) that leaders were born, not made. The result of these notions was an extensive search for the traits of the leader. A further notion was implicit in this approach— if leader types could be identified and selected, the problems of leadership in organizations would be solved. Enthusiasm for this approach cooled, however, when experience made it evident that while two individuals might possess the same traits, group leadership was exercised effectively by one case but not the other. As an example, the leader of the department-sponsored basketball team is not necessarily the most qualified supervisor. Moreover, although leaders possess some traits more markedly than do followers, the differences cannot be too great in either direction if the group is to operate effectively. In fact, good leaders are judged to be good followers. To put it another way, the ability to follow might be considered one critical component of good leadership.[4] To sum up the argument against traits, "While individual traits cannot be ignored, a knowledge of the individual leader yields a very imperfect understanding of leadership itself."[5] The rejection of the trait approach caused a shift toward analysis of leadership as social role (expectations of other organizational members) as determined by the situation. The salient implication of this newer approach is that leadership takes place in a situation and is specific to that situation. Situation, position, and people combine in a particular way to produce leadership. More is said about the situational approach in the forthcoming section devoted to leadership style.

The assignment of supervisory responsibilities and the delegation of authority for their accomplishment indicates that the right to command is expected to be exercised. To do so, however, requires a specified level of influence. Merely relying on the influence inherent in the position does not make the police supervisor a leader. If he draws upon his personality and uses the characteristics of the situation to enhance his influence, then he is an organizational leader. Influence derived exclusively from the position is routine and thus usually results in suboptimal performance. Influence based on one's personality, situation, and position allows a person to engage

---

[4] For research findings supporting this contention, see E. P. Hollander, *Leaders, Groups, and Influence* (New York: Oxford University Press, 1964).

[5] Herbert Bonner, *Group Dynamics* (New York: The Ronald Press Company, 1959), p. 176.

in behavior which extends beyond required performance and to realize more fully the potential of a given position for organizational influence. Therefore, the essence of *organizational leadership* is the influential increment over and above mechanical compliance with the routine directives of the organization. This is our definition of leadership. It is constructed out of five basic assumptions. First, leadership is behavior that not only meets established organizational requirements, but also the needs of individuals as well. The fulfillment of organizational requirements is expected of the police supervisor, therefore, in doing this he is acting as expected, as a supervisor. When his behavior extends beyond the traditional role and provides individual need fulfillment, the supervisor is acting as a leader. Second, leadership is, consequently, not equivalent to position or authority. Third, leadership is dispensable, in that the organization can function (in most instances not very effectively) without it. In other words, the police department can attain its goals if the individuals perform their routine duties properly. Fourth, authority is vested by an organization in a position, thereby creating for the incumbent a certain degree of influence. Fifth, the individual's personality and work situation adds to the degree of influence that the incumbent possesses. It is in the relationship of the supervisor's personality to the work situation that we find the possibility of developing sufficient influence to make the police supervisor a leader.

In conclusion, all police supervisors at a given level in the police hierarchy are created equal. They do not, however, remain equal. Some of them are much more knowledgeable about the technical aspects of the situation than others; some have a better understanding of organization. Because of their personality, some have a better understanding of people and are more acceptable to their superiors and subordinates. An individual whose influence is chiefly derived from his supervisory position is referred to as a supervisor. One whose ability to influence others is chiefly personal is referred to as an informal leader. One who commands both positional and personal influence is a supervisory leader. We can see that the police supervisor who can assume, because of his personality and the situation, the role of a leader optimizes his potentiality for supervisory effectiveness (effectiveness equals goal accomplishment plus human need fulfillment) within his particular department.

THE NEED FOR LEADERSHIP

Including a section on the need for leadership in a police organization and, more directly, on the part of a police supervisor can generate two opposing responses. First, who needs a "needs" section? After all, leadership is so crucial to the proper functioning of the department that it must be covered. Or, second, who needs leadership to begin with? After all, once a police organization has attained a state of maturity, there is no requirement for leaders, leadership, and influential increments. Does not the exertion of influence in the organization automatically flow from its structural nature rather than from the people who happen to fill command and supervisory positions? Both responses can be answered. To the first response we ask "Why?" and to the second response we are compelled to say that the reader has completely missed the message thus far.

The need for those in positions of authority to assume the role of an organizational leader can be justified in four ways. First, and most significantly, a supervisor who is successful in his attempts to become a leader immensely increases the degree of influence that he possesses. The supervisory, that is, formal, leader can thus exert greater pressure on his subordinates for more effectively handling their assigned tasks. Further, the supervisory leader can use the social situation to improve worker job satisfaction. Second, organizations are by nature imperfect structures. They are much more complex than one is led to believe by an organization chart or policy manual. Perhaps this complexity is quickly understood by mentioning the intricacies and unwritten norms, values, and overlays of the previously discussed informal organization. It takes more than routine performance by those in positions of authority to keep the structure running smoothly. In other words, formal leadership is one way to offset the incompleteness of organizational design. Third, changing environmental conditions affect the goals and functions of formal organizations. Effective supervisory leadership enhances the department's capability for responding appropriately to these demands for change. Adaptation on the part of the organization necessitates that it be innovative over and above the performance of traditional duties; it requires leadership of a high order. This requirement holds true for changes that must occur in both the level and quality of service and the internal relationships among men and materials. Fourth, the nature of human involvement in organizations dictates the need for leadership. People belong to more than a single organization, and they express varying levels of competence, loyalty, cooperation, and personal growth. Much of what the leader has to do deals with these properties. Essentially, leadership includes the responsibility for building the human components into an integrated operating unit whereby optimization can result for individual and organization alike.

THE ROLE OF THE LEADER: FOUR DETERMINANTS

Let us begin by accepting the fact that a new theory of leadership, supported by considerable empirical research, is emerging. This theory states that *leadership is primarily determined by the organizational situation of which it is an integral part.*[6] Since leadership is an organizational activity, one cannot either understand or employ it successfully before coming to grips with the specific organizational situation. As indicated previously, the trait approach to leadership generally breaks down when the context of the leadership changes. Assertively, it is the situation that provides the fundamental determination of "who" (that is, which type of personality) shall be the leader. Bavelas puts it thusly:

> For example, a man who shows all the signs of leadership when he acts as the officer of a well-structured authoritarian organization may give no indication of leadership ability in a less-structured democratic situation. A man may become influential in a situation requiring deliberation and planning but show little evidence of leadership if the situation demands immediate action with no opportunity for weighing alternatives or thinking things out.[7]

Consequently, the position held and the expectations of the members of a particular group determine whether the assigned supervisor becomes a leader. Of course, one can, based on the demands of the situation, adapt to meet certain expectations. Therefore, it is the perceptive, sensitive, flexible, and knowledgeable individual that has the best chance of being appointed to a formal position such as police supervisor and of becoming a leader.

Next, let us briefly examine the nature of an organizational role.[8] *A role is determined by the behavior requirements of a position in an organization.* The human personality can be defined as an arrangement of the particular needs and dispositions of the individual. It is interesting to note that there are research studies on leadership which conclude that the organizational role tends to be a more basic determinant of behavior than the personality. Also, it has been found that it is possible to predict the behavior of a new man in a leadership position more accurately on the basis of the behavior of his predecessor in that post than on the behavior of the man himself in his previous position.[9] Ouch! Such findings tend to question the scope, method, and validity of our traditional civil service selection process. Similarly, if leadership training is not reinforced by the role requirements, then the

---

[6] Daniel Katz and Robert L. Kahn, *The Social Psychology of Organizations* (New York: John Wiley & Sons, Inc., 1966), p. 302.

[7] Alex Bavelas, "Leadership: Man and Function," *Administrative Science Quarterly*, 4 (March 1960), 495.

[8] For a comprehensive overview of role theory, see Bruce J. Biddle and Edwin J. Thomas, eds., *Role Theory* (New York: John Wiley & Sons, Inc., 1966).

[9] Carroll L. Shartle, *Executive Performance and Leadership* (Englewood Cliffs, N.J.: Prentice-Hall, Inc., 1956), p. 94.

training acts as a hindrance or may, in fact, prevent the person from becoming a leader.[10]

The formal and more traditional aspects of the police supervisor's role are best found in a position statement. The first chapter contained such a statement and we repeat it here.[11]

Police sergeant

Definition
Under general supervision to supervise patrolmen engaged in investigative, patrol, traffic, records, and juvenile duties; to receive the public and to answer inquiries; and to do related work as required.

Examples of duties
Supervises police patrolmen, policewomen, and clerical personnel in investigative, patrol, traffic, records, and juvenile divisions, supervises dispatching of personnel and personnel cars to investigate complaints; gives information to the public; assists officers in completing crime reports and arrest records and reviews and corrects completed reports; writes crime reports; supervises the maintenance of the radio log; searches and books prisoners; confiscates or stores and gives receipts for prisoners' property; tags exhibits in evidence; and fingerprints and assists in questioning prisoners; supervises the inspection of the city jail and enforces discipline, cleanliness, and order.

Minimum Qualifications
Knowledge of:
   Criminal law with reference to apprehension, arrest, and prosecution of persons committing misdemeanors and felonies, including rules of evidence pertaining to search and seizure
   Preservation and presentation of evidence in criminal cases and elements of typical misdemeanor and felony offenses
   The geography of the city and of the organization, operation, rules, and regulations of the police department
Ability to:
   Analyze situations and adopt quick, effective, and reasonable courses of action
   Supervise others
   Understand and follow directions
   Write clear, concise reports

Further, in regard to this statement, we also mentioned that it either explicitly or implicitly recommended (1) that the police supervisor is expected to accomplish the cited tasks, consequently he must possess specified basic

---

[10] Robert J. House, "Leadership Training: Some Dysfunctional Consequences," *Administrative Science Quarterly*, 12 (March 1968), 571.

[11] Taken from an announcement for a supervisor's promotional examination. Through the courtesy of the City of Torrance Police Department, Torrance, California (Code 7312, January 1966).

qualifications, (2) that the police department expects the incumbent to behave in a prescribed manner while accomplishing the assigned responsibilities, and (3) that entirely absent is any inference that the supervisor is expected to act as a leader. This statement reflects a static picture of police supervision because it stresses the end result. Any worthwhile consideration of a formal position must deal also with its dynamic aspects, that is, the expected behavior on the part of the person in the position. To sum up, the position statement indicates only the minimal or routine required behavior for a police supervisor. Only in the broader concept of a supervisory role can we discern four role determinants which comprise leadership:[12]

1. support-subordinate
2. interaction facilitation
3. goal emphasis
4. work facilitation

These four role determinants emerge from a host of current leadership studies.[13] While discussed separately, these dimensions are both interdependent and susceptible to further division. In fulfilling his responsibilities to the police department for assuming the role of leader, the police supervisor engages in behavior that can be described as follows: (1) support—behavior that promotes some other member's feeling of personal worth and importance within the department; (2) interaction facilitation—behavior that influences police personnel to develop close, mutually satisfying work relationships; (3) goal emphasis—behavior that creates an enthusiasm for meeting the department's goals or achieving excellent performance; and (4) work facilitation—behavior that helps achieve goal accomplishment by deploying, coordinating, and planning, and by providing organizational resources such as required materials and technical knowledge. The crux of the message contained in this section is that if the police supervisor also wants to be an organizational leader (and let us all hope that he does want to be a leader), he must engage in four types of behavior: support, interaction facilitation, goal emphasis, and work facilitation. We now look at each role determinant in more detail.

---

[12] Bowers and Seashore, "Predicting Organizational Effectiveness."

[13] Obviously there are other lists of role determinants. For example, Wager identifies eight areas of supervisory role determinants or obligations: identification with the total organization, attractiveness of members of formal work unit, perceived solidarity of members of formal work unit, work autonomy, promotional opportunity, layoff equity, general work satisfaction, and the intent to remain with the organization. Similar to other researchers, he believes that the supportive style of leadership assists the supervisor in fulfilling these role obligations. The importance of the leadership style variable is indicated by the fact that even when supervisors with low influence manifest the supportive style of leadership, it still contributes positively to the fulfillment of nearly all the areas of role obligations. Wesley L. Wager, "Leadership Style, Hierarchical Influence, and Supervisory Role Obligations," *Administrative Science Quarterly*, 9 (March 1965), 409–17.

Support-Subordinate

Likert is perhaps the foremost advocate of the supervisory leader applying the principle of supportive relationships. He states the principle as follows:

> The leadership and other processes of the organization must be such as to ensure a maximum probability that in all interactions and in all relationships within the organization, each member, in the light of his background, values, desires, and expectations, will view the experience as supportive and one which builds and maintains his sense of personal worth and importance.[14]

In applying this principle, the relationship between the police supervisor and subordinate is crucial. This relationship, as the principle specifies, should be supportive and ego-building. The more often the supervisor's behavior is ego-building, rather than ego-deflating, the better the effect of his behavior on organizational performance. In using this principle, it is essential that we keep in mind that the interactions among the leader and the subordinates must be perceived in the light of the subordinate's background, values, and expectations. "The subordinate's perception of the situation, rather than the supervisor's, determines whether or not the experience is supportive."[15] Both the behavior of the police supervisor and the police officer's perceptions of the situation must be such that the subordinate, in the light of his background, values, and expectations, sees the experience as one which adds to his feeling of self-esteem and importance, one which increases and maintains his sense of self-identification and human dignity.

The principle of "support-subordinate" is substantiated by empirical research findings. First, the formal leader is more faithfully followed the easier he makes it for subordinates to achieve their private goals, along with the organization's goals. Second, in small groups (three to 15 people), autocratic leadership is less effective than group-centered leadership in holding the group together and getting its work done. Group-centered leadership is more effective with respect to the durability of the group, the subordinates' job satisfaction, and their productivity on the task. Third, the more supportive the supervisor, (1) the less the absenteeism, (2) the more the productivity, (3) the more likely the subordinates are to feel that the organization requirements are reasonable, and the more willingly they accept change in organizational practices, (4) the better liked the leader is, (5) the more strongly the subordinates identify with the organization, (6) the less tension within the organizational unit and therefore the more internal cohesion, and

---

[14] Rensis Likert, *The Human Organization: Its Management and Value* (New York: McGraw-Hill Book Company, 1967), p. 47.

[15] *Ibid.*, p. 48.

(7) the higher the subordinates' morale as a member (one with supervisory responsibilities) of his particular work group, not as an external agent with authority. It can be concluded that *the better organizational leader firmly keeps the goal before his subordinates and urges them to meet it; at the same time, he treats them like human beings*, by recognizing and fulfilling their individual needs.

Interaction Facilitation

The critical need and nature of interaction has already been established. In review we mean by this term supervisory behavior that aids (makes easier) in the maintenance of healthy interpersonal relations. This role also finds considerable support in research data. To begin, it has been found that the leadership of subordinates must simultaneously satisfy two necessary but often conflicting individual needs: the need for initiative, guidance, contribution of ideas, etc. (the intellectual leader), and the need for harmony, liking, belongingness, etc. (the social leader). Next, within an organization, conflict between leaders and subordinates tends to increase along with the number and the concreteness and proscriptive nature of the organization's regulations concerning human interaction, and vice versa. One example of this last point can be found in the strict use of the chain of command as the only channel for interaction between organizational members.

Goal Emphasis

The leadership role of goal emphasis differs significantly from another role discussed in the preceding chapter, organizational perspective. The latter is primarily concerned with an explanation to and indoctrination of subordinates in the goals of the police organization. Goal emphasis denotes the setting of high performance aspirations. In other words, the leader must stimulate himself and others to greater levels of goal performance. Supervisors in police organizations, consequently, should have high performance aspirations, but every member should have high performance aspirations as well. Since these goals should not be imposed on police personnel, there must be a mechanism through which the police officers can help set the high-level goals which the satisfaction of their own needs requires. Such a mechanism has already been discussed; essentially it is comprised of (1) group decision making, (2) team policing, and (3) multiple overlapping groups. Since personal need fulfillment is important to the members of a police department, the goal-setting processes just mentioned most frequently lead to high performance goals for each unit and for the entire department. Any time these high performance aspirations do not exist, there is a deficiency in the interaction processes and in the supportive relationships in the organization. Furthermore, the more likely a person is to be rewarded by an organization, the more closely he identifies with the organization's stated goals. Also, when authority and responsibility within an organization do not at least roughly correspond to the (perceived) contributions of the members, there is likely to be more than the normal amount of loss of goal emphasis within the organization. And, lastly, the more personal support given by the police supervisor, the greater the probability that the subordinate will emphasize the goals of the police organization.

Work Facilitation

To repeat, work facilitation is supervisory behavior that assists the subordinate in the accomplishment of job tasks. Here the police supervisor has a responsibility for designing the job so that it is more pleasing and easier to perform. Davis' research basically proposed three different ways of designing a job:

1. Line Job Design. An assembly operation, paced by a conveyor, typical of classical job design in all respects except that workers rotated between hard and easy work stations every two hours. This deviation from routinization was due only to the inability to equalize skill requirements at each of the nine work stations.
2. Batch Job Design. The conveyor was eliminated and workers set their own pace. No other changes from the line job design were made.
3. Individual Job Design. Each worker performed all nine operations at his own station. In addition, the employee controlled the sequence of assembly, procured necessary supplies, and inspected his own output.[16]

His experimentation with the three designs showed that individual job design resulted in increased worker output. Moreover, he found that this design

1. Increased the flexibility of the production process.
2. Permitted the identification of individual deficiencies in productivity and quality.
3. Reduced the service functions of the department such as materials delivery and inspection.
4. Developed a more favorable attitude toward individual responsibility and effort —after experience with individual job design, workers disliked the lack of personal responsibility characteristic of line job design.[17]

---

[16] Louis E. Davis, "Job Design and Productivity: A New Approach," *Personnel*, 33 (March 1957), 421.

[17] *Ibid.*, p. 427.

These data provide a strong recommendation for work to be so organized, to allow for individual differences while preserving the administrative simplicity of salary systems and job requirements for those working on the same job. While the findings are derived from production-oriented enterprises, they hold true for police organizations, which evidence a high degree of job specialization.

The gist of the argument goes one step further by calling for a job design based on job enlargement. Job enlargement does not hark back to some supposedly idyllic state where everyone does everything. It does, however, advocate an effort on the part of the police supervisor to make the best of a significant proportion of the existing technology and human resources. Figure 13 illustrates two alternatives to organizing a set of operations. The letters *a*, *b*, *c*, and *d* designate the component tasks; the rectangles contain the task or tasks assigned to individual jobs. The work cycle in both cases is the same, *abcd*. The total work cycle is that set of operations necessary to advance one material unit of production, or in our case service, by one whole stage in the process of organizational output. The unit cycle consists

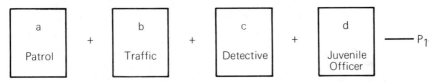

13.1. Traditional organization of simple tasks in a flow of work

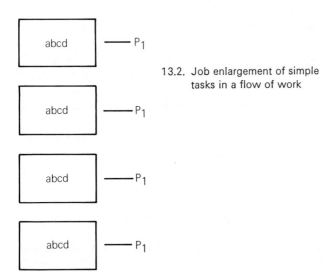

13.2. Job enlargement of simple tasks in a flow of work

FIG. 13. TWO APPROACHES TO ORGANIZING SIMPLE TASKS INTO JOBS

of *a* or *b* or *c* or *d* in Figure 13.1, and of *abcd* in Figure 13.2. Job enlargement, in these terms, means designing unit cycles to include either more or all of a work cycle. In conclusion, we should be aware that the leadership of a work group tends to be instilled in the supervisor (or, if he lacks the capability, in some other member of the group) when he possesses requisite information, resources, and skill directly related to the tasks constituting the various job designs.[18]

To briefly summarize, the above four role determinants are behaviors that the supervisor must exhibit to be a leader. Together, they serve the organization and the individual. Most important, however, is the recognition that *the leader's role is primarily devoted to aiding the members of the organization in the satisfaction of their individual needs.*

LEADERSHIP STYLES

Evidence supporting any one leadership style can always be countered by evidence supporting its precise opposite. The bewildered police supervisor that has tried and abandoned one style after another may well be pardoned for asking, "Where do I go from here?" On the classification of leadership styles, fortunately, there is more agreement. Most authorities recognize three basic types: "leader centered," or "authoritarian"; "group centered," or "democratic"; and "individual centered," or "laissez-faire."

In the authoritarian, or leader-centered, style all determination of policy and procedure is made by the leader. In the group-centered style, policies and procedures are a matter for group discussion and decision. The individual-centered approach provides complete freedom for group or individual decision. The supposedly modern view, of course, is that the group-centered style is the most conducive to improving organizational effectiveness. By contrast, the traditional view admits only the leader-centered style, regards the group-centered style as an idealistic notion of psychologists, and dismisses the free-rein style as constituting not leadership, but rather its abandonment.

Supporters of any all-or-nothing view have one thing in common: they will be surprised to learn that the research literature does not consistently support any one leadership style. The reason for this lies not in any failing of the research itself but in the fact that there is no best style. Indeed, the question, "Which kind of leadership should we use?" prevents any useful answer. The question should be, rather, "Which kind of leadership when?"

---

[18] For those interested in a comprehensive treatment of job design, see Ralph M. Barnes, *Motion and Time Study: Design and Measurement of Work* (New York: John Wiley & Sons, Inc., 1968).

In other words, "Give us the conditions and we'll be better able to recommend a particular leadership style." Consequently, we see, and expectedly so, that the style of the leader is determined more by the expectations of the subordinates and by the requirements of the situation than by the personal traits of the leader himself.[19] And, for those of you that are now or soon to fill managerial positions, it is well you remember that *the leader's style of leadership tends to be influenced by the style in which he himself is led.*

What, then, are the conditions in a situation that should be taken into account in the supervisor's choice of a leadership style? There are many. Six, however— personality, task characteristics, task roles, group characteristics, time, and decisions—are particularly important and have been explored in a number of leadership, time, and decisions studies. The characteristics of these six factors determine the leadership style that the police supervisor should use. Moreover, since they are subject to change, so must the particular leadership style be susceptible to modifications. Therefore, at one point in time the conditions in a supervisory situation can be conducive to a group-centered style. Within a few moments, however, the conditions can change to favor an autocratic style.

Interestingly, Fiedler does not believe that training can help most leaders develop a flexible style.[20] Training should therefore concentrate on helping him diagnose the leadership situation and then adapt the situation to his style. Fielder does not say just how this is to be done and is quick to admit that there are numerous difficulties to resolve before such a procedure can be put into practice. He proposes, as an alternative to changing leadership style, a form of organizational engineering in which leaders are matched to tasks or steps are taken to change the leader's position power or the leader-member relations. Position power and leader-member relations, he suggests, can be modified by manipulating the membership constitution of the subordinate group in terms of their expertise, status, and such personal attributes as attitudes, opinions, and cultural background. Besides the practical problems involved in manipulating an entire organization in this fashion, Fiedler's suggested approach seems unduly pessimistic regarding the potential flexibility of leadership style. In fact, our approach is just the opposite, in that we envision the successful supervisor as being one who easily and swiftly adapts his leadership style to the various and changing conditions contained in any situation.

Let us briefly examine the six conditions constituting a particular supervisory situation. Each supervisor is confronted by them, but if properly

---

[19] Bernard Berelson and Gary A. Steiner, *Human Behavior: An Inventory of Scientific Findings* (New York: Harcourt, Brace & World, Inc., 1964), p. 343.

[20] Fred E. Fiedler, *A Theory of Leadership Effectiveness* (New York: McGraw-Hill Book Company, 1967).

adjusted to, they can make him an organizational leader. First, a man's personality can make him suitable for a particular style of leadership and unfit for another. Consequently, we find a person able to provide group-centered leadership and not the authoritarian type, and vice versa. Second, the nature of the task to be performed influences the leadership style most appropriate to the given situation. Consider, for example, the difference between directing traffic and conducting a vice investigation. Each requires a particular style of leadership because of the nature of the involved tasks. Third, the job role plays an important part in determining the correct style of leadership. Basically, subordinates expect to be led in a certain manner. Fourth, groups develop their own norms and objectives and look to the supervisor for assistance in their fulfillment. If the supervisor does not help, it is highly improbable that he will be given the role of leader—in fact, the group usually creates an informal leader from within their ranks. Fifth, time acts as a constraint and a determinant of leadership style. Time, tasks, and problems lend themselves to a group-centered leadership approach while others demand a leader-centered style. To illustrate, the leadership employed during routine police operations may be group-centered. However, a civil riot or natural disaster requires a leader-centered style because time normally does not permit soliciting opinions and information from all concerned. Sixth, decision making can vary the needed leadership style. Time figures into the decision-making process to some extent. Perhaps of greatest significance is the philosophical approach to the making of decisions. The next section expands on the subject of decision making.

To conclude, we return to something written earlier about leadership style, "The supposedly modern view, of course, is that the group-centered style is the most conducive to improving organizational effectiveness." While group-centered leadership may be the modern view, it is questionable whether it is the practical course of action. Our argument here remains that the situation determines the most appropriate leadership style. Hence, based on the situation, and remembering that it is dynamic and changing, the supervisor will form his particular style of leadership. In some circumstances it will be leader centered, in others, group centered. Again, our example of routine police operations versus riot conditions emphasizes the point. There appears little room for an individual-centered leadership style in a formal organization; thus we give but mere mention of its existence.

Our hope here is, however, that when possible the group-centered leadership style would be used by those in supervisory positions. The arguments for its use are many and have permeated this text. Research findings have overwhelmingly shown that group-centered leadership (employee participation in those decisions that affect them) enhances organizational effectiveness and job satisfaction.[21] Bell draws a bleak picture for the building into our formal organizations of an environment that allows group-centered leadership. Using the term *democratic leadership* to encompass both group-centered and individual-centered leadership, he writes:

> But how ready is an individual in our society to assume the maturity of choice in evaluating critically the claims of a democratic leader? The problem of democratic leadership is shaped by the fact that while we live in a society of political democracy, almost all basic social patterns are authoritarian and tend to instill feelings of helplessness and dependence. We begin as dependent beings in the family situation. The nature of middle-class morality drives parents to impose basic patterns of conformity which will be subsequently demanded in the schools and in the factory. Our schools, despite the long years of effort toward progressive education, still operate largely on authoritarian models. Our factories, hierarchical in structure, are still, for all the talk of human relations programs, places where certain men exercise arbitrary authority over others. And from these questions any inquiry inevitably turns to the problem of bureaucratization. How, within the framework of impersonality and alienation which is modern society, can we create areas of genuine spontaneity in which group participation can be satisfactorily obtained?[22]

The answer to Bell is, "New organizational forms have been and will continue to be constructed to provide people with a greater say in those decisions that influence their lives."

This author has witnessed too many cases of growing employee participation in formal organizations not to be optimistic at this time for more group-centered leadership situations. And, police organizations are (or will soon become) an integral part of this trend. Therefore, the police supervisor will see more situations calling for a leadership style that, while flexible, is primarily group centered. Granted, in most cases, the traditional characteristics of a police organization do not provide a situation that fosters police leadership. That is, little formal support is given to the police supervisor for developing his leadership role. Moreover, this situation frequently hinders a police supervisor in assuming the role of a leader. Thankfully, this problem is being remedied daily by progressive police administrators.

---

[21] To cite another case in point, the TVA was one of the pioneers in the area of a group-centered approach. But a recent study of the TVA experience shows employee dissatisfaction to be high and suggests that the indirect involvement used by TVA must be balanced by direct employee participation in decision making if optimum productivity and commitment are to be realized. See Arthur A. Thompson, "Employee Participation in Decision Making: The TVA Experience," *Public Personnel Review*, 28 (April 1967), 82–88.

[22] Daniel Bell, "Authoritarian and Democratic Leadership," in *American Democracy: Essays on Image and Reality*, ed. Leonard J. Fein (New York: Holt, Rinehart & Winston, Inc., 1964), p. 72.

These administrators are in the process of creating organizational situations that encourage a police supervisor to also become a leader. Which is to say, the characteristics of the organizational situation in many of today's police departments are undergoing meaningful changes in terms of supporting a leadership role. Indeed, the present outlook for a police supervisor behaving both as a supervisor and as a leader is very promising. In sum, our position is that (1) it is vitally important that the police supervisor also be the leader of his work group and (2) the supervisor's leadership style must be flexible in order to meet both the needs of the group and the department. Thus, the police supervisor must have a capacity not just to issue orders, but to engage in behavior (support, interaction facilitation, goal emphasis, and work facilitation) that provides organizational leadership.

DECISION MAKING

It seems almost a truism that police supervision and leadership in a police department are key factors in achieving organizational effectiveness.[23] Hence, we can say that police leadership, when exercised by a police supervisor, is usually salutary in its effect and most often enhances the effectiveness of the police organization. As Likert puts it: Supervision and the general style of leadership throughout the organization are usually much more important in influencing results than such general factors as attitudes toward the organization and interest in the job itself.[24] This is to say that the police supervisor can either be a positive or a negative factor in fostering organizational effectiveness. If he decides on the correct leadership style and then makes the right decision he is more than likely to be a positive factor.

> Clarity of thought in decision making and strength of character are a necessary ingredient in democratic leadership because the decisions about the correct use of social power are far more complex and difficult. It is far easier to be autocratically simple minded than to make the necessary refined and complex distinctions about the use of social power within organizations and in all human affairs.[25]

As we noted at the outset, supervision is usually conceived in static terms: It has a certain amount of authority that permits the role occupant to make certain decisions, and these decisions must be carried out by subordinates

---

[23] Kendrith Rowland and William Scott, "Psychological Attributes of Effective Leadership in a Formal Organization," *Personnel Psychology*, 21 (Autumn 1968), 365–77.

[24] Rensis Likert, *New Patterns of Management* (New York: McGraw-Hill Book Company, 1961), p. 25.

[25] Sven Lundstedt, "Administrative Leadership and Use of Social Power," *Public Administration Review*, 25 (June 1965), 160.

who have the responsibility to follow his instructions. This conception of supervision and the supervisor's role produces the neat organization pyramids, with their unquestioned hierarchical characteristics, and, in the process, deludes many of us into viewing a formal organization as a monolithic structure. More realistically, decision making is an organizational process. It is shaped as much by the pattern of interaction of supervision as it is by the contemplation and cognitive processes of the individual. As such, supervision becomes a dynamic process—decision making sees to it. The newly appointed police supervisor is soon to recognize that he has not only a new position but new risks.

> The gradual recognition that rules are not absolute, that standards are not inflexible, and that one must live with the risks of being "in the wrong" guarantees insecurity. For this reason, the modern organization, with its appearance of bureaucratic rigidity and conformity, is anything but the perfect haven for the timid. The supervisor in the textbook checks his decision against the rules and knows whether he is "right." The supervisor in the effective organization has no such guarantees; when he tries to use as an excuse for failure that he had been hamstrung in using ingenuity and initiative, he is well on his way to demotion.[26]

Considering the tremendous interest in decision making one would be on thin ice if he did not accept its role as a major function of formal police leaders (supervisors and managers). It is accepted by many, in fact, as the central activity in supervision and as a key subject for attention in supervisory training. In his *Functions of the Executive*, Barnard was one of the first to characterize decision making as "the essential process of organizational action" and to outline how the performance of an organization could be analyzed into an interlocking, hierarchical system of decisions.[27] The initial paragraphs of Simon's *Administrative Behavior* argue that

> The task of "deciding" pervades the entire administrative organization quite as much as the task of "doing"—indeed, it is integrally tied up with the latter. A general theory of administration must include principles of organization that will insure correct decision-making, just as it must include principles that will insure effective action.[28]

From the arguments in these two books has come much of the impetus for making the decision process a primary focus of organization theory and of

---

[26] Leonard Sayles, *Managerial Behavior* (New York: McGraw-Hill Book Company, 1964), p. 215.

[27] Chester I. Barnard, *The Functions of the Executive* (Cambridge: Harvard, 1938), p. xiii.

[28] Herbert A. Simon, *Administrative Behavior* (New York: Macmillan Company, 1945), p. 1.

research on administrative action. Today, the proposition seems so obvious that we tend to forget how new it is and so clear that we can easily overlook the different approaches, types, and techniques the "decision-making" label covers. Before a discussion of the various approaches, types, and techniques of decision making, let us define what we mean by the use of this term. Our definition of decision making relies on the thinking of Herbert A. Simon, who is generally credited with fathering the school of decision theory in public administration. The classical model of decision making portrayed the decision maker as a man at the moment of choice. This image tends to misconstrue decision making by stressing its final moment. It ignored the whole lengthy, complex process of alerting, exploring, and analyzing what precedes that final moment.[29] Simon recently defined decision making in terms of three interrelated phases: (1) finding occasions for making a decision, (2) finding possible courses of action, and (3) choosing among courses of action.[30] The first phase he called intelligence activity, the second, design activity, and the third, choice activity. He goes on to relate that the cycle of phases is, however, far more complex than this sequence suggests. Each phase in making a particular decision is itself a complex decision-making process. For example, the design phase usually requires new intelligence activities; problems at any given hierarchical level create sub-problems that, in turn, have their intelligence, design, and choice phases, and so on. Notably, the implementation of decisions is an integral part of this process. A decision generates a new condition for the design and choice of a program for operationalizing the decision. Therefore, broader decisions once made are indistinguishable from making more detailed decisions for implementation.

Decision Making: Approaches

Etzioni identifies three conceptual approaches to the making of decisions: (1) rationalistic, (2) incrementalist, and (3) mixed-scanning.[31] The rationalistic model tends to posit a high degree of control over the decision-making situation on the part of the decision maker, asserting that an individual first becomes aware of a problem establishing a goal, then carefully weighs alternatives, and finally chooses among them according to his estimates of their respective merit, with reference to the state of affairs he prefers. The incrementalists' criticism of this approach is that it requires greater resources than decision makers command. Specifically, the rationalistic model fails

---

[29] Herbert A. Simon, *The Shape of Automation: For Men and Management* (New York: Harper & Row, Publishers, 1965), p. 53.

[30] *Ibid.*, p. 54.

[31] The majority of this section is based on Amitai Etzioni, "Mixed-Scanning: A 'Third' Approach to Decision-Making," *Public Administration Review*, 27 (December 1967), 385–92.

for four reasons. First, decision-making centers seldom have an agreed-upon set of values that could provide the criteria for evaluating alternatives. Values, rather, are fluid and are affected by, as well as affect, the decisions made. Second, in practice the rationalistic assumption that values and facts, means and ends, can be clearly distinguished is erroneous. Third, information about a potential outcome is fractional. Decision makers have neither the assets nor the time to collect all the information required for rational choice. While technology, especially that of computers, does aid in the collection and processing of information, it cannot supply the computation needed by the rationalist model. Fourth, decision makers are not confronted with a neat and bounded universe of relevant consequences. On the contrary, decision makers face a world in which all consequences cannot be surveyed. A decision maker, attempting to comply with the tenets of a rationalistic model, will become frustrated, exhaust his resources without coming to a decision, and remain without an effective decision-making model to guide him. The rationalistic model should be rejected as being unrealistic and undesirable. However, it has not received such rejection; in fact, it remains the most oft cited way for making decisions.

The incrementalist approach is less demanding and more pragmatic. Essentially it attempts to tailor decision-making strategies to the limited capacities of decision makers and to reduce the scope and cost of information collection and processing. Lindblom summarizes the six main requirements of the model in this way:[32]

1. Rather than attempting a comprehensive survey and evaluation of all alternatives, the decision maker focuses only on those policies which differ incrementally from existing policies.
2. Only a relatively small number of policy alternatives are considered.
3. For each policy alternative, only a restricted number of important consequences are evaluated.
4. The problem confronting the decision maker is continually redefined, incrementalism allows for countless ends-means and means-ends adjustments which, in effect, make the problem more manageable.
5. Thus, there is no one decision or right solution but a never-ending series of attacks on the issues at hand through serial analyses and evaluation.
6. As such, incremental decision making is described as remedial, geared more to the alleviation of present, concrete social imperfections than to the promotion of future social goals.

However, the incrementalistic approach is not without its problems. In essence, it fails to tackle the big picture. In other words, it is unable to adequately handle the more significant fundamental questions.

---

[32] Charles E. Lindblom, *The Intelligence of Democracy* (New York: Free Press, 1965), pp. 144–48.

... it is often the fundamental decisions which set the context for the numerous incremental ones. Although fundamental decisions are frequently "prepared" by incremental ones in order that the final decision will initiate a less abrupt change, these decisions may still be considered relatively fundamental. The incremental steps which follow cannot be understood without them, and the preceding steps are useless unless they lead to fundamental decisions.[33]

It is obvious that, while a city council or another policy-making agency does make many incremental decisions without confronting the fundamental one implied, many other decisions which appear to be a series of incremental ones are, in reality, the implementation or articulation of a fundamental decision.

Hence, we can now see rather clearly that decision making requires an approach that permits (1) high-order, fundamental policy-making processes which set basic directions and (2) incremental processes which allow for fundamental decisions. These requirements are fulfilled by mixed-scanning. In the use of mixed-scanning, it is essential to differentiate fundamental decisions from incremental ones. Fundamental decisions are made by exploring the basic alternatives the person sees in view of his conception of his goals, but—unlike what rationalism would suggest—details are omitted so that an overview is feasible. Incremental decisions are made but within the contexts set by fundamental decisions. Consequently, "each of the two elements in mixed-scanning helps to reduce the effects of the particular shortcomings of the other; incrementalism reduces the unrealistic aspects of rationalism by limiting the details required in fundamental decisions, and rationalism helps to overcome the conservative slant of incrementalism by exploring longer-run alternatives."[34]

From a practical viewpoint mixed scanning provides a particular procedure for the collection of information (for example, the surveying or "scanning" of crime conditions), a strategy about the allocation of resources (team policing), and guidelines for the relations between the two. The strategy combines a detailed (rationalistic) examination of some sectors— which is feasible—with a "truncated" review of other sectors. The relative investment in the two kinds of scanning—full detail and truncated—as well as in the very act of scanning, depends on how costly it would be to miss, for example, the apprehension of one robber, the cost of additional scanning, and the amount of time it would take.

Decision Making: Types

Simon informs us that there are two types of decisions: programmed and nonprogrammed.[35] A programmed decision may be regarded as primarily

---

[33] Etzioni, "Mixed-Scanning," 387.
[34] *Ibid.*, 390.
[35] Simon, *The Shape of Automation.*

(but not completely) a sequence of choices evoked by demands so frequently made that they can be predicted. The program is a shorthand expression for the rules, directions, and criteria that specify how people are to respond. Portions of some programs are set in print, generally in manuals presenting standard operating procedures; more complicated and subtle decision-making routines are likely to be filed away in the memories of the organizational members. A programmable decision reduces each component of the job to a standardized and settled routine. Programs may be simple or highly detailed. An example of a simple routine is the procedure followed by a patrol officer in asking questions of a victim for reporting purposes. Most of the information to be collected is contained on the face of the report.

Distinguished from such recurrent choices are the largely unprecedented actions called nonprogrammed decisions. Unlike programmed decisions, they cannot be resolved by a sequence of simple routines. They commonly call on the decision makers to construct unique procedures that summarize and define the situation confronting them. The procedures typically contain enough detail to promote comprehensive calculation of the impact that contemplated alternatives will have on the problem. For example, in deciding whether to acquire a helicopter for use by the department, the chief can either buy, lease, or contract for its usage. The standard operating procedures that govern programmed decision making furnish only slender guidance when comprehensive or unusual actions are undertaken. In fact, one key objective of a nonprogrammed decision may be to overhaul and thoroughly redo a traditional program; reformulating a police recruit training curriculum is one example.

Note that the degree to which a decision is programmed is no measure of its importance for the organization or for those whom organizational choices affect. A programmed decision is not necessarily synonymous with a minor decision, and nonprogrammed is not just another way of saying importance. These terms describe processes for making decisions; they do not evaluate the significance of the outcome. Finally, it should be understood that, while programmed and nonprogrammed decisions have been treated as though they formed separate classes, they represent little more than the end points of a continuum.

> No decision is ever wholly novel or completely repetitive, it is only more or less so. Even the municipal employees who collect garbage each morning have to improvise responses on occasion, and one way of reducing the uncertainties inherent in making nonprogrammed decisions is to compare proposed alternatives with established routines that have worked in the past. . . . If one could devise criteria for ranking decisions according to their relative saturation by settled routines, it would be possible to transpose the beguiling simplicity of this classification into a more finely calibrated serial order. Since these criteria

are not available, it was necessary to force each decision to one extreme or the other of what is known to be a continuum.[36]

Decision Making: Techniques

The techniques for making decisions can likewise be dichotomized into techniques for making programmed decisions and techniques for making nonprogrammed decisions. Table 8 depicts, by type of decision, the various

TABLE 8: TRADITIONAL AND MODERN TECHNIQUES OF DECISION MAKING

Types of Decisions	Decision-Making Techniques	
	Traditional	Modern
Programmed: Routine, repetitive decisions Organization develops specific processes for handling them	1. Habit 2. Clerical routine: Standard operating procedures 3. Organization structure: Common expectations A system of subgoals Well-defined informational channels	1. Operations Research: Mathematical analysis Models Computer simulation 2. Electronic data processing
Nonprogrammed: One-shot, ill-structured novel, policy decisions Handled by general problem-solving processes	1. Judgement, intuition, and creativity 2. Rules of thumb 3. Selection and training of executives	Heuristic problem-solving technique applied to: (a) Training human decision makers (b) Constructing heuristic computer programs

Source: Herbert A. Simon, The Shape of Automation *(New York: Harper & Row, Publishers,* © *1965), p. 62.* Reprinted by permission.

techniques. We limit ourselves to only brief explanations concerning those techniques listed under the modern heading. First, there is operations research.[37] Through its quantitative methods activities, many classes of administrative decisions have been formalized, mathematics has been applied to determine the characteristics of the best or good decisions, and myriads of arithmetic calculations are carried out routinely in many organizations to reach the required decisions. A number of sophisticated mathematical tools—linear programming, queuing theory, dynamic programming combinatorial mathematics, and others—have been invented or developed to this end.

---

[36] Benjamin Walter, "Internal Control Relations in Administrative Hierarchies," *Administrative Science Quarterly*, 11 (September 1966), 187.

[37] A thorough treatment of operations research can be found in Russel L. Ackoff and Maurice W. Sasieni, *Fundamentals of Operations Research* (New York: John Wiley & Sons, Inc., 1968).

Second, the modern digital computer has provided both a language for expressing our theories of decision making and a machine for calculating their empirical implications. Theories can now be quickly compared with data of the real world of organizations.

Third, the heuristic method can be broadly described as the method of solving problems through self-teaching. To explain further,

> Many qualitative problems are solved using the heuristic method. A *method* including the heuristic method is founded on the tradition of independent investigation. The stimulus for investigation is the individual's experience or familiarity with the problem area. The heuristic method brings a wide diversity of general experience to bear; it relies on heavy doses of common sense; the heuristic method immerses the analyst in the problem to be solved. The heurist may abstain from a precise definition of the problem before starting the investigation. Ultimately, he may (or may not) present a conclusion that is a dominantly favorable solution.[38]

Some advanced computers can now be given a set of rough instructions instead of highly detailed programs and can proceed to attack a unique problem even though it may be poorly defined. In a sense, these "nonprogrammed" activities of computers are somewhat analogous to the trial-and-error method that appears to characterize human thinking. The computer is instructed to solve part of a problem at a time, working by rough increments toward a general solution. Newell, Shaw, and Simon, for example, have developed a "general problem solver" program for a computer based on step-by-step analysis rather than on a completely comprehensive analysis of data within the computer memory.[39]

The police supervisor (who primarily makes programmed and nonprogrammed decisions through traditional techniques) will soon witness the above described modern devices pushing more of his nonprogrammable decisions into the programmable class. Moreover, he is destined to become involved, in a limited way, with the modern techniques. All of this may eventually "free" the police supervisor for coping with the more difficult problems of leading subordinates toward greater organizational effectiveness and personal satisfaction.

BASICS OF LEADERSHIP

This section is devoted to those of you that have begun to grouse about an absence of "the tricky things that I can do as a police supervisor to

---

[38] Stanford L. Optner, *Systems Analysis for Business and Industrial Problem-Solving* (Englewood Cliffs, N.J.: Prentice-Hall, Inc., 1965), p. 20.

[39] Allen Newell, J. C. Shaw, and Herbert A. Simon, "A General Problem Solving Program for a Computer," *Computers and Automation*, 8 (July 1959), 10–17.

become a leader." The author will do his best to recommend, in a general way, how you as a potential leader should behave. However, you will have to grant two major concessions. First, the recommendations must be considered for what they are—recommendations. They are not unequivocal rules by which leaders are made or unmade. However, if wisely and adeptly used, the recommended techniques should provide you with invaluable support for becoming an organizational leader. Like everything else, if merely read and practiced once or twice, they will remain nothing but a set of interesting academic recommendations. The second concession, and of the two perhaps the more difficult to grant, is that the police organization has, in fact, selected for their supervisory positions qualified people. In other words, the promotional process is sufficiently analytical and evaluative to select among the various applicants those that will make successful supervisors. In turn, these concessions are to be considered more as basic assumptions, in that they provide backing for the subsequent recommended courses of action or behavior on the part of the police supervisor. Note that the recommended techniques are categorized according to the four dimensions that constitute the role of an organizational leader.

The techniques for leading or better leading a group of subordinates are tied to a core concept that comprises (1) a new leadership style and (2) a frame of mind. The trademarks of the new style are the soft voice and the low key. The frame of mind is simply that a police supervisor must think like a leader in order to become one. With these two things in the forefront of our mind, let us look at the various techniques.

Support

1. The police supervisor should support his subordinates in achieving their individual goals as long as they do not hamper the over-all objectives of the police department.
2. The police supervisor should, when the situation presents itself (nonemergency conditions), approach his subordinates in a consultative rather than in a directive style.
3. The police supervisor should make every attempt to be considered as a member (one with supervisory responsibilities) of his particular work group, not as an external agent with authority. To put it another way, *the best organizational leader firmly keeps the goal before his subordinates and urges them to meet it; at the same time, he treats them like human beings,* by recognizing and fulfilling their individual needs.

Interaction facilitation

4. The police supervisor should, through his recognition of two sets of needs (organizational and individual) make every endeavor to become both the intellectual and the social leader of his assigned personnel.
5. The police supervisor should, through his fulfilling of social needs, keep inter-

personal conflict at the barest acceptable minimum. Further, regulations and conflict feed one another; therefore, personnel regulations should be kept at a minimum.

Goal emphasis

6. The police supervisor should develop a supportive and viable interpersonal relationship in order to influence the subordinate toward achieving the goals of the organization.

7. The police supervisor should delegate authority and share responsibility based on an individual's capacity to contribute to the attainment of the organization's goals.

8. The police supervisor should reward subordinates for goal-directed behavior.

Work facilitation

9. The police supervisor should seek to develop a system for first obtaining and then supplying his subordinates with the information, resources, and technical assistance needed to more easily do the job.

SUMMARY

Supervisory leadership occurs when the police supervisor makes correct decisions about (1) supporting his subordinates, (2) facilitating their interaction, (3) emphasizing high goal performance, and (4) facilitating the work of his subordinates. The importance of a police supervisor assuming the role of a formal leader is dual in nature. First, the work or productivity of an organizational unit is affected by the type of leadership it receives. Second, individual satisfaction in a work group is significantly enhanced or lessened by the style of leadership employed.

Leadership is the *ability* to command others. It resides in the position of supervisor, the individual assigned to the position, and the characteristics of the total work situation, including the expectation of his subordinates. Our definition of leadership is that influential increment over and above mechanical compliance with the routine directives of the police organization. Three basic styles of leadership have been proposed for mustering beyond the ordinary influence in dealing with people: (1) leader centered, (2) group centered, and (3) individual centered. The type to employ depends on the particular organizational situation. Within the situation are six conditions that the supervisor must take into consideration: (1) his own personality, (2) task characteristics, (3) task roles, (4) group characteristics, (5) time, and (6) decisions. The successful leader is one who can adapt his leadership style to the various and changing conditions contained in the situation. Hopefully, this person is, at the same time, the police supervisor.

The supervisor as a leader finds himself in the position of having to make effective decisions about people, processes, and situations Currently, there are three ways to view decision making: (1) rationalistic, (2) incrementalistic, and (3) mixed-scanning. Further, there are two types of decisions made by the supervisory leader, programmed and nonprogrammed. There are modern techniques and devices, both in existence and being created, for the making of both programmed and nonprogrammed decisions. Therefore, the police supervisor is either now or soon will be experiencing them. These techniques, if properly used, can be of significant assistance to him. Finally, this chapter concludes with the recommendation of nine basic techniques which can aid the police supervisor in becoming a formal leader. All nine are best employed through a soft voice and low key, and the thinking of oneself as a leader.

PROBLEMS

1. List, define, and discuss the four major dimensions of a leader's role in an organizational setting.
2. What do you feel is the most significant finding cited in the section on findings and recommendations? Why?
3. The leader is primarily determined by the situation and the expectations of his subordinates. Explain this finding. Give an example.
4. Think about implementing one of the recommendations. For a moment, consider yourself a leader and describe how you might attempt to implement one of the recommendations.
5. Select one of the four major dimensions that constitute the role of our organizational leader. Next, place yourself into the position of a police supervisor interested in also becoming the leader of your subordinates. What specific acts would you perform in light of the dimension you have chosen?

10

Job Satisfaction
and Morale

A connective link between this and the preceding chapter is furnished by
Athos and Coffey:

> If the view is accepted that man behaves primarily to satisfy his various needs,
> then the implications for supervisory or leadership behavior are important.
> The job of the supervisor becomes that of providing an environment and work
> that enables people, at least to some degree, to have interesting, challenging
> work, satisfying social relationships, and some recognition and autonomy in
> carrying out their duties. This suggests that supervisors would be most successful
> if they de-emphasized their authority and instead emphasized their role as
> facilitator and supporter. It also suggests that people derive much satisfaction
> from things other than the external incentives and rewards offered by the
> organization.[1]

All of us have, at one time or another, used the terms *satisfaction* or *morale*
to indicate our own or others' feelings. And, it is quite likely that we have
used both of these terms in an occupational sense. Moreover, either implicitly or explicitly, we have included the notions of "attitudes" and "values"
toward a particular job. The above words are seldom defined or dealt with
consistently. Added to this lack of precise understanding of terms are some
commonly held beliefs, such as that more satisfied people produce more
simply because of human nature—but do they? Hence we are heading toward a rather large problem. Is the effort worth it? Our unequivocal answer
is yes! The reasons underlying this response will become clear later.

Our problem, to some, may appear quite academic, a matter of semantics.
But the problem is not just one of terminology; it involves feelings, emotions,
happiness, and organizational effectiveness. Since terminological problems
are involved, we spend some time on definitions. Because of the existing
confusion between the concepts of job attitudes and job values, let us first
consider the term *attitude*. An attitude is the predisposition of an individual
to evaluate some symbol or object or aspect of his world in a favorable or

---

[1] Anthony G. Athos and Robert E. Coffey, *Behavior in Organizations: A Multidimensional
View* (Englewood Cliffs, N.J.: Prentice-Hall, Inc., 1968), p. 177.

unfavorable manner.[2] One develops an attitude concerning an external thing; that is, an attitude has an objective reference. Next is a closely related term, *value*. A value is a personally weighted preference for a thing that has been evaluated. Simply, values express "good," "bad," "should," and "rights." When values are organized into a hierarchical structure, they comprise a value system. Further, values clarify the self-image and, at the same time, mold that self-image closer to the heart's desire. Third is the concept of *personality*. As previously defined, personality is a hierarchical arrangement of the particular attitudes, needs, and values of the individual. Fourth is the term *role*, or *work role*. The reader should recall that a work role is a derivative of the behavior requirements of a position in a formal organization and that it should be viewed as the dynamic aspects of a position, in other words, as a set of functions to be performed by the role occupant.[3] Finally, we come to the most difficult concepts to define—job satisfaction and morale. Unfortunately, there is little standardization in either the meaning or the measures of these two terms. In fact, they are often used interchangeably, "Since *satisfaction* means the same thing as *morale*."[4] However, there is ample reason to separate job satisfaction and morale. They are similar, in that both refer to affective orientations on the part of individuals toward work roles which they presently occupy. The difference between the two concepts is that job satisfaction is an individual feeling while morale is a group phenomenon. To put it another way, job satisfaction is the degree of liking that a person has for his work role. Morale is the degree of liking that a group has for its particular work assignment. Before leaving the subject of definitions, it should be understood that positive attitudes toward the job are conceptually equivalent to job satisfaction, and negative attitudes to job dissatisfaction. Findings from recent studies indicate that job satisfaction and job dissatisfaction are located at two different points on a continuum. Between these two points is a very important third point of neutrality (neither pleased nor unhappy).[5] An individual's position on a job satisfaction continuum (or a group's position on a morale continuum) is *determined primarily by the amount of value fulfillment provided by the work role.*[6]

---

[2] Daniel Katz, "The Functional Approach to the Study of Attitudes," in *Psychology in Administration*, eds. Timothy W. Costello and Sheldon S. Zalkind (Englewood Cliffs, N.J.: Prentice-Hall, Inc., 1963), p. 253.

[3] Victor H. Vroom, *Work and Motivation* (New York: John Wiley & Sons, Inc., 1964), p. 6.

[4] James L. Price, *Organizational Effectiveness* (Homewood, Ill.: Richard D. Irwin, Inc., 1968), p. 150.

[5] See Frederick Herzberg, B. Mausner, and B. B. Snyderman, *The Motivation to Work* (New York: John Wiley & Sons, Inc., 1959).

[6] In support of this contention, Ernest G. Palola and William R. Larson were able to demonstrate that job satisfaction involves not only different work value dimensions, but also different numbers of work value dimensions for varying occupational categories. See Ernest G. Palola and William R. Larson, "Some Dimensions of Job Satisfaction Among Hospital Personnel," *Sociology and Social Research*, 49 (May 1965), 205. B. Blai also provides research findings in line with this thinking. See B. Blai, Jr., "An Occupational Study of Job Satisfaction and Need Satisfaction," *Journal of Experimental Education*, 32 (June 1964), 383–88.

It should be apparent now that the variables relating to job satisfaction and morale are quite numerous and complicated, ranging from physical working conditions through the social environment surrounding the job to external economic factors. But this approach to listing the components of morale and satisfaction is subjective. The only way to see what the components are is to enter an organizational setting and ferret out, by social research methods, the relevant variables. Our analysis now carries us into a general and, on occasion, detailed discussion of (1) job satisfaction, (2) morale, and (3) their relationship to other organizational variables, specifically, productivity. We end the chapter with a listing of some basic techniques for promoting job satisfaction and morale in a police organization.

JOB SATISFACTION

For approximately three decades social scientists have been using quantitative methods in an attempt to determine the events and conditions which result in different levels of job satisfaction.[7] The principal assumption guiding investigations of this problem is that differences in job satisfaction reflect differences in the work role or in personal job values. Researchers have sought to measure the effects on job satisfaction of such aspects of work roles as the type of supervision the employee receives, the kind of work group of which he is a member, the requirements of his job, the amount of his salary, and his chances for promotion. These studies have been rewarding. A large number of work role dimensions have been identified and their approximate impact on job satisfaction determined. The results of these studies have served to create a typical model of a generally satisfying work role.

Much of what we say here about job satisfaction holds true for morale. (Again, the major distinction is the level of complexity—the former is individual, while the latter is group oriented.) Consequently, the reader should keep this in mind in order to develop an appropriate appreciation and understanding of morale. In regard to job satisfaction, we cover, in the following order, (1) its significance, (2) its determinants, (3) the research methods, and (4) the research studies and findings.

Job Satisfaction: Its Significance

Directly and briefly stated, the employee's work role can either satisfy or dissatisfy basic human needs. Every worker enters his assigned organiza-

---

[7] The number of job satisfaction researches has grown to the extent that the *Personnel and Guidance Journal* has for 23 years published an annual review of such studies. See, for example, H. Alan Robinson, Ralph P. Connors, and G. Holly Whitacre, "Job Satisfaction Researches of 1964–65," *Personnel and Guidance Journal*, 44 (December 1966), 371–79.

tional role with certain values and attitudes in mind. Together they form a set of needs, which can in part be fulfilled by the occupational role itself. However, it is important that the worker's role be structured to meet his needs (values + attitudes). Sayles and Strauss summarize the argument for and against the use of the worker's role to provide job satisfaction.[8]

Job Satisfaction Important	*Job Satisfaction Unimportant*
1. People want self-actualization.	Some people prefer unchallenging work.
2. Those who don't obtain job satisfaction never reach psychological maturity.	Individual personality becomes fixed before people start working. Work is not to blame.
3. Those who fail to obtain job satisfaction become frustrated.	Most people have relatively low levels of aspiration for job satisfaction and expect only routine work.
4. The job is central to man's life.	This is a professor's value. Many people focus their lives on family and community.
5. Those without work are unhappy. People want to work even when they don't have to.	Even though there are social pressures to have a job, this does not mean the job must be challenging, etc.
6. Lack of challenging work leads to low mental health.	Poor mental health may be due to low income or low status of routine jobs. Anyway, research findings are not conclusive.
7. Work and leisure patterns spill into each other. Those with uncreative jobs engage in uncreative recreation.	A new bohemianism off the job will make up for increasing boredom at work.
8. Lack of job satisfaction and alienation from work lead to lower morale, lower productivity, and an unhealthy society.	We can provide challenging work for everybody only at the cost of eliminating our mass production technology and high standard of living—and society is unwilling to pay this price.

This author casts his lot with those who favor the organization's making an attempt to satisfy a worker's human needs simply because it seems the right thing to do. For those of a more utilitarian bent, there are some very real rewards for developing high levels of individual job satisfaction, including reduced turnover and absenteeism, the probability of increased productivity, and heightened cooperation and innovative behavior. Thus, job satisfaction can be viewed as both morally good and organizationally wise.

---

[8] Leonard R. Sayles and George Strauss, *Human Behavior in Organizations* (Englewood Cliffs, N.J.: Prentice-Hall, Inc., 1966), p. 27.

Job Satisfaction: Its Determinants

The majority of research on job satisfaction seems to support the generalization that "Even under the existing conditions, which are far from satisfactory, most workers like their jobs. Every survey of workers' attitudes which has been carried out, no matter in what industry, indicates that this is so."[9] However, and this is very important, most of these studies, which seek to determine the ratio of workers who are satisfied or dissatisfied with their jobs, ignore the cultural pressures on workers to exaggerate the degree of satisfaction.

Although it is difficult, therefore, not to accept the proposition that the majority of American workers are fairly satisfied in their work, such a finding is neither particularly surprising nor scientifically interesting. Under standard conditions workers naturally tend to identify with, or at least to be somewhat positively oriented toward, the formal organizations in which they are involved. Attitude surveys show that the "majority of employees like their company, that the majority of members are satisfied with their unions, and undoubtedly research would show a preponderance of positive over negative attitudes toward one's own marriage, family, religion, and nation-state."[10] It is the reason for the presence of marked occupational differences in work attitudes that we now turn to.

In essence, the degree of job satisfaction varies for two fundamental reasons. First, occupational status is a major determinant of a person's job satisfaction. Relevant to our position are the findings in Table 9, which indicate that, in general, reported job satisfaction declines with occupational level. To put it another way, the greater the professionalization, the higher the probability that people will report intrinsic job satisfaction, and vice versa. Second, each job contains numerous characteristics related to job satisfaction. These characteristics, to an individual, are looked upon as needs. Obviously, the intensity of need-fulfillment varies with the individual, but the point remains that all of us experience some degree of satisfaction through our job satisfying our human needs. Numerous studies have shown that the following items are associated with a person's job satisfaction: (1) salary, (2) security, (3) prestige, (4) job uncertainty, (5) working conditions, (6) physical distance from work, (7) psychological distance from the product produced, (8) number of years on the job, (9) number of friends on the job, (10) absenteeism, (11) ratings by immediate superiors, and (12) desirability of living in the area around the plant. This list can be easily extended to include other needs. Sufficient at this time is an awareness that job satisfaction is a complex mix of needs.

---

[9] Robert Blauner, "Extent of Satisfaction: A Review of General Research," in *Psychology in Administration*, p. 81.

[10] *Ibid.*

TABLE 9: *RELATIONSHIP BETWEEN OCCUPATIONAL STATUS AND JOB SATISFACTION AMONG EMPLOYED MEN*

Job Satisfaction	*Occupational Status*							
	Professional, Technician; per cent	*Managerial, Proprietor; per cent*	*Clerical Workers, per cent*	*Sales Workers, per cent*	*Skilled Workers, per cent*	*Semiskilled Workers, per cent*	*Unskilled Workers, per cent*	*Farmers per cent*
Very satisfied	42	38	22	24	22	27	13	22
Satisfied	41	42	39	44	54	48	52	58
Neutral	1	6	9	5	6	9	6	4
Ambivalent	10	6	13	9	10	9	13	9
Dissatisfied	3	6	17	16	7	6	16	7
Not ascertained	3	2	—	2	1	1	—	—
Total	100	100	100	100	100	100	100	100
Number of cases	119	127	46	55	202	152	84	77

Source: Gerald Gurin, Joseph Veroff, and Sheila Feld, Americans View Their Mental Health (New York: Basic Books, Inc., 1960), p. 163.

Unfortunately, it is difficult to match the needs of individuals with satisfiers. (Keep in mind that you cannot see a need; it must be inferred.) Costello and Zalkind have pointed out the following three reasons why this difficulty exists.[11] One is that, although two people may have an identical need (with the same intensity), they may behave differently in attempting to satisfy it. For example, both may have a need for friends, but one may invite people to his house, while the other tries to develop friends but waits to be invited by others. A second reason is that two people may have the same need but find different means of satisfying it. Both may have a need for status, but one may satisfy it through his participation in a formal work organization, while the other may do so through a social association. A third reason is that two people may behave similarly but be trying to satisfy different needs. For example, both might work very hard, one to achieve status recognition from others, the other to satisfy his need for monetary gain.

Further, as discussed in earlier chapters,

> People's past backgrounds are different. Their various successes and failures and assumptions about the conditions and behavior that led to both are different. These things have influenced their aspirations, which, in turn, influence the kinds and intensities of behavior directed toward the satisfaction of their needs. . . . In addition, the different values, assumptions, and feelings of people cause them to have different perceptions. Thus, different individuals may view the same environment but see quite different potential need satisfiers. Also, because of their past experiences and present aspirations, their expectations are likely to differ also.[12]

To summarize this section, one's satisfaction depends on the amount of need-fulfillment and the level of professionalization in a specific job. Thus, we can infer that the higher the need fulfillment and/or the greater the professionalization, the higher the probability that people will report work satisfaction. The lower the need-fulfillment and the less skilled the work, the lower the probability that people will report work satisfaction.

Job Satisfaction: Research Methods

The scientific methods used for analyzing job satisfaction and relevant work values can be separated into three categories: (1) organizational, (2) situational, and (3) personal. All three approaches naturally overlap a great deal through the sharing of similar objectives and methodological procedures. Let us first consider the organizational approach to job satisfaction.

---

[11] Timothy W. Costello and Sheldon S. Zalkind, eds., *Psychology in Administration*, pp. 64–67.
[12] Athos and Coffey, *Behavior in Organizations*, p. 178.

Golembiewski seems to best reflect the organizational theorist's point of view when he writes that, ". . . research permits the articulation of an alternative pattern of organization that is congenial to values generally held in the Western world and that encourages the high satisfaction and the high productivity of organization members."[13] The vast majority of behaviorally-oriented organization theorists include in their writings, to a greater or lesser degree, a concern for what McGregor calls, "the human side of enterprise."[14] The concern is explicit in such organizational concepts as (1) exchange theory,[15] (2) organizational reciprocity,[16] (3) organic-adaptive models,[17] and (4) fusion process (mix model).[18] Bennis provides an appropriate summary for the above mentioned organizational constructs:

> However, on all sides we find a growing belief that the effectiveness of bureaucracy should be evaluated on human as well as economic criteria. Social satisfaction and personal growth of employees must be considered, as well as the productivity and profit of the organization.[19]

Next is the situational approach for determining job satisfaction. This method is by far the one most frequently utilized and, therefore, most widely recognized among the various investigators. In essence, the situational approach is also environmental in that it endeavors to elicit from the work role the determinants of job satisfaction. One might safely assume that the majority of job satisfaction researches reviewed by the *Personnel and Guidance Journal* are predicated on a situational approach. The most exhaustive survey of job satisfaction using this approach is found in the monographs by Herzberg and his associates.[20]

---

[13] Robert T. Golembiewski, *Men, Management, and Morality* (New York: McGraw-Hill Book Company, 1965), p. 18.

[14] See Douglas McGregor, *The Human Side of Enterprise* (New York: McGraw-Hill Book Company, 1960).

[15] See Edgar H. Schein, *Organizational Psychology* (Englewood Cliffs, N.J.: Prentice-Hall, Inc., 1965).

[16] See H. Levinson, "Reciprocation. The Relationship between Man and Organization." Invited address presented to the Division of Industrial and Business Psychology, Washington, D.C., Sept. 3, 1963.

[17] See H. H. Shepard, "Changing Interpersonal and Intergroup Relationships in Organizations," *Handbook of Organizations*, ed. James G. March (Chicago: Rand McNally & Company, Inc., 1965), pp. 1115–43.

[18] See Chris Argyris, *Integrating the Individual and the Organization* (New York: John Wiley & Sons, Inc., 1964).

[19] Warren G. Bennis, *Changing Organizations* (New York: McGraw-Hill Book Company, 1966), p. 9. For an interesting study focusing on the interrelationship of many of the organizational variables subsumed in the above theories, see Jerold Hage, "An Axiomatic Theory of Organizations," *Administrative Science Quarterly*, 10 (December 1965), pp. 289–320.

[20] See Herzberg, Mausner, and Snyderman, *The Motivation to Work*; Frederick Herzberg *et al.*, *Job Attitudes: Review of Research and Opinion* (Pittsburgh, Pa.: Psychological Service of Pittsburgh, 1957); and Frederick Herzberg, *Work and the Nature of Man* (New York: The World Publishing Company, Inc., 1966).

The third and final method for researching job satisfaction is the personal approach. The primary object of concern in this instance is the individual. The approach recognizes that individuals differ greatly in their motives, values, and abilities and that these differences probably have an important bearing on the optimal characteristics of their work role. Such personality differences have traditionally played little part in research on job satisfaction. If differences in the attractiveness of a work role to persons about to enter the labor market can be accounted for in terms of personality differences, it seems reasonable to assume that such personality differences might have similar effects on the attractiveness of the work role to those occupying it. Therefore, differences in job satisfaction can be the direct result of individual differences in personality. An example of a study using this approach is *The Image of the Federal Service*.[21]

If used separately, neither of the latter two approaches—one based on situational and the other on personality values—is likely to enable the researcher to proceed very far in improving the understanding of the causes of job satisfaction. Job satisfaction must be approached as the outcome of an interaction between both situational and personality values. It is only through simultaneous study of these two sets of factors that the complex nature of their relationship can be revealed. Very few investigators have attempted to deal with work roles and individual values in the same study. However, the results of those studies in which this has been accomplished are promising and indicate the importance of such an effort. The works by Palola and Larson,[22] and Vroom[23] reflect concrete illustrations of an integrated personal and situational research approach.

Job Satisfaction: Research Studies and Findings

The clearest and most consistent body of findings in the behavioral sciences has to do with the determinants of job satisfaction. Studies corroborate one another in demonstrating that the more varied, complex, and challenging tasks are higher in worker need fulfillment than the less skilled, routine jobs. As disclosed earlier, comparisons of occupational groups show that the more skilled the vocation, the more its members enjoy their jobs. Notably, in most of these studies, job satisfaction is used loosely to encompass over-all liking for the job situation as well as intrinsic job satisfaction deriving from the content of the work process. Hence the greater need fulfillment of

---

[21] Franklin P. Kilpatrick, Milton C. Cummings, Jr., and M. Kent Jennings, *The Image of the Federal Service* (Washington, D.C.: The Brookings Institution, 1964). This study deals mainly with occupational values and devotes only limited attention to value fulfillment or job satisfaction.

[22] Palola and Larson, "Some Dimensions of Job Satisfaction."

[23] Vroom, *Work and Motivation*.

the higher occupational levels could result from the higher pay, the greater prestige of the calling, the hours, the working conditions, or the like. It is important, therefore, to hold constant any factors other than the nature of the work in comparing the satisfaction derived from jobs varying in level of skill and complexity. This rigid control is, of course, impossible when dealing with broad occupational groupings where wages and conditions of work are tied to type of occupation. Within a single company or police department, however, it is possible to make meaningful comparisons of intrinsic job satisfaction within a restricted range of differential skill levels. The department may have the same working conditions and the same program of employee benefits for all police officers within this range. Moreover, the wages may reflect seniority as well as skill level. Hence it is possible to find police personnel at more complex tasks earning no more than their co-workers at less skilled jobs. And, significantly, those assigned to the more complex tasks are usually more satisfied with their job.

Further, the old contention that people do not like to make decisions is also refuted by recent job satisfaction studies. Related to this finding are other data showing that job satisfaction and the perceived opportunities for self-expression are positively correlated. The studies on job enlargement also report greater satisfaction with an increase in the meaningful cycle of activities. In summary, considerable evidence indicates that workers prefer jobs which challenge their skill and which provide them a high measure of decision-making opportunities and responsibility. That the great majority of jobs offer a routinized work content is a constant source of frustration to the man who still has some craftsmanship and drive in his personality. Thankfully, the job of police officer is one of tremendous challenge and opportunities for the making of decisions.

Two researches in job satisfaction pertaining to police and criminal justice personnel are presented at this time. The first investigation used, in combination, both the situational and personal methods for measuring work relevant values in three related occupations. Consequently, both work relevant and individual values are analyzed in order to provide an empirical foundation for predicting relative job satisfactions. The second study employs the situational approach.

Field Research Findings I

The environmental setting of this particular study was a major metropolitan area in California. The data were collected through the use of questionnaires administered by field interviewers. The result provided a sample of 56 employees responsible for the performance of juvenile-criminal justice activities. The sample was divided into three groups: (1) parole agents (n = 20) (state employees), (2) police officers (n = 18) (city employees), and (3) probation officers (n = 18) (county employees). Two research instruments were used: one to measure the importance of certain work relevant values, and a second to measure the perceived level of fulfillment of these same work relevant values. Each instrument contained 30 items covering various aspects of the job situation, such as value of the work to society, recognition for job success, freedom to make decisions, opportunity for self-expression, etc. For each item the respondent first indicated its importance and then on a separate but identical continuum his perceived achievement of the same work values. From these two instruments a value fulfillment score was calculated by subtracting the work value achievement score for each work value item from the work value importance score for each work value item. This procedure provided 30 fulfillment scores and a total score for each one of the occupational areas. A 5 per cent significance level of the computed *r*s was used as a criterion in the selection of major findings for the occupational categories both aggregatively and separately.

The study reported here has been designed to assess (1) the patterning of occupational values and (2) the probable amount of job satisfaction among three occupational categories previously mentioned. The short-term purpose is to furnish information that may prove useful to public personnel managers in modifying organizational policies and personnel procedures relative to parole, police, and probation officers. To estimate the level of satisfaction provided by the three criminal justice work roles, it is necessary to learn what the occupants of those particular roles value in a job. The long-range goal is to provide an impetus to public personnel administrators either to begin or to continue their investigation of job values and satisfaction.

Before describing the general design of the study, a brief rationale for selecting the particular work roles to be analyzed is pertinent. Parole, police, and probation agencies are currently engaged in a competitive struggle for manpower with pertinent skills. All three of these criminal justice agencies are either now or soon will be attempting to recruit and retain college-educated human resources. And, there is a paucity of such employables. In other words, these agencies are simultaneously confronted with a constantly decreasing supply of potential candidates, primarily because of higher job standards and offers by other institutions of more satisfying work roles. To suggest that these three criminal justice agencies should at all times have priority claims on the finest of this nation's human resources would reflect a distorted concept of their relationship to the other institutions of our pluralistic society. It is clear, however, that the rapid pace of social and technological change has for some time been changing the employment needs of parole, police, and probation agencies relative to other institutions.

The majority of the job satisfaction researches mentioned thus far substantiate the thinking that there is a direct relationship between the fulfillment of work values and job satisfaction. In general, the results of this particular study suggest that the respondents should possess a reasonably high level of job satisfaction. Table 10 presents aggregate work value fulfillment scores. When totaled, it is seen that each occupation is not only meeting but surpassing the fulfillment of felt importance assigned to the work values. Further, the results of this survey showed that most of the respondents perceived of their occupation as making a very important contribution to society. Related to this contribution was their sense of being respected by family and friends. Ironically, more than half of those interviewed reported that they were reasonably satisfied with their current income. There appeared to be some doubt as to sufficient opportunity for upward mobility in the agency. That is, many thought of their job as not providing adequate opportunity for advancement. Apparently, however, the respondents did not attribute a lack of upward mobility to intraorganizational politics of luck because they overwhelmingly felt that their occupational success was based on what and not on who they know. Those interviewed indicated a sense of task accomplishment regardless of situational constraints or personal dissatisfactions. Finally, Table 10 indicates that, of the three occupational categories, the police juvenile officer seems to possess the highest amount of overfulfillment. This finding in turn implies that it is likely that they also have the greatest degree of job satisfaction—based on the questions used in the research instrument.

TABLE 10: TOTAL OCCUPATIONAL VALUE FULFILLMENT SCORES FOR PAROLE, POLICE, AND PROBATION OFFICERS

	Questionnaire I Total Score Possible = 230 (Importance)	Questionnaire I Total Score Possible = 230 (Perceived Fulfillment*)	Difference between Questionnaires I and II
Parole agents (n = 20)	156.4	172.0	+15.6
Police officers (n = 18)	128.5	164.8	+36.3
Probation officers (n = 18)	144.1	179.0	+34.9
Total (n = 56)	150.0	180.4	+30.4

*The scores, when compared to those in the first column, indicate that all respondents were experiencing an overfulfillment of their work-related values.

In summary, the rationale for conducting this specific research study encompasses four purposes: (1) to augment existing findings on work relevant values in order to provide a better understanding of the dimensions of job satisfaction, (2) to incrementally validate and improve methodological approaches for gathering the required research data, (3) to add to a very small body of empirical knowledge concerning juvenile criminal justice work roles so that a more viable and satisfying interface may occur between the individual and his job, and (4) to suggest future research direction and, in general, to provide a stimulus for additional research to those in public and police personnel administration who could conceivably use the findings. Previous sections of this study have briefly attempted to satisfy concerns one through three. Let us now proceed to the fourth and final one.

As might be anticipated, the fourth concern, in broad terms, is for an expanded research effort on the part of public personnel agencies concerning work relevant values and job satisfaction, and also, is to focus future research efforts on the organizational components of the criminal justice system. More specifically, it appears that five research problems are in need of either initial or further analysis.

First, it is safe to say that there is a great deal of variance in job satisfaction that remains to be explained. Progress in job satisfaction researches can undoubtedly be made by the identification of relevant work values in the public sector which, if fulfilled, optimize the satisfaction an individual receives from his work role.

Second, once the appropriate work values have been determined, there comes a problem of data interpretation. It is common for social science research findings to be reported in a statistically anonymous format. However, the fundamental worth of any knowledge regarding individual job values is in knowing it on an individual rather than on a collective basis. This is not to say that aggregated findings on work values are meaningless. Both types of findings are useful in that they facilitate different organizational and individual changes.

Third, at the center of the above two problem areas is the propensity for job satisfaction research findings in most cases to have little, if any, influence on operating public managers or supervisors. The failure to "operationalize social science findings" is probably caused predominantly by the not too unusual communications gap existing between the academic and workaday environments. Certainly, one way to close the gap is to translate all findings into action programs difficult for any thinking personnel administrator to ignore.

Fourth, one significant research area, which deserves more attention than it has received, concerns whether the nature and manner of overfulfillment and underfulfillment are identical. Intuitively it seems possible that feelings of inequity produced by overfulfillment may be less frustrating and less stable, since they may be resolved by an increase in the value which the person attaches to his own inputs to the job. Much remains to be accomplished in this area.

Fifth, alluded to previously is the methodological problem of varying approaches to the same phenomena. Currently, there is a growing recognition that the level of job satisfaction is determined by the interaction of job situation, personal work values, and the values of a particular organization. It now appears that a three-dimensional research approach is required to effectively investigate the area of concern. Such an approach creates a two-part, instrumental and conceptual, problem. The first portion of the problem is being remedied daily through improved social science techniques and modern data handling devices. The latter remains in the form of loosely developed thoughts derived from recent research findings. Hopefully, sufficient conceptualization will be soon afforded the crucial next step of designing a single method which interrelates the three approaches presently used in job satisfaction researches.

Field Research Findings II

The second job satisfaction study was conducted by Reiss for the Office of Law Enforcement Assistance (now known as the Law Enforcement Assistance Administration), U. S. Department of Justice. This section is excerpted, in part, from his study.[24] Briefly, the research reported on the following major features of police work as an occupation and of police organization: the nature of police careers, of police work, and of officer job satisfaction; police officer orientations toward their tasks in policing and toward their relationships and transactions with the public policed; and officer perceptions of how organizations and systems that affect law enforcement have influenced or changed police work. We concern ourselves, in this instance, with those findings pertaining to job satisfaction.

The observational studies of the police, for reasons of economy, were undertaken in selected police precincts, or districts, of Boston, Chicago, and Washington, D. C. Two precincts each were selected in Boston and Chicago and four in Washington, D. C. Only precincts with fairly high crime rates were selected, to insure observation of a large number of police and citizen transactions within a relatively short period of time. Within each precinct a probability sample of officers was selected for interview. Although the number of officers varies somewhat among the precincts, from 20 to 25 per cent of the officers in any precinct were interviewed. Almost no one refused to be interviewed.

As we have seen, satisfaction in work involves a rather large number of

---

[24] Albert J. Reiss, Jr., "Career Orientations, Job Satisfaction, and the Assessment of Law Enforcement Problems by Police Officers," in *Studies in Crime and Law Enforcement in Major Metropolitan Areas*, vol. 2, eds. Donald J. Black and Albert J. Reiss, Jr. (Washington, D.C.: U.S. Government Printing Office, 1967). The study is companion to one on the observation of police behavior with citizens which investigated how officers and citizens behave in one another's presence. By comparison, this study reports on how officers orient themselves to their work and the publics with which they deal or which affect their work. It is a study in perceptions and attitudes, not in behavior.

attributes that relate to the salary and perquisites of the job, to the specific nature of the assignment and relations with others in it, to one's opportunity to move ahead and one's rate of movement, and to conditions of work. Not all these features of police work were investigated in the survey. In this section the major features of salary and service rewards, the opportunity for and rate of promotion, the character of supervision, and how the rules and regulations of the department affect the officer are examined in terms of officer satisfaction with them.

The large majority of police officers are somewhat dissatisfied with their rate of pay (see Table 11). Only 1 per cent are completely satisfied with their salary; 27 per cent are generally satisfied with it. Almost a third are not at all satisfied with their salary. Police officers in Chicago are least satisfied with their rate of pay despite the fact that they enjoy about the same pay scale as officers in the other departments. Negro officers are somewhat more likely than white officers not to be at all satisfied with their salary.

Despite their dissatisfaction with their rate of pay, police officers generally entertain rather modest aspirations for starting salaries in the department— the modal recommendation for a starting salary is $6501–$7500. Fewer than 5 per cent of the officers believe it should be as high as $8500; no Negro officer set a starting salary that high. Given aspirations for professional status, salary aspirations of police officers are generally closer to the salary of public school teachers than to that of other professionals.

Any rank system of promotion has built within it restricted opportunities for movement in the system, since the most common ranks are low in status and pay within the system. For police departments, the common rank is that of patrolman; the large majority of police officers at any time are patrolmen and a substantial majority of any cohort never progress beyond the rank of patrolman unless there is considerable attrition from the cohort.

For this reason it is difficult to assess the opportunities for promotion in a system beyond that built into the rank system. Since one-half of all police officers believe their opportunities for promotion are excellent or good, it seems that they are more optimistic than would seem to be indicated by the number of opportunities for advancement provided by the rank system. That one-half regard their opportunities as fair or poor is not at all surprising since it is likely that at least that many will never get beyond the rank of patrolman. Negro officers are inclined to view their opportunities for promotion less optimistically than do white officers. Yet four of every ten Negro officers regard their chances as good or excellent. Only half as many Negro as white officers believe their chances are excellent, however (Table 12).

Officers are likely to express dissatisfaction with the promotion exams. More officers express some dissatisfaction than satisfaction with the promotion exams in their department. There is striking variation in satisfaction

TABLE 11: PER CENT DISTRIBUTION OF SATISFACTION WITH SALARY FOR POLICE OFFICERS IN EIGHT PRECINCTS OF THREE CITIES AND BY RACE OF OFFICER

City, Police District, and Race of Officer	Would You Say That You Are:				How Much (Salary) Do You Think a Beginning Officer in the Department Ought To Get Now?						Total Per Cent
	Completely Satisfied	Generally Satisfied	Not Too Satisfied	Not at All Satisfied	$6,500 or Less	$6,501 to $7,500	$7,501 to $8,500	$8,501 to $9,500	$9,501 or More	Cannot Say	
All districts:	1	27	40	32	22	47	24	3	2	2	100
All white officers	1	26	42	30	24	44	23	3	3	3	100
All Negro officers	3	28	30	39	14	58	28	—	—	—	100
Boston:											
Dorchester	4	48	28	20	60	8	12	—	8	12	100
Roxbury	—	40	36	20	40	32	20	—	—	8	100
Chicago:											
Town Hall	—	11	39	50	33	33	28	6	—	—	100
Fillmore	—	19	44	37	6	38	31	19	6	—	100
Washington, D.C.:											
6	4	24	56	16	8	68	20	4	—	—	100
14	—	22	37	41	19	59	18	—	4	—	100
10	—	19	42	39	15	62	19	4	—	—	100
13	4	42	23	31	8	69	19	—	4	—	100

Source: Albert J. Reiss, Jr., "Career Orientations, Job Satisfaction, and the Assessment of Law Enforcement Problems by Police Officers," in Studies in Crime and Law Enforcement in Major Metropolitan Areas, vol. 2, eds. Donald J. Black and Albert J. Reiss, Jr. (Washington, D.C.: U.S. Government Printing Office, 1967), p. 45.

TABLE 12: PER CENT DISTRIBUTION OF HOW POLICE OFFICERS ASSESS PROMOTION OPPORTUNITIES AND EXAMS IN THEIR DEPARTMENT FOR EIGHT POLICE DISTRICTS IN THREE CITIES AND BY RACE OF OFFICER

City, Police District, and Race of Officer	Promotion Opportunities Are:				How Satisfied Are You with Promotion Exams?					
	Excellent	Good	Fair	Poor	Completely Satisfied	Generally Satisfied	Not Too Satisfied	Not at All Satisfied	Don't Know Exams	Total Per Cent
All districts:	12	38	26	24	9	29	20	24	18	100
All white officers	13	39	26	22	10	32	19	23	16	100
All Negro officers	6	33	25	33	8	17	25	25	25	100
Boston:										
Dorchester	20	32	28	16	16	60	12	4	8	100
Roxbury	28	36	8	28	24	48	16	12	—	100
Chicago:										
Town Hall	6	44	22	28	6	44	17	33	—	100
Fillmore	6	31	44	19	—	31	19	44	6	100
Washington, D.C.:										
6	8	44	24	24	4	12	28	12	44	100
14	15	37	18	30	4	11	26	22	37	100
10	—	35	39	23	—	12	27	46	15	100
13	8	46	15	31	19	19	12	23	27	100

Source: Albert J. Reiss, Jr., "Career Orientations, Job Satisfaction, and the Assessment of Law Enforcement Problems by Police Officers," in Studies in Crime and Law Enforcement in Major Metropolitan Areas, vol. 2, eds. Donald J. Black and Albert J. Reiss, Jr. (Washington, D.C.: U.S. Government Printing Office, 1967), p. 47.

TABLE 13: PER CENT DISTRIBUTION OF OFFICER ASSESSMENTS OF MERIT OF PROMOTION EXAMS FOR EIGHT POLICE DISTRICTS IN THREE CITIES AND BY RACE OF OFFICER

City, Police District, and Race of Officer	Promotion Exams:							Total Per Cent
	Give Unequal Opportunity to Get Ahead	Are Arbitrary or Unfairly Prepared	Place Too Much Emphasis on Memory	Given Too Infrequently	Should be Sole Criterion for Promotion	Are Good As They Are	Don't Know About Them	
All districts:	12	14	10	3	7	27	27	100
All white officers	12	12	13	3	6	29	25	100
All Negro officers	11	22	—	3	11	17	36	100
Boston:								
Dorchester	—	4	28	—	—	48	20	100
Roxbury	8	4	16	—	—	52	20	100
Chicago:								
Town Hall	28	17	6	—	—	44	5	100
Fillmore	13	13	6	6	—	25	37	100
Washington, D.C.:								
6	12	8	8	4	16	12	40	100
14	11	11	—	11	15	7	45	100
10	27	15	15	4	8	4	27	100
13	—	35	4	—	11	23	28	100

Source: Albert J. Reiss, Jr., "Career Orientations, Job Satisfaction, and the Assessment of Law Enforcement Problems by Police Officers," in Studies in Crime and Law Enforcement in Major Metropolitan Areas, vol. 2, eds. Donald J. Black and Albert J. Reiss, Jr. (Washington, D.C.: U.S. Government Printing Office, 1967), p. 48.

with promotion exams by city, however. Officers in Washington, D. C., are least likely to be acquainted with the examination system and more likely to be dissatisfied with it if they do know it than are officers in Boston or Chicago, though the difference between officer satisfaction in Washington and that in Chicago is less substantial. Table 13 provides information on officers' assessment of the specific merit of promotion exams. While about one-fourth did not believe they could assess their merit, the remaining officers are not in substantial agreement as to their merit. (One-fourth believe they are fine as they are. Roughly 10 to 15 per cent attribute the inequality of opportunity to get ahead to the exams, mentioning the arbitrary or unfair nature of them and their great reliance on rote learning or memory (see Table 13). Some of these complaints are not uncommon for any form of examination. Such complaints should be quite evident for examinations that have as important consequences for advancement as do promotion examinations in police departments. Perhaps the surprising fact is that police officers regard promotion examinations with as much satisfaction as they do, given their centrality in deciding an officer's fate in the system.

Table 14 summarizes officer satisfaction with service ratings. The general picture is not unlike that for promotion examinations, with only slightly less than one-half of all officers expressing some satisfaction with the system of service ratings. Officers who comment on the fairness of the ratings are roughly equally divided on the fairness of them, and indeed 42 per cent of the officers did not mention any negative quality for the ratings. The main dissatisfaction with the ratings stems from the fact that they are personal judgements. Officers are well aware of the fact that the extent of the acquaintance a superior officer has of an officer can affect his rating. Such ratings are less likely to have universalistic criteria than do examinations. Hence officers mention the fact that personality conflicts or favoritism enter into such ratings or that they are based on special discriminatory standards or upon insufficient knowledge and observation; 41 per cent of the negative criticism of ratings dealt with this general absence of universalistic criteria for service ratings.

Given both the rank structure of police departments and their bureaucratic organization around a supervision rather than a professional model of decision making, the supervisor and the supervisory process are central to an operating police department. Almost a third of all officers are not satisfied with the supervision system. While there are no substantial differences among the cities, there is somewhat greater satisfaction with the supervision system in Chicago than in the other cities. No officers in Chicago said they were not at all satisfied with the supervision given them, hence, provision for supervision does not necessarily entail dissatisfaction. Officers in Washington, D. C., were most critical of the supervision given them and most likely to mention factors that could be improved. They were also the most

TABLE 14: PER CENT DISTRIBUTION OF OFFICER ASSESSMENT OF SERVICE RATINGS IN HIS
DEPARTMENT BY RACE OF OFFICER

Service Rating Assessments	All Officers	White Officers	Negro Officers
How satisfied are you with service ratings?			
Completely satisfied	11	11	11
Generally satisfied	36	35	39
Not too satisfied	15	12	28
Not at all satisfied	29	32	17
Cannot say	9	10	5
Fairness of ratings:			
Ratings are fair/just	25	27	14
Ratings are unfair/unjust	28	28	25
Ratings affect officer adversely	*	1	—
Ratings affect officer positively	8	5	19
Officer does not comment on fairness	39	39	42
Negative qualities of ratings:			
Standards are unjust or discriminatory	9	6	20
Ratings based on insufficient observa- tion/knowledge	18	18	19
Personality conflicts affect ratings	6	7	—
Favoritism in ratings	8	9	6
Other negative features	6	6	5
Cannot say	11	11	11
No negative qualities to ratings	42	43	39
Has officer received merit citations or awards?			
Yes	56	57	47

*0.5 per cent or less
Source: Albert J. Reiss, Jr., "Career Orientations, Job Satisfaction, and the Assessment of
Law Enforcement Problems by Police Officers," in Studies in Crime and Law Enforcement in
Major Metropolitan Areas, vol. 2, eds. Donald J. Black and Albert J. Reiss, Jr. (Washington,
D.C.: U.S. Government Printing Office, 1967), p. 49.

likely to criticize the kind of leadership in their supervisory system and to
criticize their supervisors for failure to support them in their work role (see
Table 15). Negro and white officers do not differ substantially in their ratings
of satisfaction with the supervision system.

An attempt was made to assess some particular characteristics of the
supervisory system in the departments. In general, there appears to be
considerable dissatisfaction with the communication with the supervisor,
particularly with the capacity of men to affect or influence their supervisors
by suggestions about policies and procedures. More than one-half of all
officers do not believe they can influence their supervisors and 65 per cent
of them seldom or never make suggestions to their supervisors about police
policies or procedures. Indeed, almost one-third never made any suggestions
to their supervisors (see Table 16).

While it cannot be assumed that all suggestions are equally valuable,
or that officer suggestions are necessarily in the best interest of the system,

TABLE 15: PER CENT DISTRIBUTION OF HOW SATISFIED POLICE OFFICERS ARE WITH SUPERVISORS IN THEIR DEPARTMENT FOR EIGHT POLICE DISTRICTS IN THREE CITIES AND BY RACE OF OFFICER

City, Police District, and Race of Officer	Would You Say That You Are:				Things That Could be Improved About Supervision:						Total Per Cent
	Completely Satisfied	Generally Satisfied	Not Too Satisfied	Not at All Satisfied	Nothing in Particular	Give Men More Support	Provide More Leadership	Seek Advice of Men	More Constructive Attitude	All Other	
All districts:	18	51	27	4	39	14	14	10	7	16	100
All white officers	19	51	27	3	41	15	13	9	6	16	100
All Negro officers	14	53	25	8	31	8	17	14	8	22	100
Boston:											
Dorchester	28	36	32	4	52	—	12	12	—	24	100
Roxbury	12	64	24	—	48	8	4	4	16	20	100
Chicago:											
Town Hall	45	33	22	—	61	6	—	—	11	22	100
Fillmore	19	69	12	—	50	13	6	13	—	18	100
Washington, D.C.:											
6	8	28	60	4	8	20	36	4	8	24	100
14	8	56	22	11	26	19	19	15	7	15	100
10	8	65	23	4	39	23	8	—	15	15	100
13	15	62	15	8	23	23	27	15	4	8	100

Source: Albert J. Reiss, Jr., "Career Orientations, Job Satisfaction, and the Assessment of Law Enforcement Problems by Police Officers," in Studies in Crime and Law Enforcement in Major Metropolitan Areas, vol. 2, eds. Donald J. Black and Albert J. Reiss, Jr. (Washington, D.C.: U.S. Government Printing Office, 1967), p. 51.

TABLE 16:   PER CENT DISTRIBUTION OF OFFICER ASSESSMENT OF SUPERVISORS AND THEIR
BEHAVIOR TOWARD THEM BY RACE OF OFFICER

Assessment of Supervisors and of Own Behavior Toward Them	All Officers	White Officers	Negro Officers
How often in 1965 and 1966 have you suggested a different or better way of doing police work to your supervisory officers?			
Never	37	36	44
Once or twice	30	30	28
Three to five times	10	9	14
Six to ten times	6	8	—
More than ten times	17	17	14
How often do your supervisory officers go along with your suggestions of different or better ways of doing police work?			
Very rarely or never	26	24	36
Occasionally	16	17	11
About half of the time	8	9	3
Almost all of the time	16	16	13
Has no way of knowing	3	4	3
Never gives suggestions	31	30	44
When you don't like some policy or procedure concerning police work, how often do you tell your opinion to one of your supervisory officers?			
Very rarely or never	38	38	42
Occasionally	27	27	28
About half of the time	6	6	3
Almost all of the time	29	29	27
How satisfied are you with the influence men at your rank have on how things are done in the department?			
Completely satisfied	6	7	2
Generally satisfied	35	36	28
Not too satisfied	26	25	31
Not at all satisfied	32	30	39
Cannot say	1	2	—

Source: Albert J. Reiss, Jr., "Career Orientations, Job Satisfaction, and the Assessment of Law Enforcement Problems by Police Officers," in Studies in Crime and Law Enforcement in Major Metropolitan Areas, *vol. 2, eds. Donald J. Black and Albert J. Reiss, Jr. (Washington, D.C.: U.S. Government Printing Office, 1967), p. 53.*

the general characterization of relations with supervisory officers would not permit a very high professionalization of the police work role. Nor are the changes in rules or procedures that officers would make (see Table 17) largely changes in the direction of more professionalization of their work role. Only 7 per cent expressed dissatisfaction with the paramilitary features of police departments, features that hinder effective professional police work in their judgement. Most other recommended changes (see Table 17) would or should affect their professionalization very little.

TABLE 17: PER CENT DISTRIBUTION OF CHANGES IN RULES OR PROCEDURES THAT POLICE OFFICERS WOULD LIKE TO SEE MADE FOR EIGHT POLICE DISTRICTS IN THREE CITIES AND BY RACE OF OFFICER

City, Police District, and Race of Officer	What Changes/Improvements Could Be Made?							
	None	Changes "In Paper Work"	Court Time Policies	Policies about Hours/ Assignments	Promotion Policies	Paramilitary Organizations	All Other	Total Per Cent
All districts:	43	12	1	10	2	7	25	100
All white officers	44	12	1	8	1	6	28	100
All Negro officers	36	11	3	17	6	11	26	100
Boston:								
Dorchester	52	12	—	12	4	—	20	100
Roxbury	60	8	—	12	4	—	16	100
Chicago:								
Town Hall	61	6	—	—	—	11	22	100
Fillmore	56	—	—	13	—	—	31	100
Washington, D.C.:								
6	32	16	4	12	—	16	20	100
14	30	15	—	19	—	7	29	100
10	23	15	8	12	4	—	38	100
13	34	15	—	4	4	23	20	100

Source: Albert J. Reiss, Jr., "Career Orientations, Job Satisfaction, and the Assessment of Law Enforcement Problems by Police Officers," in Studies in Crime and Law Enforcement in Major Metropolitan Areas, vol. 2, eds. Donald J. Black and Albert J. Reiss, Jr. (Washington, D.C.: U.S. Government Printing Office, 1967), p. 54.

MORALE

The basic fact with which one is impressed upon reviewing research findings concerning morale is that there is no clear-cut, commonly agreed-upon definition of this word. Consequently, we find that morale is an in-vogue subject of which there are as many definitions as there are definers. Psychologists would say that morale relates to the individual, while the sociologist would probably see it as a group phenomenon. As mentioned previously, the majority of scientific investigators consider morale an attitude or feeling possessed by an individual as he relates to the group. For example, Applewhite distinguishes between individual and group morale, indicating morale should apply to groups and not to individuals except when the individual is directly related to the group. He alleges that

> . . . an individual can be said to have high morale only when he is related to a group. It makes little sense to say a person has high morale when he stands alone, divorced from a group. The key, then, to morale is the group, which is defined as at least two persons working together toward some common goal.[25]

Further, group morale is "a measure of the summed motivations of group members to work together toward a common goal" and individual morale is "just a measure of an individual's motivation to pursue with others the common goal of the group of which he is a member."[26] In relation to police supervision, a considerable body of evidence and opinion indicates that both the morale and the effectiveness of employee groups vary as a function of the quality of supervision, tenure, education, the ages of the group members, the dynamic interplay of individual personalities, and the emerging social aspects of the job.[27]

One study of employees identified some rather specific determinants of morale: (1) general attitude toward company, (2) general attitude toward supervision, (3) satisfaction with job standards, (4) the consideration the supervisor shows workers, (5) work load and work pressure, (6) degree of treatment as an individual by management, (7) pride in company, (8) satisfaction with salary, (9) attitude toward formal communication system in company, (10) intrinsic job satisfaction, (11) satisfaction with, and chances for, progress, and (12) attitude toward co-workers.[28] It can be said, in terms of an operational definition, that high morale is a complex combina-

---

[25] Philip B. Applewhite, *Organizational Behavior* (Englewood Cliffs, N.J.: Prentice-Hall, Inc., 1965), pp. 22–23.

[26] *Ibid.*, p. 23.

[27] John M. Larson, Jr., and W. A. Owens, Jr., "Worker Satisfaction as a Criterion," *Personnel Psychology*, 18 (Spring 1965), 33.

[28] Darrell E. Roach, "Dimensions of Employee Morale," *Personnel Psychology*, 11 (Winter 1958), 419–31.

tion of these, and possibly more, determinants that make people do what the organization expects them to do and the organization do what the people want them to do. Conversely, low morale is a combination of determinants that prevent or deter people from doing what the organization expects them to do and the organization from doing what the people want them to do. In looking again at the previous determinants of morale, we can see that the police supervisor is in a key position to significantly influence a group's morale.

It is important to keep in mind that satisfaction is part of morale and contributes to it. In fact, job satisfaction must be present before morale can be considered high. This is to say that, if high morale is to be present, high job satisfaction must also be present, because it provides further energy for use in pursuing group goals. In examining other morale studies, it is obvious that the relationship between job satisfaction and morale approaches one-to-one. Two conclusions are immediately apparent. First, the naming of the factors is rather subjective and thus, while the factors seem the same, they may differ. The technique of factor analysis essentially attempts to separate out factors, say morale or satisfaction, and to define them by connecting a title to each factor. Second, morale and satisfaction are the same because the components of each are the same. Operationally, this must be the situation because of equivalent factors. "The distinction between the two must be made at the definitional (i.e., semantic) level reserving the term satisfaction for individuals and morale for groups."[29] Since the same components apply to both terms, the distinction at present can only be made at this level. Hence, if an individual displays these factors, he has job satisfaction; if the group he is in possesses them, it has morale. Satisfaction and morale are the same in that their components are the same, but they apply to different levels within the organization, that is, individuals and groups. Consequently, what was said in the section in job satisfaction applies here, but on a different level.

There are two ways to measure morale. First, morale can be measured by analyzing the extent to which the organization is achieving results—measurement of productivity, profits, or other indications of goal achievement. However, note that high morale and high production are not causally related. Second, if a social science definition is accepted, another approach is called for. In this case morale is tested by eliciting the feelings (attitudes) of employees toward the organization. Feelings are known as emotion-packed attitudes. Where the indicators point toward low morale it may often be desirable to conduct an attitude survey, which may be done by polling or by depth interviews, which are often used in termination interviews to ascertain why people leave voluntarily. To repeat, low morale can be

---

[29] Applewhite, *Organizational Behavior*, p. 25.

raised by supervision, the pattern for such improvement being implicit in all the pages of this text.

THE RELATIONSHIP OF JOB SATISFACTION AND MORALE TO PRODUCTIVITY AND OTHER ORGANIZATIONAL VARIABLES

To begin, we emphasize that research has established that, "There is in fact no positive correlation between morale, job satisfaction, and high productivity."[30] It was assumed by most in the early days of the human relations movement that a positive relationship existed between morale and productivity. Katz and Heyman's study of morale in U. S. shipyards during World War II indicated morale and job satisfaction to be highly correlated with productivity.[31] Since job satisfaction is definitely related to challenging work calling for skill and responsibility, one can expect that it would also relate to productivity, that is, that higher job satisfaction would be connected to better performance. This prediction would also be made from a theoretical analysis, in which we assume that sincere involvement in work activity would result in greater quantity and better quality of productive work.

The results of the widely known studies of the Survey Research Center of the University of Michigan destroyed these earlier assumptions. In these studies, of which the one by Kahn is probably the most outstanding,[32] meaningful differences were found between employees in high and low productivity sections on such morale measurements as job satisfaction, employee involvement in the company or participation in company activities, and financial satisfaction. In essence, it was learned that employees could be quite happy with their job and accomplish nothing. Moreover, employees could dislike their work, yet be productive.

The reasons for this failure to confirm the correlation between job satisfaction and productivity are not difficult to find in further analysis. Essentially, three reasons are involved: (1) pride, (2) level of aspiration, and (3) the nature of the work. Let us consider each one in more detail. First, pride in the work group has proven to be the only attitudinal variable showing a distinct relationship to productivity. In Kahn's study there was a significant difference between the ratio of employees in the high and low performance sections who displayed high pride in their work group. The high performance

---

[30] Albert R. Martin, "Morale and Productivity: A Review of the Literature," *Public Personnel Review*, 30 (January 1969), 42.

[31] Daniel Katz and H. Heyman, "Morale in War Industry," in *Readings in Social Psychology*, eds. T. Newcomb and E. Hartley (New York: Henry Holt and Company, 1947), pp. 437–47.

[32] Robert L. Kahn, "Productivity and Job Satisfaction," in *Psychology in Administration*, pp. 98–105.

sections indicated a greater degree of pride and loyalty.[33] Second, Morse has suggested that the levels of aspiration of the workers influence the relationship.[34] Workers with higher job involvement were probably setting higher levels of aspiration for themselves and hence reacted more negatively to blocks in their progress than did less aspiring workers. Thus, a job satisfaction measure which does not take into account the aspirations of the worker is an inadequate measure of his degree of job involvement. Third, certain factors have to be present in the work itself before high satisfaction can cause improved productivity, or vice versa. Simply expressed, when tasks are more varied and require more skill, the expected positive correlations do occur. Many jobs have been so thoroughly standardized that individuals have little opportunity to express their talents, with the result that the basic motivation is to maintain an acceptable level of performance rather than to excel. In other words, one's job should be so designed (and this is the rationale behind such things as group decision making and team policing) that the individual can acquire greater need fulfillment through greater productivity.

Hence, an individual's satisfaction with his work and group morale can be linked to high productivity. The so-called link is the quality of supervision in the organization. In the preceding chapter, we found that the employee- or group-centered leader was more apt to become a supervisory leader. Pertinent here are the studies which have revealed that group-centered supervisors are higher producers (in terms of group productivity) than production-centered supervisors! The supervisors with the better production records appear to be persons who show in a variety of ways that the individual is important to them, that they understand and appreciate him. The specific characteristics of high production supervisors were that they spent more time on supervision, displayed a closeness to and an identification with the employees, showed personal interest in the employees, both on and off the job, were nonpunitive in their behavior toward the employees, and were accessible for communication with their employees. All of this is to say that the supervisor acted as a leader.

In regard to productivity, we conclude that if all three conditions are met—pride, aspiration, proper job design—the probabilities are very good that high job satisfaction and group morale will cause high productivity. If they are not met then we must abide by the following:

> . . . the overwhelming research evidence to date supports the conclusion that there is no positive correlation between morale, job satisfaction, and productivity. This is not to say that there can not exist high morale and high productivity, but rather that when this is found, variables other than morale or

---

[33] *Ibid.*

[34] Nancy Morse, *Satisfactions in the White Collar Job* (Ann Arbor, Mich.: Survey Research Center, 1953).

variables interacting with morale are probably responsible for the high productivity.[35]

Another major relationship is that of satisfaction and morale to absenteeism and job turnover. Morse asserts that the "level of general satisfaction may be a predictor of the individual's desire to stay or leave the organization."[36] Further, she relates this does not mean the individual will definitely leave, for this leaving depends upon the state of the labor market. In other words, the worker whose personal needs are satisfied through his work role is more likely to remain in the organization. Moreover, low satisfaction leads to grievances, turnover, absenteeism, and tardiness on the job.

Research has indicated also that morale and job satisfaction differ according to age and skill of the worker. In dealing with age, though, the evidence available suggests that in studying the relationship between age and morale, length of service should be considered. Otherwise, it might be the length of service in the organization that relates to satisfaction, for as the age of the employee increases, usually his length of service with the company does too. Morse, again, provides an excellent discussion of the age and skill level relationships to morale and satisfaction. "In general, the shorter the time the employee has been with the company the more satisfied he is with his salary and his chances for progress in it."[37] Conversely, the older employees become dissatisfied when their expectations of advancements and salary increases are not met quite so rapidly. All this seems to say that there is a positive correlation between job satisfaction and salary level. It has been shown previously that salary is a component of job satisfaction and morale, but now further analysis is necessary. To begin, skill level is related to job satisfaction and salary—the higher the skill level, the higher the salary. "Therefore, the apparent relationship of salary to job satisfaction is, in fact, indirect. The higher skill level results in greater job satisfaction at *all* age levels."[38] The older employees are more satisfied with the job content because they have, in most cases, acquired the more skilled jobs. Thus, we can expect to find that police supervisors are more satisfied than police officers as a whole because supervisors are generally older and have more highly skilled jobs.

Finally, studies on job satisfaction and morale have either proven or strongly implied that:

1. There is no relationship between worker popularity and job satisfaction (morale).[39]

---

[35] Martin, "Morale and Productivity," 44.

[36] Morse, *Satisfactions*, p. 52.

[37] *Ibid.*, p. 68.

[38] Applewhite, *Organizational Behavior*, p. 29.

[39] B. J. Speroff, "Job Satisfaction and Interpersonal Desirability," *Sociometry*, 18 (January 1955), 69–72.

2. There is no relationship between worker job satisfaction (morale) and in-plant communications.[40]
3. There is a positive relationship between worker job satisfaction (morale) and an increased role in the organizational decision-making processes.[41]
4. There is a negative relationship between worker job satisfaction (morale) and the size of the organization.[42]
5. *There is a positive relationship between worker job satisfaction (morale) and the attitudes and behavior of the supervisor.*[43] In case the reader might have forgotten, such a finding is one of the primary reasons for writing this text!

Applewhite suggests for us what the next step in the subject of job satisfaction and morale should be.

> This raises an important point: what are the relative weights of each of the components of job satisfaction and morale? If they were known (which they really are not at present), then a multiple regression equation could be written. This would be an equation predicting job satisfaction as a function of its four or five components. It would then be possible to say, for example, that increasing the attitude toward monetary rewards by X amount would have the same effect upon satisfaction as increasing the attitude toward supervision by Y amount. With this equation at hand, different combinations of the components could be used to obtain different levels of satisfaction or morale. Then, if a regression equation could be written to predict labor absences, turnover, and grievances as a function of satisfaction or morale, it could be seen what combination of satisfaction factors would be the most effective in reducing absences, etc. . . . Changing these amounts according to the equation could either increase or decrease the satisfaction or keep it the same but with different proportions of the attitudes entering in. In any case, the satisfaction would be brought up to a desired level, using a proper "mix" of the attitudes, to reduce absences according to the relationship established between satisfaction and absences.[44]

To Applewhite's "next step" can be added four others described earlier: (1) augment existing findings on work relevant values as they relate to job satisfaction and morale, (2) improve and standardize the methodological approach for conducting research in this area, (3) dig into the highly critical

---

[40] Dallis Perry and Thomas A. Mahoney, "In-Plant Communications and Employee Morale," *Personnel Psychology*, 8 (Winter 1955), 339–53.

[41] Nancy Morse and Everett Reimer, "The Experimental Change of a Major Organizational Variable," *Journal of Abnormal and Social Psychology*, 52 (June 1956), 120–29.

[42] Sergio Talacchi, "A Critique and Experimental Design for the Study of the Relationship between Productivity and Job Satisfaction," *Administrative Science Quarterly*, 5 (June 1960), 309–12. Concerning job attitudes, see Bruce G. Lawson, "Employee Attitude Surveys: An Aid to Administrators," *Public Personnel Review*, 30 (April 1969), 97–101.

[43] Morse, *Satisfactions*.

[44] Applewhite, *Organizational Behavior*, p. 31.

fold of criminal justice occupations, and (4) *use* the resultant findings for increasing worker job satisfaction and morale.

Basic Techniques of Job Satisfaction and Morale

Clearly the police supervisor has a basic responsibility for attempting to improve his subordinates' job satisfaction and morale. His method and tools for doing so are, to some limited extent, suggested in the preceding chapters. Instead of reviewing these techniques at this time, we provide a measuring device for determining if they are in use. The reader should carefully examine and respond to each question listed below. The over-all numerical score indicates your level of satisfaction. Combining your score with others in the same work group indicates the level of morale present. The police officer and supervisor should find the device of particular interest. In one way, the score is suggestive of how successful the subordinates feel their immediate supervisor is in meeting their personal needs. Where low scores are evident, further analysis of the 15 items is necessary. Spotting those items that received a low or dissatisfied check should provide to the supervisor a warning sign for remedial action. Corrective action on the part of the supervisor should begin with an examination of the various supervisory techniques described in this text. It should continue through the selection and application of the most appropriate alternatives for the solution. It ends if, after further measurement, the individual's level of job satisfaction has been increased. If not, then back to the drawing board.

Notice that we have provided a space for answering which allows you to show several degrees of satisfaction or agreement. There are no correct answers to these questions, but only answers as you see them.

1. How satisfied are you with the sort of work you are doing?

	1	2	3	4	5	
Very dissatisfied						Very satisfied

2. What value do you think the community puts on your service?

	1	2	3	4	5	
None						Very great

3. In your daily work, how free are you to make decisions and act on them?

	1	2	3	4	5	
Not at all						Very free

4. How much recognition does your supervisor show for a job well done?

	1	2	3	4	5	
None						Great deal

5. How satisfied are you with the type of leadership you have been getting from your supervisor?

	1	2	3	4	5

Very dissatisfied   Very satisfied

6. To what extent do you get to participate in the supervisory decisions that affect your job?

	1	2	3	4	5

None   Great deal

7. How closely do you feel you are observed by your supervisor?

	1	2	3	4	5

About right   Too closely

8. Are you satisfied with the department as it now stands?

	1	2	3	4	5

Very dissatisfied   Very satisfied

9. How satisfied are you with your prestige within the city government?

	1	2	3	4	5

Very dissatisfied   Very satisfied

10. How satisfied are you with your possibilities of being promoted to a better position?

	1	2	3	4	5

Very dissatisfied   Very satisfied

11. How satisfied are you with your present salary?

	1	2	3	4	5

Very dissatisfied   Very satisfied

12. How satisfied are you with your status in the community?

	1	2	3	4	5

Very dissatisfied   Very satisfied

13. Would you advise a friend to join this department?

	1	2	3	4	5

No   Yes

14. Do you receive a feeling of accomplishment from the work you are doing?

	1	2	3	4	5

Very dissatisfied   Very satisfied

15. Rate the amount of pressure you feel in meeting the work demands of your job.

	1	2	3	4	5

Very dissatisfied   Very satisfied

SUMMARY

Job satisfaction and morale are similar since both refer to the feelings an individual has toward his present work role. They differ in that the former is concerned with the feelings of the individual worker and the latter, with the feelings of a group of workers. The levels of job satisfaction and morale are based on the amount of value fulfillment provided by the work role. To explain, each of us approach our work with certain needs or values we seek to be fulfilled. To the extent that the job either meets or does not meet these needs, we experience some form of satisfaction or dissatisfaction with our work.

Daily we see our formal organizations falling into line behind an ethos that asserts, "work should be made more satisfying to the worker." This ethos has some highly pragmatic overtones, however. Besides being an expression of a Judeo-Christian ethic, it provides a firm footing for reducing worker turnover and absenteeism, increasing his productivity, and developing cooperative and innovative patterns of behavior. Job satisfaction depends on two interrelated areas: (1) the levels of skill and professionalization in the job and (2) the amount of human need-fulfillment that a particular job gives to a particular person.

Essentially, three methods are used for studying job satisfaction: (1) organizational, (2) situational, and (3) personal. Clearly there is a need to integrate these approaches into a single framework. From research in job satisfaction we have learned that workers are more satisfied with jobs having variety, complexity, and challenge. Consequently, police administrators and supervisors alike are furnished a highly important guideline for making police work more gratifying to the individual officer.

Morale is an attitude possessed by an individual as he interacts with a group. Hence a police supervisor is in a highly critical position, both as a member and as a superior, to affect the level of morale in a group. That morale and job satisfaction differ has already been established. However, they are also quite similar in that the components of one are the components of the other. If an individual manifests these components, he possesses job satisfaction; if a group displays them, it has good morale.

Both job satisfaction and morale have been analyzed for possible relationships with other organizational variables. The major finding here is that neither is causally related to productivity. However, if a worker or work group has pride, high levels of aspiration, and the nature of work is challenging, the chances are that one will find both high job satisfaction and high productivity. Further, research has shown that job satisfaction and morale are related to absenteeism, age, skill, shared decision making, and—most importantly—effective supervision.

PROBLEM

The reader is invited to take a look at Police Department X. During your perusal, keep in mind certain questions that may be posed regarding job satisfaction and morale. Discuss these questions with your co-workers. What are some of the issues and problems? More importantly, what might be some reasonable alternatives for correcting the situation? Finally, what did the reading of the case do to your own level of satisfaction?

Police Department X: Job Satisfaction and Morale

The police department discussed in this study is approximately ten years old. The city functions under a city council–city administrator form of government and is a general law city. The population is approximately 58,000, and the area, approximately 12 square miles.

The history of municipal government in city X is one of instability, coupled with scandals, including corrupt city councilmen, who were prosecuted and found guilty of bribery; frequent replacement of the city administrator (sometimes under mysterious and sudden conditions); and the firing and subsequent rehiring of the present chief of police.

City X has not had the benefit of a master plan, and almost no industry has been attracted to the city. Major business firms such as car dealerships have in the last one or two years come into the city to take advantage of vacant land near major thoroughfares. An unusually large number of trailer parks have sprung up, but the great majority of the city consists of individual homes in the middle and lower price ranges. Ironically, the last year has been one of increased and refreshing stability and professionalism on the part of the city council and the city administrator. Both the council members and the administrator are recent replacements of their predecessors.

The police department has an authorized strength of 53 sworn officers, but only 40 officers are currently employed, primarily because of numerous resignations during the past year. Of the 40 officers now employed, 15 hold supervisory ranks from sergeant to chief.

The traffic division, which normally consists of 1 sergeant, 1 investigator, and 3 traffic officers, has had to discontinue use of the traffic officers and their motorcycles to transfer that strength to the patrol division. Further, the detective division normally has 1 lieutenant, 2 sergeants, and 7 detectives. At the present time it functions with the 3 supervisors and 4 detectives. The sergeants, who usually concentrate on supervision, now carry investigative case loads (robbery and auto theft respectively); 2 detectives who resigned have not been replaced and 1 detective has been transferred to patrol because of that division's shortage of manpower. Also, case assignments have been changed so that the vice and narcotics divisions no longer have anyone assigned to them because of other and more pressing cases, such as burglary. In addition, a shortage of patrolmen has made it mandatory for them to work 6 days a week instead of the normal 5 days. The pay is comparable to salaries paid in similar jurisdictions but below the salary paid by larger departments, such as Los Angeles Police Department and Sheriff's Department.

The male juvenile detective serves as coordinator of the reserve officers when his time permits. The department has approximately 12 reserve officers who are required to work at least 16 hours per month, usually as a second man in a patrol car. Recently, however, they have been permitted to operate a patrol car provided that at least two reserves are in the vehicle.

Department X's police chief has served as chief for ten years. He had prior police experience as a lieutenant in another department and entered this department as a chief. He has a bachelor's degree which he obtained in his younger days. Both the captains entered the department as policemen and were promoted by examinations. Neither captain has any appreciable college background. The operations captain, who has most of the personnel under him, has a history of being very successful in public relations. His smooth handling of citizens has won many friends for the department. His similarly smooth way of handling the officers has become too smooth for the officers who feel that he is so anxious to "make them feel good" that he becomes too flowery and insincere; promises are not always kept. Although friendly in his approach to the employees, he operates on a completely authoritarian theory and proudly announces that "we don't operate here as a democracy."

Both the chief and the captains act prudently on citizens' complaints. If the investigation shows misconduct on the part of the officer, appropriate disciplinary action is always taken. If, on the other hand, the officer acted properly under the circumstances, management does not yield to citizen pressure but supports the officer fully. However, management performs little inspection or control. Many obvious errors and inefficiencies exist in procedure and performance without being recognized or acted upon by the chief or the captains.

The chief has no communication with his men, while the captains occasionally speak with the personnel, although no effort has been made to make such communication relevant or regular. Under this management, the department has maintained facilities and performance approximately equal to those of other, average departments in the county, but at no time has this administration been first at anything, pioneered a new procedure or tool, or sought to experiment with any departure from traditionalism. These administrators have, on the contrary, greeted news of other departments' new ventures with scorn and ridicule. Granted, management has been instrumental in securing for the police department a new, attractive police building and has also, at approximately the same time, changed the department's uniform from a disharmonious, four–color one to a plain blue police uniform.

Department X has 3 lieutenants assigned as patrol watch commanders and one lieutenant assigned as detective commander. Eight sergeants are assigned as follows: 1 as traffic commander, 1 in services, 2 in detectives, and the rest as patrol field supervisors. All the lieutenants have extensive police backgrounds. Two of them hold bachelor's degrees in criminology, and the other two are high school graduates with no interest in college education. Three lieutenants function in a very professional manner, while one is moody, vacillating, and primarily interested in not "rocking the boat." The sergeants have from 3 to 15 years of police experience. Two hold bachelor's degrees—one in criminology, one in social sciences—and two have acquired A. A. degrees in police science. The other four have very little college background. With the exception of two quite senior sergeants, all usually perform their duties effectively. One detective sergeant, although an excellent investigator, is noted for his almost total lack of social understanding; nonconformists have, in his opinion, no right to exist.

The 25 policemen are currently doing the job ordinarily performed by 38 men. Even when all positions are filled (38 policemen and 15 supervisors), the policeman-citizen ratio is only 0.93 policeman per 1000 citizens, a figure below average both regionally and nationally. During the last year, 9 officers and 1 sergeant have resigned, and 1 officer has been asked to resign. Some reasons given for resigning are entering private business, entering private investigation, seeking employment in federal law enforcement, seeking employment on same level in neighboring police agencies, and preferring local law enforcement employment on same level in other parts of the nation.

The officers going into business and private investigation did so because of their desire for higher income. One officer went to the Office of Naval Intelligence because he saw this as an opportunity to later enter the Federal Bureau of Investigation with higher prestige and income. Those going to nearby police departments were very senior officers whose performance was inferior and who could not pass promotional examinations. Yet they were bitter because they had not been promoted, and they felt their chances would be better in another agency. One officer took a pay reduction to join a two-man department in Northern California because he preferred rural surroundings.

The majority of those officers remaining daily express their dissatisfaction with a variety of conditions. While they appreciate the extra pay, they are getting tired of having to work a six-day week on a mandatory basis. They complain that the city should have engaged in some type—any type—of recruiting effort to avoid the present manpower situation. They complain that it is unfair that the supervisors have to work only five-day weeks. A recent memo from the chief advising the personnel that they will not be granted more than half their normal vacation this year was met with further despair. Most of the officers feel that they are able to contribute some ideas and thoughts on the operation of the department, but they have no avenue of expression. Some have given their suggestions to their sergeants, but no result ever appears. Those officers who have attended college for many years feel their education is a waste because no one in the department allows them to use it. Those same officers sometimes state that they think it odd that, while they go to college three or four nights a week year after year, many supervisors, including captains, do not even attend one class per year and have done nothing to further their education for many years.

It is generally agreed among the men of policeman rank that the morale is lower than they can recall it ever having been previously. One reason this belief is reinforced is that no member of supervision or management is apparently aware of this condition, and it is felt that even if they were, it would not make any practical difference because the administration does not care. Furthermore, discontent exists because the department never does anything to cause particular pride in the organization. It acquires new equipment usually after the majority of other departments have done so. One hears complaints such as "Why do we still have to write our reports in the field by hand when the Sheriff's Department has been able to telephone their department and dictate their reports for several years." While the relationship between the policemen and their sergeants is generally a pleasant one, few of the complaints are passed on to the sergeants.

An example of the attitude toward the chief is found in the incident in which a citizen commented upon the chief to an officer with two or three years on the force. The officer responded, "I wouldn't know. I don't know the chief."

Some officers express amazement that the department does not require them to practice shooting at the range regularly (they are supposed to do so once a month but no one enforces it), that they are not required to keep physically fit or to stay within a healthy weight limit, and that they are not exposed to any real in-service training. Most of the officers state that they would welcome enforcement of such rules in the interest of a better police department with better personnel.

Two cliques have emerged in the detective bureau. One comprises the juvenile officers, whose cases stack up in hopeless numbers. The other clique is formed by the adult investigators, who also realize that they cannot handle all their cases but clear them out and are better organized than the juvenile officers. The poorly organized juvenile detectives spend much time complaining about their case load and are good customers in the local coffee shops. They regard the adult detectives as unfriendly and callous. The detectives investigating adult crimes have resigned themselves to the fact that their investigative task is impossible, and they are better able than the juvenile officers to select the important cases for careful investigation, while quickly clearing the less important and less promising cases out. They regard the juvenile officers as gossipers, chronic coffee drinkers, and poorly organized detectives. All detectives have offered to work evenings or weekends in return for overtime pay or compensatory time, but this has not been approved by the department. The officers assert, "If the Department or the public doesn't care, why should I worry too much."

Every man on the department is pleased with the new police building but has not forgotten how everyone had to work in substandard facilities for too many years. One matter which bolsters the morale of many is the fact that the city pays 5 per cent extra salary for individuals possessing the intermediate training certificate and 10 per cent extra for those having the advanced certificate.

11

The Police
and their Community*

Community relations are not the exclusive business of specialized units, but the business of an entire department from the chief down. Community relations are not exclusively a matter of special programs, but a matter that touches on all aspects of police work. They must play a part in the selection, training, deployment, and promotion of personnel; in the execution of field procedures; in staff policymaking and planning; in the enforcement of departmental discipline; and in the handling of citizens' complaints.[1]

Please reread the above quotation! The President's Crime Commission indicated that they perceived police-community relations as identical with the police organization. Hence, they are inseparable—good police-community relations is good police work. This author fully concurs with their thinking. Moreover, the commission asserted that

A community-relations program is not a *public*-relations program to "sell the police image" to the people. It is not a set of expedients whose purpose is to tranquilize for a time an angry neighborhood by, for example, suddenly promoting a few Negro officers in the wake of a racial disturbance. It is a long-range, full-scale effort to acquaint the police and the community with each other's problems and to stimulate action aimed at solving those problems.[2]

Reread the last quotation. It can be put another way: police-community relations (PCR) is a concerted departmental effort to develop viable and mutually supportive relationships among the police and their community. All of the above creates a dilemma, however, for this author. To explain,

---

*This chapter is, with cordial admiration, dedicated to Chief of Police R. Fred Ferguson, City of Covina, California. His wise counsel, willingness to experiment, leadership, and interest in police-community relations are worthy of commendation by police administrators, educators, and researchers alike.

[1] *The Challenge of Crime in a Free Society*, a report by The President's Commission on Law Enforcement and Administration of Justice (Washington, D.C.: U.S. Government Printing Office, 1967), p. 100.

[2] *Ibid.*

currently there is a wealth of sound, applicable information on PCR, covering everything from field training programs through grievance procedures to the changing role of the police in an ever-changing community—certainly too much terrain to cover in a single chapter. Therefore, we have no other choice but to delimit our analysis to the following areas: (1) a definition of PCR, (2) the significance of PCR, (3) PCR programs, (4) an experimental case study concerning PCR, (5) grievance mechanisms, and (6) concluding remarks.

PCR—WHAT IS IT?

Too many of us, by far, view PCR as an organized attempt to gain a workable level of acquiescence from the minority-group community. Indeed, the President's Crime Commission relates that

> This is the problem that is usually—and politely—referred to as "police-community relations." It is overwhelmingly a problem of the relations between the police and the minority-group community, between the police and Negroes, Puerto Ricans, and Mexican-Americans. It is as serious as any problem the police have today.[3]

Granted, the PCR problem is most serious in the area of minority-groups, but clearly the problem does not stop here. We find majority-groups (teachers, attorneys, clergymen, and so on) manifesting reservations, if not hostility, toward those who have been chosen to enforce their laws. Consequently, to carry out, with proper efficiency and discretion, the complicated law enforcement and community-service tasks the police are expected to perform is a formidable assignment. It is, we might add, at times even impossible.

It is time to define what *we* mean by PCR. PCR is a process, to be engaged in by all members of the department, for constantly interacting with its environment so as to obtain the general support of external organizations and people for facilitating the accomplishment of its assigned goals. Where does the police supervisor fit in?—at the very focal point of any PCR process. He does so by his role as controller and trainer. In other words, better supervision can very likely lead to better PCR. Conversely, the possibilities of successful PCR are nil if the police supervisor fails to make it his business.

Every formal organization is in constant need of environmental support. Hence, units develop within the organization to institutionalize environmental relationships and guarantee such support. An organization often has a separate division for public relations and contact with the larger society. We find that the operation of any organization depends not only

---

[3] *Ibid.*, p. 99.

upon the specific reception of its product or service but upon *the support and legitimation of its activities by the larger social structure.* Corporations deal with the federal government with respect to policy and practice on mergers and monopolies and tax laws, among other things. Corporations also relate to the general public on support for private enterprise and types of restrictions on private power. Awareness of this problem has led to concern about the image of the company in the public mind. In a similar way, the police department interacts with the community. A person selected as chief of a police department soon finds that little of his time is available for administration within the organization. He is primarily its external representative, dealing with service groups, professional associations, governmental officers, civic and other public groups. The term *community relations* tends to be restricted to departmental advertising and is not an adequate concept to cover this important function of relating the organization to the total social system of which it is a part. Our approach to PCR, therefore, conceptualizes it within a much broader framework.

THE SIGNIFICANCE OF PCR

> The Commission believes that a police-community relations program is one of the most important functions of any police department in a community.[4]

That the police and its public, or perhaps better stated the public and its police, are a timely and urgent subject cannot be denied. Bowser in the *Saturday Review* provides a provocative treatment of their relationship.[5] His thinking is here presented in an abridged form. Bowser begins by stating that whether we like it or not the police

> ...are right in the midst of a great debate about the growing disaffection between the police and large segments of the American public. This disaffection is, of course, not altogether new. What is new is the intensity and passion with which the subject is now being argued in kitchens, clubrooms, corner bars—in all the places where Americans talk freely and from the heart. Are policemen brutal and contemptuous in their dealings with Negroes? With antiwar demonstrators? With university rebels? With hippies and other unconventionally clad youngsters? Is the Supreme Court handcuffing the police? Should police, as public servants, have the right to strike or stage slowdowns? Should policemen be expected to keep "hands off" a crowd taunting them in filthy language? It is a rare American indeed who will not give you impassioned answers to all these questions. . . .

---

[4] *Ibid.*

[5] Hallowell Bowser, "The Public and the Police," *Saturday Review*, 251 (November 2, 1968), 26.

Thus, depending on one's place of dwelling, income, racial background, and political convictions, the local police tend to be seen as a decent, long-suffering, much-put-upon lot—or as foulmouthed, minority-hating, club-swinging brutes. The problem is, in fact, becoming heavily ideological—i.e., when they hear reports of an alleged police excess, more and more people feel they know *in advance* what the rights and wrongs of the case are.

This ideological cleavage runs along curious lines. Many people who a decade ago were confirmed umpire-baiters, cop-haters, and authority-defiers generally have now become converts to the notion that policemen can do no wrong. And many young people whose families have for generations venerated policemen as guarantors of justice and exemplars of rectitude, now go about calling the police Fascist pigs.

This mixed situation leaves the average citizen all at sea. He probably gets to see little real police action, either brutal or benevolent. And when, as with the Chicago convention, he sees apparent police brutality on TV, he later learns that the police claim they were only responding to shocking provocation and assault not shown on TV. . . .

To learn more about PCR, Bowser suggests:

. . . the police-public question, the interested citizen would also do well simply to keep his eyes open and his common sense in working order. He should, for instance, know better than to swallow the notion that hurling a taunt at a policeman is just as grievous an offense as hurling a brick at him. Nor should he buy the contention that it is all right to throw a brick at an innocent patrolman so long as the thrower claims to have in mind some high philosophic purpose.

Above all, the citizen should try to remain sympathetic to all sorts of constructive initiatives, such as the upgrading of police salaries and recruitment-and-training standards; and the development of special police-trained service corps, staffed by local young people, to be assigned to aid work in neighborhood communities within the big cities.

In reviewing and perhaps reformulating his thoughts about the police-public interaction, it would also pay the concerned citizen to keep his sense of humor bright. When an over-thirty-five friend tells him in all seriousness that no body of men, even trained policemen under orders, can be expected to control themselves when they are called bad names, he should remind the friend of the case of Ted Williams, the Boston Red Sox great. When Williams was taunted by the Red Sox fans for days on end, in quite foul and explicit language, he finally turned to the bleachers one afternoon and made an obscene gesture to his tormentors. Howls of outrage promptly went up from clergymen, sportswriters, youth leaders—and, of course, from the bleacherites who had cursed Williams. Almost to a man, the American public cried that ballplayers held positions of high trust, were examples to youth, and should not let "mere taunts" upset them. It would be ironic if we Americans went down in history as a people who expected more of our ballplayers than we did of our police officers.[6]

---

[6] *Ibid.*

The National Advisory Commission on Civil Disorders was equally at odds with the issue of developing and maintaining PCR. They were quick to recognize that

> One side, disturbed and perplexed by sharp rises in crime and urban violence, exerts extreme pressure on police for tougher law enforcement. Another group, inflamed against police as agents of repression, tends toward defiance of what it regards as order maintained at the expense of justice.[7]

Thus far, in general terms, we have alluded to the significance of PCR. Before focusing on it in detail, let us briefly cover its historical background. When reviewing an area such as PCR, it is difficult to select a starting point. Texts in police administration, dating back to the early years of this century, indicate that questions involving the police and the community were recognized by students of law and society at that time. At first, PCR came under the popular title of public relations (PR). While progressive police executives gave recognition to this function over the years, police participation in the ever-growing problems of traffic regulation and control intensified the need for the development of more effective PR programs. Spurred by the success of the Federal Bureau of Investigation's efforts to gain public cooperation and support, and influenced by the difficulties of the task at hand, many municipal police agencies adopted appropriate PR policies and initiated formal training in the area. Finally, PR was blessed with organizational status, by PR or public information units being created in the police departments of such cities as New York and Los Angeles.

Specialized police training in community relations goes back about 25 years. Its development has been described as a phase of the broader context of professionalization of the police during the same period. However, the primary impetus for formalized training in PR stemmed from growing racial problems in our urban centers. The sociological factors are readily apparent; for example, unprecedented migration of southern Negroes (and whites) to northern and western big cities in search of better economic opportunities in war production industries. The rapid social change created serious problems of adjustment for the newcomers, problems which made the police task of maintaining civic peace more challenging. "Logically, police training programs began to reflect efforts to meet this need."[8] PR began to be conceived of as a broader area because of an ever-increasing concern for the police image and public attitudes toward the police.

At first PCR was designed as a tactical reply to civil disorder. During

---

[7] *The National Advisory Commission on Civil Disorders*, report of the Commission (Washington, D.C.: U.S. Government Printing Office, 1968), p. 157.

[8] A. F. Brandstatter and Louis A. Radelet, *Police and Community Relations: A Sourcebook* (Beverly Hills, Calif.: The Glencoe Press, 1968), p. iii.

World War II we also saw numerous city police agencies beginning quite systematic approaches to the development of special training for police officers in the subject matter of race relations, racial tensions, the police and minority groups, and so on.[9] Few of these programs dealt with tactics only. There was an awareness of the importance of preventing violence. This awareness meant police training that included attention to the causes of interracial friction, attention to understanding somewhat better the groups involved in the struggle for justice in race relations, and attention to the civil role of the police service in these situations. All these dimensions represented a tremendous challenge for the police.

It was not, however, until the 1950s that a "police-community relations concept" was identified in the literature beginning to converge in "the sociology of the police." The goals of PCR programs were formulated as a result of expanding experiences as follows:

1. To encourage police-citizen partnership in the cause of crime prevention.

2. To foster and improve communication and mutual understanding between the police and the total community.

3. To promote interprofessional approaches to the solution of community problems, and stress the principle that the administration of justice is a total community responsibility.

4. To enhance cooperation among the police, prosecution, the courts, and corrections.

5. To assist police and other community leaders to achieve an understanding of the nature and causes of complex problems in people-to-people relations, and especially to improve police-minority group relationships.

6. To strengthen implementation of equal protection under the law for all persons.[10]

These goals are primarily an outgrowth of the National Institute on Police and Community Relations at Michigan State University. The Institute, repeated annually since 1955, brings together police officers from across the country and a representative assortment of other community leaders. A wide variety and a considerable number of related or parallel programs in police and community relations have also been conducted in the years since 1955. Some of these other programs have involved police only; others have brought police officials together with other community leaders to discuss problems of mutual concern in what is billed as "an inter-professional approach to community problems."

Relatedly, in 1961, the School of Police Administration and Public

---

[9] The National Center on Police and Community Relations, *A National Survey of Police and Community Relations*, report to the President's Commission on Law Enforcement and Administration of Justice (Washington, D.C.: U.S. Government Printing Office, 1967), p. 3.

[10] Brandstatter and Radelet, *Police and Community Relations*, p. iv.

Safety, Michigan State University, conducted a national survey of 168 law enforcement agencies. The results of this survey established a strong case for the creation of a National Center on Police and Community Relations. The Institute was recast in 1965 into such a center, and it presently operates with year-round services available at Michigan State. Similar to our definition of PCR is the one they offer.

> Properly understood, Police and Community Relations in its generic sense means the variety of ways in which it may be emphasized that the police are indeed an important part of, not apart from the communities they serve. Properly understood, Police and Community Relations is a concept for total police organization, functionally speaking—a total orientation, not merely the preoccupation of a special unit or bureau within the department. It bears upon administrative policy, it bears upon supervision, it bears upon every aspect of personnel practices, it bears puon records and communications, it bears upon complaint practices, it bears upon all aspects of internal as well as external relations, it bears upon planning and research, and perhaps most significantly, it bears upon line service through the uniformed patrol division. In short, Police and Community Relations, ideally, is an emphasis, and attitude, a way of viewing police responsibilities that ought to permeate the entire organization. Every major issue in American law enforcement today is, in a substantial sense, a challenge and an opportunity in terms of Police and Community Relations. For it is only in an effective partnership of police and community that there is any prospect of dealing constructively with these issues.[11]

Wherein lies the fundamental significance of PCR? As with most phenomena, in its goals. The goals have been described. In summary form, then, what might be said about the importance of PCR? PCR is the attempt by one organization serving society to elicit support in the accomplishment of its assigned goals. It is much more than a communications effort. Indeed, it is an action-oriented program designed to better relate the needs of law enforcement to the needs of society. The significance of PCR is, therefore, that its goals are the goals of our local police. However, the goals are not as much in question as are the means. In other words, "It isn't what a policeman does, it is the way he does it!"[12]

PCR PROGRAMS

Basically, a PCR program should be designed to fulfill the six goals specified in the preceding section. Considerable effort has and is being made

---

[11] *Ibid.*, p. v.

[12] A comment made by Chief of Police R. Fred Ferguson, Covina Police Department, Covina, California, March 24, 1969.

by our police in the area of PCR. To further their efforts, the federal government has been quick to furnish monies for PCR programs. Significantly, 34 grants were made to police departments for PCR planning and development.[13] Slightly over $500,000 was spent on such programs during a 30-month period. Considerably more was spent on PCR education and operations programs. In fact, in reviewing the entire list of federally sponsored programs during fiscal years 1966–1968 (April 1), it can be seen that well over one-half of the total $19 million spent was allotted to PCR. (For example, the City of Newark Police Department received $99,284 for a PCR pilot project.) It is reasonable to expect that the Law Enforcement Assistance Administration will see to it that much of its funds, both now and in the future, are committed to PCR endeavors.

The Status of PCR

Research surveys do not portray a very satisfactory picture of existing police-community relations. (Clearly this is the main reason for the above mentioned federal support of PCR programs.) There are bright spots; however, they are few and far between. Moreover, areas considered successful are in most cases situations in which a police and community relations program has developed only within the past several years, largely as a pacification effort on the part of local government.

One case in point regarding the status of PCR is a recent survey of public attitudes toward the police conducted by the National Opinion Research Center.[14] It showed a variety of opinions. Twenty-three per cent of all white people thought that the police were doing an "excellent" job, while only 15 per cent of nonwhites held that view. At the opposite end of the scale, 7 per cent of all whites thought the police were doing a "poor" job, compared with 16 per cent of nonwhites. Approximately the same response was obtained to a question about how well the police protect citizens. Graphically it looks as follows:

Do Police Do "Excellent" Job?
White—23 per cent
Nonwhite—15 per cent

Do Police Do "Poor" Job?
White—7 per cent
Nonwhite—16 per cent

Additional information showing that a sizable proportion of our population is either dissatisfied with or distrusts the police is furnished by another study (see Table 18). The question asked and the replies given were, "How

---

[13] *Third Annual Report to the President and the Congress on Activities Under the Law Enforcement Assistance Act of 1965* (Washington, D.C.: U.S. Government Printing Office, 1968), p. 1.
[14] *The Challenge of Crime in a Free Society*, p. 99.

TABLE 18: RATINGS OF LAW ENFORCEMENT

	Good–Excellent Rating		
	Federal, per cent	State, per cent	Local, per cent
Nationwide	76	70	65
By size of place			
Cities	80	67	57
Suburbs	79	71	72
Towns	75	72	65
Rural	71	72	66
By race			
White	75	71	67
Negro	81	63	51

Source: The National Center on Police and Community Relations, A National Survey of Police and Community Relations, report to the President's Commission on Law Enforcement and Administration of Justice (Washington, D.C.: U.S. Government Printing Office, 1967), p. 10.

would you rate the job the Federal (state, local) Government does on law enforcement—excellent, pretty good, only fair, or poor?"[15]

Any attempt to examine the present status of the police and community relationship on a nationwide basis is difficult, if not impossible. Of the numerous reasons for this, three are paramount.[16] First, the police and community relationship cannot be separated from some of the most challenging issues of our time—it is at the crux of such problems as civil rights, urbanization, and poverty. Second, the relationship is a dynamic series of interrelationships among the national and local levels of government. While there are identifiable issues which in general characterize the national level, the local situation to a greater degree is the product of the interplay of local personalities, practices, problems, and values. Third, the status of the relationship is masked behind emotional words, ideological phrases, and slogans, most of which are either ill-defined or not understood at all. For example, what does police brutality, law and order, and so on, mean to you?

It must be understood clearly that no police and community relations project or program, no matter how carefully conceived and conducted, can totally eliminate the causes of the social ills prevalent in our society and especially malignant in the minority group areas of our large metropolitan centers. Consequently, to seek to establish who is to blame for this state of affairs, and to what degree, is to engage in an absurd game. In all social relationships in which there is a problem, the responsibility for this problem is spread among many institutions and people. In other words, the police and the disaffected elements in the community are both wrong in holding one another culpable. Admittedly, however, too often the police insist it is

---

[15] As reported in *A National Survey of Police and Community Relations*, p. 10.
[16] *Ibid.*

the community that is at fault, and the community claims that the blame lies with the police. This is a senseless argument, for, in fact, the police are the community, and the community is the police.[17]

All studies of PCR to date emphasize the tremendous need for additional studies and research on this subject. The researchable areas and questions, especially types, involving evaluation of carefully constructed operational models, are many. The resources of the social sciences have barely been touched with regard to PCR, and their relevance has only recently been suggested in the literature and publications of such scholars as Gordon E. Misner, James Q. Wilson, Jerome Skolnick, Arthur Stinchcombe, Albert J. Reiss, Jr., Herman Goldstein, Walter Gellhorn, Marvin Wolfgang, Albert C. Germann, and others.

While we continue to research the area of PCR, there remains the ever-growing need for PCR programs—not soon, but *now*! Why now? Lohman and Misner, in speaking of the relationship between the police and the community, inform us that we are now

> . . . witnessing a breakdown in this dialogue. We are witnessing too, paradoxically, a development not only of distance but of *polarities* between the police and groups within the community they serve. Rather than standing "in relationship to," we find them in the unfortunate position of being "in confrontation with," among others—racial and ethnic groups, social action and civil rights groups, the adolescent community, and the court. More than at any other time in our history, the police are estranged from other agencies and from groups within the community. This is the most urgent problem facing our police today. This is perhaps the most urgent problem facing our cities today.[18]

As might be imagined, their field studies have likewise reported PCR problems. If one is sufficiently optimistic, however, he is able to see favorable signs pointing in the direction of better PCR. Namely, our citizenry are becoming more concerned with a viable approach to PCR. Similarly, so are the various levels of government, educators and researchers, business firms, and police administrators, in other words, society in general.

PCR Programs: Approach and Content

Lohman and Misner provide us with wise counsel when they write:

> The strongest caution should be directed toward police assumption that Police-Community Relations is equated with or is a function of Police Public Rela-

---

[17] *Ibid.*, p. 375.
[18] Joseph D. Lohman and Gordon E. Misner, *The Police and the Community: The Dynamics of Their Relationship in a Changing Society*, vol. 1, a report prepared for The President's Commission on Law Enforcement and Administration of Justice (Washington, D.C.: U.S. Government Printing Office, 1966), p. ii.

tions. The latter stresses one-way communication, the former two-way. This study has shown that a constant request of those who are alienated from the general community is that they be "understood." Their assumption is that they are not heard and thus not understood. "Hearing" requires that the police listen to varying viewpoints, as well as present their own.[19]

Further, they have, based on their research experiences, assembled a list of recommended actions in regard to improving PCR. Space does not permit citing all of them. We concern ourselves with those directed at the local level of government. Note, significantly, that they use the term *local level of government.* In other words, Lohman and Misner did not single out the police as being solely responsible for PCR. They, as have others, view PCR as primarily a total local government responsibility. To begin,

1. Local public and governmental leaders, members of the public, and police personnel should give recognition to the importance which the matter of effective and meaningful police-community relations has for the peace and security of urban areas.

2. Recognition should be made of the condition of the day which characterizes the fact of our urban social existence, that is the fact that the peace and security of the community do not rest alone upon the efficient and technological performance of law enforcement. More important is *law observance* or the consent of the governed which involves meaningful participation in the formulation as well as the implementation of law as a means of social control.

3. Local community leaders should make realistic efforts to analyze the police mission, in the general sense and as it applies specifically to their own community. Opportunities must be created to make effective relationships possible between both police agencies and citizens in order to make a dialogue focusing upon the peace and security of the community possible.

4. Local communities should take immediate steps to insure and protect the confidence of the public in its police force. Concerning complaints against the police system, much of the attention of both the police and the public has been directed at arguments surrounding the advisability of Police Review Boards. In fact, however, the Police Review Board should never have been the central issue; Police Review Boards are only symptomatic of a much more serious matter, i.e., the loss of confidence by the public in some local police forces. It is the loss of confidence which is the central issue in this controversy.

5. It is recommended that each unit of local general-purpose government accept responsibility for the fact that its police force operates under political and civilian control.

6. It is recommended that the governmental and community leaders of each urban area analyze the extent to which the public is inconvenienced unneces-

---

[19] *Ibid,* p. 178.

sarily by the fact that lower, magistrate-level courts operate on a traditional work-day schedule.

7. It is recommended that efforts be undertaken seriously to examine the whole question of "public apathy."

8. It is recommended that urban police departments take immediate steps to explore ways in which the police can work in concert with the public and private school systems in order to work with school children and build an understanding of the role of policing in a democratic society.

9. It is recommended that an analysis be made of the ways in which civilians can be given an increased measure of effective participation in urban policing.

10. It is recommended that police administrators—in cooperation with other governmental and community leaders—explore ways in which police agencies can make a more meaningful and realistic use of persons with ethnic minority group backgrounds.

11. It is recommended that police departments examine their present policies and procedures with the deliberate intention of analyzing the implication which each has for police-community relations matters.

12. Police administrators should examine the immediate and long-range effects of using auxiliary and reserve police forces. Such forces of "civilians" have a potential and long-term value in assisting in the overall police-community relations program.

13. It is recommended that police administrators examine the role which "anonymity" plays in alienating the police from the public and the public from the police. If it is determined that one aspect of the police-community relations problem is caused by an organizationally-induced distance between the policemen and the citizen, the department should take immediate steps to change its policies of manpower assignment.

14. It is recommended that police administrators give serious consideration to the role which "individual involvement" can play in an effective, long-term program of police-community relations.

15. It is recommended that police administrators demonstrate their personal and administrative support of an effective police-community relations program. Such support—manifested in a variety of ways—is crucial to such programs.

16. It is recommended that the chief of police participate personally in community relations functions to the greatest possible extent. Although many of his responsibilities may be administratively delegated, police-community relations functions are so critical that he should avoid giving the impression that he feels they are secondary to his other responsibilities.

17. It is recommended that police officials on the highest levels cooperate with a representative cross-section of the community in order to assess the effects which enforcement policies and techniques have on immediate and long-term community relations programs.

18. It is recommended that police officials consult specialists to assist in analyzing any possible organizational aberrations which result from the administrative use of traditional measures of police efficiency.

19. It is recommended that, as one part of its administrative control mechanism, police officials develop a regular and systematic way of sharing information within a department about complaints against members of the department.

20. It is recommended that the police department establish a formal unit for the investigation of complaints lodged against members of the department.

21. It is recommended that police departments should make full and complete investigations of complaints lodged against police officers, complete with a full account of each stage of the investigation. Reports and statements, including an outline of the investigator's reasoning which leads to specific recommendations should be made available to any person or organization which has a legitimate interest in the case. The availability of this information should be publicized through the various mass media.

22. It is recommended that police departments make a clear distinction between "public relations" and "community relations."

23. It is recommended that each local police force give recognition in its organization to the importance of police-community relations.

24. It is recommended that the rank of the officer responsible for Police-Community Relations programs be equal to the rank allocated to other major functional units such as Patrol, Detectives, Administration, etc.

25. It is recommended that local police departments which establish Police-Community Relations Units take measures to insure that despite the formation of this special unit, the achievement of effective police-community relations remains the responsibility of the entire department.

26. It is recommended that Police-Community Relations Units be assigned the following responsibilities:

a. The centralization of information and knowledge pertinent to police-community relations, generally, and to specific problems encountered in the local community.

b. Stimulation of department-wide concern and interest in addressing problems.

c. Evaluation of department policies, procedures and activities for their short-term and long-term effect upon community relations.

d. Development of department-wide policies and programs in community relations.

e. Development of training programs for personnel in other units of the department.

f. Analysis and evaluation of experimental programs in community relations.

27. An effective police-community relations program will involve a variety of techniques. Essentially, these will fall under one of two major categories of effort: 1) those directed toward the total community, and 2) those directed toward special interest groups. An outline of suggested programs in each of these categories is, as follows:

28. Police-community relations units should be assigned full responsibility

for coordinating community relations programs in the police department. The unit should not have responsibility, however, for the exercise of tactical duties such as riot control, control of civil disobedience, etc.

29. Centralization of departmental responsibility of community relations should not relieve district (precinct) commands of their responsibility for community relations.

30. Departments should be encouraged to experiment with programs which offer promise of improving communication with and understanding within "hard-to-reach" populations.

31. The establishment of a National Association of Police-Community Relations Officers should be encouraged and supported.

32. It is recommended that a regional association of police-community relations officers should be established in each of the metropolitan areas of the nation.

33. Although the selection of all police personnel should be carefully and systematically accomplished, it is particularly important that care be exercised in the selection of officers assigned to serve with a special, centralized unit performing police-community relations functions.

34. Officers assigned to a police-community relations unit should exercise great care to avoid becoming involved in activities which are incompatible with the mission of their unit.

35. Training in police-community relations must encompass all ranks of the department. If such a training program focuses upon only one level of the department and excludes other personnel, intra-departmental communication will be stifled. It is essential that the entire department be talking "the same language" if the organizational communication process is to be effective.

36. In police-community relations work, great care has to be exercised to distinguish between communication and "intelligence gathering." Charges of violating confidence, or allegations that police personnel are interested only in finding certain information about the community and its various groups will seriously jeopardize community relations efforts.

37. Responsibility for training in such subjects as riot control and civil disobedience should be clearly divorced from the responsibilities of the police-community relations unit.

38. A regularized system for communicating information which has significance in community relations should be developed for intra-departmental purposes. This type of information could be utilized not only for passing along knowledge about current developments, but it could also serve as a special training device.

39. Since effective community relations are as important to the police department and to the community as the criminal investigation function of the department, study should be devoted to incorporating achievements in effective community relations into the assessment of individual officers. Effectiveness in community relations should be given as much credit in promotion as success in the criminal portion of police work.

40. The salaries of police personnel should be set at a level which is commen-

surate with their present responsibilities of protecting the peace and security of the community. Low salaries diminish the number of potentially capable persons who will be attracted to police careers and such low salaries perpetuate the aggravation of serious social problems. Realistic salaries permit the entrance of capable persons and also permit the imposition of strict job requirements for retention in office.

41. Police recruitment standards should be developed so that the emphasis will be upon attracting recruits with a service ideal and a desire to work with and to help people.

42. Personnel who are unable to fulfill the present service requirements of urban policing should either be reassigned to duties which exclude them from contact with the public or they should be separated from the police service.

43. The probationary period for new officers should be long enough to allow a fair appraisal of their adaptability to the demands of a police career. This probationary period should be used in a diligent effort to separate those personnel who are clearly unfit for the police service.

44. Police examinations—both recruit and promotional—should be structured in such a manner as to assure that they adequately measure abilities, aptitudes, and characteristics which are necessary for effective police service and community relations.

45. Police examinations—both recruit and promotional—should be structured so as not to discriminate either subtly or overtly against personnel of ethnic minority group backgrounds.

46. In developing promotional standards and procedures, emphasis should be placed upon assessing the performance of officers in noncriminal situations as well as their performance with the criminal public.

47. The content of present police training programs should be examined to determine their present adequacy in view of the changing character of urban policing.

48. Police training should include imparting knowledge about the social, political, and cultural organization of the community and the implications these factors have upon the police mission. Furthermore, information about community organization should be considered to be as important to the policeman as information about current crime trends.

49. Recognition should be made of the fact that the effect of training upon recruits is often seriously diminished by "experience" in the police system itself. Training should address the problem of the "informal police system."

50. Training should emphasize the fact that the bulk of an officer's time involves dealing with citizens and the noncriminal public.

51. In police training, the present emphasis of imparting knowledge about the literal interpretation of the law should be changed in favor of dealing with the law as an instrument of "reasonableness" and as an instrument of meaningful social action.

52. Police training and supervision should prominently mention the importance of police discretion.

53. An adequate police training program necessarily involves the effective training of police supervisors and administrators.

54. As a part of its recruitment and training programs, police departments should examine the desirability of establishing special internship programs for college-age youth, involving the guarantee of summer employment as a "sub-professional" in the police department.

55. Departments should be encouraged to experiment with new techniques of training, some of which will be radical departures from traditional methods of instruction. One such method is known as the "plunge" and would require the police recruit to exist for a short period of time in an area populated by lower socio-economic level people.

56. In urban areas where sizable segments of the population speak a language other than English, the police department should undertake efforts to train officers to be bilingual.

57. Each police technique and procedure for dealing with the public should be critically analyzed for its manifest and latent effect upon police-community relations. The emphasis should be placed upon discovering ways in which the number of positive police-public contacts can be increased.

58. Police departments should recognize the fact that uncritical application of the principles of "selective enforcement" may unnecessarily complicate police-community relations problems.

59. Police departments should recognize the fact that the use of field interrogation or "stop and search" procedures is subject to abuses of discretion.

60. It is recommended that police patrol operations be analyzed to determine the extent to which nonmotorized patrol methods can be effectively utilized.

61. It is recommended that police departments seriously examine the advantages and disadvantages of rotation of assignment. An attribute of an effective patrolman is that he knows his territory. It may be advantageous—from both a police-community relations and a police effectiveness point of view—to develop a deliberate policy of fixed assignment for a reasonably long period of time.

62. Large urban areas should give serious consideration to separating the traffic function from the police department.

63. It is recommended that police departments examine the effect which specialized units of the department have upon overall police-community relations.[20]

In conclusion, the above recommendations can serve as both framework and guideline for PCR programs. For our purposes, we divide formal PCR programs into specialized police units and training. First, the police-community relations unit in a police department should approach PCR as an integrated effort which utilizes both internal and external sources of support

---

[20] Lohman and Misner, *The Police and the Community*, vol. 2, pp. 295–316.

to build and sustain a high level of PCR. The content handled by the unit varies according to the particular area and its inherent problems. To put it another way, police units assigned the responsibility of PCR programs must custom-fit their efforts. Second, in regard to PCR training, the approach should cover "recruitment through retirement." Too often we give an officer "a shot of PCR" and expect it to last a career lifetime. Once administered, PCR training daily loses its influence because of changing community conditions and attitudes. The police supervisor, in his role as trainer, is in a unique position to identify PCR training needs and to see to it that sustained training in PCR is afforded his subordinates.

For those interested in a more detailed treatment of the approach and content of PCR units and training, see Chapter 6, "The Police and the Community," in *Task Force Report: The Police*.[21] Concerning PCR, it recommends:

1. Establish community relations units in departments serving substantial minority population.
2. Establish citizen advisory committees in minority-group neighborhoods.
3. Recruit more minority-group officers.
4. Emphasize community relations in training and operations.
5. Provide adequate procedures for processing citizen grievances against all public officials.[22]

To reemphasize two points: (1) Time is short, therefore, immediate and innovative action in PCR is needed now. (2) The police supervisor has a vital part to play, because of his location and role in the police organization, in any PCR effort.

PCR: AN EXPERIMENTAL CASE STUDY

The case about to be discussed is firmly entrenched in group dynamics. Hence, it may be helpful to review the summary of Chapter 3. The case, moreover, is an attempt to both operationalize and internalize PCR precepts and attitudes. It so happens that it utilizes the group process in doing so. The field study entitled "Experiment in Changing Organizational Behavior Through Group Orientation" is presented with the kind permission of Police Chief R. Fred Ferguson, Covina Police Department, Covina, Califor-

---

[21] *Task Force Report: The Police*, a report by the Task Force on the Police to The President's Commission on Law Enforcement and Administration of Justice (Washington, D.C.: U.S. Government Printing Office, 1967), pp. 144–207.

[22] *Ibid.*, p. xi.

nia.[23] As a student of behavior, and as a part of the police command, Chief Ferguson has strong feelings about the development of over-authoritarian attitudes in policemen. In essence, he feels that too many seemingly well-oriented young men are dropped from the police ranks during the first year of service for poor attitudes toward the public. If one has faith in the selection process, and he has, with certain reservations, then one must critically view the multitude of new experiences that greet a young policeman.

Like other people, a policeman, in addition to his inherent traits, tends to reflect the sum total of his experiences. During his formative years as a young policeman, he has many demanding and unusual experiences, quite different from those of ordinary citizens. At least, the experiences are crowded into a narrow span of time and stacked on top one another like building blocks. He begins to put people and circumstances into categories, cataloged by his experiences. For example, he tends to hear similar, repetitious alibis for deviant behavior, especially in the enforcement of traffic regulations. It would seem almost normal to develop some degree of cynicism. With this in mind, Chief Ferguson posited that the negative authoritarian attitudes normally developed by some segments of the police organization can be effectively reduced by the implementation of effective and well-conceived PCR group-orientation programs. To this end he experimented. The results are as follows:

The city of Covina, in the San Gabriel Valley just 23 miles east of downtown Los Angeles, is a rapidly growing white, conservative, middle-class community whose population has increased from 4,000 to 30,000 since 1950. Covina has a council–manager form of government in which five part-time Council members are elected for four-year terms. From their membership, a Mayor is selected. The Council also appoints a full-time City Administrator, who at the time of this case was Mr. Neil Goedhard (who has since accepted the City Managership of the city of Fresno, California), and he, in turn, with the approval of the Council, appointed Chief Ferguson to his present position, a position held for the past seven years.

Nearly all the 49 men and women of the police department are in a college or other continuing education program, with books and tuition paid for by the City; rotation of shifts in the police department is based on the school schedule of members of the force. The majority of the force are police science majors and attend school as individual students rather than as groups.

As one might expect, the police department received a normal number of

---

[23] R. Fred Ferguson, "Experiment in Changing Organizational Behavior Through Group Orientation" (paper presented in the course Public Organization Theory, School of Public Administration, University of Southern California, Los Angeles, Calif., January 13, 1969). For a more general description of the project, see "Profile in Innovation: Covina: Operation Empathy," *Public Management*, 51 (March 1969), 10–11.

complaints, some justified, others not, about the attitudes of policemen. The majority of complaints came from the large teenage segment of the population. Since Covina is primarily white and since its few nonwhites are thoroughly integrated, it is doubtful that any such negative police contacts would result in racial tension or a riot of any kind; however, it was still cause for concern. On the other hand, one can not ignore the broader picture, namely, the conditions leading to social disorganization in our society have resulted in a modern urban phenomenon—the riot. For example, in August 1965, Los Angeles, less than 25 miles from Covina, was terrorized by the worst riot in the nation's history, in which 34 persons were killed, 1032 were injured, and 3952 were arrested. Property damage was estimated at $40,000,000. The McCone Commission, investigating the causes of the riot, concluded that there appeared to be no single cause for the events leading to the Watts disorder; however, just as a single arrest triggered events leading to the Watts riot, strained relationships between the Negro community and the "thin thread" of police officers appears to be a critical factor in recent urban riots throughout the United States.

Although it is generally agreed that police cannot be expected to solve all the ills of our rapidly growing communities, PCR programs established by law enforcement officials can provide time for other social institutions of society—economic, political, educational, religious, and governmental—to adjust to changing urban conditions. All citizens who register complaints against the department are invited to ride for an evening in a patrol car with a police officer and see the problems of those concerned with law enforcement. Although there was some concern when this plan was initiated, the program was so successful for both officers and adult members of the community that it has been expanded to include teenagers. This action was logical and necessary because the teenager was the problem area involving policemen's attitudes. The "getting to know you" program was good but not really adequate in that it handled the problem after the fact. It was the staff's hope that, through group orientation, attitudes might be changed to a degree that mopping up exercises would literally be unnecessary. Too, it must be realized that only a portion of those offended bother to report the incidents. For these and other reasons, a formal training program plan was developed, using the services of two behavioral scientists.

The program content focused on philosophical and behavioral science perspectives on individual ethical and value systems as they relate to responsible leadership behavior in a democratic society, with emphasis on improving interpersonal effectiveness, creative use of time, improving skills in group communication and decision making, planning for organizational change, research findings on intergroup tensions and race relations, and community leadership in urban growth and development. Seminar teaching and training techniques included lecture discussions, directed outside reading assignments, management exercises, directed field experiences among the clientele groups, and sensitivity training.

This training project was to equip a selected group of uniformed and nonuniformed members of the Covina Police Department with the greater knowledge and skill essential to better understand and deal more effectively with members of the Covina community and with their own department. The project represented an attempt to combine PCR training with a comprehensive leadership program. The design philosophy held that modern law enforcement officials must clarify their personal value commitments and adapt their attitudes and behavior to meet the changing law enforcement needs of contemporary society. Not only must the traditional rights of life and property be protected, but a redefinition of the police role within the framework of our pluralistic democracy must include protection for people who hold values and behavior that differ from those of the majority. The seminars, then, were designed to help participants examine their personal values and attitudes and to develop certain professional skills and knowledge. Therefore, the specific objectives of this PCR training program were

1. To obtain knowledge about the traditional Judaic-Christian, democratic view of man generally held in the United States and about the application of this view to police-community relations
2. To acquire skills in interpersonal and intergroup relations
3. To gain information from the behavioral sciences about the human individual, interpersonal and group relationships, complex organizations, and the community as an environment

Twenty members of the department were selected by Chief Ferguson on the basis of their interpersonal relationships and departmental work schedules. These members included three women dispatcher-clerks, three police investigators, 11 policemen, and three police sergeants, all of whom made up a group of several sub-groups. The two-day overnight retreat which began the program was conducted at California Polytechnic's Voorhis campus in San Dimas, California, which had excellent conference facilities for discussions, training exercises, recreation, eating, and sleeping. The seven regular sessions were held in Covina in the conference room of the public library. This room was well-equipped with movable tables, a large portable blackboard, and coffee-making equipment. The field exercise took place within the confines of the Riverside County Jail and in the Los Angeles skid row area. (It should be stated at this time that any organization which attempts to embark on such a program must be prepared to make a substantial man-hour investment.) The seven regular sessions were held Friday afternoons from 2: 00 until 6: 00. The field exercise at the Riverside County Jail took place with approximately five different participants going together to the jail on each of four occasions. The skid row experiences were spread over a period of time with male participants only, working in two-man teams.

A number of standard psychological tests were administered to the group by the program directors, including a balanced Authoritarian Personality (F) Scale. The testing was repeated at the end of the seminar. Ideally, to justify the project there should have been substantial changes in the test patterns. There were none! For example, the F score for the group only dropped from a 4.2 to a 4.0; not a substantially significant change. However, in the Chief's observation, the group experience was not given sufficient time to sink in, and a retesting would be more meaningful in the future.

When a policeman is arrested, handcuffed, booked, and thrown into a jail tank overnight, one can reasonably assume that he will emerge with a new set of values in understanding. When he lives as a bum on skid row, sleeps in two-bit flophouses, mingles with derelicts, and ends up being searched spread-eagled against a wall, he literally experiences the terror that often motivates an arrestee's negative actions. Hopefully, he will discover that empathy, the understanding of another human's feelings, can often have more impact than a show of force.

The jail tank, the two-bit flophouse, these are situations where normally a policeman stands on the outside looking in. As an observer, how can he understand the feelings and the emotions of the individuals on the inside who come under his scrutiny? He cannot—not until he becomes a part of "the inside" through an experimentation program. The retreat, the seminar sessions, the eight text books, the personal confrontations in the group process —all benefit, but none are so stirring as living it as it is.

As in most cities, in addition to academy training, the policemen of Covina learn about arrest, search, and booking procedures by assisting in actual arrests. Their knowledge of fingerprinting, mugging, and the normal jail routine comes as a result of jailer assignment. From this the officer learns a great deal about rational procedure. But he knows very little about either the arrestee's point of view or the arrestee's emotional reactions to police procedure. One might ask, "Is this really necessary—to know the arrestee's emotional state?" The writer need only point out the number of officers killed on so-called routine arrests. Why do arrestees, who have never before been in real trouble, panic and lash out at the officer? Why do some jails have problems with their inmates, while others do not? The prisoners could tell, but they won't—or perhaps law enforcement just doesn't listen.

With the cooperation of Ben Clark, Sheriff of Riverside County, California, located some 30 miles from Covina, a plan was formulated. Riverside was chosen because it seemed unlikely that inmates or employees of that county jail would recognize Covina personnel. Sheriff Clark agreed to tell none of his personnel that an exercise was taking place, the only exception being the chief jailer. His confidence was necessary so that the booking records, including mugs and fingerprints, could be retrieved after each release.

As a format for the experiment, Covina investigators were supposedly working a large forgery-burglary ring that had moved operations to Riverside, taking with them a quantity of stolen checks from Covina. All prisoners were to be booked as overnight-holding for the city of Covina. It was felt that with the large existing jail population, shift changes, and jailers' days off, Covina people would be swallowed up without arousing suspicion in either jailers or inmates. Teams of four and five Covina Police personnel were to be booked-in on afternoons and released to Covina investigators the following day.

On the day of arrest, the "prisoners" were handcuffed and transported the 30 miles to Riverside. The handcuffs served to further condition the prisoners for the treatment they would receive in custody during the course of the experiment. The arrest and booking procedures and the overnight incarceration created many anxieties for the counterfeit prisoners, yet they all learned a great deal about the jail procedure. They gained a new insight— from the arrestee's point of view. One lesson that stands out is that policemen seldom tell an arrestee what is going to happen to him. Covina's personnel now believe that a simple explanation would help to reassure the prisoner and make him easier to handle.

Picture, if you can, your own reaction to arrest. You have been booked, showered, deloused, and issued jail clothing. You are given a mattress and the only place to put it is on the floor of the overcrowded tank, or perhaps in the "head." Your emotional reaction would undoubtedly be one of depression. You would feel pretty low. It might be normal for you to create friction with the other inmates, to make yourself difficult to handle. You might, rightfully, feel that you had lost your identity and your dignity.

It is impossible here to sum up all the experiences, all the lessons learned in handling prisoners, the values and the effects of the jail procedures garnered by Covina Police personnel in their "Operation Empathy" experience. Suffice it to say that every successful salesman knows the value of understanding his customer. The same should be true of every policeman. Further, it is extremely difficult to immerse the average policeman into situations that will reveal the feelings of the down-and-outer, the social outcast, the have-nots, and show *their* perspective of normal law enforcement procedures. Obviously, the officer in his police role would not fit into a ghetto of any kind. But suppose he were a man with a great deal of courage, willing for the sake of experimentation to become a bum, a skid row habitant.

For some time the University of Southern California has used the skid

row experience for special seminar students, with positive results. They
had not, however, placed city policemen in such a position. The Covina
officers, male participants of the total group training program, were conditioned for the role they were about to play. Each man was given three dollars
with which to purchase a complete outfit of pawn shop clothing. Among
his other props were such items as a shopping bag filled with collected junk
and a wine bottle camouflaged with a brown paper sack. Conditioned and
ready, the men, assigned in pairs, moved into the Los Angeles skid row
district. They soon discovered that when they tried to leave the area, walking
a few blocks into the legitimate retail sections, they were told, "Go back
where you belong!" The men knew in reality they were not bums, but they
found that other citizens quickly categorized them and treated them accordingly. Some women, when approached on the sidewalk and asked for a
match, stepped out into the street rather than offer a reply, much less a
light. During the skid row experiment, the men ate in the rescue missions
and sat through the prayer services with other outcasts and derelicts. They
roamed the streets and the alleys and discovered many leveling experiences.
Some were anticipated, others were not. Perhaps the most meaningful
experience of the skid row exercise occurred to Tom Courtney, a young
officer in the juvenile division with five years police service.

It was dusk, and Tom and his partner were sauntering back to a prear-
ranged gathering place. Feeling a little sporty, the pair decided to "polish
off" the bottle of wine (which had but a few drops in it to begin with). They
paused in a convenient parking lot and Tom tipped the bottle up. As if
from nowhere, two uniformed policemen materialized before the surprised
pair. Tom and his partner were spread-eagled against a building and
searched. Forgetting the admonishment not to reveal identities and purpose
unless absolutely necessary, Tom panicked and identified himself. Later,
Tom found it difficult to explain why he was so quick in his revelation. "You
wouldn't understand," he said; then he blurted out that he had thought he
might get shot. Tom stated that as he was being searched, he suddenly
thought of every negative thing he had ever heard about a policeman. He
even perceived a mental flash of a newspaper headline: "Police Officer
Erroneously Shot While on Field Experiment." "I know better now," Tom
continued, "but when you feel that way about yourself, you believe—you
believe."

The only negative aspect of the confrontation Tom could remember
was, while the officers were firm and courteous, "They didn't smile, or tell
me what they were going to do next." Tom had discovered a new emotional
reaction within his own personal makeup, and it left a telling impression.
Today, Tom Courtney is still telling the department's personnel, "For God's
sake, smile when you can. And above all, tell the man you're shaking down
what you are going to do. Take the personal threat out of the encounter,

if you can." Equally as important as Tom's experience is the lesson learned about personal judgment. The men in the skid row experience found they were judged by the so-called normal population as "being like" all the other inmates of skid row, simply because their appearance was similar.

As stated at the outset, policemen must guard against the natural tendency to lump people into categories simply because they look alike. An illustrative example of categorizing can be found in the nationwide hippie movement. Long hair, beards, odd clothing, unkempt appearance—these are the hippie labels, and when they appear in a city, they bring with them the undertones of fear and distrust and occasional outbursts of violence, and some policemen tend to overreact.

In conclusion, what has transpired since the group orientation program is most reassuring. The other half of the Covina Police Department was exposed to the same program, with the exception that training was done on consecutive days as opposed to weekly sessions. The group members have since been rotated and mixed, but they have become stronger and more self-confident as a whole. Indeed, public interest was aroused, and some national attention was focused upon the Covina Police Department; a new kind of pride became evident. People expected them to be a cut above average, and they themselves began to act that way. Complaints against officers, especially against the younger men who are usually equated with a certain air of arrogance, have become nearly nonexistent.

The Chief's opinion that a substantial, positive change has taken place in the accepted attitude and conduct of the Covina Police Department member is reinforced by statements of many Covina citizens and, perhaps more objectively, by the former City Administrator, Neil Goedhard, and by members of the City Council.

The real test of these attitude changes came recently when a hippie group moved into town and later brought with it a "love-in," comprising about 3500 hippie types. Needless to say, the event was a traumatic one for the small conservative community. That the love-in was held without negative incident, that the officers were effective but did not act or react in the traditional authoritarian manner (which would have been welcomed by a fairly large segment of the adult population) can, in the writer's opinion, be accepted as a valid test of group orientation. As a matter of fact, policemen even assisted the hippies in planning the love-in, since it was inevitable. The planning of the love-in, the policemen's roles, the acceptance of hippies as real people by the establishment, and the community reaction of pride are all worthy of a separate case, which could reasonably be entitled "An Alternative to Flexing Police Muscle" or "The Returns on an Investment in Group Orientation to Change Organizational Behaviors."

Further indications that the group-orientation project was successful can be found in public reaction, both local and national:

1. Each Covina policeman now meets with a small neighborhood group, some-where in his patrol beat, once each month, to discuss community involvement as one solution to law enforcement problems. The main hitch in the program hasn't been how to find receptive hosts and hostesses, but rather, how to limit the appearances.
2. Local and national news media have carried stories of unusual police attitudes in Covina. Two television stations, KABC and KNBC, each devoted ten minutes of color video tape to Covina policemen doing their job.
3. The Urban League recommended to the Avanti Film Corporation, producers of educational films, that they use the Covina Police Department in a motion picture depicting positive relationships between Negro children and the police.
4. The *Reader's Digest* (April 1969) has printed an article (11 pages) about the Covina Police Department as a model.
5. *Esquire Magazine*, in their February 1969 issue, devoted two pages, one a full color photograph, to "Five Good Cops." One of these men is Tom Courtney, mentioned earlier in this chapter. *Esquire's* editors contacted Chief Ferguson and requested that a resumé of one representative Covina officer be submitted. This was done, and Tom Courtney was taken to New York by *Esquire*, as were four other officers who were from large eastern cities. Covina was selected, according to *Esquire* representatives, because of its reputation, earned since the group orientation.

Granted, Covina policemen still make mistakes, but they are less frequent; and perhaps even more important, they are never covered up. Problems are most often solved by "the group" and the group has gained a very special pride. And so has, I might add, Chief Ferguson.

GRIEVANCE MECHANISMS

Strange as it seems, grievances of citizens against our local police are primarily focused on human alienation and the demand for increased decentralization of—and participation in—police activities. This is to say that our community is looking for ways to have its interest represented. Clearly the quest for representativeness in this generation is not limited to the police alone. All public agencies are being subjected to demands to become more representative. Admittedly, malfeasance on the part of a police officer remains the reason behind some grievances. The fundamental reason behind most of the grievances against our police departments, however, is their lack of representativeness. Essentially there are three proposals for making public agencies more representative.

1. *Situating spokesmen for the interests affected in strategic positions within the organizations.* Often, this means nothing more than filling vacancies on existing boards and commissions with appointees enjoying the confidence of, or perhaps even

chosen by, those interests. In the case of the controversial police review boards, it involves injecting into administrative structures new bodies, dominated by ethnic minority groups or their friends, to survey and constrain bureaucratic behavior.

2. *A centralized governmental complaint bureau, with legal powers of investigation, to look into citizen complaints against administrative agencies and to correct inequities and abuses—the office of "ombudsman."* Once, it was chiefly through his representative in the appropriate legislative body, or through the local unit of his political party, that a citizen of modest status and means petitioned for a remedy of a grievance. . . . Today some observers contend that only a specialized, full-time official, wise in the ways of bureaucracy, having a vested interest in correcting its errors, and supported by adequate staff and authority, can perform this function effectively; *apparently*, it takes a bureaucrat to control a bureaucrat.

3. *Decentralization.* The most sweeping expression of *the unrest over lack of representativeness is the growing demand for extreme administrative decentralization, frequently coupled with insistence on local clientele domination of the decentralized organizations.* Dramatic manifestations of this movement occurred in the antipoverty program and in education. (In terms of the police department, we find some now experimenting with "neighborhood policing.")[24]

As mentioned, grievances concerning our police are twofold, involving a lack of representativeness and misconduct. Let us briefly review the second problem. The solution to it is plain:

> The best way to deal with police misconduct is to prevent it by effective methods of personnel screening, sufficient training, constant retraining, and *supervision*. A department that clearly articulates its community-relations policies and holds its members to abide by them should receive a minimum of complaints from citizens. However, there will always be citizen complaints, warranted and unwarranted, about treatment by the police. And there will always be misconduct by individual officers about which no complaint will be made. How complaints should be handled and how misconduct should be dealt with has been the subject of perhaps the fiercest of the many controversies about the police that [have] raged in recent years.[25]

Significant for our purposes is the above emphasis placed on the role of the police supervisor for handling problems of organizational deviance. Without question, the best way to insure that police personnel comply with departmental policies and general notions of fairness is through the use of effective supervisory procedures. Supervisory discipline can be swifter and, because it is imposed by the officers' own superiors, more effective. If properly administered, discipline can assure the public that the department's policies

---

[24] Herbert Kaufman, "Administrative Decentralization and Political Power," *Public Administration Review*, 29 (January–February 1969), 5–6.

[25] *Task Force Report: The Police*, p. 193.

concerning community relations are fully meant and enforced, particularly when the department's own investigation discovers misconduct without a complaint from an external source. Basically, the machinery for handling complaints can be divided into internal and external procedures. Internally, the police organization has at its disposal supervision, or a specialized internal affairs officer or unit, or both. Externally there are the: court, civilian review boards, ombudsman, and a variety of human relations commissions. The *Task Force Report: The Police* contains a description of each procedure.[26]

In conclusion, we have seen that grievances concerning the police are not exclusively caused by their misconduct. In numerous instances grievances attributed to police misconduct are actually due to a lack of community representativeness in its police organization. Corrective devices have been tried but usually with poor, if any, success. Of those devices listed above, it appears timely to experiment with the more innovative approaches. First, in terms of grievances over a lack of representativeness, decentralization of services may be the most effective solution. Second, in terms of organizational deviance, vastly improved selection and training processes seem to be the more viable approach.

CONCLUDING REMARKS: A CALL TO ACTION

> Neither simplistic polemics, nor delineation of criminal justice complexities, will solve current police-community relations problems. Even though the problems persist and fester, affirmative progress *is* possible.[27]

This author is quick to defend the content presented in this chapter. A "Basic Techniques" section is obviated for two reasons: (1) the previous list of recommendations can, and should be, envisioned as a list of PCR techniques and (2) much of the material in Part One can, and should be, looked at as being a basis for effective PCR. Undoubtedly, a few individuals will take exception to the heavy use of government research documents devoted to the subject of PCR. This is summarily answered by the futility of "reinventing the wheel." In other words, why attempt to create another list of recommendations pertaining to PCR when we have them at hand? The intent here, therefore, has been both to reemphasize and to add a few additional spokes to this wheel and to provide a stimulus for action.

---

[26] *Ibid.*, pp. 193–205.

[27] A. C. Germann, "The Problem of Police–Community Relations," a paper prepared for The Task Force on Law and Law Enforcement, National Commission on the Causes and Prevention of Violence (Long Beach, Calif., California State College at Long Beach, 1968), p. 6.

First, in regard to a reemphasis, the list of recommendations on PCR is certainly worth a review. All are well thought through and designed to promote PCR. A few are provocative and must be given careful consideration. The majority are innovative and require change—change in terms of the organizational structure and the behavior of its members. We should again evaluate each one of the above recommendations.

Second, a few items not expressed but perhaps implied should be enlarged upon. Namely, PCR training must not be limited to recruit, advanced officer, supervisory, or management courses. Clearly, although PCR is included in these programs, it is sufficiently crucial at this point in time to be made a continual part of programs updating our local law enforcement. Depending on the state of affairs in a particular community, officers might well be furnished a one-full-day-per-month program in PCR (obviously other subjects may also be covered during this period). Naturally, the program should be structured to meet the specific situation. Consequently, standardized materials and generic concepts will be of only minor assistance in generating a relevant PCR program. Note the use of a single day devoted to PCR. This is another way of saying that roll call training is not an adequate vehicle for establishing a meaningful dialogue between trainer and trainee. If PCR is as important as many say that it is, then (1) we ought to devote sufficient time to it, (2) we ought to include every member of the department in the program, (3) we ought to design the program so as to make it directly pertinent to the needs of the police and the community alike, (4) we ought to see to it that the PCR unit or officer both talks and listens, and (5) we ought to assign the police supervisor the responsibility for the daily instruction of line officers in the use and benefits of good PCR.

Third, one would have to stick his head in the sand to avoid the obvious: PCR is becoming more important to our local police agencies. The majority, if not all, of urban police administrators know this only too well. Let this, then, provide a call to action. Where PCR training and specialized units exist, strengthen and improve them Implement those recommendations that appear helpful! Where PCR training and specialized units do not exist, create them.

Finally, in terms of what is an adequate PCR program:

> Our reply to this question would be: a police department is adequate when it is viewed as *our* police by all segments of the population of the community it serves. This, it seems to us, is the measure of the professional integrity of law enforcement in our time and society.[28]

---

[28] Brandstatter and Radelet, *Police and Community Relations*, p. vi.

SUMMARY

To summarize Chapter 11 is, at best, very difficult First, and most importantly, PCR is not a public relations or crime prevention program. Second, it is a departmental program (for all members of the organization) to gain the support of the environment for achieving its assigned goals. Third, the significance of PCR, therefore, lies in the goals of local law enforcement. Even with this high degree of significance, much remains undone in the area of PCR. However, of late some rather major strides have been made in the direction of improved PCR. Similar to most other areas undergoing change, the problem is not one of "What to do now?" but of "Put what we know into action!" The recommendations contained in this chapter are indicators of what can be done now. Of relevance to the police supervisor is the fact that his position and role in the organization makes him an ideal candidate for implementing a PCR program.

Finally, we spoke of grievances against our local police agencies as being caused more by a desire for police representation and less by a feeling of police brutality. The solutions to the first type of grievance are contained in the over-all administration of the department. The solution to the second grievance lies in improved selection and training processes. As stated before, the police supervisor plays a prominent part in an officer's training and, hence, in the abatement of grievances due to misconduct.

12

Job Safety:
Human Preventive Maintenance

The mission of safety is changing. No longer does safety strive to prevent individual accidents. Rather, attention is directed toward the factors that cause the accident to happen. The effort is to identify and to recommend correction of *management system errors* that permit loss to occur. Reduction of medical symptoms does not remove the cause of disease. Catching drops of water does not turn off the faucet. Neither does individual correction of a particular accident situation prevent similar accidents from recurring in an unpredictable and unending series. We need to find effective means to use the intelligence gained from analysis of past accidents to reduce the probability of future accidents.[1]

Let there be no doubt about three things. One, police personnel are the most valuable resource of a department; both humanitarian and commonsense considerations dictate that we should safeguard this asset with the greatest of care. Two, employee safety is a supervisory responsibility and a problem of growing significance. Three, the relationship between training and safety is a very close one; reducing accidents is largely a problem of creating a safety-consciousness, which in turn is dependent upon educational and training efforts. It is stressed that our concern here, while primarily with safety, includes the related subject area of employee health (physical and mental).

The first point is sufficiently self-evident and obvious to warrant no additional discussion. The other two points, however, need further examination. In regard to the second point, job safety is a supervisory responsibility and problem because police employee injuries interfere with the efficient provision of police services. It is growing in significance because of the dramatically increasing costs connected with worker injuries. The costs are, in essence, twofold: (1) loss of skilled talent to the organization, and (2) organizational and personal expenses connected with job related injuries. Because of the

---

[1] William C. Pope and Trenton Crow, "Safety: Pay Dirt for the Personnel Manager," *Personnel Administration*, 31 (September–October 1968), 8. Copyright 1968, Society for Personnel Administration, 485–87 National Press Building 14th and F Streets, N. W., Washington, D. C. 20004. Reprinted by permission.

attitude held by some administrators and supervisors that accidents are uncontrollable acts of misfortune, the problem of police employee safety demands special emphasis. This emphasis can take the form of specialized safety training, safety inspections, educational programs, and so on, but in no instance will an accident prevention effort be successful without the support and continuing interest of police management and supervision. Moreover, the attitude that employee injuries must be held in check must start from the top and pervade all levels of the organization down to the first line supervisor. The first line police supervisor is the most critical link in the whole management chain from the standpoint of accident prevention. The police supervisor must be the one to demonstrate management's interest in safety to the employees. Clearly, the police supervisor is the one who influences employee behavior on a day-to-day basis.

As far as point three is concerned, special safety training programs are necessary to assist in reducing accidents.[2] However, care must be taken to insure that these programs are designed to support police supervision, rather than supplant it, in the area of safety. Too often supervisors have come to view employee safety as a technical specialty outside their regular supervisory role. The safety program must always be designed to aid supervision, thus giving supervisors assistance in carrying out their responsibility for police employee safety.

JOB SAFETY: PHILOSOPHY, GOALS, AND POLICY

Historically, police supervisors have regarded safety as an activity of only incidental interest to the organizational role. The safety mission has been only vaguely defined, even to people engaged in safety work. The end product of the safety programs was periodic safety analyses that had doubtful utility for the supervisor. Further, neither was the information in usable form nor was it the basis for program development.

Over the years, the rise of police officer injuries has seriously hampered the economy and efficiency of police operations and indirectly affected the health and well-being of all employees. This needless waste of human and material resources must be halted. The answer lies in the adoption of a department-wide safety program to eliminate injuries before they happen— not after. (Tables 19 and 20 show police work-related injuries for 1965 in California.) Fundamentally, this means that each member of this department must lend his full support and active participation to a program eliminating those unsafe conditions or acts causing the bulk of industrial accidents.

---

[2] For a pragmatic overview of safety training programs, see the feature articles in *National Safety News*, 97 (January 1968).

TABLE 19: INDUSTRY, DISABLING WORK INJURIES, CALIFORNIA, 1964 AND 1965

	1964			1965		
Industry	Total	Fatal	Nonfatal	Total	Fatal	Nonfatal
Government, state and local*	21,599	120	21,479	22,616	100	22,516
State	4,475	46	4,429	4,690	38	4,652
Local	17,124	74	17,050	17,926	62	17,864
Police protection	2,708	32	2,676	2,889	21	2,868
Fire protection	2,158	23	2,135	2,195	23	2,172
Education	5,951	3	5,948	6,341	7	6,334
Park and recreation	897	—	897	921	—	921
Road, street, public works	2,044	6	2,038	2,037	4	2,033
Hospitals	1,630	2	1,628	1,610	4	1,606
Other local government	1,736	8	1,728	1,933	3	1,930
Industry not reported	49	1	48	46	2	44

Injuries to employees of publicly operated utilities included in the transportation, communication, and utilities division.

Source: California Work Injuries—1965 (*San Francisco, Calif.: Department of Industrial Relations, 1966*), p. 11.

The ideal goal of modern safety programs is completely error-free performance. The minimum goal of such programs is to reduce the frequency of errors to the level police management decides it can permit. This goal is consistent with the goals of all police managers and their supervisory personnel. Management decisions are influenced by economics, employee safety, public relations, impact of error on the organizational mission, operational urgencies, and other human factors. The best safety programs for a police organization are not necessarily those that demand perfect performance. Effective safety programs should seek the greatest reduction in human injuries at the lowest possible cost to the performance of the organization.

Safety must be a major ingredient in every police employee's orientation, in all job training, and in the planning, organizing, and execution of all work assignments. This ingredient is most effectively fostered through departmental policy. A safety policy should encompass the following:

1. Safe standards of work performance for each position promoted through proper training and direct supervision.

2. The development of safety rules and regulations, protective equipment, and work instructions that will assure that each employee is aware of appropriate safety practices in performing his work assignment.

3. Safety rule violations similar in nature and penalty to operating rule violations.

4. The reporting and investigation of all unsafe conditions and practices, whether or not they result in property damage or injury.

5. The analysis of all positions for potential hazards and the application of proper remedial measures when hazards are pinpointed.[3]

---

[3] Detailed examples of safety-accident analysis can be found in a series of articles in *National Safety News*, 92 (December 1965).

TABLE 20: INDUSTRY AND ACCIDENT TYPE, DISABLING WORK INJURIES, CALIFORNIA, 1965

Organization	Total	Struck by or Striking Against	Caught in or Between	Fall or Slip	Accident Involving Moving Motor Vehicle	Strain or Over-exertion	Contact with Temperature Extreme	Inhalation, Absorption, Ingestion, Swallowing	Contact with Electric Current	Explosion, Flareback, etc.	Foreign Substance in Eye	Other and Not Reported
Government, state and local*	22,616	4,980	763	5,748	1,795	6,040	391	1,165	42	75	665	952
State	4,690	984	188	1,130	431	1,209	65	300	11	14	118	240
Local	17,926	3,996	575	4,618	1,364	4,831	326	865	31	61	547	712
Police protection	2,889	656	41	558	704	467	42	67	2	3	65	284
Fire protection	2,195	389	29	619	58	599	112	132	6	8	95	148
Education	6,341	1,529	255	1,918	153	1,817	74	297	11	26	152	109
Park and recreation	921	241	35	225	42	252	7	53	1	1	43	21
Road, street, public works	2,037	421	89	422	217	607	27	104	7	10	96	37
Hospitals	1,610	350	53	318	23	652	43	103	2	3	32	31
Other local government	1,933	410	73	558	167	437	21	109	2	10	64	82
Industry not reported	46	8	3	12	4	7	—	2	—	—	—	10

*Injuries to employees of publicly operated utilities included in the transportation, communication, and utilities division.

Source: California Work Injuries—1965 (San Francisco, Calif.: Department of Industrial Relations, 1966), p. 28.

THE RESPONSIBILITY FOR SAFETY

The prime responsibility for suggesting, implementing, adopting, observing, and enforcing safety (health and welfare) measures rests in the normal employee-supervisor-management chain of command in the police department. The success or failure of fulfilling safety responsibilities should be taken into consideration when the effectiveness of the organization is under study. In practice, the responsibility for safety can be divided into three levels—line employee, supervisory, and managerial.

Police Employee's Safety Responsibility

The responsibility for the performance of each work assignment in the safest manner possible is part of each police officer's job. Safety is an element that cannot be divorced from the proper day-to-day performance and completion of a given work assignment. In large degree, the success of the departmental safety program depends on each police employee's compliance with these essential elements of the program:

1. Each police employee must work in accordance with accepted safe practices, observing all rules and regulations for his and others' safety.
2. Every police officer is responsible for reporting in the prescribed manner any on-the-job accident or injury which occurs to him or which he has observed to occur to another employee. Every employee shall also report any property damage resulting from an accident occurring to himself or others.
3. When injured, an officer must seek medical treatment in the manner prescribed by his department.
4. Each police employee must report to his immediate supervisor any unsafe condition or practice that exists and that may endanger himself or his fellow officers. Should an employee know of such conditions and fail to report them for correction, he violates his safety responsibility and is subject to appropriate action.
5. An officer faced with a job whose safety features he does not fully understand should ask for the proper instruction from his police supervisor before attempting the job.

Police Supervisor's Safety Responsibility

The great bulk of police injuries are caused by human failure, not by equipment failure. For a variety of reasons police employees at times commit unsafe acts which result in injury to themselves or their co-workers, or in damage and destruction of police equipment. Through observant supervision, these employees can be made aware of their unsafe behavior and trained and counseled to correct it. This is a part of every supervisor's role.

Only when each police supervisor recognizes that he is responsible for the safety of his subordinates can his department effectively reduce injuries, deaths, lost time, and all of the human and material costs that go with these. To further this program, each supervisor must know and observe the following policies:

1. Each police supervisor is responsible for the safety of subordinates and their work place. His success or failure in fulfilling this responsibility is to be considered when promotional opportunities exist and when ratings of performance efficiency are given.

2. All injuries or property damage reported by police subordinates or observed by supervisory personnel are to be reported in the manner prescribed by the police department and the civil service commission.

3. Each police supervisor will investigate each injury or damage incident that occurs in his area to ascertain the causes and take action to prevent recurrence.

4. When a subordinate is injured and requires the care of a physician, the police supervisor will refer the employee for medical treatment in the manner prescribed by the city or county health officer.

5. Each supervisor is to perform a safety analysis for each job under his supervision to identify potential hazards and then develop courses of action to eliminate or guard against the hazards.[4]

6. Each supervisor must orient and train all new police employees in safe work practices.

7. Each supervisor is to inform his subordinates of all departmental safety rules or regulations, as well as the work procedures that have been adopted as a result of job safety analysis. These safety measures must be enforced by each police supervisor. Little good results from the purchase of protective equipment, for example, if the supervisor does not issue work instructions on its use. When these work instructions are not observed by an employee, the police supervisor must take corrective action through training, counseling, and, when necessary, discipline.

8. To assure that workplaces are safe, each supervisor is to make periodic safety inspections. When technical assistance is needed—from an hygienist, electrician, and so on—the supervisor should request these services through his immediate superior.

9. Each police supervisor should hold periodic safety meetings with subordinates and, at all times, actively encourage subordinates to make safety suggestions which may eliminate hazards. Each supervisor is encouraged to discuss safety periodically with individual police officers. A mutual interchange of ideas and suggestions can help achieve a higher degree of safety.

10. When an employee returns to work after an absence for injury or a prolonged sick leave, the police supervisor should obtain from him a physician's release

---

[4] *Ibid.*

to return to work and then contact the personnel office to clear him for return to the job. Each supervisor should also furnish the personnel office with any information that he may have on the need for a special work assignment.

11. Whenever a police supervisor questions an employee's ability to do his job because of an apparent physical incapacity (obesity, increases in marginally unsafe acts, eye failure, lack of coordination, evidence of senility, emotionally erratic behavior, or the like), a medical reevaluation should be requested.

Police Management's Safety Responsibility

Clearly, the responsibility for preventing employee injuries also falls upon departmental management. To achieve the major objectives of the safety program, police management must properly assess the progress being made, and where progress is unsatisfactory, take steps to bring about improvement. To carry out this evaluation of departmental safety progress, the injury or property damage procedure must be maintained; a statistical analysis made of each unit, section, and division; and definite plans established whereby management is assured that the action taken by a police supervisor to prevent recurrence of an injury or property damage is proper. Management may delegate the authority for safety coordination to a responsible person who will act in a staff capacity, that is, as advisor to police management on matters pertaining to safety. Furthermore, some matters relating to the reassignment, rehabilitation, or retraining of employees who have been disabled can be handled for management through the personnel office. Others, dealing with legal representation before the personnel office, are of primary concern to the police chief. But the police department's safety concerns remain an integral and proper part of every activity in the organization. Every police employee is a member of the safety team. Only by continuous emphasis on working safely can one avoid the personal and financial losses that result from injury to police employees.

SUPERVISING FOR SAFETY

Good police supervision and accident prevention are one and the same. In fact, it is unrealistic to expect accident prevention to be effective when supervision is poor. With specific reference to safety, a police supervisor should consider the following points:

1. In a work situation, employees instinctively follow the example set by their work leader. The police supervisor who consciously follows safe work procedures will find his employees receptive to an accident prevention program. On the other hand, the supervisor who advocates safety while setting a poor example

cannot expect a conscientious effort to work safely on the part of his subordinates.

2. No matter how knowledgeable a newly trained employee appears, he deserves a complete orientation to his specific assignment plus specific training on each of his tasks. In introducing a new employee to his job, his supervisor should (1) discuss the mission, organization, and policies of the city or county government, the department, and the work unit, (2) encourage the reporting of all unsafe conditions and all injuries irrespective of the degree of severity, and (3) cover specific procedures relating to safety including methods of reporting unsafe conditions, making safety suggestions, and reporting injuries. Seasoned as well as new employees need to be trained regarding new or changed procedures. Every time a new job assignment is given, safety considerations should be discussed.

3. Frequently policemen do not realize that they are committing unsafe acts. On the other hand, they may know better, but underestimate the degree of risk involved. In any case, police supervisors must make a conscious effort to observe the work of their subordinates and correct unsafe work habits that may be observed.

A PROGRAM OF HUMAN PREVENTIVE MAINTENANCE

Safety programs are now being expanded to include the over-all *health* of the individual worker. Accident prevention programs, for example, express concern for the employee's mental as well as his physical well-being. Consequently, our approach is one of programmed (formalized) human preventive maintenance. It encompasses three dimensions: (1) accident and safety, (2) physical working conditions, and (3) physical and mental health. In the following sections each dimension is examined in more detail.

Accident and Safety

The accident-safety movement which swept over private industry after World War I was caused by (1) the workmen's compensation movement, stemming from a recognition of the employer's responsibility for industrial accidents, and (2) the desire of employers to eliminate production losses due to accidents. There has been less progress along this line in the public services than in private industry. This lag is due to the frequently noted tendency for governments to be less concerned with their own employees than with those of private employers because most public employees are covered by compensation laws, and these laws ordinarily do not make the cost of accidents a charge against the budget of the department or bureau involved. Whereas industry has been forced to develop safety programs for its own protection, most government agencies seem not to have been under any such compulsion.

In the design of an accident reduction or prevention program, the point of departure is the determination of the number, character, and causes of accidents. This means reports on prescribed forms, investigations by competent supervisors, and management analysis. Accidents are due either to working conditions, machine failures, and the like, or to primarily personal or human factors, such as carelessness and ignorance. In the case of the former, a safety engineer may be able to improve the conditions of work so that a large number of accidents are prevented.

The second type of accidents, those caused by carelessness or inexperience on the part of employees, can be reduced by safety education. The techniques involved in a program of safety education have been extensively worked out in industry, and it is unnecessary to consider them in detail here. The particular program adopted may take a number of forms, depending partly upon circumstances. It may include safety instruction, the use of posters, the institution of organization safety committees, and interorganization contests. But whatever the program, it can be successful only if someone is specifically charged with its functioning.

The importance of an accident-safety effort is attested to by O. Glenn Stahl.

> The utility of putting a safety program into effect in a public jurisdiction has been demonstrated time and again. Dramatic reductions in accidents and resultant injury compensation payments have been made in a number of municipalities, states, and federal agencies. . . .[5]

Naturally, there will always be a certain number of unpreventable accidents. The problem presented by these is one of amelioration, decreasing the seriousness of the results of accidents. At this point the safety program ties into the general health program. The potential seriousness of accidents can be reduced, of course, by immediate emergency treatment and by proper hospitalization. The safety program therefore requires the provision of emergency medical facilities. These are briefly discussed in the following section.

Physical Working Conditions

The fast and expanding growth of the police service since World War II has necessitated a vast amount of enlargement, and replacement, of outworn buildings. The sheer volume of modern facilities has made the acceptable standards for good work space widely evident, even to the casual

---

[5] O. Glenn Stahl, *Public Personnel Administration*, 5th ed. (New York: Harper & Row, Publishers, 1962), p. 313.

observer. All that is needed here is a brief reference to the main conditions involved in good physical working conditions. These conditions are (1) ventilation, (2) seating, (3) lighting, (4) space, (5) noise, and (6) sanitation.

First, by proper ventilation we mean the quality and temperature of the air in the working area. Correct ventilation affects both the physical and mental states of police personnel and thereby their output. Police administrators are paying more and more attention to the matter of ventilation for their employees. For one example, although conditions are still not fully satisfactory, most of the newer police buildings are air conditioned. Further, there is a decided trend toward equipping the newer police vehicles with air conditioning units. Second, both seating and one's work must be so arranged that posture can be varied and that good posture is possible. Too little attention has been given to the seating of police officers in the police vehicles. Third, poor lighting conditions, if long continued, may result in a permanent impairment of the sight of police employees. Moreover, the fact that there is a close connection between productive efficiency and illumination has been established by a number of investigations. Whether one depends on natural or artificial light or both, adequate standards should be maintained by means of systematic tests. Again, much room for improvement remains where the police vehicle is concerned.

Fourth, the importance of adequate space in a person's working environment is receiving greater recognition. We find police agencies engaging space consultants and interior decorators to provide both functional and emotional spacing. Fifth, unnecessary noise is expensive in a number of ways. It makes telephone conversations or interviews difficult and complicates the taking of dictation. In police office buildings, noise can be reduced by providing a soft floor covering and noiseless typewriters, and by treating the walls with effective sound-absorbents. Planning departmental layout can help by isolating noisy machines, keeping typing operations separate from investigative interview rooms, and the like. Regretfully, a common error in police departments, even in modern police buildings, is to require investigative and clerical employees to sit at desks close together—often four, or as many as ten to a dozen, to a small room. Concentration on a problem or a report becomes almost impossible when one or more others in the room are engaged in necessary telephoning or interviews with witnesses or suspects on a case. The amount of continuing output lost is immeasurable. Certainly it is far greater than any temporary savings in space or in the cost of installing simple and movable partitions. The solution is simply to provide small, quiet private or semiprivate offices for all police employees who are responsible for doing investigative work or who solve supervisory or management problems, carry on extended telephone or personal interviews, write reports, or otherwise perform more than repetitive or manual tasks. The total space required need be little greater than that of the open type of office space. Finally, while covered last, sanitation is the first requirement for proper working conditions. Floors should be cleaned, windows washed, and desks dusted regularly. Further, attention must be given to drinking water, toilet facilities, and wash and locker rooms. The police officer who spends eight hours every day in clean, cheerful, and comfortable surroundings is likely to have a very different outlook from the man who is forced to spend his days in a drab, dirty, or uncomfortable working environment. This is true for buildings and vehicles alike.

Physical and Mental Health

To keep police employees fit, in the interest of effective work output as well as of their own welfare, is a motive that should actuate all personnel. Maintenance of the physical and mental health of the working staff is certainly more important than the maintenance of physical equipment. Clearly the police supervisor has a stake in his subordinates' health because he is charged with the development of an efficient staff. At this point let us examine the nature and scope of a modern employee health program.

Fundamental to any physical health program is the establishment of regular physical examinations. The Philadelphia Fire Department provides a case in point.

> Because of the biennial physical, knowledge of a member's physical condition has saved the Department embarrassing incidents. This is particularly true as it concerns the appointing authority's responsibility of declaring disabilities nonservice or service connected. The author also is of the opinion, although such cannot be factually supported, that this early discovery of remedial conditions of all sorts has contributed to our high retirement (for time and service) and low mortality rate. Of great importance is the fact that the procedural development of the routine physical examination program has evolved into a tight control over sick leave.[6]

Directly related to physical examinations is a program for the treatment of injuries and the diagnosis and treatment of minor illnesses. Such a program usually involves the health department or an assigned medical staff. Finally, some of the most effective work of the medical staff may be done in connection with health education through the police supervisor. This education should include the dissemination of information on ordinary matters of personal hygiene, such as sleep, cleanliness, and diet.

There is growing recognition today that the connection between a man's work and his mental health is basic to human satisfaction and productivity.

---

[6] Albert Dector, "A Program of Human Preventive Maintenance," *Public Personnel Review*, 27 (April 1966), 109.

The national mental health program is today concerned with man and his total environment, because it is in the subtle interplay among biological, biochemical, physical, psychological, and environmental factors that the key to prevention can be found. The concern with the industrial environment is not new to the field of occupational mental health, but there is still much to be done.[7]

One example of a specific problem that lends itself to greater interaction between mental health centers and business organizations is alcoholism. Considering the size of the problem, industry has initiated few alcoholism control programs, but those it has started have been relatively successful. Studies have shown that when industry makes an intensive effort with employees who have drinking problems, the recovery rate ranges between 65 and 85 per cent, as compared with a general public recovery rate of 30 per cent or less.[8]

The current revolution in mental health has serious implications for all managers. Namely, the growth of community out-patient mental health services is changing the nature and direction of treatment for mental illness and has important bearing on managerial decisions to allow more liberal sick leave for disturbed workers. Where once custodial care was the only choice for persons who did not respond to treatment, today's treatment methods, including drugs and other therapies, can change the behavior of a patient so that he can work effectively in his organization.

There is a similarity between the functions of the therapist in the office and those of the police supervisor. Frequently, the supervisor is used as a confidante by his subordinate. A great many feelings related to the present problems of the individual employee are thoroughly discussed. The worker gets "things off his chest," which helps the individual to maintain his emotional stability and his efficiency on the job. Whether he realizes it or not, the police supervisor deals with the worker's actual or fancied needs and problems as well as the worker's personality problems. In relation to the latter, the supervisor should attempt to determine how much help the worker can receive from him, from the department, and from private or public professional services. Many business firms have added professional psychologists and even psychiatrists to their full-time staff. Therefore, an important part of the role of the supervisor is quasi-therapeutic in that he needs to be aware of the neurotic problems of his workers and to make important decisions in regard to these problems.[9] From this statement the question quite

---

[7] Wilber J. Cohen, "Revolution in Mental Health," *Personnel Administration*, 32 (March–April 1969), 7.

[8] *Ibid.*

[9] Leon A. Dale, "The Quasi Therapeutic Functions of the Supervisor," *Personnel Administration*, 30 (November–December 1967), 10.

naturally arises as to just what a police supervisor, who is uninformed on medicine and psychology, can do in the way of handling employees with mental problems. Clearly it is not the function of supervision to cure and rehabilitate an emotionally disturbed adult. This is not within the province of the police department any more than is diagnosing a case of appendicitis and performing the requisite surgery. If a police employee is ill, either physically or emotionally, he should be directed to a competent specialist. The police supervisor, however, can be useful both in abating the external conditions that give rise to emotional problems and in recommending to the employee that he seek professional assistance.

Several steps can be taken to enhance the chances of a supervisor properly handling an individual's personal problems.[10] These steps are treated in the subsequent section on basic techniques of job safety.

BASIC TECHNIQUES OF JOB SAFETY

Many techniques for achieving job safety are contained in the preceding pages. A few of the more pertinent points in regard to safety are covered again in this section. Not in the following list, however, are the items discussed in the section on physical working conditions. See that particular section again for indicators of "what to do." The last four points below deal with a person's physical and mental health.

1. The first and most important step is to sell yourself on the vital need for the police supervisor to be concerned with his subordinates' safety and mental well-being.
2. When accidents do occur, investigate carefully and communicate on the basis of facts. Be specific in the analysis, identifying those causes which are still active. Also keep a record on the subordinates.
3. Enforce safety rules! Establish a definite routine to check for violations and take action when safety infractions are found.
4. Instruct the new men. Let them know what has happened in the past, what the most probable causes of accidents are.
5. Let the subordinates help. By listening to them, one may spot new causes for accidents and get suggestions for improvement.
6. Be a good example. Supervisory actions must reflect safety.
7. The supervisor must make every attempt to furnish the police officer with a well-planned and clean working environment.
8. The supervisor should expect (and sometimes encourage) the recital of personal

---

[10] For an easily read and meaningful text in the area of mental health, see Harry Hevinson, *Emotional Health in the World of Work* (New York: Harper & Row, Publishers, 1964).

problems whose intensity may interfere with the employee's work. Even in police agencies where psychologists (or psychiatrists) are available for this purpose, it is likely that at least some police employees will prefer talking to their immediate supervisor (depending on their feelings toward him).

9. In our age of anxiety, the police supervisor can provide reassurance—reassurance of the employee's identity, of his existence and functioning as a human being. This is accomplished by recognizing the police employee as a human being, particularly in an age in which personal relationships have a tendency to become impersonal, as, for instance, when people deal with each other on the basis of titles. This dehumanization can be lessened if first names are used instead of titles, social gatherings are encouraged, and so forth.

10. The police supervisor, once having identified a person in need of psychotherapy, should be quick to assist him in seeking out professional help.

SUMMARY

The quotation beginning this chapter serves as an appropriate ending.

The mission of job safety is changing. No longer does safety merely strive to prevent individual accidents. Rather, attention is directed toward the factors, both physical and psychological, that cause the accident to happen. The effort is to identify and to recommend correction of organizational errors that permit loss to occur. Reduction of medical symptoms does not remove the cause of disease. Catching drops of water does not turn off the faucet. Neither does individual correction of a particular accident situation prevent similar accidents from recurring. We are in need of an effective means for using the intelligence gained from analysis of past accidents to reduce the probability of future accidents.[11]

The effectiveness of safety programs is reflected in their contribution to organizational goals. Safety does not exist to operate safety programs; safety exists to make a worthwhile contribution to organizational goals. To make its contribution, safety needs to help supervision meet its organizational responsibilities. Exploitation of the complementary functional interest of safety and supervision is the best approach.

A quick examination of physical working conditions, safety, and health and welfare activities in the larger and more progressive public jurisdictions in the United States reveals encouraging signs, but the more progressive private business concerns historically have devoted more attention to the problems involved than have most government units. This fact is ironical in view of the social character of government enterprise. Safety in a police department is closely allied to training in that it depends mainly on the

---

[11] Pope and Crow, "Safety."

creation of an awareness of the problem. There is a growing recognition that the development of a safety consciousness can save money for the police organization and reduce risks for the personnel. Again, the success of such programs depends on the police supervisor. If he doesn't sell himself on the importance of safety, chances are his men will not be convinced either.

PROBLEMS

1. As a police supervisor (if you are not one, you will have to play the role for the next few minutes) you have received numerous complaints about your fleet of patrol vehicles. The complaints vary from poor maintenance to uncomfortable surroundings. What steps would you take to rectify this situation? Further, what changes would you make to create a more acceptable working environment out of an automobile?

2. As an enlightened supervisor you are shocked to learn that one of your subordinates is an alcoholic. He does not drink on the job but is constantly intoxicated while off duty. What is your course of action, if any?

3. Your supervisory instincts are stimulated when a report shows that your unit is experiencing sizable increases in the number of job-related accidents. What is your approach to this situation? In discussing your approach cite your reasons for each thing you do.

TRAINING

FOR

DEVELOPMENT

part three

Introduction

Never in history has the policeman's job been more difficult. The days when you could take a man who was honest and physically superior, hand him a stick, a gun, and a badge and make a good policeman out of him are gone forever. Today a policeman must be well educated and trained. He must know a good deal about criminal law and evidence. He must know something about fingerprinting and photography. He must be part soldier, part scientist, and part human relations expert. But he can take comfort from the fact that if his job is more difficult, it is also more important than ever before. If his mistakes will be more costly, so will his victories be greater.

To be truly professional, the law enforcement officer must take advantage of every educational opportunity, do everything possible to improve his own proficiency, then do his best to pass along his knowledge and experience to his subordinates. In every free nation, the urgent need is for more, better educated and better trained police officers. We must be much smarter than our adversary because he is not burdened by high moral standards and he doesn't have to adhere to the rules as we do. The policeman must do everything he can to upgrade law enforcement at all levels of government.[1]

There is a clear and immediate need to train and educate police personnel. Indeed, policy makers at all levels of government, college educators representing a variety of disciplines and fields, police practitioners, and the general populace are now arriving at concrete conclusions about the training and educating of our local police. Briefly and directly stated, their conclusions can be summarized as: (1) "Needed: New Expertise in Local Policing," (2) "Let's Train Our Police," and (3) "The Time Is Now!" Significantly, many of the recommendations of the President's Commission on Law Enforcement and Administration of Justice dealt with the concern for improved training and education.

Recruit more actively, especially on college campuses and in inner cities.

---

[1] Evelle J. Younger, "The Policeman's Evolving Job," *Los Angeles Times*, Feb. 9, 1969, Sec. G., p. 9.

Set a goal requirement of a baccalaureate degree for general enforcement officers.

Require immediately baccalaureate degrees for supervisory positions.

Require a minimum of 400 hours of training.

Improve training methods and broaden coverage of nontechnical background subjects.

Require a 1-week yearly minimum of intensive in-service training and encourage continued education.

Emphasize community relations in training and operations.[2]

The above recommendations, along with other sources of similar support for training and advanced forms of education, too numerous to cite here, indicate the growing interest in this subject. In fact, those possessing even a limited awareness of the mission currently assigned to local law enforcement by our society appreciate the fact that the complexity of the police task is as great as that of any other profession.

It is interesting to note that the need for highly educated personnel was recognized as early as 1931 in the report of the Wickersham Commission.[3] Despite this early awareness of a need to improve low entrance standards, educational requirements today remain minimal in most departments. This writer fully recognizes and appreciates the few exceptions. However, recent surveys continue to present data reflecting low academic achievement. For example, in a survey of 6,200 officers conducted in 1964, only 30.3 per cent had taken one or more college courses and only 7.3 per cent possessed a college degree.[4] Another survey of over 5,700 police officers employed by police agencies in the metropolitan area of Detroit revealed that over 75 per cent had not attended college.[5] It was further shown that nearly 13 per cent of the officers had not received high school diplomas. Next, it was recently reported by 289 city and county law enforcement agencies in California that their minimum educational requirements for employment are as follows: 4-year degree required—1 department; 60 college units required —13 departments; 20–30 units required—9 departments; and 12–16 units required—9 departments.[6] Hence, approximately 11 per cent of the report-

---

[2] *The Challenge of Crime in a Free Society*, The President's Commission on Law Enforcement and Administration of Justice (Washington, D.C.: U.S. Government Printing Office, 1967), p. 295.

[3] *Report on Lawlessness in Law Enforcement*, The National Commission on Law Observance and Enforcement (Wickersham Commission) (Washington, D.C.: U.S. Government Printing Office, 1931).

[4] George W. O'Connor and Nelson G. Watson, *Juvenile Delinquency and Youth Crime: The Police Role* (Washington, D.C.: International Association of Chiefs of Police, Inc., 1964), p. 79.

[5] Michigan State University, Institute for Community Development, *Police Training in the Detroit Metropolitan Region: Recommendations for a Regional Approach* (Detroit, Mich.: The Metropolitan Fund, 1966), p. 69.

[6] *A Career in Law Enforcement: There is No Greater Challenge* (Sacramento, Calif.: State of California, Commission on Peace Officer Standards and Training, 1969).

ing agencies indicated some college work is presently required. The major cause for this figure is probably located in the results of a 1968 survey of all police chiefs and sheriffs in California. The purpose of the survey was to solicit individual opinions on needed improvements in local law enforcement. In general, the 239 respondents did not cite the need for more training and education as being very critical (increased salaries and a statewide criminal justice information system were listed as the top priority items).[7] More specifically, in-service training was rated as being absolutely necessary, while college-educated recruits, supervisors, and managers were only of average interest.

This author predicts that the 11 per cent figure and indicated average level of interest in career training and educational programs will soon increase for three reasons. First, eventually there will be a reduction in our military manpower needs, thus expanding the pool of available talent. Second, there will be continued and growing support for local law enforcement by the federal government. Third, and most important, the community at large will, through their demands for constantly better law enforcement, force upon our policing agencies increased levels of training and education.

The job of police officer is an occupation that requires the incumbent frequently to function in unpredictable situations, and thus to make difficult judgments which require sound knowledge of society and human behavior. This knowledge can best be attained through advanced education. Even a recent statement by a prominent practitioner is now in need of updating in order to include not just superior officers but all police personnel.

> A superior officer of any police department should certainly be conversant with the structure of our government and philosophies. He must be well grounded in sociology, criminology, and human relations in order to understand the ramifications of the problems which confront him daily. He must understand what makes people act as they do and what impact his activities in the performance of duty will have on them.[8]

Figure 14 depicts a model career development program for local law enforcement. Further, the model serves both as an approach and as a criterion for necessary organizational changes.

Hopefully the reader has been sufficiently convinced of the need—the urgent and growing need—for advanced education in the police service. Thankfully, the challenge for providing the required education has been accepted by many colleges and universities. The federal government is

---

[7] "California Opinions on President's Crime Commission Recommendations for Improving Law Enforcement," *Univac: All Points Bulletin*, 2 (February 1969), 2–5.

[8] Statement of Stephen Kennedy, former Commissioner of Police, cited in Franklin M. Kreml, *The Role of Colleges and Universities in Police Management: The Police Yearbook* (Washington, D.C.: International Association of Chiefs of Police, 1966), p. 40.

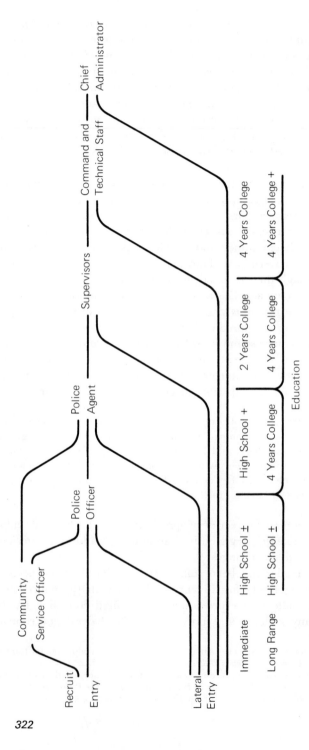

Source: Task Force Report: The Police. *The President's Commission on Law Enforcement and Administration of Justice (Washington, D.C.: U.S. Government Printing Office, 1967). p. 124.*

FIG. 14. CAREER DEVELOPMENT AND EDUCATIONAL STANDARDS

presently endeavoring to support their efforts through programs of direct financial assistance. More will be said later about the activities of the Office of Law Enforcement Assistance (OLEA) and the Law Enforcement Assistance Administration (LEAA), U. S. Department of Justice.

Let us consider for a few moments the status and trend of academic programs for law enforcement officers. It is obvious that there is a rapidly growing trend among colleges, especially community (two-year) colleges, to develop degree programs for potential and existing law enforcement personnel. In 1966, 134 degree programs could be identified as oriented toward police service, of which 100 were two-year degree programs in police science offered at community colleges.[9] While presently vocational in nature, we are now witnessing curricula changes that promise a broader educational background to the participants.

> The Commission's examination of these programs disclose that many of them are highly vocational in nature and are primarily intended to provide technical skills necessary in performing police work. College credit is given, for example, for such courses as traffic control, defensive tactics and patrol procedures. Although there is a need for vocational training, it is not and cannot be a substitute for a liberal arts education.[10]

This author, as are other educators and an increasing number of police administrators, is firmly convinced that academic programs designed for police personnel should emphasize the social sciences and liberal arts. The complex community responsibilities and duties of police work require that field personnel understand their environment and conditions which breed criminal and delinquent conduct. Such an understanding can best be gained through an educational program designed to broaden an individual's capacity for dealing with his work-relevant problems.

The next two chapters are constructed upon three underlying cornerstones. First, training and education are sufficiently vital to the police service that they must become continuing and developmental processes. Second, there is a mutual responsibility on the part of the police and the colleges and universities to improve the standard and quality of training and education within the ranks of the police personnel. Third, and directly pertinent to this text, the role of the police supervisor subsumes a major responsibility for training and developing line personnel. Indeed, it is here recommended that the police supervisor act as the primary vehicle for train-

---

[9] "Police Science Programs of Universities, Colleges, Junior Colleges in the United States," *The Police Chief*, 33 (August 1966), 50–64.

[10] *Task Force Report: The Police*, The President's Commission on Law Enforcement and Administration of Justice (Washington, D.C.: U.S. Government Printing Office, 1967), p. 127.

ing, while the present position of training officer be assigned the staff function of supporting supervision in its training role. Chapter 13 looks at training in terms of its involved goals and strategies; Chapter 14 discusses the training phase from the starting point through evaluation.

13

Training:
the Supervisor as a Developer
of Human Resources

It is becoming increasingly recognized that efficiency in an organization is not enough; that the real wealth of the nation is in trained and skilled manpower. Every organization therefore has the obligation of developing its employees to their maximum potential; and in most cases this responsibility must fall to the supervisor. Not only must he do what he can to help create such opportunities for his subordinates, but he himself must engage personally in a program of self-development.[1]

From what has been said so far in describing the supervisory pattern, it may well be wondered whether a book on police supervision is necessary. Why not simply read a book on general supervision? Certainly much would be gained from such a reading. However, it must be remembered that work takes place within a certain organizational setting and environment. While it is true that the police sergeant and the senior clerk have things in common, it nevertheless is quite apparent that there are substantial differences in the situation in which the two must operate. The police supervisor operates in an organizational setting that includes uniforms and a rather exacting system of authority. His environment is filled with "people problems," which vary from "Help! My husband and I are fighting," to "Help! My husband has just shot me." Consequently, the environment of the work situation does condition, to a considerable degree, the extent to which supervisory practices may be universally applied. To put it another way, the problems of supervision are universal; the answers must be conditioned by the setting in which the supervision occurs.

In the past ten years, police training and education has mushroomed into a large-scale activity. The immediate question should be whether all this training activity, or even the greater part of it, can be justified by its results. My answer is no, with a growing number of honorable exceptions. The next question then is how it can be improved. That is what this and the following

---

[1] Frank P. Sherwood and Wallace H. Best, *Supervisory Methods in Municipal Government* (Chicago, Ill.: The International City Managers' Association, 1958), p. 9.

chapter are about. Involved in answering the question are police administrators and training officers now numbering in the thousands, as well as
participants in police training programs and their parent organizations, who
are entitled to receive good value for their investment in training.

A few sample figures indicate the broad dimensions of what we are concerned about. First, the investment in skills acquired through training now
accounts for over half of the expenditures on all formal education in the
nation. Second, $600 million is spent on management development programs
alone. Third, and more specifically, note how the Office of Law Enforcement
Assistance (now known as the Law Enforcement Assistance Administration)
during its three years of existence allocated the majority of its funds. Table
21 reports on the distribution of the federal monies. Certainly training was
primary in mind. The funds were used to establish more than 70 OLEA
projects, providing training for an estimated 33,000 local law enforcement
personnel. The latter figure does not include personnel who benefit from
the ancillary training accorded by OLEA operations programs or by police
curriculum development projects or by programs concerned with the production and dissemination of training films and annuals.

*TABLE 21: PROJECT EXPENDITURES, OFFICE OF LAW ENFORCEMENT ASSISTANCE, FISCAL
YEARS 1966, 1967, AND 1968 (TO APRIL 1)*

Type of Activity	Millions
Training—Law enforcement—General recruit and in-service	$2.7
Training—Law enforcement—Command and management	1.2
Training—Law enforcement—Special subject	0.7
Training—Law enforcement—Higher education	1.3
Training—Corrections (all levels)	1.4
Training—Criminal justice (all levels)	0.4
Operations—Law enforcement—General	2.1
Operations—Law enforcement—Information and communications system development	2.2
Operations—Law enforcement—Scientific and technological research	1.5
Operations—Law enforcement—Community relations and public support	0.8
Operations—Corrections	1.4
Operations—Criminal justice	1.1
General crime prevention and program coordination	0.7
General studies (including their dissemination)	1.5
Total:	$19.0

Source: Law Enforcement Assistance Administration, Third Annual Report to the President
and the Congress on Activities Under the Law Enforcement Assistance Act of 1965 (*Washington,
D.C.: U.S. Government Printing Office, 1968*), p. 6.

Interestingly, the OLEA divided their law enforcement training efforts into four areas of program concentration: (1) general recruit and in-service training, (2) command and management training, (3) specialty and special subject training, and (4) higher education.[2] Although all four areas are important, we discuss only one in detail. Passing comment is made, however, in regard to areas (2) and (3). Briefly, in regard to the second area, police leaders and those involved in professional education are placing continuing and increasing emphasis on the importance of command and management training for police administrators. Accordingly, new training opportunities for law enforcement personnel in top level and middle management positions have received special OLEA emphasis. The question arises, "What about the supervisor?" It appears this all vital "neither management nor line" level received the short end of the training stick. Further, it should be noted that most of the grants under the heading of specialty and special subject training were for police-community relations.

Now let us look at the subject area of higher education. The OLEA supported higher education for police at both the undergraduate and graduate levels. Nearly 50 awards were made, totaling $1.2 million in allocated funds. Further, the OLEA took prompt action to encourage new undergraduate programs in police science. When the OLEA program began, there were 30 states in which no institution of higher education offered a police curriculum. Today, encouraged in part by OLEA special grants, police curriculum programs are offered in over 40 states, Guam, and the Virgin Islands. In addition, the OLEA sponsored a pilot program of graduate fellowships for in-service police personnel who show promise as administrators. This program, initially funded for 30 fellowships, provides for a year of study toward a master's degree in police or public administration. It was established at three universities currently offering such degrees—eastern, central, and western U. S. institutions—in September 1967. The program offered the general range of educational expense support. A final advantage of OLEA's investment in higher education is its benefit to other forms of police education. The existence of strong police science and criminal justice departments with qualified full-time faculties in the nation's two- and four-year colleges and universities offers law enforcement a valued resource for quality in-service instruction, consultation, and research which can strengthen the programs of local police departments. Such aid to local departments may take the form of training institutes, special courses, command seminars, or other help not otherwise available, thus making the degree program schools centers for increased professionalization.

Encouraged by OLEA participation, the LEAA has provided funds for

[2] Law Enforcement Assistance Administration, *Third Annual Report to the President and the Congress on Activities Under the Law Enforcement Assistance Act of 1965* (Washington, D.C.: U.S. Government Printing Office, 1968), pp. 3–12.

continuation and expansion of academic aid. Part D of Section 406 of the 1968 Omnibus Crime Control and Safe Streets Act authorizes programs of academic educational assistance to improve and strengthen law enforcement. LEAA is responsible for administering this program and deals directly with the educational institutions concerned. In late 1968 the Office of Academic Assistance of LEAA furnished guidelines and application forms to over 2200 eligible colleges and universities, in every state. The LEAA allocated $6.5 million for the educational program in fiscal year 1969. The awards were made to some 485 institutions of higher education. The money awards provide a program of student loans or grants to state and local public law enforcement personnel and to persons who intend to enter the law enforcement field. The loans may be of up to $1800 per academic year. Grants are only available to currently employed law enforcement personnel and may be of up to $300 per semester or $200 per quarter and may not exceed the cost of tuition and fees. Future years will see the 6.5 million figure increase considerably. The majority of the LEAA funds will, in all probability, continue to be designated for action-oriented grants (operations, and the like). However, often hidden in action programs are sizable training endeavors.

The preceding material was included to provide the reader with a necessary adjunct to his recognition of a training need. Namely, not only is there such a need but we now have an avenue for meeting it. And, the police supervisor should play a greater part in the training process. In the following order, this chapter contains (1) training—the goals, (2) training—the process, (3) training—employee appraisal, and (4) training—the strategies. This chapter does not include a section on the basics of training; Chapter 14 depicts a model program for human resource development and training, and, consequently, the basics of training are either stated or implied.

TRAINING: THE GOALS

A word of explanation is needed here about the basic concept of training and the terminology used throughout the book. Training, as I see it, has two fundamental goals: to make lasting improvements in the performance of one's organizational role and to develop one's capacity for handling higher levels of responsibility. In other words, training ought to help a person do his job better, while at the same time prepare him for more challenging duties. Consequently, training means a change, that is, a change on the part of the individual and the organization. Both are interdependent partners in any process of change. Further, training means integration, that is, unifying man and organization in a concerted attempt to more effectively achieve assigned goals.

Underlying its goals and characteristics is a certain philosophy, or perhaps better, attitude, of what training is. Little attention is furnished this notion. In nearly every case, an organization possesses an attitude toward training. An attempt to discern the training philosophy of an organization requires a knowledge of the policies and values of that organization. Rather than tackle the complex considerations included in the determination of an over-all police training attitude, a sense of direction is reviewed to provide an indication of present and future training objectives. Since the two goals cited previously are, if not universal, certainly accepted by the vast majority of formal organizations, we focus on attitudes expressed by local police agencies, which indicate the present objectives of police training efforts.

Training for the police service, in and out of the department, during the recent decades has tended to focus on training in operational techniques. In other words, the attitude on police training is one of concern for the substantive field in which the line officers work. Granted, this type of training is vital to police personnel, and organizational effectiveness. However, it should be viewed as but one type of training in the professional life span of a police officer. Thankfully, the police are changing their attitudes toward the training of their personnel. The list below compares the existing traditional with the emerging newer attitudes on police training.

Traditional Attitudes

1. The acquisition of information by a police officer leads to action.

2. The police officer learns what the trainer teaches. Learning is a simple function of the capacity of the person to learn and the ability of the trainer to teach.

3. Individual learning automatically leads to improvement on the job.

4. Training is the responsibility of the training unit. It begins and ends with the course.

5. It is not necessary to repeat training once provided.

Emerging Attitudes

1. Motivations attached to skills lead to action. Skills are acquired through practice.

2. Learning is a complex function of the motivation and capacity of the individual, the norms of the training group, the training methods and the behavior of the trainers, and the general climate of the police organization.

3. Improvement on the job is a complex function of individual learning, the norms of the working group, and the general climate of the organization. Individual learning, unused, leads to frustration.

4. Training is the responsibility of three partners: the organization, the trainee, and the trainer. It has preparatory, pretraining, and posttraining phases.

5. Training is a continuous process and a vehicle for consistently updating the skills of the individual human resources.

When it is analyzed we are afforded a fairly clear picture of current and future police training objectives. One can say that the present objectives are to provide

1. required entry level information of a technical nature
2. new information as necessary
3. required training for upper levels only after the person has been promoted
4. a unit or individual to the agency for conducting in-service training

The newer objectives are designed to provide[3]

1. required entry level information of a technical and a social nature
2. new information on a sustained and planned basis
3. developmental learning and training experiences for all members in the department
4. required work experience and training for upper levels before the person is promoted
5. the police supervisor with the major responsibility for training and developing his subordinates
6. the police training officer with the responsibility for planning a total program including all members—officers, supervisors, and managers—of the police agency in a set of learning experiences both within and without the organization.

Note the key training position the police supervisor holds in the newer set of objectives. The reason for this should be evident: the police supervisor who takes an interest in his subordinates, and perceives teaching as a part of his normal role, provides a real base upon which a training program can be built. If, on the other hand, the supervisor separates training from the rest of the work experience and is concerned only with its contribution to the output of the police organization, the chances of effective training are sharply reduced. This latter point is extremely important. Nothing contributes so much to job satisfaction and morale as a sincere interest in employee development. This author has seen more than one police department where, for example, nearly every member goes to college; there are many in-service training activities; and the supervisors spend much of their time helping newer men. These departments have no trouble attracting or holding officers, and their effectiveness (the real payoff) has increased steadily since the new attitudes and leadership took over.

---

[3] Many of the more futuristic attitudes pertaining to police training are found in a comprehensive document by Ronald M. Stout, ed., *Local Government In-Service Training: An Annotated Bibliography* (Albany, N.Y.: Graduate School of Public Affairs, State University of New York at Albany, 1968), in particular, pp. 42–56.

How can you develop the newer set of attitudes? In the selection of police supervisors, this question has not yet been paid great heed. Unfortunately, too, little is known about creating such an attitude. However, recognition of the importance of this developmental attitude throughout the department would seem to be an important first step. The next step would be to improve the process and devices for selecting supervisors. Most police supervisors are currently promoted on the basis of (1) their ability to respond well during an oral interview and on a written examination and (2) their prior performance as line officers. Here is the problem—the written, oral, and performance appraisals are designed to evaluate how well the person did in regard to memorizing technical information and was a good detective, vice officer, etc. Based on this kind of an examination, police managements predict that a person will be an effective supervisor. This author has seen excellent officers become poor supervisors. In essence, the selection criterion ought to be the ability to deal with people; that is, to control and train them. Rather broad changes must occur in the selection process before we can be assured of capable talent in supervisory positions.

Training is neither easy nor inexpensive. The goals of organizational training cause it to be so. However, the question remains, "Is it worth it?" The answer for local law enforcement is "Yes." For the police supervisor, moreover, training must be incorporated in his daily thinking about the job; it must be an integral part of his method of getting work done and of his total working attitude. Such complete endorsement will enable him to visualize training opportunities in his normal relationships with subordinates, to plan employee experience in terms of individual development, and to enhance the motivation and morale of his subordinates.

TRAINING: THE PROCESS

At the focal point of training is the trainee. The changes in his behavior are the measure of the effectiveness of training. To effect needed behavioral changes, training subjects the participant to a process of change that includes three overlapping and circular stages: preparation, implementation, and evaluation (follow-up and repreparation). Naturally, participants other than the trainee are involved; namely, the organization and the trainer. The three partners—organization, trainer, and trainee—in the training process and their interrelationships are shown in Figure 15. The presence of all three is required to identify their relevant training needs. To put it another way, far too often organizations dictate to trainers what knowledge and skills should be imparted. This author has also observed numerous trainees looking out windows or falling asleep during the training process. (Admittedly, at times I have been both the cause and the observer.) In

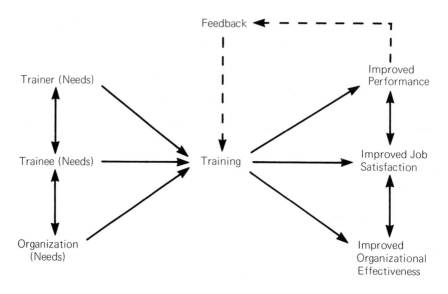

FIG. 15. THE TRAINING PROCESS

most cases, this lag in attention is caused by a lack of trainee need fulfillment. This lag can be avoided by involving the trainee in deciding which needs should be met through both formal programs and developmental experiences.

The trainee and the organization are subjected to the same stages in the process but with different purposes in mind. The function of the trainer relates to his style. In regard to the trainee, we find (1) preparation—the trainee identifies his needs and develops certain expectations and levels of motivation concerning the program, (2) implementation—the trainee selects the items he feels he must learn, and (3) evaluation—the trainee transfers the learning to application. Concerning the organization, we find (1) preparation—the organization identifies its needs, and selects and motivates the trainees, (2) implementation—the organization provides an environment conducive to learning, and (3) evaluation—the organization provides support for the transfer of learning into application.[4] Finally, as mentioned, the trainer inserts his particular style into the setting. Every trainer and therefore every police supervisor develops a personal style of his own. He grows to prefer certain kinds of training events and methods and is most effective when using these. One study has delineated seven styles among a group of adult teachers, all assessed as effective.[5] A trainer's

---

[4] Tactics on the transfer of training are discussed in Timothy W. Costello and Sheldon S. Zalkind, *Psychology in Administration: A Research Orientation Text With Integrated Readings* (Englewood Cliffs, N.J.: Prentice-Hall, Inc., 1963), pp. 222–23.

[5] Daniel Solomon and Harry L. Miller, *Exploration in Teaching Styles* (Chicago, Ill.: Center for the Study of Liberal Education for Adults, 1961).

style is defined as his consistent behavioral pattern which distinguishes him from other trainers. The categories used and the seven styles delineated in the study are set out in Table 22. Two points should be kept in mind concerning a trainer's style of training (or a supervisor's style of supervising): (1) there is a wide variety of training styles through which trainers can promote learning and development and (2) the style should vary in conjunction with the type of training; that is, effective trainers are more flexible in their style compared with poor trainers. Hopefully the reader recalls that the same thinking has already been expressed about the supervisor in his role of providing organizational control and leadership.

TRAINING: EMPLOYEE APPRAISAL

The basic design of any training program stems, or should stem, from some form of employee appraisal.[6] The term *employee appraisal* or *performance evaluation* (or whatever is being used to denote the judging by one person of another's contribution to the organization) typically raises feelings of hostility and anxiety. Significantly, in most cases it is the police supervisor who is saddled with this onerous task of appraisal. The traditional use of employee appraisals has caused this delegation because of their use as either punitive or competitive devices.[7] Moreover, the whole process of critical review is resented both by subordinate and superior as partaking of surveillance. The police subordinate, in wanting to know how well he is doing, really wants to have his merits recognized and to know how to develop his own talents more fully. Another major reason for the unpopularity of supervisory appraisal is that many employees have little individual discretion in task accomplishment and little opportunity to excel. Both the departmental norms and the informal standards of the work group set a uniform rate of accomplishment. The frequent complaint of the police officer is that he does not know where he stands with his superiors. Often a police employee is identified as a major problem for an organization so late in the game that his poor performance seems beyond remedy and even transfer or discharge is difficult. There is belated recognition that there should have been an earlier review with him of his performance. Yet procedures for rating and review of the work of employees by their superiors have not proved helpful. The problem, in essence, is not as much one of poor technique as it is one of wrongful application.

---

[6] Robert Tannenbaum, Irving R. Weschler, and Fred Masserick, *Leadership and Organization: A Behavioral Science Approach* (New York: McGraw-Hill Book Company, 1961), p. 124.

[7] Most employees, and the police officer is no exception, view the appraisal of their performance as a device for wage and salary adjustment, or to promote, transfer, or fire them. See Stanley Sloan and Alton C. Johnson, "New Context of Personnel Appraisal," *Harvard Business Review*, 46 (November–December 1968), 14–32.

TABLE 22: SEVEN TYPES OF TRAINING

	Type 1 Business/like, Objective, Impersonal	Type 2 Emphasis on Communication	Type 3 Personal Approach	Type 4 Self-Involvement	Type 5 Sensitivity toward Students	Type 6 Protective Behavior	Type 7 Stimulating the Student
Goals				To provide greater self-awareness, emotional discovery		To give student ability to relate subject to problems	To get student excited and involved in subject
Direction of interest	Subject matter			The art of teaching	Students		
Class orientation	Unitary						
Control components		Low dominant (responsive)					
Sequence	Fluctuating: medium and high dominant (responsive)	Fluctuating: low, medium, and high dominant (responsive)					
Emotional quality	Relaxed (accepting)		Relaxed (accepting)				
Methods of stimulating students	Presents materials without expressing opinions	Encourages class discussion of students' work	Gives student chance to practice particular method of discipline Poses problems and asks questions regarding individual experience	Presents material and expresses opinion Uses small groups	Is sensitive to the need for continuation	Actively supports group process from interference Encourages agreement among students	"Playing the ham"
Of allaying anxiety		Opportunity to communicate with instructor				Acceptance of expansion of students' contribution	Use of humor
Of presenting subject matter					Use of analogy		

Source: Adapted from Daniel Solomon and Harry L. Miller, Exploration in Teaching Styles (Chicago: Center for the Study of Liberal Education for Adults, 1961).

Why few articles and studies are being produced on the subject of employee appraisal should be apparent in the difficulties described above. The more modern concept of employee appraisal includes such terms as *constructive, developmental,* and *clinical.* In essence, we are beginning to approach it as an indicator of individual training needs—hence, the reason for the reader finding this topic in a chapter on training.

In the development and use of performance evaluation systems there has been a tendency to overlook the fact that appraisals themselves influence motivation of the worker. Whether periodic ratings or evaluations are handled in such a way as to improve employee work satisfaction and foster productivity is doubtful. Little research has been conducted directly on the subject, but considerable evidence does indicate that positive incentives—the opportunity of reward and recognition for good work—are good motivators. Further, it is recognized that present rating and reporting systems provide rather crude and imperfect means of estimating and recording abilities and work habits. But, since they are better than random unrecorded judgments of individual supervisors, the personnel profession should accept the challenge of the situation and seek to provide more adequate and useful instruments to the supervisor.

The most important single criterion of an effective evaluation program is whether it fosters the development of good employee performance. If it fails to do this, it should be discarded. One of the important keys to this development is employee participation, both in planning the program and in the individual evaluations. From the point of view of the line policemen such a program has a heartening effect. He realizes that his merits are known, that good service is recognized, and he may further become aware of habits that deter progress in his career. Performance evaluation must stimulate interest and respect on the part of all concerned.

It is the responsibility of the police supervisor not only to train persons to perform in various police roles, but also to take part in his subordinate's total development. In these efforts emphasis must be placed upon that which goes on in the primary work group, the interaction of superiors and subordinates within the organization, and the relationships of persons in the organization to outside organizations. In other words, identification of potential should not take place on the basis of certain selected character traits. The criteria must be developed as a result of a searching look at the work environment. The police supervisor and supervision in general have a large stake in making such a look and developing the necessary criteria.

Methods of Appraisal

It is strange that after nearly half a century of experience with employee appraisals, there are still no commonly accepted and applied norms. The methods used in rating and evaluating employees still tend to be generally weak procedures. Also, there is no universal standard as to what method of evaluation produces the best results. There is not even consensus as to what these methods are called; they are labeled types, plans, systems, scales, as well as methods. The only factors agreed upon are those methods including some measuring device or scale, a processing procedure, and some form on which to record the results of an employee's endeavors. Among the numerous methods of appraisal, nine are in vogue today. They are as follows:[8]

"Yes-no" scale. The "yes-no" scale is the simplest method of rating employees. The rater indicates with a yes or a no whether the employee has each of the characteristics listed, such as cooperation, initiative, and attitude.

Adjectival. The adjectival scale uses adjectives to describe differences in the traits of human behavior. Its validity is questionable because it erroneously assumes that the adjectives describing the employees mean the same thing to each rater.

Graphic rating scale. The graphic rating scale normally consists of a line with varying degrees of each characteristic or qualification upon it. The rater indicates the degree of each person's qualifications by the point he marks on the line. This scale is a continuum from one extreme, which is negative, to the other, which is positive. The midpoint is considered average. Since there is a tendency to attribute a negative connotation to anything average, there is a pressure to rate people between average and superior, rather than along the entire scale.

Trait or group rating. The trait, or group-standing, method of rating rates all the employees on one trait, such as responsibility, before any of them are rated on a second trait, for example, judgment. Subsequently, the rater evaluates all the workers for each of the traits one at a time until all employees have been evaluated for all the characteristics.

Checklist. The checklist method uses a list of qualities considered to lead to more effective performance. A check is placed by the police supervisor after each of the qualities possessed by the person being rated. This method allows for easy scoring and quantification, which, in turn, permits easy follow-up and analysis. This method is favored by many local law enforcement agencies. Figure 16 illustrates such a device.

Forced distribution. Under the forced-distribution method, the police supervisor is forced to distribute the ratings of the officers along a scale from "most valuable" to "least valuable." In essence, each officer is rated against all other officers. The advantage of this method is that all the officers cannot

---

[8] The nine methods of employee appraisal are adapted from Leon C. Megginson, *Personnel: A Behavioral Approach to Administration* (Homewood, Ill.: Richard D. Irwin, Inc., 1967), pp. 422–25.

LOS ANGELES COUNTY CIVIL SERVICE COMMISSION
REPORT OF PERFORMANCE EVALUATION

1

EMPLOYEE NAME   EMPLOYEE NUMBER   ITEM NUMBER   STATUS   DATE

FROM

POSITION   DEPT.   DIV   SUB   TO   PERIOD

RATE EACH FACTOR	OUTSTANDING COMPETENT IMPROVEMENT NEEDED UNSATISFACTORY

Checking items OPTIONAL with department
+ Strong   **✓** Standard   **—** Weak

Use COMMENTS space to describe employee's strengths and weaknesses. Give examples of work well done and plans for improving performance.

(Factor ratings of Unsatisfactory, Improvement Needed or Outstanding must be substantiated by comments.)

1. QUANTITY
☐ Amount of work performed
☐ Completion of work on schedule

2. QUALITY
☐ Accuracy
☐ Neatness of work product
☐ Thoroughness
☐ Oral expression
☐ Written expression

3. WORK HABITS
☐ Observance of working hours
☐ Attendance
☐ Observance of rules and regulations
☐ Observance of Safety Rules
☐ Compliance with work instructions
☐ Orderliness in work
☐ Application to duties

4. PERSONAL RELATIONS
☐ Getting along with fellow employees
☐ Meeting and handling the public
☐ Personal appearance

5. ADAPTABILITY
☐ Performance in new situations
☐ Performance in emergencies
☐ Performance with minimum instructions

6. OTHER

7. SUPERVISORY ABILITY   (only for supervisors)
☐ Planning and assigning
☐ Training and instructing
☐ Disciplinary control
☐ Evaluating performance
☐ Leadership
☐ Making decisions
☐ Fairness and impartiality
☐ Approachability
☐ Maintaining an effective safety program

(Continue COMMENTS on attached sheet)

OVER-ALL EVALUATION

UNSATISFACTORY	IMPROVEMENT NEEDED	COMPETENT	OUTSTANDING

SIGNATURES OF REPORTING OFFICERS

This report is based on my observation and/or knowledge. It represents my best judgment of the employee's performance.

RATER _____ DATE _____

(The use of Reviewer OPTIONAL with department)
I have reviewed this report.

REVIEWER _____ DATE _____

I concur in and approve this report.

DEPT. HEAD _____ DATE _____
(or authorized representative)

Copy of report given to employee   DATE_____
Copy of report mailed to employee
Address _____ DATE _____
Report discussed with employee
BY _____ DATE _____
This report has been discussed with me.

EMPLOYEE'S
SIGNATURE _____ DATE _____

FIG. 16. LOS ANGELES COUNTY SHERIFF'S DEPARTMENT DEPUTY EVALUATION FORM

be pushed to one end of the scale; there must be a distribution of the individuals over the entire curve, from best to worst.

Paired comparison. Under the paired comparison arrangement, every police officer is paired with every other officer in the group. Then the police supervisor must decide which of the two subordinates in each pair is more valuable to the department. This procedure is repeated until each officer has been paired with every other officer and his rank relative to each other person has been ascertained. The officer's score is determined by the number of times he is preferred over the other person with whom he is paired. If the procedure is completed effectively, each officer must be rated with all his co-workers for every factor being considered, such as attitude, responsibility, and so forth.

Peer or buddy rating. The peer, or buddy rating, method is also called the mutual rating system. It consists of each policeman evaluating, by secret ballot, each of the other members of his work group. This rating is made not only by the officer's supervisor but also by the members of his peer group. Although it is not a panacea for all personnel problems, this method does have the advantages of usually being more candid and also of obtaining a greater number of ratings for each person. Relatedly, we find the peer group method being used by private organizations as one criterion for selecting supervisors.

Forced-choice rating. The forced-choice rating method is growing in acceptance. Although its applications differ, in general it includes an arrangement of several pairs of statements concerning the job performance of each officer. There are two comments which appear to be equally favorable and two which appear to be equally unfavorable. These two sets of statements and one other irrelevant statement are placed together in a group. From this group of observations, the supervisor must choose the one statement most descriptive of the man under consideration and the one least descriptive. Significantly, the supervisor does not know that only one of the statements which appears to be favorable is really meaningful as far as job performance is concerned, and only one of the apparently unfavorable statements really counts against the officer. The results of this method, through research with similar jobs and employees, have been found to be valid predictors of success. Because the supervisor does not know which of the apparently favorable responses really counts in favor of the policeman, or which of the factors that appear to be unfavorable are really detrimental to the officer, there is less bias in the ranking procedure.[9] Therefore, theoretically, the supervisor doing the rating would choose the comments truly most descriptive of the man under consideration. Importantly, in addition to eliminating more of

---

[9] In regard to such biases, see James L. Quinn, "Bias in Performance Appraisal," *Personnel Administration*, 32 (January–February, 1969), pp. 40–43.

the factor of bias than any other method, the forced-choice rating scale also eliminates the "halo effect," whereby the supervisor gives his subordinate a good rating, and the "horn effect," whereby he gives the man a poor rating.[10] Under the former, the police supervisor tends to hang a halo over the ranking of a favored employee and thus emphasizes favorable factors and glosses over those that are unfavorable. Under the latter effect, the supervisor may tend to rank employees lower than they deserve; therefore, their disadvantages are dramatized and their advantages ignored.

Improving Employee Appraisals

If police officer appraisals are to act as developmental factors, the officers must be made aware of what the appraisal represents, how the decision was arrived at, and how significant the appraisal is compared with other departmental standards. Without an awareness of these facts, the developmental aspect of employee appraisals tends to be minimized.

Basically, two steps can be taken to improve employee appraisals. First is a general overhaul of the program, second a specific examination and a change in the method. The first step includes two critical procedures: (1) The supervisor must set standards of performance and relate them to the officers so that each policeman knows what is expected of him. Ideally, the police chief should obtain the approval of the personnel before installing an appraisal system; if this is possible, the value of the system is increased. When the standards of performance have the social approval of the work group, they are more effective as incentives for personal development. (2) In the second step to improve the developmental effect of performance appraisals, the police supervisor must compare his subordinates' performance with predetermined standards. He should then tell each subordinate which areas need development and which are satisfactory. This procedure may be continuous or periodic, formal or informal, but it must be performed. In most instances in the past these interviews have not been very effective. The skill with which the police supervisor handles the appraisal feedback is the key factor in determining whether the performance appraisal program is an effective developmental factor in changing employee behavior. Pertinently, one study indicated that, among middle managers in a large manufacturing firm, those who took some form of positive action as a result of the appraisals did so because of the way their superiors had performed the appraisal feedback interview and discussion.[11]

In summary form, if formal employee appraisal programs are to be used

---

[10] George S. Odiorne, *Personnel Policy: Issues and Practices* (Columbus, Ohio: Charles E. Merrill Books, Inc., 1963), pp. 312–19.

[11] H. H. Meyer and W. B. Walker, "A Study of Factors Relating to the Effectiveness of a Performance Appraisal Program," *Personnel Psychology*, 14 (Autumn 1961), 291–98.

and if they are to have the greatest possible developmental effect, the following items should be done:

1. The organization should determine what it hopes to achieve by using this procedure.
2. The employees' goals must be related to and in agreement with the organizational objectives.
3. As the only true measure of how well an employee performs is whether he achieves results, the characteristics that lead to achieving these results should be rated, not personal traits which do not affect productivity.
4. The discussion of the person's performance should be held either when he reaches his goal and receives recognition or when he fails to reach it and is not rewarded.
5. Even the best performance appraisal is worthless unless immediately followed by some firm commitment from the person regarding what he understands to be expected of him in the future.[12]

In regard to the appraisal itself, the following suggestions should improve its use. They should also be kept in mind when constructing the form to be used.

1. While the traits included in the rating scale should be comprehensive, only those related to productivity on the job should be included.
2. Each term used should have a single meaning; none should be ambiguous.
3. The items included should be of uniform length, as raters tend to give undue weight to longer items.
4. Specific statements of employee behavior should be used, rather than abstractions, and only necessary adjectives should be included.
5. If feasible, the statements of behavior should be worded in the past tense to encourage the rater to report actual happenings rather than to make value judgments concerning the future.
6. Negatively worded items tend to give greater validity than positive ones.
7. Items should be specifically and distinctly worded so the rater can truly differentiate between the individual abilities.
8. The items should be unrelated and independent.
9. If feasible, the results should be stated in quantitative terms easily understood by the employees.[13]

A few final words of warning: First, if the police supervisor does not have a fairly accurate understanding of himself and his reactions to others, his efforts to identify potential and to evaluate and subsequently develop police officers will go for naught. Second, the preferred function of an

---

[12] See Allan Young, "On the Line," *Personnel Administrator*, 29 (March–April 1966), 60.
[13] Megginson, *Personnel*, p. 425.

employee appraisal program is to indicate needed training, in other words, to point out to the police officer where he should be making strides to develop his skills, talents, and character. Third, no appraisal should be used as an ominous tool for "putting on record" an individual's errors or weaknesses. In conclusion, the appraisal of police officers, if properly directed, designed, and implemented, can provide the police department with a more relevant training program and improved employee performance.

TRAINING: THE STRATEGIES

> Preparing the subordinate to respond adequately by briefing, training, and the like is an obvious support for directive leadership. This requires long contacts at the outset—a kind of capital investment which many leaders are reluctant to make.[14]

In practice, the aims of training are external to the process itself; that is, the goals to be achieved are modifications in organizational performance or capabilities. Further, the results obtained from training are ultimately assessed in terms of organizational criteria and not by standards that are an inherent part of training itself. In short, the common quality of training is its intended aim of moving something from an initial state in which problems or needs exist to an end state in which the problems have been solved or the needs met. In all cases the action involves modifications in human objects— the trainees—whose knowledge, skills, and attitudes are the targets. Moreover, there is an expertise of training, comprised in part of systematic knowledge and in part, too, of an empirical technology expressed in principles derived from experience. Thus one finds in this section various strategies now practiced in the field of training. However, the consideration of strategies for training involves the broader issue of effectiveness. In other words, the desire for effective training structures the entire program, including the employee strategies. Hence, we turn briefly to an examination of what is meant by effective training.

First, effective police training requires proper selection of both courses and trainees. This means that all concerned, trainees and their supervisors, should know the objectives of the course. It also means that the selection decision should consider the employee's training needs in his present job and in his career development.

Second, to be effective, police training must support operations. In other words, both trainees and supervisors should be able to specify in advance how the employee is expected to use the training in his work. Furthermore,

---

[14] Leonard Sayles, *Managerial Behavior* (New York: McGraw-Hill Book Company, 1964), p. 148.

if the training has been effective, they should be able at some later date to point to ways in which the trainee has used it.

Third, effectiveness of police training depends upon positive action, not only by the trainee but also by the police supervisor. The aim of training is to change a man's behavior. However, the effects of training evaporate unless supervision and management are prepared to accept the changed man, and have changed the work situation to accommodate him. As has been pointed out more than once, the organizational climate must reinforce the training experience, thereby increasing the probability that the employee will apply the training in his work. If this reinforcement does not take place, training can be nonrewarding, or even a hindrance, with correspondingly less chance of successful application.

Effective training calls, therefore, for clarity of objectives and means. Both the ends and the means must be appropriate to the purpose. Relating them demands clear specifications for each part of the training task, including the time, skill, and facilities required to complete it. Insuring this clarity is a primary responsibility of the police supervisor. Unless this task has been accomplished, a new police training program is launched into a void, doomed to problems and failure. One final question remains, however, "How do we know when we have succeeded in providing an effective training program?" The answer is obvious—by evaluating the training effort! In summary, then, effective training calls for (1) establishing relevant training goals, (2) defining training specifications, (3) selecting the appropriate strategy, (4) creating suitable structural arrangements, and (5) evaluating and improving the program.[15]

Establishing Training Goals

In the first place, any training goal is based on the goals of the police department. Consequently, the main question is whether the goals of the department are realistic. Further, is the training input of a program envisaged also realistic? Or, is training in danger of being misused? For example, is it too little and too late? All of this is to say that (1) training goals must support organizational activities and (2) training goals must be realistic. These two basic needs suggest that three steps are necessary to insure that departmental and training goals are met.

The first step is to be certain that a needed change calls for training. What many police organizations need is not training, at least not immediately, but lots of detailed, operational planning and implementation of plans. Training at this stage would be a disservice if it deprived the organization of skilled people currently needed for action.

---

[15] The majority of the thinking contained in the following sections is derived from Rolf P. Lynton and Udai Pareek, *Training for Development* (Homewood, Ill.: Richard D. Irwin, Inc., 1967), pp. 31–53.

The second step is to define the part that police training can play in the change. What new competences does the department require and which of these can be acquired through systematic training? Training strategy determines which goals can reasonably be achieved through a training program and which cannot. And, vice versa, the goals determine which training strategy is most appropriate.

The third step is more taxing and worthy of the most careful consideration; it concerns questions of quantities and levels of police personnel to be trained, and of timing the training well. The training of one police officer is seldom enough to achieve a change in a department. While one person goes for a special program elsewhere, others need to be trained. It is important to decide what minimum concentration of trained police personnel of all kinds is required to achieve the change. If the police training program as a whole does not reach this minimum, the endeavor amounts to treading water instead of moving toward the goal. Or worse, it leads to frustration among police personnel.

Defining Training Specifications

The responsibility is reversed when one reaches the point of defining training specifications. The police organization has specified the new knowledge, understanding, and skill required for a needed change. The department has pinpointed those aspects which can be developed through systematic training. How this is to be done, which training designs and methods are to be used, is strictly the business of the police supervisor. By matching methods to requirements, the total timetable of training for the change can be established.

Training specifications also have to cover two other aspects. First, they need to state precisely the contributions to training that agencies other than the department have to make. The provision of opportunities for field work placement in other criminal justice agencies is an example during the course, adequate support after participants return from training and start the new work is an example for later. Second, the training specifications must take into account the minimum concentrations of trained personnel required to effect a change. This has been referred to earlier. To summarize, defining of training specifications requires (1) the matching of methods to requirements, (2) the assessment of the contribution of the training to the organization, and (3) the probability of effecting change within the organization.

Appropriate Training Strategies

Any attempt to train, that is, to change, an individual automatically means a "freezing-up of relations" between people. The freezing-up of relations involves three stages: "unfreezing," "moving," and "refreezing."

Unfreezing is necessary because the police officer (and his organization, family, and locality) comes with habits, values, practices, the very opposite of a clean slate. To affect him through training, his normal habits have first to be questioned and disturbed, or unfrozen. Training can do this by focusing on needs that police trainees cannot satisfy by habitual behavior. The supervisor then introduces other events which allow participants to try new ways of behaving, that is, changing. If the police trainees find the new behavior more useful in meeting the "new" needs, they can then be helped to make it habitual. Each officer thus gains a new set of behavioral patterns, which he then freezes.

The guiding principles for training strategies lie in these dynamics of the development process and in the minimum critical concentration of effort required at each stage of it. Training differences occur along two axes. The first axis delineates the subject matter that policemen are to learn. At one extreme it points toward learning about a specific task or piece of knowledge, such as the pros and cons of using certain investigative techniques. This kind of knowledge is "content." At the other extreme are general understanding and insight into how people and things function. This kind of knowledge is "process." For example, participants could learn how investigative techniques are developed and the principles that underlie them. This first axis then has content for one extreme and process for the other.

The second axis shows the basic function of police training. Is it to be used for constructing new concepts and theory? That would be one extreme, which we call "concept." Or is it to improve action on the job? That extreme we call "job." Along these two axes are six major training strategies, as shown in Figure 17.

For greater comprehensiveness, we ignore here the distinction noted in the first chapter between education and training and encompass both in this exposition. Table 23 relates the general characteristics of each training strategy. A more thorough description can be found in *Training for Development.*[16]

The selection of a strategy depends on a number of factors. One is the training goals. Once the police department is clear about its goals, it can choose a strategy that leads to them. The second consideration when choosing a strategy is the resources (human, physical, and financial) available for training.

It is of interest to note that a study of management training techniques used by business companies indicated they use one or more types of management training techniques in developing their management personnel.[17] It

---

[16] *Ibid.*

[17] For more information on this study, see Wayne J. Foreman, "A Study of Management Training Techniques Used by Large Corporations," *Public Personnel Review,* 28 (January 1967), 31–35.

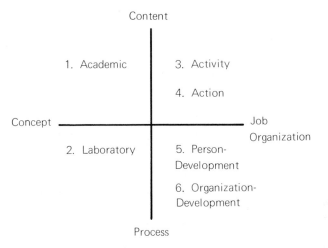

Source: Rolf P. Lynton and Udai Pareek, Training for Development (Homewood, Ill.: Richard D. Irwin, Inc., 1967), p. 40.

FIG. 17. SIX TRAINING STRATEGIES.

was shown that on-the-job training was used in more companies than any other technique, with 43, or 96 per cent, of the corporations using this training means. Of the 43 corporations using this method, 30, or 70 per cent, ranked it as the management training technique used most often. The method using conference and discussion groups followed with 42, or 93 per cent, of the corporations employing this means. Of the 42 corporations using this technique, nine ranked it as the training technique used most often.

In descending order of frequency, the other techniques or strategies used were:

Job rotation	76
Special projects	71
Case studies	49
Problem solving	49
Management games	18
Role playing	18
Programmed instruction	16
Sensitivity training	9
Brainstorming	7
Other	7

More specific to our interests is a survey by the International City Managers' Association reporting on the teaching techniques used during recruit

TABLE 23: COMPARISON OF SIX TRAINING STRATEGIES

Strategy	Emphases	Characteristic Methods	Assumptions	Action Steps
1. Academic	Transmitting content and increasing conceptual understanding	Lecture Seminar Individual reading	1. Content and understanding can be passed on from those who know to those who are ignorant. 2. Such knowledge and understanding can be translated in practice.	Building a syllabus to be covered in the program Examination to test retained knowledge and understanding
2. Laboratory	Process of function and change Process of learning	Isolation Free exploration and discussion Experimentation	1. It is useful and possible to pay attention to psychological factors for separate attention. 2. Understanding of own and others' behavior helps in the performance of the jobs.	Unfreezing participants from their usual expectations and norms Helping participants see and help others see own behavior and develop new habits
3. Activity	Practice of specific skill	Work on the job under supervision Detailed job analysis and practice with aids	1. Improvement in particular skill leads to better performance on the job. 2. Production and training can be combined rather simply.	Analyzing skill and dividing it into parts Preparing practice tasks, standards, and aids
4. Action	Sufficient skills to get organizational action	Field work, setting and achieving targets	1. Working in the field develops people. 2. Individual skills and organizational needs will fit together.	Preparation of field programs Participation according to schedule

346

TABLE 23: (Continued)

Strategy	Emphases	Characteristic Methods	Assumptions	Action Steps
5. Person development	Improved individual competence in wide variety of tasks and situations	Field training, simulation methods, incident and case sessions, and syndicate discussion	1. Training in job requirements with emphasis on process will help a participant develop general skills and understanding. 2. Organization will support the individual in using understanding and skills acquired.	Identifying training needs Preparing simulated data
6. Organization development	Organizational improvement	Study of organizational needs Work with small groups from the organization	1. Attention to organizational needs as process develops understanding. 2. Organizational change will result in individual's change.	Survey of organizational needs Determining strategic grouping for training Working on organizational requirements

Source: Rolf P. Lynton and Udai Pareek, Training for Development (Homewood, Illinois: Richard D. Irwin, Inc., 1967), pp. 50–51.

training.[18] Regretfully it was reported that 18 per cent of the 1475 municipal police departments surveyed indicated that no recruit training at all is provided. For a listing of the recruit training techniques, see Table 24.

Suitable Structural Arrangements for Training

It is not sufficient to make police training supplemental to work; police work must be organized to facilitate training and development. Several factors support this conclusion. First, any help in training provided by the organization must be welcome because the training demands are ever expanding in local law enforcement. Second, even if repetition has made the point trite, we live in an age of revolution in processes, systems, and products in public and private organizations. The training burdens are great. Increasingly, training must be part and parcel of the work itself and it should be increasingly supplied and directly monitored by the immediate supervisor. Third, the concept of organizing work to decrease the need for substantial training must be suspect, even if the two factors just discussed were unimportant. The matter is a complicated one, but one facet permits easy illustration. Namely, high satisfaction is an unlikely outcome of over-specialization. Such an interpretation seems to fit available data. On one assembly line, for example, fully two thirds of the workers interviewed in one department desired transfer to some other job in their department. Significantly their choices for a new job reflect their needs for a job with more content and scope: about half of the men wanted repair or utility jobs; one quarter had set their caps for supervisory positions; and the remainder would settle for any production job as long as it was not on the main assembly line, which exhibits the most extreme devotion to classical job design. Significantly, few of the discontented traced their desire for mobility to higher pay. Their typical explanations were: "On the job I want, I could do a lot of different things." "It would give me a chance of learning more." "It would be easier, not so much work."[19] The relevance of employee satisfaction must be put in perspective. The workers quoted were well paid, their workplace was modern and safe, their lavatories were sparkling. But to paraphrase one of them: "These things are well and good, but it's what you do most of the time that's important." Organizing for training in the process of work suggests a way out of this unattractive cul-de-sac, and a profitable way in the bargain.

---

[18] For details, see J. Robert Havlick, "Recruit Training: Police Chiefs' Dilemma," *Public Management*, 50 (December 1968), 300–303.

[19] Charles R. Walker, "The Problems of the Repetitive Job," *Harvard Business Review*, 28 (May 1950), 56–57.

TABLE 24: *TEACHING TECHNIQUES FOR RECRUIT TRAINING (990 CITIES REPORTING)*

Teaching Technique	Rank for All Cities over 10,000	Number of Cities Using Technique	Rank by Population Groups					
			10,000 to 25,000	25,000 to 50,000	50,000 to 100,000	100,000 to 250,000	250,000 to 500,000	Over 500,000
Lecture and discussion	1	973	1	1	1	1	1*	1
TV, films, recordings, and other audio-visual aids	2	874	2	2	2	2	1*	1*
Actual practice (field experience under supervision of selected police officers)	3	796	3	3	5*	4	6	3*
Practice in use of work devices	4	782	4	4	4	6	5	5*
Simulation of practice (such as acting out the apprehension and arrest of a shoplifter)	5	764	5	5	3	5	1*	5*
Field observations of police facilities (such as communication facilities, lab facilities, etc.)	6	704	7	7	5*	3	1*	3*
Discussion of assigned readings	7	699	6	6	7	8	8	5*
Field observations of street problems (such as traffic control, crowd engineering, etc.)	8	673	8	8	8	7	7	8

*Ranked equally.
Source: J. Robert Hovlick, "Recruit Training: Police Chiefs' Dilemma," Public Management, 50 (December 1968), 33.

Evaluating and Improving Training Programs

Most are interested but few ask whether our training and development programs are of value. Those police departments that have sought to answer this question typically take a "popularity poll" among participants. Such questions as, "What did you get out of the training?" or "How did you like the course? the instructors? the manner of presentation?" are asked each participant. Such an approach, while useful, can be improved upon. Some organizations are now gathering empirical evidence of the effects of training upon the employee's job performance and then evaluating the information so as to actively encourage, in the work setting, positive reinforcement of what has been learned. Harmon and Glickman offer one example of this approach.[20]

The Harmon and Glickman study assumed that any operationally meaningful assessment of training must be made within a systems concept, of which the trainees, the instructors and instructional methods, and the supervisors and the management methods are component parts, all influencing the total effectiveness of training. They designed and tested two sets of three open-end questionnaires (see Table 25). One set was used on a group of government employees who participated in a training seminar and the other on their supervisors. The questionnaires were administered prior to training, immediately after training, and eight months following completion of the training.

The answers to each question were analyzed, then sorted into categories according to the quality level of the answer. No more than three categories were used in any case. A value of 2 was always given to the best, or preferred, answer, which usually involved a reference to specific operational gains or changes derived from training. A value of 0 indicated no report of change or benefit, 1 was in between. For "yes-no" questions, only the 1 and 0 categories were needed. The results of their study showed that the training program needed considerable improvement.

Practically speaking, the most significant outcomes of this research were the indications of specific ways to improve the effectiveness of training, providing that one is willing to take the necessary trouble. Therefore, in the first place, their results showed that asking about follow-up plans increased the likelihood that follow-up would occur. To illustrate, one group of participants was not asked Posttraining question Four: "What plans do you have for discussing this course with your supervisor?" Of those who were asked, 29 out of 35 did engage in subsequent discussions as reported by their supervisors; while, of those who were not asked, only one in eight did so.

---

[20] Francis L. Harmon and Albert S. Glickman, "Managerial Training: Reinforcement Through Evaluation," *Public Personnel Review*, 26 (October 1965), 194–98.

Their results clearly show that feedback promotes follow-up. Of 11 supervisors who indicated that they had seen the first report on the project, eight related that they had held posttraining discussions and taken specific follow-up steps with one or more of their employees. Of 20 who had not seen the first report, only six had taken both of these steps. "But," one may ask, "does follow-up really make a difference in determining whether the participant will find applications of the training in his work?" Figure 18 suggests that the answer is "Yes." As Figure 18 shows, there were 17 participants whose supervisors related that they had both discussed the training and followed up on the employee's use of it. Of these 17 participants, 16 indicated that they had found some application of the course in their work.

TABLE 25:   PRE-TRAINING, POST-TRAINING, AND FOLLOW-UP QUESTIONS FOR PARTICIPANTS AND SUPERVISORS

Pre-training	
Participants	*Supervisors*
1. What do you think are the specific objectives of the course?	1. What do you think are the specific objectives of the course?
2. How does this seem to fit into your own career plans?	2. How does this fit into your Agency Training and Development Program for this participant?
3. On the basis of information available to you now, in what particular ways do you expect to apply this training in your future work? Give examples.	3. On the basis of information available to you now, in what particular ways do you expect this employee to apply the training in his future work? Give examples.
4. Have you discussed points 1, 2, and 3 with your supervisor? If yes, do you feel that he shares the same expectations as you do? If not, how do your expectations and his differ as you see it?	4. Have you discussed points 1, 2, and 3 with the employee? If yes, do you feel that he shares the same expectations as you do? If not, how do your expectations and his differ as you see it?
5. Looking back over your work during the past six months or so, has anything happened to bring home to you a need for this kind of training? Give actual examples.	5. Looking back over his work during the past six months or so, has anything happened to bring home to you his need for this kind of training? Give actual examples.
6. Is there any other advance information you should have been provided about the course?	6. Is there any other advance information you think should have been provided about the course?
7. Who participated in deciding that you were to attend?	7. Who participated in deciding that this employee was to attend?
8. Other comments?	8. Other comments?
Post-training	
1. In what ways, if any, have your ideas changed as to objectives of the course?	1. In what ways, if any, have your ideas changed as to the objectives of the course?

TABLE 25 : *Continued*

Participants	*Supervisors*
2. a. Give examples of situations in your own work in which the concepts and methods taught in this course would be applicable. b. Give examples of situations in which they would not be applicable.	2. In what ways do you plan to follow up on this employee's use of what he learned in the course ?
3. a. Can you recall any situations during the past six months or so that you might have handled differently if you had already taken the course ? b. If yes, in what ways do you think that the outcome might have been different ? Give specific examples.	3. Other comments ?
4. What plans do you have for discussing this course with your supervisor ?	
5. Other comments ?	

Follow-up

1. a. Have there been any situations in which the Kepner-Tregoe concepts and methods were helpful to you in your work ? b. If yes, give specific examples.	1. Has this employee discussed the Kepner-Tregoe concepts and methods with you during the past six months or so ?
2. a. Have there been any situations in which you tried to use these concepts and methods, but they did not help you much ? b. If you have not been able to apply the training at all, what do you consider to have been the reasons ?	2. a. Have you been able to follow up on his use of the Kepner-Tregoe training ? b. If yes, in what specific ways ?
3. a. Have you made use of these concepts and methods in discussions with your supervisor during the past six months or so ? b. If yes, give examples.	3. a. Have there been any situations in which these concepts and methods seem to have been helpful to this employee in his work ? b. If yes, give specific examples. c. If no, what do you consider to be the reasons he has been unable to make use of these concepts and methods ?
4. a. Have you seen the Personnel Research Staff report, "A Path to Management Development and to the Measurement of Its Growth ?" b. If yes, do you have any comments on the findings ?	4. a. Have you seen the Personnel Research Staff report, "A Path to Management Development and to the Measurement of Its Growth ?" b. If yes, do you have any comments on the findings ?
5. Other comments ?	5. Other comments ?

Source: Francis L. Harmon and Albert S. Glickman, "Managerial Training: Reinforcement Through Evaluation," Public Personnel Review, 26 (October 1965), 195–96.

By contrast, the supervisors of 22 participants had not taken both of these steps, and only 13 of these participants succeeded in using the training.

The previously described method of evaluating yields empirical evidence

Employee Applied Training

		No	Yes	Total	%
Both Discussion and Follow Up by Supervisors	Yes	1	16	17	44
	No	9	13	22	56
	Total	10	29	39	100
	%	26	74	100	

Source: Harmon and Glickman, "Managerial Training: Reinforcement Through Evaluation," Public Personnel Review, *26: 198.*

FIG. 18. DISCUSSION AND FOLLOW-UP BY SUPERVISORS
AND EMPLOYEES' USE OF TRAINING

susceptible to statistical analysis. The information obtained by this method, despite its obvious limitations, is pertinent to training in industry and government. Furthermore, the results of this research seem to support the importance of the managerial climate as reflected in supervisor-trainee communication. To this end, we find in this study that the greatest value will come from its use in action programs. As a one-shot study, its value is questionable, but implemented on a sustained basis, the value of the procedure can be fully exploited. Significantly, the procedure can trace changes in the effectiveness of a training program over time. By pinpointing weaknesses, either in the training program itself or in its administration, it can lead to better results from the training effort.

Finally, to be of maximum utility the results of any evaluation must logically provide for the growth and development of the training program itself. Improving the training program includes, as priority items, the development of its trainers, of its other resources, and of close professional and working relations with other institutions and concerned criminal justice agencies outside—in short, equipping the training program in every way for performing even more effectively its primary responsibilities. In the specific context of this text, improving the training program also means improving, upgrading, the police supervisor's ability to train and develop his subordinates.

SUMMARY

The police department has an obligation to the community it serves and to the members of its work force. Concisely stated, it is to develop its personnel to their full potential. Significantly, the police supervisor is the best candidate for seeing to it that the police organization meets this obligation. In the role of trainer, the police supervisor must improve an individual's work performance while simultaneously developing his capacity for dealing with higher levels of responsibility. This task is most effectively achieved by incorporating training into a police officer's daily job.

The training process is comprised of a matrix of needs (trainee, trainer, and organizational) which, once fulfilled, tend to improve one's job performance, job satisfaction, and organizational effectiveness. Training needs can be identified in a variety of ways. Clearly, employee appraisal is a highly useful means for identifying the training needs in a police department. Further, there is a growing trend away from the use of the employee appraisal as a negative device and toward its use as a motivator and as an indicator of needed improvement in skills and attitudes.

Finally, an effective training program is based on (1) establishing relevant training goals, (2) defining training specifications, (3) selecting the appropriate training strategy, (4) creating suitable structural arrangements, and (5) evaluating and improving the program. All five of these components are related to one another. Further, a training program that fails to include all five components can expect to obtain only marginal results with the participants. Regretfully, component five—evaluation and improvement of the training effort—is all too often absent.

14

Career Development:
Planned Employee Experience

We see today a growing trend which emphasizes training as the most effective means of personnel development. Police training is coming of age. By most, it is now considered an integral part, rather than a burdensome appendage, of the police organization. A police organization can usually be divided into four professional levels, each with its own requisite understandings.[1] Remember, each higher level in the hierarchy subsumes that knowledge required by the level beneath it. And, while the amount of knowledge may not change, the combination of understandings does. The beginning, or first professional, level is comprised of police officers who are in the process of acquiring a total knowledge of their operational duties and skills. This classification pertains to the patrolman as well as to the plainclothes investigator. In other words, those commonly referred to as line employees are within the first level. The second professional level contains first-line police supervisors, who in most cases hold the rank of sergeant. For the police officer in the first level who has acquired a firm grasp of the substantive field there is an important skill he must learn before he can rise to this second echelon. It is the skill of leading others in achieving an organizational end, that is, the skill of controlling and directing others. The skill involves the understanding of face-to-face human relations at two levels—relations with subordinates and relations with equals and superiors. The third pyramidal level is similar to what we often refer to as middle management. To those skills that the employee has developed through his activities within the two previously described professional levels, he now must add even more difficult skills. Fundamental for an effective performance of the middle management role is knowledge of the basic concepts of management, organization, and administration, as well as knowledge of the practices related to the professional duties and responsibilities. Also, the middle manager, a police lieutenant

---

[1] The majority of this section is taken from Paul M. Whisenand, "Equipping Men for Professional Development in the Police Service: The Federal Law Enforcement Assistance Act of 1965," *The Journal of Criminal Law, Criminology, and Police Science*, 57 (August 1966), 223–27.

or captain, needs to learn about other functions of the department and related government agencies. This learning is best accomplished by becoming involved in their various activities. There is much he can learn by reading, but there is equally as much he must learn by participating in the work. Finally, the middle manager must increase his knowledge about the environmental realm within which his department operates.

The chief of police and deputy chiefs constitute the top professional level in a police department. It is at this level that an executive first realizes that he, and he alone, bears the ultimate and whole responsibility for the department or bureau he heads. The dimensions of most public executive positions have changed markedly since the 1930s. First, urbanization has caused the numbers for whose work they are responsible to grow by leaps and bounds. Second, modern specialized skills and complex technologies have greatly increased, thereby making the coordinative and integrative role of the police executive a Herculean feat. Lastly, police functions and police goals are both multiplying and constantly changing in accordance with societal needs. While coping with the above pressures with one hand, he must, with the other, steer his department by the application of correct policies and programs.

Training occurs in many ways. Much of it, of course, is informal. At the formal level there are several different programs with which we should have some familiarity. These are normally defined in the following terms:

1. *Preentry education*—involves the education acquired by the person before he is accepted as an employee.
2. *Preentry training*—involves that portion of preentry education which may be given an individual in anticipation of his entering a specific occupation prior to his employment.
3. *In-service education*—occurs after acceptance on the job and involves work taken in a regular educational institution, usually for degree purposes.
4. *In-service (recruit, supervisory, etc.) training*—includes that portion of postentry education intended to improve performance in, or to prepare for, a specific employment.

The areas covered by the terms *training* and *education* overlap one another. With the development in recent years of professional police curricula, it is particularly hard to tell when a course serves a general education purpose and when it contributes specifically to performance on the job. At any rate a rather firm line can be drawn between (1) preentry and (2) postentry, or in-service, education and training.

Basically, there are two approaches to in-service police training: group and individual. Each professional level in the police department should have a training program employing different combinations and techniques of these two approaches. The individual approach includes such training techniques as on-the-job training, coaching, counseling, job rotation, and directed study. Some of the techniques employed by the group approach are lecture, discussion, case study, role playing, incident process, risk technique, brainstorming, sensitivity training, and simulation exercises.

Preentry training and education are usually acquired through an academic program undertaken on the employees' own initiative. It is recognized that many concepts can best be gained in a formal academic setting. However, it is becoming increasingly clear that much of the education, and certainly the majority of the vocational training, of the future policeman will occur after he is at work in a department. Preentry education, even in the broad field of law enforcement specialization, is stressing more and more the general principles of police administration and operations, and less and less the unique and specific techniques that are experiencing constant change because of new findings.

CAREER DEVELOPMENT: ENTRY TO EXIT

This section indicates broad guidelines for the construction of an integrated and multilevel training program. The key is for us to conceive of career development as (1) a constant process which begins once the person enters the police organization and does not stop until he leaves, (2) a varying process, which differs according to both the professional level and the trainee, (3) an integrative process, which assists in the coordination of resources, and (4) a total process, which involves all members of the police organization in an effort to improve their performance and adapt to changing conditions.

As previously stated, each level, because of the mix of requisite understandings, requires a custom-fitted combination of group and individual training approaches. Time, budget, employees, and policies of the department determine the approach combination. It appears that as one progresses upward in the organization the amount of individual training should increase along with a commensurate decrease in group training. As far as the first professional level is concerned, the police officer should have at least some college training before joining the department. Once he is a member of the department, in-service training should occur prior to field assignment. This training should give the officer a sound foundation in substantive police techniques. The following training techniques may prove useful (the percentages indicate the approximate amount of the total training program that should be allotted to that particular technique): classroom lecture, 60 per cent; directed discussions, 20 per cent; simulation exercises, 10 per cent; case studies, 5 per cent; sensitivity training, 5 per cent.

The second professional level, hopefully, will require some external academic training. The first-line supervisor should receive advanced specialized training in supervision and the substantive police field prior to appointment. This training should normally be provided on departmental time. The group techniques to be considered are: classroom lecture, 40 per cent; directed discussions, 10 per cent; simulation exercises, 10 per cent; case studies, 10 per cent; sensitivity training, 5 per cent. The individual techniques might well include: on-the-job training, 15 per cent; intradepartmental job rotation, 10 per cent. Training for the third level, middle management, is based on the axiom that *no single program of experience, of training, or of academic education will suffice to improve the performance of middle management training.* Appropriate group techniques are: lectures (not necessarily of the classroom variety), 20 per cent; nondirective discussions, 10 per cent; simulation exercises, 10 per cent; case studies, 10 per cent; sensitivity training, 5 per cent. Individual techniques are: on-the-job training, 15 per cent; intradepartmental job rotation, 15 per cent; interdepartmental job rotation, 15 per cent. At this point, formal academic training should be mandatory.

The fourth, or executive, level of training revolves around the notion of planned experience. At this level the majority of effort goes into a rather informal and individualized training program. Group techniques involved are: lectures, 10 per cent; nondirective discussions, 20 per cent; case studies, 20 per cent. The individual techniques are: interdepartmental rotation, 20 per cent; academic training as a part of work, 30 per cent.

Training and development programs at the first and second professional levels have been accepted as necessary elements of police management, and there is steady growth in the number and quality of such programs.[2] The needs of the police officer are just now beginning to be viewed in terms of his total career. It is recognized that as the officer moves upward in the department he experiences a demand for differing requisite understandings. Each professional level requires a new combination of skills and knowledge for the fulfillment of its tasks. Consequently, each level should have a training program tailored to impart relevant skills and, at the same time, to equip men for career growth in the police service. For the career officer, professional training programs, whether offered by government or academic institutions, should be made available at all levels in the department. In summation, the police training program of the future should be conceived and designed as an integral element of career development for supporting each stage in a policeman's career.

---

[2] Further evidence of the nationwide growth in police training is documented in the article "State Training Legislation in the United States," *The Police Chief*, 32 (August 1965), 9–19. It reports preliminary findings which indicate that there are 21 statewide laws dealing with minimum standards for police selection and training.

TRAINING: THE PROBLEM AREAS

Before proceeding further a few rather serious barriers to police training should be discussed. First, training is not cheap. It costs money, for materials, fees, salaries, and the like. Second, training is time consuming, and many police organizations lack sufficient manpower to "cut personnel loose" for training periods. Interestingly, in early 1969, the Riverside County Sheriffs Department sent all 17 of their lieutenants and captains to a police middle management training program one day a week for 16 weeks! In doing so, they strongly implied two things: (1) most personnel are well trained and motivated enough to do their job without the presence of management and (2) their sergeants have the capacity to assume higher-level challenges. Pointedly, O. Glenn Stahl recently predicted that in the near future at least one quarter of the time a person spends in a professional or managerial career will be devoted to formal training—whether provided directly by the agency or in facilities away from the job.[3] One might predict, based on his prediction, that the supervisor will also soon be spending more of his working day in training. Third, there have to be some rather positive incentives to motivate the departmental personnel to a training endeavor. In fact, at times outright pressure may have to be employed. Fourth, the upgrading of educational requirements means a reassessment of recruitment and retention programs is in order. A highly skilled and well educated officer is going to demand more from his organization. That is to say, it will take more to attract and to hold him to the department.[4]

The remainder of this chapter provides the reader with recommended programs for career development and educational incentive. While the programs are described primarily in terms of the line officer, the basic concept and plan can be applied to supervisory and to managerial training. The required body of knowledge changes, however, with each level in the police department. This text indicates what information and ideas a supervisory training effort should include.

POLICE TRAINING: PLANNED EMPLOYEE EXPERIENCE

To reemphasize a point made earlier, it is axiomatic that no single program of experience, of training, or of academic education will suffice to

---

[3] Letter received from O. Glenn Stahl, "Challenges to Personnel," a message from Dr. Stahl as the incoming President of the Public Personnel Association, Chicago, Illinois, January, 1965.

[4] For more information on this problem area, see Paul M. Whisenand, "The Upgrading of Educational Requirements for Police," *The Police Chief*, 33 (August 1966), 39–43, and S. M. Klein and J. R. Maher, "Educational Level and Satisfaction with Pay," *Personnel Psychology*, 19 (Summer 1966), 195–208.

improve the performance of police personnel.[5] Activities of our local police agencies are rapidly increasing in complexity to meet the demands of a growing society. A well-rounded developmental program for police personnel is crucial if local law enforcement is to continue to meet its obligations to the community effectively and economically. The subsequent sections present a conceptualized continuous developmental program which encompasses planned experience, agency or interagency training, and academic education.

Recommendations

Proposed training program

1. All police personnel shall participate in a development program consisting of individual planned experience, in-service group training, out-service specialized training, and academic education.

As mentioned above, we have conceptualized a continuous developmental program which encompasses planned experience, agency or interagency training, and academic education (see Figure 19). A three-year period for completion of the minimum program is recommended. The total program lasts a career lifetime. Obviously, police personnel who have completed the prescribed academic portion of the program should be able to complete the total program in a shorter period of time. The following sections outline the four phases of the program.

1.1 *Basic Academic.* An academic program undertaken on the police employee's own initiative to provide him with the basic concepts of government, organization, management, and criminal justice administration is crucial. It is recognized that many concepts can best be gained in a formal academic setting. These concepts are reflected in courses in the following subject areas available to police employees through colleges and universities throughout the nation. Fundamentals of Criminal Justice—The role of criminal justice agencies in modern society; significance of administration to policy processes and criminal justice effectiveness; criminal justice service and the community (world, national, state, and local) as the setting; relation of culture to the administration of criminal justice.

The Role of Our Local Police—The role of police in modern society; departmental organization; problems of authority; delegation and control; line and staff concepts; managerial and specialized functions; functionalization and

---

[5] This section is based upon the thinking contained in the *Task Force Report to Governor's Committee on Personnel and Training: Middle Management Training* (Sacramento: California Department of Justice, 1965).

Source: Task Force Report to Governor's Committee on Personnel and Training: Middle Management Training (*Sacramento, Ca.: California Dept. of Justice, 1965*) *p. 7.*

FIG. 19. CONTINUOUS CAREER DEVELOPMENT

coordination; centralized and decentralized services; tools and leadership; planning and communications; authority and power.

Criminal Law, Procedure, and Evidence—Statute and case law, rules of evidence, and criminal justice procedures.

The Etiology and Ecology of Crime—The roots, causes, and prevention of criminal behavior.

Supervision of Police Personnel Resources—Human resource development and supervision; values and processes in civil service career systems; training practices; human relations in supervision; personnel theory; evaluation of police personnel systems.

Administration of Financial Resources, or Fiscal Management—Problems of financial management in governmental units; alternate revenue sources; tax enforcement; budgeting; financial planning and control; debt management; public credit; and intergovernmental financial relationships.

Program and Sustaining Activities—An overview of current functions and resources used in the provision of police services; program (line) and sustaining (staff) activities and relationships; deployment of organization resources.

This author believes also that police personnel should have a reasonable understanding of the three subjects listed below. College and university courses help to develop competency in these areas; therefore, formal courses are probably the best means for gaining competency.

Advanced Oral and Written Communications—Police personnel deal with the day-to-day operations of public business. It is imperative that any written or oral communication be clear, concise, and factual.

Statistics—There is an increasing requirement for analysis of information and data to assure logical deployment of personnel and other resources in the accomplishment of the police mission.

Information Processing—There is growing usage of modern data processing technology which requires an awareness of the concepts, uses, and involved hardware and systems design.

1.2 *Core Training*. The core training program should consist of a series of courses administered on a departmental basis. The subject matter should cover organization, management, and field operations of a general nature. The courses must be designed to provide police personnel with knowledge pertaining to the police policies, processes, and practices.

The author feels strongly that the contents of specified courses listed shortly are needed by all police personnel to effectively perform their duties and to meet their responsibilities. The subject matter in these courses may be covered in an average of 800 hours of formal classroom instruction. Further, the universal nature of the curriculum content allows offering the courses on a multidepartmental basis. However, it remains the responsibility of each police department to assure availability of the courses for its police employees.

The core training begins with an 800-hour academy basic training program. The program includes courses in

The Mission of Local Law Enforcement
Criminal Law
Field Operations
Sustaining Activities (for example, jail, records, communications)
Departmental Policies
Community Relations
Physical Training
Weaponry
Disaster Operations
Report Writing
Simulated Field Problems

The above list must vary according to current departmental needs.

Core training continues with a minimum of ten days of training for each employee annually. The curriculum should be provided on departmental time as an integral part of the police employee development program. The courses should involve the imparting of new skills, the updating of previously learned information, and the introduction of new concepts and practices.

The program must be flexible and incorporate changing and required information.

    1.3 *Departmental On-The-Job Training.* The specialized nature of many police departments requires training programs peculiar to the individual department. Training relating to these specialized needs can best be met within the department—on the job—and are a responsibility of the police supervisor. Each department should develop a year-round training program to provide police officers with additional on-the-job training in the techniques of police operations and in the substantive content of the agency's programs. Each supervisor should plan such training as an integral part of the departmental operations. The training program is followed by more formal classroom training programs.

    1.4 *Advanced Technical Training.* Many activities performed within the community by police personnel require a technical competency of a professional or vocational nature. The specialized nature of many departments puts a particular imposition on the police officer. Training should normally be provided on departmental time as part of the employee developmental program. Courses may be offered by the department or agency, or through release time programs in colleges or universities, either on a full-time or part-time basis. Examples of such advanced technical training are new field techniques, the handling of newly acquired technology, changes in departmental procedures, and crime problem areas. Roll call training is one means now in use for accomplishing such training.

    1.5 *Planned Experience.* Police personnel development should include a planned series of organizational experiences to supplement formal training courses. This phase of the program is a responsibility of the chief administrator. As a part of personnel development programs, police departments should identify the principal duties of higher-level positions and develop line personnel by brief assignments to these duties. The whole police agency benefits from such planned experience. The policeman gains a new understanding of higher-level responsibilities and is better able to work with supervision and management. Managers and supervisors gain experience and confidence in delegating responsibility and often discover new capabilities in their subordinates.

Total personnel management

    2. Police personnel development should be coordinated into an over-all personnel program tailored to the general requirements of police officers and the specific requirements of each particular position in a department.

The objectives of performance appraisal and individual development planning are (1) to help each employee perform his present job more effectively, more easily, and with greater satisfaction and (2) to prepare for advancement promotion, job enlargement, and job change or transfer.

The important goal toward which these objectives are directed is to help the police agency insure the effective performance of every job. A second goal is to insure a reservoir of replacements for every job opening in the future. The performance appraisal process should identify what knowledge, abilities, and personal characteristics are required for the specific police positions. The supervisor, using the official job specification as his reference point, should identify with the employee his strengths and weaknesses. Furthermore, increasing efforts should be made in promotional examinations to reflect the outstanding concepts and materials contained in the prescribed training, education, and experience program for police personnel.

Departmental training policy

3. The police training policy should be sufficiently broad to include the previously proposed police training program.

Such a policy might read as follows: The police department has an obligation to its employees and to the people of the community to utilize and develop in full measure the talent and ability of each employee. Managerial and supervisory personnel are accountable for the development and utilization of human resources even as they are accountable for the execution of other administrative instructions, rules, and statutes. In training and development, the responsibility falls on:

3.1 *The Individual*—to himself and to the community for his own development.

3.2 *All Administrators and Supervisors*—to promote and encourage the development of each of their subordinates; to create a situation in which it is possible for police employees to develop themselves; and to provide the appropriate training, experience, and coaching made necessary by present and future job requirements.

3.3 *Departments*—for developing a climate which provides a continuing development process so that competent and industrious employees are available to fill higher-level vacancies as such vacancies occur. Agencies are also responsible for establishing a police supervisor's accountability for the training and development of persons he supervises.

3.4 *The City Personnel Department*—for providing assistance in: organizing for training, developing of line personnel (including administration of a program of interagency courses), securing training resources, setting standards, determining needs, securing and disseminating information on resources for specialized training, giving advice concerning current methods, and consulting with agencies on training and development problems.

3.5 *The City (County) Council and Manager*—to encourage and review departmental and interdepartmental activities which forward the training and development process of all local government personnel.

Record keeping

4. Individual records on training should be maintained by departments for those employees who participate in a development program.

The purpose of training records and reports is to allow police management and supervision to keep informed on the progress of employee development. Individual records on developmental activities of police officers make it possible for management to determine if an individual policeman is completing the appropriate training. This knowledge aids in the evaluation of training and in the selection of police employees for promotion and special assignments and gives an annual summary of police personnel development activities. The mechanics of maintaining personnel development records are not difficult. Individual records should include in-service and other courses taken, as well as any planned special assignments made for the specific purpose of development. Significantly, the experience of agencies using individual development records shows that records are not kept up to date unless used regularly by management and supervision. Unless kept up to date, the records are of little use to anyone. Reviewing the employee development records every time a man is considered for promotion or reassignment will make these records a valuable tool and, incidentally, add a great deal of emphasis and prestige to the whole development program.

Tuition refund for specialized out-service police training

5. Tuition refund for police training should be expanded to allow the employee to participate in out-service programs.

Out-service police training courses presented by colleges, universities, and professional associations provide opportunities for policemen to fill individual needs not met by in-service programs. Business and industry use these out-service resources extensively and their use is increasing. This author predicts the day will come when police science and criminology schools around the country will be conducting regular seminars, directed at policemen, with the same regularity with which classes are now being offered to undergraduate and graduate students in other fields. Besides offering training not available through in-service programs, these out-service courses allow police personnel to associate with other criminal justice members. This association results in a broader viewpoint of the over-all criminal justice system. Assignments to out-service courses should be limited to needs which cannot be met by in-service programs.

Training facility

6. Interagency regional training facilities are required for police training.

The learning process must be carried on in surroundings conducive to maximum effect. The adverse effects of poor lighting, poor ventilation, and crowded conditions on learning are well known. Equally important is the requirement that the facility be suitable and appropriate to the training. Police training is no exception. There is no better way to indicate to the trainee the importance of his training than to provide proper and adequate facilities for his learning. While the initial budgeting of funds for regional facilities might be difficult, economy of scale and strength of classroom offerings can be vastly enhanced.

Evaluation

7. Regular evaluation of police training programs should be made by the department and by the city personnel department.

Quite naturally, training and education should relate to the needs of the employee's department and thereby broaden his knowledge and increase his professional skills. Too few training and development programs are based on these kinds of criteria.

Financing

8. Police training programs should be adequately financed and include provisions for an adequate staff. Also, funds should be provided for police departments to contract for training consultants.

Adequate resources and supervisory manpower should be supplied by the departments to carry out the police training program. This author draws attention to five areas that will need such assistance if the program is to be implemented.

8.1 Large police departments should have a training officer to develop and coordinate departmental programs.

8.2 The police department should increase the amount of money allotted for training.

8.3 The practice of hiring consultants from the universities, management consultant firms, or private industry has proven its usefulness in police work as it has in industry and in the federal government. The author therefore suggests that a standard for consultant appropriations be established so that a department can plan its police training programs and budgets appropriately. This suggestion does not negate the policy that agencies are responsible for doing their own training, but does recognize that occasional assistance is needed from specialists in academic or other fields.

TRAINING AND EDUCATION INCENTIVE PROGRAMS

> In addition to requiring higher educational standards for such advanced positions, all departments should provide pay incentives for college education. For example, a pay increase could be provided for each year of college education completed, with a substantial increase for personnel completing the work required for a degree.[6]

This section is included with due recognition and respect for built-in training and educational incentives provided police personnel. To put it another way, good programs of training and personnel development without formal organizational incentive to participate have minimal, if any, impact upon an officer's behavior. One might look at the "push" for greater and better training as vitally in need of an organizational "pull." California's Commission on Peace Officers Standards and Training (POST) has a recommended program of action which furnishes the all important pull. As one might suspect, POST linked education to pay. Their recommended program is as follows:

1. Must possess the POST Basic Certificate to qualify for the final step in the pay scale for police officer, deputy sheriff, or higher ranks.
2. Possession of POST Intermediate Certificate shall qualify the officer for a 5 per cent pay increase.
3. Possession of POST Advanced Certificate shall qualify the officer for a 10 per cent increase.
4. To remain eligible to receive the incentive program pay increase, the applicant must requalify each year by completing no less than 50 hours of education or training which would be recognized by POST as courses credited toward intermediate or advanced certificate or by completing a project approved by the department head. All education, training, or projects approved under this section (annual qualification) shall be completed on the officer's own time unless otherwise approved by the department head.

   For the purpose of annual qualification, the department head may specify and approve credit courses other than those recognized by POST when, in his judgment, the course has added to the professional development of the training or education specified.

Note that the above program requires an officer to engage in educational activities on an annual basis. The police department of San Carlos, California offers one illustration of an educational incentive program (the pay

---

[6] *Task Force Report: The Police*, The President's Commission on Law Enforcement and Administration of Justice (Washington, D.C.: U.S. Government Printing Office, 1967), pp. 140–41.

scale given here is as of 1969 and probably has increased by 5 per cent annually over the quoted figures). To begin, all newly hired policemen must have one year of college and start at a salary of $666 a month. After climbing the five salary steps common to most departments and reaching a salary of $810 a month, the patrolman can go two steps higher if he continues his education. The sixth step, which requires completion of two years of college, pays $851 a month. To reach the seventh and top step of $894 a month, the officer must take three units of additional college work (usually 45–50 classroom hours) or its equivalent in department approved research or training. To continue in the top bracket, he must fulfill the same requirement for study every year. Interestingly, this department has had no difficulty attracting applicants who meet the one-year college requirement. There are no vacancies in the department at the time of this writing. All 29 uniformed officers have had some college. Nine hold an associate of arts degree from a junior college and three have bachelor's degrees.

The police department of Culver City, California has gone one step further in providing educational incentives. Besides connecting pay to education, they have also included promotion. The President's Crime Commission alluded to the benefits of such a relationship when they stated:

> Few departments today provide sufficient encouragement for personnel to return to school. For example, the fact that an officer has an advanced degree does not, in most cases, qualify the officer for a pay increment and is not normally one of the factors considered in promotions. A department should provide these additional incentives to encourage officers to advance their education.[7]

Since the Culver City education incentive program reflects many of those now or soon to be in existence (the Culver City Police Department reports that 40 city police departments in California currently have some form of educational incentive program), we will look at it in more detail.

In mid-1968 the Culver City Police Department (CCPD) presented to their city council a career development program entitled "Building for the Future."[8] In the recommendations, the incentive for education is developed within the patrolman and supervisory levels. The mandate for educational achievement is instituted at the recruitment level. By this process, incentive and aspiration for promotion inspires voluntary personal upgrading by the incumbents, bringing immediate benefits; and the higher educational requirements at recruitment levels assures eventual evolvement into an era when all personnel will possess a degree. At last, the officer who thought enough of the job to better equip himself for it is compensated for his efforts.

---

[7] *Ibid.*, p. 140.

[8] Culver City Police Department, "Building for the Future," paper presented to the city council and chief administrative officer, Culver City, California, August 20, 1968.

Method for Phasing into the Program

The program recommended is designed in phases to allow incumbents sufficient time to acquire the necessary educational credits needed for promotion. Failure on an incumbent's part to upgrade his education keeps him in the lower pay bracket and eventually prohibits his advancement. Active participation by the incumbent enables him to become a better officer and gain even more advantage from his years of dedicated service. The area of incentive covered by a 5 per cent education incentive award establishes what is commonly referred to as the "grandfather clause." This clause provides coverage for an incumbent's present scholastic achievement and longevity (experience); however, it limits the use of years of experience until the incumbent meets the requirements of a 10 per cent education incentive award. Conversely, the newer officers, while meeting higher educational requirements in the 5 per cent education incentive award area, must gain commensurate experience before being eligible for a 10 per cent award. See Table 26 and Figure 20 for details. Table 26 depicts the direct link

TABLE 26: MONETARY INCENTIVE FOR EDUCATION

Five per cent Award					
Prior to Jan. 1, '49	Jan. 1, '49 to Jan. 1, '54	Jan. 1, '54 to Jan. 1, '59	Jan. 1, '59 to Jan. 1, '64	Jan. 1, '64 to Jan. 1, '69	After Jan. 1, '69
20 E	15 E	10 E	5 E	3 E	2 E
0 P	10 P	20 P	30 P	45 P	AA, BAC
PB	PB	PB	PB	PI	PI

Ten per cent Award		
Prior to Jan. 1, '59	Jan. 1, '59 to Jan. 1, '66	After Jan. 1, '66
10 E	5 E	3 E
AA	90 P	BAC
PA	PI	PI

KEY: E   —Years of approved Experience
       P   —Training and education Points
       PB —POST Basic Certificate (200 hours of recruit level training)
       PI   —POST Intermediate Certificate
       PA —POST Advanced Certificate
       BAC—Baccalaureate degree
       AA —Associate of Arts degree or 60 units at college or university

Source: Culver City Police Department, "Building for the Future." Paper presented to the City Council and Chief Administrative Officer, Culver City, California, August 20, 1968.

	1969	1970	1971	1972	1973	1974	1975	1976	1977	1978	1979
Chief	BAC. or P.A. →					BAC. →					
Assistant Chief	BAC. or P.A. →						BAC. →				
Captain	BAC. or P.A. →							BAC. →			
Lieutenant	H.S.	30 U or P.I.	45 U or P.I.	A.A. or P.A.	A.A.+ 15 U or P.A.	A.A.+ 30 U or P.A.	A.A.+ 45 U or P.A.	BAC. or P.A.	BAC. →		
Sergeant	H.S.	15 U or P.I.	30 U or P.I.	45 U or P.I.	A.A. or. P.A.	A.A.+ 15 U or P.A.	A.A.+ 30 U or P.A.	A.A.+ 45 U or P.A.	BAC. or P.A.	BAC. or P.A.	BAC.
Agent	Same As Sgt. →										
Policeman	H.S.* or A.A.** →										
Community Service Aide	*** H.S. →										

KEY: *BAC* Baccalaureate degree.
      AA Associate of Arts degree or 60 units at college or university.
      HS High school graduation.
      PA POST Advanced Certificate.
      PI POST Intermediate Certificate.
      U Accredited college semester units.
      * Must attain A.A. degree within 4 years or become Y-rated.
      ** Starts at second pay step.
      *** Must maintain 12 college semester units per semester.

Source: Culver City Police Department, "Building for the Future." Paper presented to the City Council and Chief Administrative Office, Culver City, California, August 20, 1968, p. 24.

FIGURE 20: EDUCATIONAL REQUIREMENTS FOR PROMOTION

between education and pay incentives. Figure 20 expresses present and future educational requirements in terms of promotional incentives. Further, in Figure 20 one can see how the CCPD proposes to implement the President's Crime Commission recommendations regarding community service aides and police agents. Briefly, this program (the Community Service Aide Program) promotes the concept of cadet status prior to permanent appointment. It is proposed that the "aide" be unarmed, although in a distinctive uniform, and be required to perform only the less hazardous police tasks.

Certain educational standards, outlined in the program, must be met by the aide, and performance capabilities must be manifestly displayed before permanent appointment is granted.

The Police Agent Program is designed to answer the need for recognition of superior performance of a consistent nature. The designation of Police Agent provides an officer additional monetary compensation as well as increased status. The selection of officers for this title would be based on educational achievement combined with proven ability and consistent contribution of accepted value. Such a scheme allows a latitude of rewards for individuals who fail to advance through the promotional process but are, nonetheless, excellent officers.

Requirements: Experience and Education

POST, as well as many other agencies similar to it in other states, has established a certification program under which appropriate awards are given to peace officers based on a combination of experience and education. Two of these certificates, Intermediate and Advanced, have been mentioned already. (The Basic Certificate is awarded for 200 or more hours of extra level training.) Based on the minimum amount of education and training points needed for qualification, and disregarding the value of the experience factor, the requirements, as listed shortly, indicate that the POST Advanced Certificate is most nearly equivalent to educational achievement represented by two years of college.

The intermediate certificate. The CCPD police officer:

1. Shall possess or be eligible to possess a Basic Certificate.
2. Shall have acquired the following combinations of education and training points combined with the prescribed years of law enforcement experience (education and training points are given—one for each semester unit from an accredited college, or one for every 20 hours of approved classroom training):

Education and Training Points and	30	60	90	Baccalaureate Degree
Years of Law Enforcement Experience	8	6	4	2

The advanced certificate. The CCPD police officer:

1. Shall possess or be eligible to possess the Intermediate Certificate.
2. Shall have acquired either the following combinations of education and training points combined with the prescribed years of law enforcement experience or the college degree designated combined with the prescribed years of law enforcement experience:

Education and Training Points	60	90	Baccalaureate Degree	Masters Degree or Equivalent
and Years of Law Enforcement Experience	12	9	6	4

Education and Training Qualifications

Qualification for the CCPD incentive program is determined by a combination of education or training and experience. A point system is used to establish and maintain eligibility in this program. The points are accrued in the following manner:

1. One college unit equals one point.
2. Twenty classroom hours of police training equals one point.
3. Experience is acquired as a police officer for the CCPD unless other law enforcement experience is determined by Board to be of equal or proportional value. The "Board" is explained in the first item of the section on general provisions.
4. Use of any credits acquired from Basic Training courses is not valid until at least 30 credits in approved college courses are first obtained, at which time the Basic Training credits can be added.
5. Courses necessary for a degree in police science, police administration, criminology, public administration, law, or sociology are considered approved courses. (The author suggests that other courses and majors such as psychology and history also be acceptable.)
6. All sworn personnel of the CCPD are eligible to apply for an award. (The author recommends that some civilian positions, such as dispatchers, also be eligible for incentive awards.)

Maintenance of Incentive Increment

After meeting the requirements for the percentage increases for the 5 per cent and 10 per cent awards, to maintain this percentage increase the officer must complete at least 65 hours of approved study or training during the calendar year preceding each annual application.

1. The CCPD may from time to time schedule approved in-service training or study (not to include departmental firearms training) that will apply toward the 65 hours of required study, providing it is conducted on the officer's off-duty time.
2. One 3-unit college course, or the accumulation of 65 hours by any combination of training, teaching, or public speaking activities approved by the Board, will satisfy the requirements for 65 hours.

3. Officers can take courses in accredited public or private schools, colleges or universities, which are undertaken to improve their efficiency, knowledge, or competency in the performance of their duties or are necessary to obtain a degree in an approved field.
4. Officers who wish to enroll in an outside school, college, or university must submit for approval (in advance of enrollment) a report to the Board listing the name of the school, the subject, the number of credits or hours, the name of the instructor, and the class schedule.
5. Officers attending outside schools are required to complete the selected course of study with a grade of at least "C." If, for departmental reasons, an officer is unable to complete a semester, credit may be granted to the point of completion.
6. Approved outside seminars, lectures, workshops, and similar educational meetings may be designated by the Board.
7. Officers may secure credit for awards by teaching without compensation in a departmental or accredited law enforcement training school.
8. Officers who wish to teach or to make public appearances must submit, in advance, an acceptable outline of their material to the Board.
9. As much as 3 hours of credit may be granted for each hour spent in teaching or public speaking, depending upon the amount of preparation time necessary for the assignment. When the same material is presented on successive occasions and advance preparation is not required, credit is given only for the time needed to complete the assignment.
10. Research projects may be undertaken with advance approval of the chief of police. Approval to conduct a project depends on the current departmental need for the project and the potential benefit to be derived by the CCPD, the city government, or law enforcement in general. Credit time for officers' projects are discussed on an individual basis at the time of approval.
11. Officers' projects must be submitted in writing to the Board and shall include a statement of: objective; scope; estimated time and cost; and value to the CCPD, city government, or law enforcement.
12. Officers are required to file an acceptable final report on all projects.
13. The Board may determine other circumstances wherein persons would be eligible for an award.

General Provisions

1. A police Education and Training Evaluation Board comprised of personnel selected by the chief administrative officer is established to determine standards of acceptance for study and training.
2. Acceptability of each course of study, training, or project must be determined by the Board in advance of participation, if credit is requested.
3. An officer who wishes to take a course in a public school, institute, college, or university, or who undertakes a special project to fulfill the training requirement, must do so on his own time.

4. Any education or training, except Basic Academy (which is attended on duty with expenses paid for by the city), does not count toward the maintaining of, or gaining eligibility for, the pay percentage in the officer's particular classification. In the case of a city-sponsored program, where some officers attend on their own time and some attend on duty time, those attending on duty time do not receive credit for the program for maintaining their percentage.

5. Routine refresher courses, such as firearms, are not approved for award credit.

6. All time spent in preparation for awards is off-duty time, of no cost to the city, and not compensated for by any other agency. (There are a few agencies that also provide tuition funds for attending, plus the awards.)

7. Candidates do not receive compensable time for any part of a class used to fulfill all or part of the requirements for the award classification.

8. An officer who wishes to attend an approved training course, make a personal appearance, undertake a special project, or teach during regular duty hours to qualify for the award may do so by arranging with his supervisor to be relieved from duty so that the activity is performed on his own time. The time is deducted from accumulated overtime.

9. Expenses and assistance may be granted in unusual cases involving award project work and public appearances outside the greater metropolitan area, if warranted and with the advance approval of the Board.

10. Normal expenses, such as travel, parking, registration fees, and meals, are not provided if the training, teaching, public appearance activity, or special project is undertaken to qualify for an award.

11. Candidates who desire information on activities not covered by the above set of regulations are invited to discuss the subject with the CCPD training officer.

To summarize, the CCPD has designed an educational incentive program that affects the officer from the moment of induction into the police service and throughout his career with the department. Consideration is given to those who have voluntarily submitted to educational improvement in the past by supplying a percentage increase to their salary, commensurate with individual achievement. The benefit, however, cannot be automatically obtained by the individual merely by the accumulation of unrelated college credits or by longevity. Controls are devised to maintain quality of performance and studies. These controls extend beyond the acquisition of college degrees and require continued studies each year, in order for the recipient of the educational increment to retain the benefit. With this program, provisions are made for the recruit who enters the service already armed with a degree or a sizable number of credits. In addition, measures must be established to safeguard against the recruit who enters the police service and fails to maintain scholastic standards. Provisions for such contingencies basically require revisions in employment announcements. In essence, the crux of the entire program is the department's endeavor to effect educational upgrading. Naturally, to inaugurate this whole plan, all levels of the structure must be altered. At the lower level, the Community Service Aide Program is suggested; at the intermediate stage, the Police Agent Program is recommended; and at the upper stages (supervisory and managerial levels), new promotional requirements are needed.

STATEWIDE COMPREHENSIVE CRIMINAL JUSTICE PLANNING ON EDUCATION AND TRAINING

The 1969 California Statewide Comprehensive Plan for action programs to be funded by the Law Enforcement Assistance Administration provides an indication of the direction to be taken by at least one state.[9] The comprehensive plan brought together the findings and recommendations of numerous task forces in 11 regions. The output was voluminous—24 books with a total of 5896 pages. Further, it was the result of the work of more than 1500 local law makers, city and county officials, law enforcement personnel, and community representatives.

Of relevance here is that one of eight major subject categories is education and training. Since the comprehensive plan will serve as a guideline and stimulus in the area of education and training in criminal justice, its recommended goals, objectives, and priorities for education and training are contained in the following paragraphs.

First, the members of the State Task Force on Education and Training expressed two primary goals which they would constantly strive to meet.[10]

1. To determine in a broad sense the manpower needs and the education and training needs of personnel throughout the criminal justice system and to develop suggested priorities for action programs and projects designed to meet these needs.
2. To assist all state task forces and committees in providing a meaningful training and information system in conjunction with the California Council of Criminal Justice (CCCJ) and to study and report upon such special subjects as may be referred to it by the CCCJ. (The CCCJ is a 25-member statewide planning agency comprised of eight task forces: (1) education and training, (2) police services, (3) judicial process, (4) corrections, (5) juvenile delinquency, (6) narcotics, drugs, and alcoholic abuse, (7) organized crime, and (8) riots and disorders.)

Second, the comprehensive state plan for education and training has the following specific objectives.

---

[9] California Council on Criminal Justice, *Statewide Comprehensive Plan: Plan for Action*, vol. 2 (Sacramento: California Council on Criminal Justice, 1969).

[10] *Ibid.*, pp. 444–46.

1. To encourage quantitative and qualitative studies and research necessary to provide, on a continuing basis, comprehensive data on manpower needs for all elements of the criminal justice system.
2. To solicit and review information from all interested agencies, organizations, and units of local government to determine the immediate and long-range educational training needs of personnel throughout the criminal justice system and to make recommendations for fulfilling these needs.
3. To encourage educational programs designed to develop broad citizen support for a responsive, efficient, and progressive criminal justice system.
4. To encourage the establishment and continuation of programs in elementary and secondary schools to develop student understanding and support of agencies involved in the criminal justice system.
5. To cooperate with other task forces and committees in furthering the basic purposes of the CCCJ.
6. To encourage innovation and experimentation in methods and techniques of education and training particularly suited to the field of criminal justice.
7. To develop and disseminate modern training policies and to encourage their adoption by state and local government.
8. To develop continuing priorities for programs designed to carry out the education and training element of the state plan.

Third, the CCCJ has given the following 15 items funding priority.

1. A project designed to determine in depth and in minute detail the roles and tasks of personnel in the criminal justice system, commencing as a first priority with the police officer in today's society and the identification of a model in police education and training.
2. An itinerant team of well-qualified persons to conduct one-day institutes to inform local government officials about existing and changing criminal justice practices. To develop support for local criminal justice agencies, it is essential that local policy officials be fully informed as to modern and efficient practices in the areas where they have a responsibility for decision making. Attendance at the institutes (held in perhaps as many as 15 to 20 locations in the state) would be stimulated to the point where it would be possible to reach 1500 or as many as 3000 policy-making officials.
3. Study of the feasibility of establishing regional training centers for personnel in the criminal justice system.
4. A summer institute to train coordinators and teachers now involved in teaching courses to personnel in the criminal justice system.
5. The organization of education and training programs to improve the competency of regular and special criminal justice units in the prevention, detection, and control of riots and other civil disorders.
6. Full participation by cities and counties in the present and future programs prescribed by the Commission on Peace Officer Standards and Training.
7. Expansion of the peace officer standards and training concept to other elements of the criminal justice system.

8. The interchange of personnel among federal, state, and local criminal justice functions in an effort to develop greater understanding and comprehension of the total criminal justice system.

9. Education and training for all criminal justice personnel in the aspects of societal needs and special education and training for leaders in each discipline.

10. Adult as well as elementary and secondary school public education programs designed to develop support for a responsive, efficient, and progressive criminal justice system, including crime prevention and encouraging respect for law and order, looking toward public understanding of and cooperation with criminal justice agencies.

11. The establishment of Area Training Resource Centers to develop, produce, and maintain training aids such as films, tapes, overlays, electronic aids, and related visual aids and devices pertaining to the administration of criminal justice. Such aids will be made available to educational institutions and criminal justice agencies involved in training.

12. Improvement of the quality of criminal justice instructor training by (1) attendance at Area Training Resource Centers to develop new teaching techniques and to renew teaching enthusiasm and (2) establishing in-service workshops to provide new and innovative programs among training instructors and coordinators in the criminal justice system.

13. The development of administrative and staffing policies and patterns to insure a full complement of operational personnel, in recognition of the fact that a measurable percentage of criminal justice system personnel are always in training status and thus unavailable for normal operational assignments.

14. The development of training opportunities for criminal justice personnel to acquaint them with the special characteristics of adolescents, particularly those of social, racial, and other specific groups with which they are likely to come in contact.

15. The training and employment of paraprofessional aides, including police community service officers, to provide assistance in the broadest possible number of criminal justice agencies.

SUMMARY

General education is used here as a term denoting educational experience for living, for understanding, and for satisfying man's desire for knowledge. General education must provide man with a background for further educational growth so that he can develop as a self-directing individual and prepare for the on-going continuum of life, personal and organizational. This growth is accomplished by developing the qualities of reasoning and critical inquiry while providing the individual with a broad understanding of himself and the world about him.

The need is apparent to the astute and concerned observer that the present-day police officer be prepared to encounter extraordinary events. The alert citizen perceives; the policeman anticipates; the victim employs hindsight; the legislator concurs that we can no longer accept an outmoded concept of the police officer. Because of this awareness educational programs and priorities are submitted as a declaration that our local law enforcement agencies, after critical self-evaluation, must again exercise their ability and flexibility to respond to the demands of the citizenry. The population is entitled to more than just adequate police protection, it must receive superior service. Supervision, rank and file, and cooperative outside agencies can contribute to establish programs which undoubtedly could provide superior police service. This chapter was prepared for those responsible to pick up the gauntlet and face the social issues and ills of our day.

PROBLEMS

1. Identify a police training need. From the need develop an effective program for fulfilling it. Be certain to include training goals, strategies, means for evaluating the results, and so on.

2. Write two or three paragraphs on why training in the police service is growing in importance.

3. Write two or three paragraphs on what you see in store for police training at the end of five and ten years.

THE
FUTURE

part four

Introduction

It may seem strange to elevate a single chapter to the level of a "part" of this book. But it seemed most urgent to take a brief venture into the future. In doing so, we are provided with a reason for asking some highly important questions as to benefits and problems connected with certain anticipated changes. Further, we are furnished a look at the future role of the police supervisor during the next few years. The reader will be quick to recognize that more than the supervisory role or organizational changes are previewed. The vehicle for arriving at given points, products, or policies is emphasized. This vehicle has a "dual engine"—change and innovation. Consequently, our concern in the following chapter is with both the process itself and the end results. Our focus is naturally on the police supervisor: the challenge of change is growing more intense to him and his organization each day.

There is no need to elaborate on the urgency and importance of planned organizational changes. All of us feel a need for a basic understanding of the critical changes taking place in our society; we need this understanding at a philosophical level as well as at the level of technical solutions. In a brilliant article titled "Revolution and Counterrevolution," Brzezinski has analyzed some of the underlying elements of our current unstable environment:

> A revolutionary situation typically arises when values of a society are undergoing a profound change. The crisis in values in its turn is linked to profound socioeconomic changes, both accelerating them and reacting to them. For example, the transition from an agrarian to an industrial society produced very basic changes in outlook, both on the part of the elites ruling the changing societies and also of the social forces transformed by the changes and produced by them. Similarly, it can be argued that today in America the industrial era is coming to an end and America is becoming a technetronic society, that is a society in which technology, especially electronic communications and computers, is prompting basic social changes.[1]

---

[1] Zbigniew Brzezinski, "Revolution and Counterrevolution," *The New Republic*, 33 (June 1, 1968), 23–25.

This new era automatically produces a profound shift in prevailing social and organizational values. Quite obviously the police are swept up in the process. Granted, we may be on our way to a technetronic society; however, our major problems and solutions in such a futuristic society are not technical but social. The formal organization, in our case the police organization, with its human components will play a prominent part in bringing about needed and planned change. For it is clear that

> ... decisions about change in any enterprise often depend on the attitudes of the existing role holders, and in a settled stable task system their attitudes are likely to be resistant: "it will last my lifetime" is perhaps a more prevalent attitude than is sometimes thought. The difficulty is that, even if it does, their successors are likely to inherit a bankrupt enterprise; more frequently, however, it fails to last, with consequent conflict, compromise, and chaos.[2]

In summary, our subject is twofold: (1) what the future holds for the police supervisor and (2) his emerging role as an agent of change.

---

[2] E. J. Miller and A. K. Rice, *Systems of Organization: The Control of Task and Sentient Boundaries* (New York: Tavistock Publications, Ltd., 1967), p. 258.

15

The Police Supervisor
and the Future:
Innovation and Change

The most noticeable fact about modern society—the root fact necessary to comprehend so many other confusing aspects which distinguish our times from the past—is the "change of scale" in our lives. Urbanization, the population explosion, the accelerated pace of our activities, the constant input of new ideas, new knowledge, new values—all are changing continually. The simple and crucial result for the individual is that he no longer will be able to live in the same world his parents and grandparents inhabited. The complex and crucial result for the police organization is that it must live with a constantly and rapidly changing environment. For centuries formal organizations retraced their steps, were initiated into stable and ritualized routines, and maintained a basic familiarity with their environment. Today, not only is there a radical rupture with the past, but an organization must necessarily be structured and trained for an unknown future. Furthermore, our organizations are leaving old anchorages, are no longer following traditional ways, and are constantly faced with the problem of choice, with no authoritative standards or social values to guide them.

Many converging strands of thought, philosophical and practical, suggest that police organizations have entered a new period in human history, one unlike any in the million years or more of the man-environment relationship. The result is a fundamental change in the police-environment relationship. Regardless of whether the police have changed, their environment has changed and is changing. Moreover, a changing environment and a changing organization (or even one that resists change) causes problems of no small consequence for the organization's members. In Part One we discussed some of the dimensions of individual and group change. Organizational change is even more perplexing and difficult. The supervisor either does or should see to it that needed individual change does occur. He can do this simply by fulfilling his role as a controller and developer of human resources. This role is accomplished more on an interpersonal and group basis. On an organizational basis, however, the police supervisor has to accept an additional component to his already complex role, that of an agent of change. This role automatically makes him responsible for thinking and acting in an innovative manner.

This chapter covers, in the following order, (1) police problems and proposals for change, (2) strategies for effecting organizational change, (3) tomorrow's police supervision.

THE POLICE:
PROBLEMS AND PROPOSALS FOR CHANGE

> Bureaucratic structures are designed to do programmable things in a stable, predictable environment. More and more, programmable things can be mechanized and automated. More and more, the environment is unstable and rapidly changing. The present need is for modes of organization which permit rapid adaptation to changing circumstances; the search is for ways in which people can organize for innovative, unprogrammable activities. The main point [here] is that a more humanistic organization theory than we have known in the past is required, and that it is realizable in practice.[1]

Change for the police is complicated by the fact that, at least in large cities, the police department is an organization with at least two primary goals, one of which causes conflict and the other of which cannot be attained.[2] The dilemmas confronting police administrators stem from their inability to obtain agreement on what constitutes satisfactory performance of the first objective and their difficulty in locating a strategy which would allow the realization of the (agreed-upon) second objective. (There are, as mentioned in an earlier chapter, additional objectives which a police organization serves, providing certain nonpolice services and handling large-scale disorders, for example.) James Q. Wilson refers to the first goal as *order maintenance:* the handling of disputes, between persons who disagree over what is right or over who is to blame for what is wrong (for example, the family quarrel, the noisy drunk, the tavern brawl, a street disturbance by teenagers, and so on). The second goal he cites is *law enforcement:* the application of legal sanctions, normally an arrest, to persons who injure or deprive innocent victims (for example by burglary, purse snatching, mugging, robbery, or auto theft). In this case, the police task is either to arrest or to deter the criminal. The problem is that the officer lacks the means—the

---

[1] Herbert A. Shepard, "Changing Interpersonal and Intergroup Relationships in Organizations," in *Handbook of Organizations*, ed. James G. March (Chicago, Ill.: Rand McNally & Company, 1965), pp. 1141–42.

[2] James Q. Wilson, "Dilemmas of Police Administration," *Public Administration Review*, 28 (September–October 1968), 407.

information, primarily—to arrest or deter more than a very small percentage of all criminals.[3]

Public apathy over these two goals has ended because violence and crime, urban riots, and charges of harassment and brutality in the ghetto have increased public concern about the role of our local police. Neither the general public nor the researcher in urban affairs now views the police as unimportant governmental instruments whose policies and procedures can be ignored as long as they are efficient in meeting law enforcement goals.

As a result of this heightened concern about the police role, local law enforcement officials have been the object of increasing attention from academic researchers and of close scrutiny by official government commissions. The purposes and conclusions of these two types of investigators have been quite different. The academic studies depict how the police behave and analyze why they behave as they do. Generally, these studies review a number of areas in which improvements might be attempted but do not evaluate specific plans for change. In fact, most often their conclusions tend to be pessimistic with regard to the prospects for significant change. Jameson Doig reflects such a defeatist attitude when he writes:

> To identify a reasonable proposal for innovation is one thing; to implement it is quite another. Like most bureaucracies, police organizations are largely composed of members who prefer to maintain familiar habits of thought and practice in the face of demands for change. In fact, the police in the United States may be more resistant to innovation than most other organizations, because of the fragmentation of policing into separate local departments, closed systems of recruitment and promotion, and an unusual degree of general isolation from the broader public.[4]

This author takes an opposite position, however. I firmly believe that local police departments, compared with other local government agencies, are more amenable to change. Witness the computer, for one example. Our local law enforcement agencies are, in nearly every instance, welcoming its arrival. Resistance can be found quite frequently in other functional areas of local government. In fact, it can be stated that our local police are more innovative than other agencies when it comes to the use of new technology. In terms of attitudinal and organizational changes, granted the police are not in line for any gold stars. But, then again, neither are such departments as planning, personnel, fire, recreation, social welfare, education, and so forth.

In contrast, the government studies are directed toward change. While

---

[3] For greater coverage on this subject see *ibid.*, pp. 407–17.

[4] Jameson W. Doig, "Police Problems, Proposals, and Strategies for Change," *Public Administration Review*, 28 (September–October 1968), 396.

recognizing the conflicts in public expectations and other difficulties that plague local law enforcement, these studies provide specific proposals to remedy these problems. Among the government studies of police problems, the most prominent are those of two presidential commissions—the President's Crime Commission (1967) and the President's Riot Commission (1968). The recommended changes can be found in their respective reports.[5] In addition to these reports are numerous national and statewide planning documents, either emanating from the Law Enforcement Assistance Administration, United States Department of Justice, or supported by their funds.[6] All include recommended changes which vary from increased salaries through more education and training to automated command force control systems. One of the difficulties resulting from this heavy outpouring of policy studies and proposals has been the problem of selecting the most important recommendations, evaluating the feasibility and probable impact of the various suggestions, and determining how the proposals can be put into effect. Again, we find skepticism on the part of many over the possibilities of anything more than marginal changes. James Q. Wilson, for one, believes that the more wide-scale changes will be few in number.[7] Again, I am reluctant to accept this thinking. In fact, I am willing to go out on an academic limb and predict that local law enforcement will not only accept but initiate many comprehensive and profound changes in their role.

Briefly, what has been said thus far is: (1) the police are, in most instances, change oriented and (2) the critical question, therefore, becomes not "Will they change?" but "How can such proposals be carefully evaluated in terms of their impact on the urban environment and the police department so that those which will produce significant net benefits can be segregated from those which will merely create more problems" and "How can the more worthwhile proposals be implemented?"

The objective of the following section is to comment on the new strategies likely to be successful in bringing about change, especially in the structure and functions of the police departments of our larger cities. The discussion emphasizes the police organization and its supervisors, although it may have wider relevance to problems of evaluating and implementing change in a complex urbanized society.

---

[5] See *The Challenge of Crime in a Free Society*, A Report by the President's Commission on Law Enforcement and Administration of Justice (Washington, D.C.: U.S. Government Printing Office, 1967), and *Report of the National Advisory Commission on Civil Disorders* (Washington, D.C.: U.S. Government Printing Office, 1968).

[6] For two examples, see Institute for Defense Analyses, *A National Program of Research Development, Test, and Evaluation on Law Enforcement and Criminal Justice*, prepared for Law Enforcement Assistance Administration, U.S. Department of Justice (Washington, D.C.: U.S. Government Printing Office, 1968); and California Council on Criminal Justice, *Plan for: Action! Statewide Comprehensive Plan* (Sacramento: California Council on Criminal Justice, 1969).

[7] James Q. Wilson, "Dilemmas," 407–16.

STRATEGIES FOR EFFECTING ORGANIZATIONAL CHANGE

Every organization, whether growing or not, is periodically faced with the necessity of bringing about some fundamental changes in the behavior of its members if it is to stay effectively related to its changing environment. Various research studies on effecting desired behavior changes in organizations have emphasized the importance of using both structural modification and education. The educational approach gives people a chance to become familiar with the proposed change, to comprehend the reasons behind it, possibly to contribute to its design, and to test out behaving in new and different ways. The structural approach sets up mechanisms that serve to reward the desired behavior and punish conduct that is no longer approved. Both approaches are based on well-established learning theories, and each can serve to strengthen the other. The findings of the present research, however, can provide some guides to the sequence and emphasis that might be given these two approaches.[8]

There will be a few readers, especially those now in supervisory roles, that approach this section with the thinking "Hey! Why talk about organizational change? There isn't anything I can do to change the way things are run around my department." My response to this thinking is "You are wrong!" The police supervisor can be, that is, if he wants to be, an agent of change. This text strongly recommends that he accept this role. Consequently, a profile of the future role of the police supervisor should look as follows:

1. organizational control
2. training
3. administrative detail
4. procedural development
5. organizational perspective
6. performance appraisal
7. formal, informal, and personal communication
8. organizational responsibility
9. safety awareness
10. community relations
11. employee morale
12. support-subordinate
13. interaction facilitation
14. goal emphasis
15. work facilitation
16. change agent

---

[8] Paul R. Lawrence and Jay W. Lorsch, *Organization and Environment: Managing Differentiation and Integration* (Boston, Mass.: Graduate School of Business Administration, Harvard University, 1967), p. 232.

There is ample literature on planned organizational change.[9] Moreover, this body of literature is growing at a very fast pace. A recent writing by Harold Leavitt provides us with a highly useful way of viewing change in an organization.[10] According to Leavitt, organizations are complex systems in which at least four interacting variables loom very large: task variables, structural variables, technological variables, and human variables. To this list of four, we should add another, environmental variables. These five are highly interdependent; change in any one usually results in compensatory (or retaliatory) change in others. It should be kept in mind that the aim may be to change one as an end in itself or as a mechanism for effecting changes in one or more of the others. In most instances, efforts to effect change are ultimately designed to influence the task variable.

If one takes such a view, he can go on to categorize major applied approaches to organizational change by using three of the same variables: structural approaches to change, technological approaches, and personal approaches. In discussing organizational change, we focus on the most difficult factor of all to change—the human variable. While doing so we must not compound an error already prevalent in dealing with problems of organizational change. Briefly stated, this error results from a disregard of the systemic properties of the organization and a confusion of individual change with modifications in other organizational variables. To illustrate, look at the systemic changes that occur with the introduction of new technological tools such as computers. The arrival of a computer may cause changes in structure (for example, in the communication system or decision network of the organization), changes in personnel (their numbers, skills, attitudes, and roles), and changes in performance, or even definition, of tasks, since some tasks may become feasible for the first time and others may become unnecessary. Changes in the human and task variables could, comparably, filter through the system to generate similar changes in other variables.

As mentioned previously, we concentrate on the individual's relation to organizational change. First, it should be recognized that considerable confusion exists in this particular area. The confusion between individual and organizational change is due mainly to the lack of precise terminology for distinguishing between behavior determined largely by structured roles

---

[9] Perhaps the most comprehensive treatment on the subject of planned change is the book of readings by Warren G. Bennis, Kenneth D. Benne, and Robert Chin, eds., *The Planning of Change* (New York: Holt, Rinehart, and Winston, Inc., 1962). For those interested in planned change, see the growing body of literature in organization development. For example, Richard Beckhard, *Organization Development: Strategies and Models* (Reading, Mass.: Addison-Wesley Publishing Co., Inc., 1969).

[10] Harold J. Leavitt, "Applied Organizational Change in Industry: Structural, Technological, and Humanistic Approaches," in *Handbook of Organizations*, ed. James G. March (Chicago, Ill.: Rand McNally & Company, 1965), pp. 1144–70.

within an organization and behavior determined more directly by personality needs and values. The behavior of personnel in organizations is still the behavior of individuals, but it has a different set of determinants than does behavior outside organizational roles. Consequently, modifications in organizational behavior must be produced in a different manner.

The weakness of the individual approach lies in the fallacy of concentrating upon individuals without regard to the role relationships that constitute the social system of which they are a part or to the other variables cited previously. The assumption has been that, because the organization is made up of individuals, we can change the organization by merely changing its members. This is an oversimplification which disregards the interrelationships of individuals in an organizational structure and fails to identify the aspects of their behavior which need to be changed. In other words, to approach organizational change solely on an individual level involves a series of assumptions, most often proven wrong, which assume, at the very least, that every individual can be provided with new ideas and knowledge; that this knowledge will inevitably produce some significant alteration in his behavior; that these newly acquired ideas and behavioral patterns will be retained after the individual leaves the protected situation in which they were learned and returns to his assigned role in the organization; that he will be able to apply his new knowledge to a real-life situation; that he will be able to influence his co-workers to accept the changes in his behavior; and that he will also be able to influence them to make changes in their own expectations and behavior. The error in such thinking can be seen in the subsequent example. It is a growing practice to pull police supervisors out of their organizational roles and train them in human relations. Then they return to their original positions to find the same role expectations from their subordinates, the same pressures from their superiors, and the same functions to perform as before their training. Even if the training program has begun to build a different orientation toward other workers on the part of the supervisors, they are likely to find little opportunity to reflect their new orientation unless the situation to which they return permits it.

To further clarify the issue, we look to Katz and Kahn, who have identified seven individual approaches to organizational change.[11] They are described in order (weakest to strongest) of their inherent ability for bringing about change.

Information. The supplying of additional information has real but limited value as a way of producing organizational change. It can support other methods, give the reason for proposed changes, and describe what will be expected of individuals. It is not, however, a source of motivation; other

---

[11] For a more detailed explanation on the seven approaches to organizational change, see Daniel Katz and Robert L. Kahn, *The Social Psychology of Organizations* (New York: John Wiley & Sons, Inc., 1966), pp. 351–90.

methods are required to provide the necessary influence to change. Moreover, the target of information is the individual and not the organization.

Individual counseling and therapy. These methods represent attempts to avoid the limitations of the information approach and to bring about individual change at a more meaningful level. It is true that the creation of new insight can lead to deeper and more lasting changes in attitudes and, therefore, to altered behavior. The target of such attempts is still the individual, however, and the deployment of his new insights toward organizational change is entirely up to him.

Influence of the peer group. A potent approach to organizational change is through the influence of the peer group. It is based on established findings that peers do exert strong influences on individual behavior, and that a process of change successfully initiated in a peer group becomes self-reinforcing. A dilemma is encountered, however, in seeking to maximize the relevance of the peer group approach to organizational change. Namely, the peer group is likely to be inhibited in its change efforts by the role and authority structure in the organizational setting.

Sensitivity training. This technique is essentially a much discussed extension of the peer group approach to individual and organizational change. The primary target of change remains the individual, although recent variations of this training technique deal specifically with the problem of adapting individual change to the organizational structure.

Group therapy in organizations. This approach has shown beneficial results and represents an original and important combination of individual therapy and the social dynamics of organizations. Its most serious limitation is the assumption that organizational tensions are primarily the expression of individual characteristics, for the most part unrecognized by the individual.

Feedback. This approach to organizational change evolved out of an attempt to make research results more useful to management. It has grown into a well-defined procedure which relies on discussion of relevant findings by organizational units, each consisting of a supervisor and his immediate subordinates. The organization-wide use of feedback begins with the chief executive and his assistants and works down through the hierarchy of organizational units in order. The targets of this highly effective technique are changes in personal and role relations within the organization.

Systemic change. This is the most powerful approach to changing human organizations. It requires the direct manipulation of organizational variables (structure, technology, tasks, and personnel). The target of change is the suitability of the variables which constitute the organization to each other.

While only passing comment is made, one should keep in mind that the significance of organizational change varies according to its source, either internal or external. Katz and Kahn point out that in the absence of external changes, organizations are likely to be reformed from within only in limited ways. More profound changes are initiated or made possible by external forces.[12] Two qualifications to the emphasis on external events should be made. First, every organization, as a unit in a supersystem, not only is influenced by events in that supersystem but also contributes to those events. It is no less true that life within the police organization feeds into the community as its members move back and forth across the organizational boundary. The contribution of a single police organization may be impossible to trace, but the relation of the organization to the community is nevertheless a two-way transaction. The second qualification has to do with the cumulative effects of small internal changes. Logically, a succession of small internally generated changes might in time produce organizational transformations of great depth without the advent of external forces. Nevertheless, the role of external forces in major organizational change remains dominant.

To conclude, regretfully space precludes an examination of implementing change. The previous seven approaches to changing an individual and therefore the organization provide but a brief overview of the process. Actual implementation is the next and final step in effecting change. In regard to implementation, two documents are recommended for the reader's perusal. First, *Managing Organizational Innovation*[13] provides a case study of planned organizational change. Second, is a highly pragmatic monograph, *Putting Research, Experimental, and Demonstration Findings to Use*.[14] Together, they furnish a guide to action.

TOMORROW'S POLICE SUPERVISION

My argument so far, to summarize quickly, is that the first assault on bureaucracy arose from its incapacity to manage the tension between individual and management goals. However, this conflict is somewhat mediated by the growth of an ethic of productivity which includes personal growth and/or satisfaction. The second and more major shock to bureaucracy has been caused by the scientific and technological revolution. It is the requirement of adaptability to the environment which leads to the predicted demise of bureaucracy and to the collapse of management as we know it now.[15]

While this author does not foresee the collapse of supervision as we know it now, I certainly anticipate some vast changes in the daily working life of

---

[12] *Ibid.*, p. 449.

[13] Jeremiah J. O'Connell, *Managing Organizational Innovation* (Homewood, Ill.: Richard D. Irwin, Inc., 1968).

[14] U.S. Department of Labor, *Putting Research, Experimental and Demonstration Findings to Use* (Washington, D.C.: U.S. Government Printing Office, 1967).

[15] Warren G. Bennis, *Changing Organizations* (New York: McGraw-Hill Book Company, 1966), p. 10.

the police supervisor. Concisely stated, the supervisor will experience an ever-increasing stress on challenge and change, with less stress on the more traditional role component of employee control. The major reason for this trend stems from the worker himself. To explain, science (social and physical) and technology, mass higher education, and the information fallout from the media explosion are reshaping the attitudes of the supervised as well as of the supervisor. Consequently, in the police organization of tomorrow, I can see enforced job changes and added responsibility as ways to promote an effective response to new challenges, for the supervisor and the police officer alike.

In describing the future of the police supervisor one is confronted by a couple of frustrating dilemmas. First, where does one start and end his look into the future? Second, there is always the chance of being wrong. Strange as it seems, the latter possibility is of little concern. The former, however, does generate the problem of what to include in the forecast. Admittedly, the items selected can be considered arbitrary. The criterion for their inclusion is one of significance. Hopefully, the future will bear me out. In summary, the horizon for police supervision appears to hold: increased professionalization, a looser and more tolerant structure, decentralization, less restricted communications, team policing when possible, rotation of assignments, greater reliance on group processes, attempts at continual restructuring, modification of the incentive system, changes in many supervisory practices, and a resultant changed emphasis in the supervisor's work role.[16]

Professionalization

Professionalization means upgraded work and workers. A professional is optimally a person who has developed himself thoroughly in some area, about to the limits of his capacities, so that he has that richness of experience and self-confidence upon which effective performance thrives. In other words, the police organization eventually will be comprised of professionals, this is to say, professional police officers, professional supervisors, and professional managers. In terms of the police supervisor, therefore, we can safely predict that he will have a broader education. Instead of being well-versed in one primary discipline (for example, police science) and conversant in one or two secondary ones (such as criminology and public administration), he may have to be the master of two or three primary disciplines and conversant in several others. In addition, tomorrow's supervisor will have a continuing education. The federal and state governments will support some of this continuing education, but the police departments themselves and

---

[16] The basic framework for this section is derived from Victor A. Thompson, "Bureaucracy and Innovation," *Administrative Science Quarterly*, 10 (June 1965), 1–20.

the universities and other centers of knowledge must provide the basic programs in this quest of learning.

The interest in professional growth provides the rising aspiration level needed to stimulate performance beyond the satisfactory level, and the perception of the police organization as a vehicle for individual professional growth harnesses this powerful motivation to the interests of the over-all department in a partial fusion of goals, both personal and organizational. In summary, the police organization and its members will be more professional than ever before.

Structural Looseness

The police organization of the future will be characterized by structural looseness, with less emphasis on narrow, nonduplicating, nonoverlapping specifications of duties and responsibilities. Some will look askance at such a proposed state of affairs. After all, isn't our primary concern for the most effective and efficient way of gaining our goals? Yes and no. Effectiveness and efficiency are not identical. We can have one and not the other. Hopefully they will occur simultaneously. If not, then our choice must be effectiveness. And, effectiveness in our rapidly changing world often calls for risk taking. Further, when we allow the taking of risks, we are placed in the position of possibly increasing the number of "goofs" committed by police personnel. The police supervisor, as well as other members of the department, must more and more engage in risk-taking behavior; therefore, the police organization will be required to back away from rigid proclamation of procedures, duties, and responsibilities. Central to the future of the police supervisor and all the changes that will challenge him are (1) management's tolerance of error and (2) an organization that uses its errors to attain success, that is one which is experiment oriented.

Decentralization

Assignment and resource decisions will be much more decentralized than is customary today. The reader has waded through strong arguments for decentralization. We do not repeat them here, but simply state that the benefits emanating from decentralization overshadow its disadvantages. Not only will there be improved decisions about the allocation of police resources, but moreover there is an enhanced probability of community acceptance (hopefully even support) of local law enforcement. In essence, the police supervisor will be in a position to better identify with his clientele, the people to be served by his activities. In spending a major part of his career at the line level, he will see that the public relations as well as the program results are highly visible. Very pointedly, the police supervisor will be just as much a member of the community as any other resident. A point of clarification, I am not arguing for what is presently referred to as neighborhood policing. On the contrary, I am attempting to avoid it through the decentralization of police services and the strengthening of the authority and responsibility of the police supervisor (centralized administrative control and standards can be maintained by such things as inspection and computer-based information systems).

Less Restricted Communications

Communications will be looser and legitimate in all directions. Again, such an anticipated future state of affairs should not surprise the reader. Obviously, the need for one-way communication with immediate response will remain. We will find, however, greater use of horizontal and upward communications. Significantly, the police supervisor will be at the hub of this multidirectional sending and receiving of messages. The input of better educated people into the police service will see to it. In fact, the trend toward freer communications is already under way.

Team Policing

The work unit will become an integrated group of professionals (patrolmen, investigators, traffic, vice, and so on) engaged in tasks demanding a high degree of technical interdependence and group problem solving. Inklings of team policing can already be seen in some organizations. And, similar to his role in loosening communications, the part the police supervisor will play in extracting the advantages out of such an organizational arrangement is prominent. Briefly put, he will be more of a leader and less of a controller. Team policing, if it is to work at all, requires the very things that constitute the role of supervisory leader: (1) support-subordinate, (2) interaction facilitation, (3) goal emphasis, and (4) work facilitation. To fulfill this more complex role he will be furnished with new and sharpened tools. He will be more facile with systems analysis, program evaluation, manpower planning, operations research techniques, computer applications, and planning-programming budgeting systems (PPBS). And, of course, there will be new tools as yet unknown to us.

Rotation of Assignments

Team policing includes the rotation of assignments; however, even if team policing is not feasible, individuals can still be rotated occasionally. Even if continuing assignments, or jurisdictions, seem to be technically necessary, police organization units will convert a large part of their activities into successive assignments, or have a number of assignments (this is especially pertinent to the police supervisor) going on at the same time, so that individuals can be constantly solving new and challenging problems and experiencing a maximum input of diverse stimulation and ideas. It will be possible for individual and unit jurisdictions and responsibilities to be exchanged occasionally. This is to say, tomorrow's police supervisor will be far more mobile. Less and less will he rise—a career rung at a time—on the ladder of his own organization. He will spend portions of his career in other police agencies, in federal, state, and local governments, in universities, foundations, research centers, businesses, and industries. In short, he will be moved by the rising trend, already advancing toward us, known as personnel interchange. Already we see the joining of forces, of heads and hands, between the components of criminal justice—a joining that is not a mere gesture of good will, but rather mutual cooperation, a sharing of resources, born of necessity. In fact, the police supervisor will lose his current exclusive identity with a single police organization. He will become more and more looked upon as a police supervisor apart from any agency affiliation. To borrow from the title of CPA (certified public accountant), we may find tomorrow's police supervisor a CPS—certified police supervisor. Though based in a single police department, he will be trained and conditioned to serve where needed. Obviously, we have included in our prediction lateral entry at the supervisory level, that is, a formal procedure whereby a police supervisor can transfer from one organization to another as a supervisor. To conclude, the police supervisor of the future will have greatly expanded career opportunities.

Group Processes

Group processes will be more openly used than at present. The freer communication system, the broader work assignments, the lack of preoccupation with overlap and duplication, and the lessened emphasis upon authority will all work in the direction of a greater amount of interpersonal communication and multiple-group membership. The person who will have the major responsibility for promoting and utilizing the group process is the police supervisor. Multiple-group membership will facilitate innovation and improved work performance by increasing the amount and diversity of ideas and stimulation. In an atmosphere which encourages and formalizes multiple-group membership, the injurious competition of fellow subordinates will no longer exercise the powerful constraints against "showing up" with new ideas or outperforming co-workers. Responsibility for new ideas and better effectiveness can be shared within the group. Wide participation in the work process will greatly facilitate change. To repeat, the police supervisor will be, at the same time, group leader and group member of a task-oriented work group. In addition, he will serve on supervisory groups and as a member of the middle management team. Overlapping memberships will result in more accurate decisions. Further, there will occur a heightened sense of participation and involvement in the operations and policies of the police department. Such a situation leads to a closer union of organizational and personal goals.

Continual Restructuring

Police organizations will be sufficiently loose for their units to restructure themselves continually in the light of the problem at hand. Thus, for generating ideas, for planning and problem solving, the police organization or unit will "unstructure" itself into a freely communicating body of equals. When it comes time for implementation, requiring a higher degree of co-ordination of action (as opposed to stimulation of ideas), the organization will then restructure itself into the more usual hierarchical form, tightening up its lines somewhat. The police supervisor will be intimately involved in this process of loosening relations and subsequently tightening them up. He will use this process of loosening relations to derive better decisions and to instill a sense of participation in his subordinates. He will tighten up relations to put the ideas to work. Naturally, group processes are involved here. Empirical evidence that certain structures are optimal for certain problems is compelling. Almost equally compelling is the evidence that the leadership role of the police supervisor needs to be changed as the situation changes. Bureaucratic rigidity makes such structural alterations almost impossible. It is hard to escape the conclusion that current police organization structures are not the best adaptations for some kinds of problem solving. Sufficient recognition of the problem has led some police managers to experiment with new forms, more fluid forms, of organization. For examples of fluid patrol, one can look at the police departments of Glendale and Richmond, California and Tucson, Arizona.

Modification of the Incentive System

What has been predicted thus far substantially hinges on changes being made in our present system for rewarding police personnel. To facilitate these changes we will abandon the use of hierarchical positions as prizes. Further, the importance of extrinsic rewards will decline. In general, the police department structure will be much more amenable to manipulation.

Clearly, everyone is not destined to become a chief of police or, for that matter, a middle manager or supervisor. However, the typical organization of today holds these positions out as prizes—extrinsic rewards—for those who have proven themselves on a promotional examination and worthy as police officers. The purchase of personal motivation and job satisfaction with extrinsic rewards is becoming more and more costly, and improved performance cannot be purchased in this way at all. What will occur is both much less expensive and much more costly—the devaluation of authority and positional status and the recognized, formal sharing of power and influence. Note the term *sharing*. We are saying here that the supervisor of tomorrow will share with his subordinates power and influence in the making of decisions that affect them. He will not, however, give away his basic responsibility for supervising. To put it another way, the police supervisor will permit others to involve themselves in the making of supervisory decisions. But, in every instance, he must make the final decision. Obviously, during extreme emergency conditions the possibilities for such sharing diminish.

What we have said is this, positions of authority will be used less and less as rewards. Involvement or a sense of participation will be used more and more as incentives to better performance. One further prediction in regard to incentives. With total career development programs in the offing, we are confronted with a scheme for matching rewards with development. The police supervisor will be, if he is not already, saddled with the responsibility for giving the police officer a meaningful sense of involvement in his work. The police organization must equal his efforts by providing to all employees a professional pay plan. This plan offers a means for each member of the department to be rewarded for his personal and positional growth. It can result in a police officer earning as much money as a middle manager. Briefly, two interrelated career routes are established. One is professional in nature, permitting an individual to receive, through examinations and performance evaluations, advanced standing in the professional ranks. The second is administrative and begins with supervisor through to the chief. Further, each career ladder allows transferring between the various levels. To illustrate, after three or four movements upward on the professional career ladder, an individual can decide to compete for the equivalent position on the administrative rung, which may be a middle manager's position. One thing is certain, this dual incentive system eliminates the tragic practice of forcing a highly qualified professional officer to become a supervisor in order to advance. How many of you have seen an excellent policeman become a poor supervisor? Or, vice versa?

Changes in Supervisory Practices

At this point the reader is provided with a potpourri of pending supervisory practices. In one way or another all are associated with the previously described changes. Only a few of the most obvious ones are described.

The present common practice of annual or semi-annual performance ratings by supervisors will probably be dropped. Many believe that this practice conflicts with effective work performance. It is clearly inconsistent with increasing police professionalism, since professional standing is not determined by a hierarchical superior. As discussed previously, rather than a single system of hierarchical positions, with corresponding salaries, there will be a dual ranking system and dual salary scales. The managerial or hierarchical ranking system will be only one career alternative. Presumably, it will not exclusively carry the highest status. The professional rankings will have equally high status.

Peer evaluations will be used as a partial substitute for supervisory performance rating of police officers. In other words, an individual's co-workers will be asked to evaluate his contribution to the group effort. Their evaluation, in conjunction with the supervisor's, will be used to determine the training needs and placement of an individual.

Furthermore, peer evaluations will be employed to assist the police organization in selecting its supervisors. Consequently, the promotional process for police supervisor will be comprised of written and oral examinations, and departmental and peer group evaluations. Considerable social science findings show that those supervisors selected by co-workers perform better compared with those selected exclusively by their superiors. At any rate, the wishes of subordinates will probably be considered a good deal more than they are in present practice.

Supervisory job descriptions and classifications will have to accommodate an increasing proportion of professionals. The duties and responsibilities approach to job descriptions was designed for a less complicated age. It does not accommodate professional work easily, especially because tomorrow's police supervisor will have greater recognition and prestige. He will, through lateral transfer, become better known and better appreciated throughout the police service. In essence, the police supervisor or professional of tomorrow will discover and enjoy many new personal interests and satisfactions. Freed of his old-style commitments and career boundaries and projected into new areas of endeavor he will meet many more interesting and stimulating situations.

Supervisory activities will be interrelated with the work level, allowing supervisory personnel to become part of integrative problem-solving work groups rather than resentful onlookers sharpshooting from the outside. When responsibilities and jurisdictions are exchanged as predicted, supervisory responsibilities will be included in such exchanges. To paraphrase a famous expression, supervisory work is too important to be left entirely to supervisors. Hence, we will find, in the absence of the supervisor, line police officers more frequently being placed in the role of acting supervisor. Moreover, as stated previously, supervisory decisions will be of a shared nature.

A series of miscellaneous functions will occur in the police supervisor's future work role and organizational environment. Rather than cite them in detail, a few current innovations are described in order to indicate what tomorrow holds in store. Examples are (1) a large portion of a supervisor's promotional chances hinging on his ability to develop his replacement, (2) the supervisor visiting new residents in his assigned area to welcome them to the community and to explain the existing local government and police services, (3) the supervisor informing his subordinates' wives of the successful performance of the assigned duties of their husbands, (4) the supervisor developing and attending community coffee meetings with concerned residents, (5) on-duty time set aside for reading pertinent journals and documents, and (6) adopting new uniforms which appear less militaristic and more businesslike.

Finally, and this is the crux of tomorrow's supervisory role, the police supervisor will be viewed primarily as a socio-psychological specialist. His duties as a controller will decrease while those as a group motivator, trainer, and agent of change will be enhanced. The future work role of the police supervisor follows.

Police Supervision: The Changing Role

> Every organization is in a continuous state of change. Sometimes the changes are great, sometimes small, but change is always taking place. The conditions requiring these changes arise from both within and without. As a consequence, there is never-ending need for decisions which guide adjustments to change. The adequacy of these decisions for meeting an organization's current and developing internal and external situations determines the well-being, power, and future of that organization.[17]

The roles constituting organizational structure and functions are changing. The future role of the police supervisor is based on the growing necessity for him to respond constructively to the challenge of leading police personnel in the direction of achieving new and ambitious goals. Further, often he will be compelled to operate effectively under crisis conditions, while supervising efficiently—and without loss of personal commitment—programs that steadily increase in scope, scale, and complexity. Interestingly, all these duties must be accomplished while developing police manpower which has the creative capacity and dedication to the community ethic required to cope with the even more difficult public problems of the future. Therefore, the new role of the police supervisor will appear as follows:

---

[17] Rensis Likert, *The Human Organization: Its Management and Value* (New York: McGraw-Hill Book Company, 1967), p. 128.

Role Components   *Change in Role*
   1. organizational control
   2. training
   3. administrative detail
   4. procedure development
   5. organizational perspective
   6. performance appraisal
   7. formal, informal, and personal
      communication
   8. organizational responsibility
   9. safety awareness
  10. community relations
  11. employee morale
  12. support-subordinate
  13. interaction facilitation
  14. goal emphasis
  15. work facilitation
  16. change agent

Finally, we can see that our increasing knowledge of the complexity of the question has outmoded the traditional designations of police supervision. These designations ought to be modified now to express the ways in which supervision continuously changes in response to changing situations. The suggestions presented previously outline future changes in the role of the police supervisor. Needless to say, though these suggestions are consistent with the available organizational trends, only the future will tell if they are appropriate or accurate.

Index